The Joan Palevsky  Imprint in Classical Literature

In honor of beloved Virgil—

"O degli altri poeti onore e lume . . ."

—Dante, *Inferno*

The publisher and the University of California Press Foundation
gratefully acknowledge the generous support of the
Joan Palevsky Imprint in Classical Literature.

The Seer and the City

The Seer and the City

*Religion, Politics, and Colonial Ideology
in Ancient Greece*

Margaret Foster

UNIVERSITY OF CALIFORNIA PRESS

University of California Press, one of the most distinguished university presses in the United States, enriches lives around the world by advancing scholarship in the humanities, social sciences, and natural sciences. Its activities are supported by the UC Press Foundation and by philanthropic contributions from individuals and institutions. For more information, visit www.ucpress.edu.

University of California Press
Oakland, California

© 2017 by The Regents of the University of California
First Paperback Printing 2024 | ISBN 9780520401426 (pbk)

Library of Congress Cataloging-in-Publication Data

Names: Foster, Margaret, author.
Title: The seer and the city : religion, politics, and colonial ideology in ancient Greece / Margaret Foster.
Description: Oakland, California : University of California Press, [2017] | Includes bibliographical references and index. |
Identifier s: LCCN 2017029447 (print) | LCCN 2017034383 (ebook) |
ISBN 780520967915 () | ISBN 9780520295001 (cloth : alk. paper)
Subjects: LCSH: Religion and politics—Greece—History. | Oracles, Greek. | Prophets—Greece. | Hero (Greek mythology) | Greece—Colonies.
Classifi cation: LCC BL795.P57 (ebook) | LCC BL795.P57 F67 2017 (print) | DDC 292.6/1—DC23
LC record available at https://lccn.loc.gov/2017029447

24
10 9 8 7 6 5 4 3 2 1

For Jon

CONTENTS

Acknowledgments ix
Conventions and Abbreviations xi

Introduction 1

1. Beyond Entrails and Omens: Herodotus's Teisamenos and the Talismanic Seer at War 23
2. Sailing to Sicily: Theoklymenos and Odysseus in the *Odyssey* 51
3. Suppressing the Seer in Colonial Discourse: Delphic Consultations and the Seer in the City 76
4. The Disappearance of Melampous in Bacchylides' *Ode* 11 88
5. Hagesias as *Sunoikistēr*: Mantic Authority and Colonial Ideology in Pindar's *Olympian* 6 108
6. Amphiaraos, Alkmaion, and Delphi's Oracular Monopoly 136

Conclusion 185

Bibliography 193
Index 209
Index Locorum 215

ACKNOWLEDGMENTS

This book began at UC Berkeley, and I would like to acknowledge first Leslie Kurke, Mark Griffith, Donald Mastronarde, and Emily Mackil for their collective wisdom and support in getting the project off the ground. As the years pass, I realize with increasing clarity the extent to which I was standing on the shoulders of giants at Berkeley. Audiences at Indiana University, Real Universidade de Santiago de Compostela, the University of Notre Dame, Florida State University, the University of South Carolina, and the meetings of the Society for Classical Studies provided helpful comments on earlier versions of chapters.

A version of chapter 5 appeared in *Classical Antiquity* as "Hagesias as *Sunoikistēr*: Seercraft and Colonial Ideology in Pindar's Sixth Olympian Ode," and I am grateful to the University of California Press for granting permission to reproduce parts of that article here. I would also like to thank the two anonymous readers of that article for their generous comments. The two readers of the book manuscript as well as UC Press's Editorial Committee helped transform the book over the last year. Their detailed reports made it better.

Eric Schmidt's interest in the project at an early stage was a highlight of my pre-tenure career. I am grateful for his subsequent patience in guiding me through the stages that followed and for his clear vision for the book. I also wish to thank Maeve Cornell-Taylor for shepherding me through the process of completing the manuscript and Cindy Fulton for overseeing its production. Marian Rogers's meticulous copyediting saved me from errors in both the English and the Greek.

Colleagues in the Department of Classical Studies at Indiana University have been wonderfully encouraging and supportive over the years. Noah Kaye helped me track down an image for the cover art. I remain indebted to Claire

Drone-Silvers, who carefully read through the manuscript and checked the Greek passages and the bibliography. Large portions of this book were written during sessions of Indiana University's Scholarly Writing Program. I am grateful to my colleagues in these sessions and to the director, Laura Plummer, for their camaraderie and contagious productivity.

I owe special thanks to Melissa Mueller for her wise advice and especially for reading a draft of the introduction at the eleventh hour. Nigel Nicholson has been unfailingly generous in providing comments that always improved my arguments. Finally, it has been the great privilege of my academic life to have been able to work with Leslie Kurke. This book has benefited at every stage from her own innovative scholarship, above all her ability to crack open and illuminate Pindaric poetry without dulling its beautiful strangeness, and her tireless dedication to her students.

The support of friends and family has helped me see the book through, especially the support of my siblings, Jack, Charlie, Dan, Pete, and Beth Foster. I am also grateful to Faith Rose, who first taught me about ancient Greece, and to Rachel Friedman and Rachel Kitzinger, who first showed me why it matters. To Susan Levin and Robert Ready, I hope that I have finally earned a place on your shelf of family authors. Two years ago, my parents, Patricia and John Foster, moved to Bloomington. This book could not have been written without both of them nearby. I owe special thanks to my extraordinary mother, who rescued me daily and who, together with my father, has made my own children's lives so much richer. If I turn out to be half the mother she is, they will be very lucky indeed. I would also like to thank Jack, Ruthie, and Bridie Rose, who were born during the writing of this book, for letting this project share their mother with them and for their patience in letting me finish it. Finally, this book is dedicated to my husband, Jonathan Ready, whom I wish to thank above all for helping me talk through what I wanted to say and how to say it, for reminding me to take the long view, and for keeping us all well fed.

CONVENTIONS AND ABBREVIATIONS

I use the standard editions of Snell and Maehler for all quotations of Pindar and Bacchylides: B. Snell and H. Maehler, eds., *Pindari Carmina cum Fragmentis*, vol. 1, *Epinicia* (Leipzig, 1987); H. Maehler, ed., *Pindari Carmina cum Fragmentis*, vol. 2, *Fragmenta, Indices* (Leipzig, 1989); H. Maehler, ed., *Bacchylidis Carmina cum Fragmentis* (Leipzig, 1992). Unless otherwise noted, I use the Oxford Classical Text (OCT) series for all other ancient authors. When there is no OCT available, I use the most recent Teubner edition.

The names of most Greek authors appear in their more familiar Latinized form (e.g., Bacchylides instead of Bakkhulides; Aeschylus instead of Aiskulos), but for most other Greek names (those of literary characters, historical figures, etc.) I have preferred to transliterate directly from the Greek. Some inconsistency is unavoidable, and this is most apparent in the spelling of place-names, which follow a criterion of perceived familiarity (thus the Latinized "Crete" but the transliterated "Oropos"). The names of Greek authors and works are abbreviated in citations following the conventions listed in the OCD^4, although Bacchylides is abbreviated as "Bacch." and Pindar is abbreviated as "Pi." The abbreviations of Latin authors and works follow the conventions listed in *OLD*. Translations are my own unless otherwise indicated.

CEG   Hansen, P. A., ed. 1983–89. *Carmina Epigraphica Graeca*. 2 vols. Berlin.
EGF   Davies, M. 1988. *Epicorum Graecorum Fragmenta*. Göttingen.
FGrH Jacoby, F., ed. 1923–58. *Die Fragmente der griechischen Historiker*. 3 vols. Berlin and Leiden. Schepens, G., ed. 1998. Vol. 4. Leiden.
GEF   West, M. L. 2003. *Greek Epic Fragments*. Cambridge, Mass.

IG	*Inscriptiones Graecae.* 1873–. Berlin.
LIMC	Ackermann, H. C., J.-R. Gisler, and L. Kahil, eds. 1981–97. *Lexicon Iconographicum Mythologiae Classicae.* 8 vols. Zurich.
LSJ	Liddell, H. G., and R. Scott, eds. 1940. *A Greek-English Lexicon.* Revised and augmented throughout by H. S. Jones, with the assistance of R. McKenzie, with a supplement (1968). 9th ed. Reprint, Oxford, 1990.
M-W	Merkelbach, R., and M. L. West. 1967. *Fragmenta Hesiodea.* Oxford.
OCD^4	Hornblower, S. and A. Spawforth, eds. 2012. *The Oxford Classical Dictionary.* 4th ed. Oxford.
OLD	*Oxford Latin Dictionary.* 1968–82. Oxford.
PEG	Bernabé, A., ed. 1987. *Poetarum Epicorum Graecorum: Testimonia et Fragmenta.* Leipzig.
PMG	Page, D. L., ed. 1962. *Poetae Melici Graeci.* Oxford.
Pfeiffer	Pfeiffer, R., ed. 1949–53. *Callimachus, Works.* 2 vols. 2nd ed. by A. Henrichs. Stuttgart.
Powell	Powell, J. U. 1925. *Collectanea Alexandrina.* Oxford.
Rose	Rose, V. 1966. *Aristotelis qui ferebantur librorum fragmenta.* Leipzig.
R	Radt, S., ed. 1985–86. *Tragicorum Graecorum fragmenta.* Göttingen.
SEG	*Supplementum Epigraphicum Graecum.* 1923–. Leiden and Amsterdam.
Tarditi	Tarditi, G. 1968. *Archilochus.* Rome.
W^2	West, M. L., ed. 1989–92. *Iambi et Elegi Graeci ante Alexandrum Cantati.* 2 vols. 2nd ed. Oxford.

Introduction

In Aristophanes' *Birds*, as Peisetairos prepares to perform a foundation sacrifice in his new city of Cloudcuckooland, he is rudely interrupted by a series of intruders. The intruders, a poet, a *chrēsmologos* (oracle monger), a surveyor, an inspector, and a decree seller, all shamelessly offer their unsolicited services in the hopes of being granted some reward. Thus, for instance, when the *chrēsmologos* arrives, he proceeds to spout a number of riddling hexameters from an oracle of Bakis that supposedly refer to the foundation of Cloudcuckooland.[1] The *chrēsmologos* is exposed as a fraud whose real purpose is to wrangle clothes and food out of Peisetairos, and he is eventually sent running off stage, beaten over the head by his own collection of oracles. Before Peisetairos physically abuses the *chrēsmologos*, however, he first defeats the charlatan's oracular claims by citing ones of his own (*Av.* 981–91):

ΠΕΙΣΕΤΑΙΡΟΣ
        οὐδὲν ἄρ' ὅμοιός ἐσθ' ὁ χρησμὸς τουτῳί,
        ὃν ἐγὼ παρὰ τἀπόλλωνος ἐξεγραψάμην·
        "αὐτὰρ ἐπὴν ἄκλητος ἰὼν ἄνθρωπος ἀλαζὼν
        λυπῇ θύοντας καὶ σπλαγχνεύειν ἐπιθυμῇ,
        δὴ τότε χρὴ τύπτειν αὐτὸν πλευρῶν τὸ μεταξὺ—"

---

1. The *chrēsmologos* (often translated as "oracle monger") was a figure separate from the seer (*mantis*) in the archaic and classical periods, but Aristophanes intentionally collapses the distinction between these two related types of diviners as a way of lampooning the more prestigious seer. I thus treat the *chrēsmologos* and the seer as roughly synonymous in this passage. For distinctions between the *chrēsmologos* and the seer, see Flower 2008b: 60–65; and below in the section "The Greek Seer: An Overview."

ΧΡΗΣΜΟΛΟΓΟΣ
    οὐδὲν λέγειν οἶμαί σε.
ΠΕ.   λαβὲ τὸ βυβλίον.
    καὶ φείδου μηδὲν μηδ᾽ αἰετοῦ ἐν νεφέλῃσιν,
    μήτ᾽ ἢν Λάμπων ᾖ μήτ᾽ ἢν ὁ μέγας Διοπείθης.
ΧΡ.   καὶ ταῦτ᾽ ἔνεστ᾽ ἐνταῦθα;
ΠΕ.   λαβὲ τὸ βυβλίον.
    οὐκ εἶ θύραζ᾽; ἐς κόρακας.
ΧΡ.   οἴμοι δείλαιος.
ΠΕ.   οὔκουν ἑτέρωσε χρησμολογήσεις ἐκτρέχων;

Peisetairos:
Well now, your oracle doesn't match this one at all, an oracle I personally wrote down from Apollo:
    "Yea when a charlatan type who arrives uninvited
    vexes the sacrificers and desires a share of the innards,
    then must you smite him in the place twixt the ribs—"
Oracle Monger:
You must be kidding.
Peisetairos:
Here's the book.
    "and spare not even an eagle midst the clouds,
    not if he be Lampon nor yet the great Diopeithes."
Oracle Monger:
That's in there too?
Peisetairos:
(*hitting him with the book*) Here's the book! now get the hell out of here!
Oracle Monger:
Oh mercy me!
Peisetairos:
Go on, scat! Do your oracle mongering somewhere else![2]

This exchange marks the culmination of an oracular duel in which Peisetairos impugns the oracle monger's prophecy with one he has personally received from Delphic Apollo. In his role as oikist (colonial founder) Peisetairos leverages his privileged connection with Delphi in order to discredit the *chrēsmologos*'s own religious authority. Peisetairos's behavior here is in keeping with his conduct toward the other unwelcome intruders. Dismissing them all, he claims sole credit for the successful foundation of his city.

The entire scene is, of course, a parody, but it is a parody that captures the central claims of this book. For Aristophanes' representation of Cloudcuckooland calls attention to the idiosyncratic way in which the Greeks often remembered the foundations of their cities: they reserved acclaim for the oikist alone and did so to

---

2. Trans. Henderson 2000.

the exclusion of other experts present during the foundation. Most notably, in colonial narratives, the oikist becomes not only a figure who wields political power but also one who, endorsed by Delphi, possesses the religious authority accorded in other contexts to the seer. We might paraphrase Peisetairos's final insult to the oracle monger—"Do your oracle mongering somewhere else!"—as "Your oracle mongering does not belong in this foundation tale!"

This book develops a new understanding of the Greek seer by illuminating the ideological motivations of colonial discourse. Seers were prominent figures in ancient Greek society, but they rarely appear in archaic and classical colonial discourse.[3] To be sure, Greek foundation tales are known for being lacunose, preferring to describe in detail certain components of a given colonial expedition while passing over others in silence. For this reason we might assume that the absence of seers from many foundation stories can be attributed to a kind of narrative indifference: seers were simply not felt to be important enough to make the cut in the Greeks' highly compressed renderings of their colonial experience. This book suggests another explanation for the absence of seers from colonial discourse: it exposes the ideology behind this discrepancy and reveals how colonial discourse's privileging of the city's founder and his dependence on Delphi, the colonial oracle par excellence, entails a corresponding suppression of the seer.

It is worth stating clearly at the outset that this book does not include a comprehensive survey of colonial narratives featuring Delphi, nor does it attempt to reconstruct the religious duties of seers during a foundation.[4] Such endeavors have been successfully carried out before, and the present study depends in many ways on those investigations. Rather, this book represents a different type of undertaking. It explains why the seer's form of authority was seen to conflict with that of the oikist (chapter 1) and then proceeds through a sequence of texts that allow us to witness colonial discourse's ideological promotion of the oikist and concealment of the seer in action (chapters 2–6). It looks to moments in which colonial discourse can be figuratively caught in the act of occluding the seer as well as to instances in which the seer appears to intrude on colonial contexts. Through close literary analyses, it tracks the maneuvers and repercussions of these concerted suppressions and disruptions. By reading the seer and the Delphi-sanctioned oikist in relation to one another, it exposes the contests for authority between them. Yet, precisely because this investigation involves central figures and institutions of Greek culture, its conclusions extend beyond this framework. Colonial discourse becomes a productive metonym for understanding both the contestatory and the

---

3. For a definition of colonial discourse, see pp. 6–8.

4. On colonial narratives that include Delphi, see esp. Malkin 1987: 17–91; Dougherty 1993: 15–80; Miller 1997: 88–144. On the possible religious duties of seers in colonial contexts, see Malkin 1987: 92–113; 2009: 386–90.

collaborative dynamics between mantic, oracular, and political powers operative in archaic and classical Greece.

KEY TERMS AND METHOD

I adopt a historicizing approach that relies on many of the theoretical tenets of Cultural Poetics (New Historicism). It will thus be useful to begin by providing definitions for certain key terms—*text, culture,* and *ideology*—and to identify how they relate to one another from the perspective of Cultural Poetics.[5] I will then outline several points of method that further clarify the application of such an approach to the study of archaic and classical Greek literary texts.

Cultural Poetics understands texts as sites in which the contestation and negotiation for power and authority are enacted.[6] Texts are not the detached reflections of culture but actively intervene in culture, receiving but also refracting and reshaping cultural norms and conditions in turn.[7] From this perspective, culture itself is viewed not as a unified, static system but as a dialectic of system and practice.[8]

This contestatory dynamic of culture, and of texts as part of culture, necessitates ideology. Catherine Bell puts it succinctly when she defines ideology as "not a disseminated body of ideas but the way in which people live the relationships between themselves and their world, a type of necessary illusion."[9] Because this "necessary illusion" is lived, because it embodies "worldliness," ideology is always evolving, incomplete, and unstable.[10] Nor is ideology singular: as a number of literary theorists emphasize, there exists at any particular point in time within a given culture a range of ideologies in play, as current ones jostle with each other, with the remnants of older ideologies, and with incipient ideologies.[11]

---

5. I follow Kurke 2011: 22–25 in offering at the outset a set of definitions for key terms and their relation to the book's theoretical apparatus.

6. In this respect, Cultural Poetics has been profoundly influenced by poststructuralism and, in particular, Michel Foucault. Its theoretical foundations also include Jacques Derrida's concept of textuality, Mikhail Bakhtin's and Julia Kristeva's concepts of dialogism and intertextuality, and Clifford Geertz's cultural anthropology. For the core theoretical assumptions of Cultural Poetics/New Historicism, see, e.g., Stallybrass and White 1986: 1–26; Montrose 1989: 15–36; Gallagher and Greenblatt 2000: 49–74. For the productiveness of Cultural Poetics for the study of ancient Greek culture, see Dougherty and Kurke 1993: 1–12; 2003: 1–19.

7. See Said 1983: 33–35; Bell 2009: 81. See also Jameson 1981.

8. See Bonnell and Hunt (1999: 12), summarizing the arguments of Sewell: "Culture is most fruitfully conceptualized as a dialectic between system and practice. It is a system of symbols and meanings with a certain coherence and definition but also a set of practices; thus the symbols and meanings can and do change over time, often in unpredictable fashion." See also Sewell 1999.

9. Bell 2009: 85, paraphrasing Althusser and Balibar 1979: 314.

10. See Bell 2009: 81.

11. Belsey 1980: 101–24; Jameson 1981: 93–102; Smith 1988; Macherey 2006.

Since texts do not exist apart from culture, their content comprises ideology or ideologies.[12] Inconsistencies, contradictions, and lapses in a text, including in the ways in which individual characters are conceived and constructed, are manifestations of the instability and tensions that inhabit ideology and arise between ideologies. By attending to textual ruptures and omissions, by looking for anomalies and discrepancies in the interstices of narrative, that is, by reading a text "symptomatically," we can identify the ideologies themselves that are operative therein. That is to say, we identify an ideology more completely when we read not only for the elements that it valorizes and makes explicit but also for those elements that, by virtue of highlighting others, it necessarily obscures. In Pierre Macherey's formulation, "meaning is in the *relation* between the implicit and the explict, not on one or the other side of that fence."[13] Thus in the following chapters I will read literary texts with a view to ideology, alert especially to a given text's strange and jarring components and to its moments of hedging ambiguity, and I will treat these aberrations and evasions as the symptomatic indices of its ideological strategies. As David Konstan observes, "Unity is not an ideal quality of a text, but a product of its ideological labor, and it is the task of the critic to lay bare the contradictory elements that the narrative welds together into an apparent whole."[14]

I turn now to three general points of method that relate this historicizing approach to the book's interpretation of ancient Greek texts, especially archaic and classical poetry. First, classicists have long recognized that archaic and classical poetry was occasional and composed for performance and thus both entrenched in and engaged with its particular (social, political, religious) setting.[15] I therefore consider it a necessary part of the interpretation of a given poem to attend to its historical and cultural framework. Epinikia (victory odes), the focus of chapters 4–6, readily lend themselves to historicizing readings, since these odes represent the "libretti" for ritual choral performances, and it seems logical to acknowledge the larger performance context as part of deciphering an individual ode's significance.[16] Yet recognizing the vibrant inextricability between texts and their contexts will inform my readings of archaic and classical literary works from a variety of other genres treated in the book as well, including Herodotus's *Histories* (chapter 1) and Homer's *Odyssey* (chapter 2).[17]

12. See Eagleton in Macherey 2006: ix.
13. Macherey 2006: 97, emphasis in original.
14. Konstan 1995: 5.
15. The shift in classics to poetry's connection to performance has produced a huge body of secondary literature. I list here only a minute fraction of important works relating to the study of Greek poetry in performance: Calame 1977; Gentili 1988; Martin 1989; Krummen 1990; Nagy 1990; Kurke 1991; Stehle 1997; Wilson 2000; Kowalzig 2007; Athanassaki and Bowie 2011.
16. "Libretti" is Kurke's (2013: 105) analogy.
17. See Morgan (2015: 5–6) for a clear defense of historicizing readings.

Second, while this book centers on a set of selected texts dated to the archaic and classical periods, it simultaneously brings to bear on its arguments an array of other evidence, including evidence drawn from later sources. The use of later sources, such as Diodorus Siculus, Apollodorus, Plutarch, and Pausanias, amplifies our paucity of evidence from the archaic and classical periods. It does so both because such authors had access to more ancient material than is available to us, and, relatedly, because these authors often directly transmit earlier cultural phenomena, without necessarily understanding their original import. Such phenomena frequently stand out within these later texts as aberrant or confused, and by attending to these anomalies one is able to excavate earlier layers of cultural meaning and signification.[18] Chapter 1, for instance, discusses an anecdote from Diodorus Siculus that presents, without explanation, how the archaic athlete Milo marched into battle wearing his six Olympic crowns, while chapter 6 traces the strange ellipses and contradictions embedded in Apollodorus's compilation of the myth of the Seven against Thebes.

Finally, while the book is informed by Cultural Poetics, its arguments are simultaneously built up from close textual analyses and explications that recruit the reading practices of literary formalism. Each chapter comprises literary readings attentive to diction, narrative patterns, intertextuality and allusion, and generic expectations. This sort of granular sensitivity to the formal features and nuances of the literary works presented will allow us to detect in a more comprehensive way the textual strategies and aberrations that the book's historicist perspective seeks to elicit.

COLONIAL DISCOURSE IN THE ARCHAIC AND CLASSICAL PERIODS

The texts I consider offer instances of or reactions to the larger conceptual category of colonial discourse. I understand ancient Greek colonial discourse to be a discourse comprising the totality of literary texts and other cultural artifacts relating to foundations (of cities, regions, groups of people) as well as the rules and practices that underlie the production of these artifacts. That is, I take discourse in this sense to be systematic in character, with rules and practices that provide the metaphors, paradigms, analogies, and concepts for how it expresses its subject matter, for how it "delimits the sayable."[19] For colonial discourse, "the sayable"—

---

18. See Dougherty and Kurke 1993: 6. On the regressive method of reconstructing history, see Kurke 2011: 23.

19. See Henriques et al. 1998: 105–6. This definition of discourse ultimately derives from Foucault (1972) but also appears in numerous adaptations of Foucauldian discourse (see Mills 2004: 43–44, 94–115). I provide a definition of discourse because of the fluidity and range of meanings accorded to the term between and even within discrete disciplines. For example, my definition of discourse differs from that of Mac Sweeney (2015: 3), for whom "foundation discourse" refers to the

the way in which a particular event or sequence of events is constructed and expressed—can take the literary form of a colonial narrative. Throughout the book, for the sake of variety, I will refer to particular colonial narratives as foundation myths, stories, or tales.[20]

There is no discrete, autonomous Greek genre concerned with *ktisis* (foundation) until the Hellenistic period.[21] Rather, colonial narratives appear in a wide range of genres, in a variety of contexts, and in both poetry and prose. Yet the relative coherence and systematicity of colonial discourse entail that colonial narratives produced across this range of genres and contexts not only exhibit recognizable narrative patterns, metaphors, and concepts but also, as this book aims to show, maintain a degree of ideological integrity, a persistent angle of vision.[22]

The late archaic to the early classical period (ca. 520–440 B.C.E.) offers a productive time frame in which to study the conjunction of seers and the ideological motivations of ancient Greek colonial discourse. During this period the confluence and imbrication of an array of phenomena created a cultural environment in which colonial discourse became especially charged. The era witnessed the Greek colonial movement, which, begun in earnest in the eighth century, was still ongoing in the fifth century. It also marked the heyday of the Delphic oracle's Panhellenic influence and the height of its status as the principal colonial oracle. At the

foundation of a specific "city, state, or group of people" and comprises the various foundation myths as well as the interaction of these myths for that particular foundation. Mac Sweeney's definition, however, importantly stresses that a discourse is not just the sum of the individual variants themselves but also includes the dialogue or interaction between these variants.

20. While acknowledging the anachronistic nature of these terms, I use *colony, colonization,* and *colonial* in this book. I also treat *colony* and *foundation* as synonyms. In an influential article, Osborne (1998) campaigned against applying the term *colony* to archaic settlements of the eighth and seventh centuries, since these sites were not established in the same organized manner of later Greek colonies. He further argued against the term because of the "strong 'statist' overtones" it connotes to our modern, Western ears (1998: 251). Osborne's stance, however, has been so influential that, paradoxically, it has mostly liberated the word from many of the misconceptions he maintained it promoted. Thus note Kowalzig's (2007: 267n3) assessment: "Thanks to Osborne (1998) much attention has been drawn to the conceptual differences between Greek colonization in the Mediterranean and the colonial movement of modern European states, and the term should by now be free of any culturally specific baggage." See also Hall (2008: 384n5): "Osborne . . . rightly points out that 'colonisation' is not an entirely appropriate term to describe the movements of Greek peoples from the 8th century, but since it has become conventional usage and since the perpetual search for synonyms becomes tedious after a while, it is here retained for the sake of convenience." See also Tandy 1997: 75; Tsetskhladze 2006b: xxiii-lxxxiii; Malkin 2016. Osborne (2016) continues to argue for the inappropriateness of these terms.

21. See Dougherty 1994.

22. As summarized below, Dougherty (1993) importantly exposes and makes sense of many of the key narrative patterns, metaphors, and concepts of colonial discourse. "Angle of vision" is Konstan's (1995: 6) phrase. Different theorists treat the relationship between discourse and ideology in different ways (see Mills 2004: 26–42). Here I follow Eagleton (2007: 194) in viewing ideology as "a particular set of effects *within* discourses" (emphasis in original).

same time, it included the florescence of the independent seer, who played a central role especially in the events during and surrounding the Persian Wars. The sixth and fifth centuries were also a period of stasis within individual poleis where the aristocracy's traditional outlets of power became threatened and where the elite sought to maintain their foothold in part through assertions of personal charismatic authority, including as athletic victors and as colonial founders.[23] Finally, the period's vibrant poetic economy produced genres that readily accommodated colonial discourse, including elegy and epinikion.[24] Thus upheaval and crisis, shifting populations and contested claims of authority, competing forms of oracular and mantic divination, each at the height of their power, and the embeddedness of Greek poetry—these are some of the main factors that, as we will see, converge in the sixth and fifth centuries and account for the ideological intensity of archaic and classical colonial discourse.[25]

PREVIOUS SCHOLARSHIP

This book brings together two major strands of scholarly inquiry, the study of Greek colonization and of Greek seers and divination. As the preeminent oracle among the Greeks as well as the oracle by far the most connected to the Greek colonial movement, Delphi straddles the two subjects and provides a crucial point of contact between them.

Modern scholarship in both areas is massive, and an overview of even the most fundamental works would prove cumbersome and interminable. For scholarship on Greek colonization, I have elected to focus on key studies that have especially shaped the objectives undertaken here, while acknowledging other major scholarly contributions mainly in the footnotes. A number of these studies will be cited again in greater detail in the coming chapters.[26] Whereas work on colonization continues to be diffuse and run the gamut from archaeological reports to modern historiography to literary studies to various combinations of these perspectives, in the case of divination it is possible to provide a brief overview of how this book

---

23. See Davies 1981: 88–131; Morgan 1990: 194–205; Kurke 1993: 153–55. See also chapter 1.
24. For the different genres of poetry associated with foundations, see Dougherty 1994.
25. A discourse's ideological strategies intensify the more forcefully it has to assert its unity and identity and overcome difference. As Laclau and Mouffe (1985: 112) argue, "Any discourse is constituted as an attempt to dominate the field of discursivity, to arrest the flow of difference, to construct a centre."
26. Important contributions and canonical works include Dunbabin 1948; Bérard 1957; Snodgrass 1980; Graham 1983, 2001; Descoeudres 1990; Londey 1990; D'Agostino and Ridgway 1994; Boardman 1999; Osborne 1996, 1998; Antonaccio 1999, 2001, 2007; Nafissi 1999; Tsetskhladze 1999, 2006a, 2008; Horden and Purcell 2000; Hall 2002, 2008; Calame 2003; Lomas 2003; Donnellan, Nizzo, and Burgers 2016. On oikists, see Leschhorn 1984; Scheer 1993. Literary representations of colonization: Miller 1997; foundation stories: Giangiulio 2001; Hall 2008; Mac Sweeney 2015.

relates to certain recent trends in the field.²⁷ I will then position this project in relation to the only book-length treatment of Greek seers to date, Michael Flower's *The Seer in Ancient Greece* (2008).²⁸

Two groundbreaking studies, Irad Malkin's *Religion and Colonization in Ancient Greece* (1987) and Carol Dougherty's *The Poetics of Colonization* (1993), divergent though they are in their respective objectives, have both been instrumental in forming the concerns of this book. In *Religion and Colonization in Ancient Greece*, Malkin sought to offer for the first time a comprehensive account of the religious components of Greek colonization. Like earlier scholars, Malkin emphasized the importance of Delphic foundation oracles in the initial stages of the foundation process.²⁹ What set Malkin apart from his predecessors, however, was his emphasis on the religious status accorded to the oikist himself and, relatedly, the significance of the oikist's close connection to Apollo at Delphi. As he argued, the oikist's session at Delphi was not merely when the oikist received a colonial oracle but also marked the moment at which Apollo was seen to confer on the oikist the necessary religious authority for the undertaking:

> Apollo's address endowed [the oikist] with a kind of religious aura which enabled him to make decisions about religion concerning, for example, the locations of sacred precincts, particular cults, and so on. In religious terms, the relationship of the oikist to the colonist was like Apollo's relationship to him: an *exegetes*, an expounder of the god's will.³⁰

Malkin's reconstruction suggests that during his session at Delphi the oikist was seen to receive an extraordinary degree of religious authority: the "divinely appointed oikist" became a human counterpart to Apollo.³¹

---

27. Donnellan and Nizzo (2016: 9) capture well the diversity of the field of Greek colonization: "This extremely dynamic and rapidly changing field comprises so many interrelated geophysical, hydrological, biological, cultural, social and economic realities which, as a consequence, allow for virtually endless varieties in scientific research."

28. Two frequently cited dissertations focus on the seer: Kett 1966 (a prosopography of seers); Roth 1982.

29. Parke and Wormell 1956 and Fontenrose 1978 remain the classic compilations of Delphic oracular responses, including those concerning colonization. For Malkin's take on the Delphic oracle and its role in colonization, as well as his own evaluation of Parke and Wormell and Fontenrose, see Malkin 1987: 17–91. See Kindt 2016: 5–10 for a concise evaluation of earlier scholarship and its singular and problematic focus on the authenticity and historicity of Delphic oracular responses.

30. Malkin 1989: 135; see also Malkin 1987: 27: "The most important aspect of the oikist's consultation at Delphoi was his personal designation by Apollo and the implied religious authority with which he was invested. . . . In this respect the religious authority with which the oikist was invested resembled that of Apollo himself, namely, the authority to expound religion."

31. See Malkin 1987: 51. On the conferral of authority by the Delphic oracle in general, see Parker 1985.

Malkin is also among the few scholars to address the role that divination played in Greek foundations. Noting the dearth of references to seers in archaic colonial contexts, Malkin accounts for their absence by suggesting that the oikist in this period was a figure in whom religious, military, and political powers all inhered and who thereby obviated the need for a separate seer.[32] At the same time, he asserts that seers, by analogy with their well-documented presence on military campaigns, almost certainly did accompany colonial expeditions as members of the oikist's retinue. For Malkin, then, the seer was most likely in attendance on archaic colonial expeditions, despite the silence of our sources, a plausible, but not crucial, presence on hand to assist the religious capabilities of the oikist himself.[33]

Malkin's interest lies in the historical reality of the religious and colonial phenomena he examines, and, to the extent possible, he attends exclusively to the historical evidence without incorporating references to these same phenomena found in Greek myths and legends.[34] By contrast, in *The Poetics of Colonization*, Dougherty seeks to understand Greek representations of archaic colonization, be they historical, mythical, or legendary. Adopting a Cultural Poetics approach, Dougherty is less concerned with the realia of actual colonial practices than with the ways in which the Greeks chose to remember their foundations. To this end, she first collates the basic elements that constitute the archaic colonial narrative: A crisis within a community generates a Delphic consultation. At Delphi, Apollo prescribes a colonial foundation as a solution to this crisis and selects an oikist to lead the expedition. Resolution of the original crisis is achieved by establishing a new, independent polis. Dougherty then sets about deciphering the concepts, analogies, and metaphors manifest in this pattern that the Greeks deployed to articulate their colonial experience. As she shows, the representational strategies of colonial discourse helped the Greeks "familiarize the unfamiliar" and make sense of the challenging, disorienting experience of leaving home and settling a new land.[35]

Dougherty demonstrates that the study of Greek colonial discourse is well served by Cultural Poetics methods of analysis as well as by the recognition of the inseparability of the historical and the mythical-legendary in the Greek cultural imaginary. *The Poetics of Colonization* accounts for much of the strangeness of

---

32. See Malkin 1987: 92–113, esp. 111–12. Flower (2008b: 4) notes our lack of Greek evidence for the progression from the concentration of mantic and political ("royal") powers in a single individual to the allocation of these powers to discrete individuals.

33. See also Malkin 2003, 2009. Malkin remains one of the few scholars to consider seers in the context of foundations.

34. See Malkin 1987: 21. For a critique of Malkin's attempt to keep myth and history separate, see Kearns 1991. Calame (2003) presents an extended argument for the inseparability of myth and history in Greek thought, using the foundation of Cyrene as a case study for demonstrating this point.

35. White 1978: 86, quoted in Dougherty 1993: 5.

colonial narrative patterns: why, for example, an oikist would be represented as a murderer, or why a foundation is figured as a marriage.[36] Her analyses also alert us to colonial narratives' tendency to suppress and transform elements that occurred in connection with actual foundations. For instance, to take the example of the oikist as murderer, although we know that crises such as land shortage and political unrest were motivating factors for launching colonial expeditions, colonial narratives themselves often ignore such explanations. Instead, a number of them cast the oikist as a murderer who must be expelled from his community. Dougherty argues that, in doing so, colonial narratives use the metaphor of the murderer who is subsequently purified by Delphic Apollo to describe the analogous experience of being forced to leave home and found a new city, an experience in which Delphic Apollo also plays a role.

Despite its markedly different objectives, Dougherty's work intersects with the more positivist aims of Malkin insofar as her analyses also highlight Delphi's prominence and the centrality of the Delphi-oikist relationship in many colonial narratives. Dougherty importantly emphasizes other ideological components of colonial discourse, but she does not address the primacy in colonial discourse of Delphi, the Delphi-oikist bond, and the characterization of the oikist as a figure of religious authority.[37] Setting Malkin and Dougherty side by side thus directs us to a neglected area of inquiry. Malkin's meticulous assemblage of a wide range of evidence underscores the oikist's privileged relationship with Delphic Apollo and also helps us to see the striking contrast between conspicuous military seers and absent colonial ones. Dougherty in turn provides a model for reading colonial discourse for ideology and for considering the discursive motivations that generate the phenomena Malkin examines. As this book will argue, colonial ideology deliberately valorizes and promotes the image of the Delphi-sponsored oikist, and this formulation, far from occurring in a cultural vacuum, requires the suppression of the seer.

To turn to divination, in her overview of the study of divination within the field of classics, Sarah Iles Johnston tracks how scholarship has evolved from primarily compilations of data (i.e., of oracles or of the technical aspects of specific rituals) to interpretive analyses of divination as, for example, social practice, as a complex semiotic system, and as cognitive process.[38] The last two decades have seen an array of diverse works on the subject, including Johnston's own survey of ancient

---

36. For the oikist as murderer, see Dougherty 1993: 31–44; for the intersections between colonization and marriage, 61–80.

37. For example, Dougherty considers how marriage ideology informs certain narrative patterns of colonial discourse.

38. Johnston 2005: 1–28. Johnston also helpfully provides an exhaustive bibliography on Greek and Roman divination.

Greek divinatory methods, which investigates the major oracular centers, independent diviners, and divination's relationship to magic.[39] Other recent work includes Hugh Bowden's consideration of the intersections between divination and democracy at Athens, Esther Eidinow's study of oracular consultations and curse tables at the oracle of Dodona, Kai Trampedach's work on the political functions of divination, and Peter Struck's approach to divination through the application of ancient and modern theories of cognition.[40] Scholarship on Delphi itself has followed the evolution from data assembly to analysis noted by Johnston for the study of divination in general. Thus H. W. Parke and D. E. W. Wormell in the 1950s and Joseph Fontenrose in the 1970s published works dedicated to the collection of Delphic oracular responses and attempted systematic evaluations of their authenticity. By contrast, Julia Kindt reads "oracle stories" about Delphi as a unified group of narratives in order to evaluate not their historicity but rather what these stories reveal about Greek religious belief in divine communication.[41]

This book is in keeping with this more general shift toward placing divination in its cultural context and within the Greek cultural imaginary and leveraging the strengths of multiple disciplines to do so. Yet this is not to dismiss earlier work focused on the practicalities and mechanisms of divination. In fact, Flower's *The Seer in Ancient Greece* (2008) offers a model for combining both objectives, synthesizing evidence of the technical expertise and actual functions of the seer with that of the perceived image and the underlying system of belief that shaped the profession. My own overview of the seer presented in the following section is greatly indebted to Flower's detailed portrait. In addition to drawing on his exhaustive survey of the role of the seer, both real and imagined, I note two further ways in which his book has informed the concerns of this one. First, Flower stresses that the independent seer could not simply rely on technical competence for his success but also must have possessed personal charisma: "In the Greek world a seer, who operated by a combination of skill and charismatic inspiration, was the most authoritative expert on religious matters."[42] Second, as part of his assertion that

---

39. Johnston 2008.

40. Bowden 2005; Eidinow 2007; Trampedach 2015; Struck 2016. See also Rosenberger (2001) on Greek oracles and the cross-cultural comparisons of Beerden (2013, on divination in Greece, Republican Rome, and Neo-Assyrian Mesopotamia) and Raphals (2014, on Chinese and Greek divination). See Santangelo (2013) on divination and the Roman Republic.

41. In addition to Parke and Wormell 1956 and Fontenrose 1978, classic works on Delphi include Lloyd-Jones 1976; Roux 1976; Parker 1985. On the procedures of the sanctuary, see Parke and Wormell 1956: 1.17–45; Amandry 1975; Fontenrose 1978: 196–228; Bowden 2005: 17–26; Flower 2008b: 215–22. See also the groundbreaking work of Morgan (1990, 1993) on cult practice and the development of the sanctuary in relation to the formation of the polis. On oracle stories as oral narratives, see Maurizio 1995, 1997. For an overview of the history of the site of Delphi, see Scott 2010 and 2014.

42. Flower 2008b: 24.

seers were central figures of Greek society, Flower observes, "They are always lurking just beneath the surface of historical texts; they rear their heads only when they are involved in some extraordinary action."[43] This book in many ways builds on these two statements by exploring through case studies of individual seers what precisely it means to be considered "charismatic" in the archaic and classical periods, especially in relation to other, nondivinatory figures similarly characterized. Further, through the lens of colonial discourse, it attempts to account both for the ideological forces that cause the seer to "lurk" out of sight and, in turn, for those moments in which the seer rises to the surface.

THE GREEK SEER: AN OVERVIEW

Detecting colonial discourse's suppressions and manipulations of seers entails a fundamental understanding of the role of the seer himself in ancient Greek society. To this end, I provide here a general overview of the seer's basic functions and attributes.[44] "Seer" serves as a translation of the Greek term *mantis* (plural *manteis*), and the two words will be used interchangeably throughout the book. The relationship of the word *mantis* to other Greek terms for religious experts associated with divination, none of which appear as frequently as *mantis*, will be discussed below.

The Greek seer or *mantis* was a professional diviner whose primary role was to interpret the will of the gods through omens. The word *mantis* is thought to derive from the Indo-European root **men* (to be in a special mental state), a root from which the Greek words for "madness" (e.g., *mania* and its related verb *mainomai*) appear to originate as well.[45] Despite the etymological link between *mantis* and "madness," the Greek seer generally did not operate as a medium or mouthpiece for a god, uncontrollably transmitting messages through ecstatic possession.[46] While there are important instances of ecstatic possession in ancient Greece, most notably the Pythia at Delphi, the seer's fundamental role was that of an interpreter, although this capacity to interpret could be connected to an exceptional ability to intuit divine will.[47]

---

43. Flower 2008b: 3.

44. I enlist for this overview a number of recent studies, above all Flower 2008b. See also Dillery 2005; Johnston 2008; Raphals 2013; Trampedach 2015.

45. See Chantraine 1968–80: 3.665 s.v.; Dillery 2005: 169. This etymological connection was already made in antiquity: Plato (*Phdr.* 244c), for example, uses this connection to discredit the role of the seer.

46. For this reason, certain scholars have rejected the link between *mantis* and madness. Casevitz (1992), for instance, argues that the word *mantis* derives from *mēnuo* (to reveal), which would connect the *mantis*'s capacity to reveal through signs to his (less-attested) role of revealing through ecstatic possession (see also Raphals 2013: 101).

47. Flower 2008b: 30. On the Pythia, see, e.g., Flower 2008b: 215–26. The instances of seers prophesying through divinatory possession are rare but include the seer Theoklymenos (*Od.* 20.351–62) and the *chrēsmologos* Amphilytos (Hdt. 1.62.4–63.1). On Theoklymenos and Amphilytos, see chapters 2 and 6, respectively. On divinatory possession, see Flower 2008b: 88–89; for evidence of female seers, 211–39.

One way to capture in general terms the idiosyncratic character of the Greek seer is to emphasize the range of skills considered part of his expertise and the relatively unconstrained nature of the role itself, especially in contrast to those of professional diviners from other ancient Mediterranean cultures.[48] Thus two of the most salient attributes of the *mantis* are his independence and itinerancy, attributes that allowed him to adapt to a variety of contexts. The *Odyssey*, for instance, preserves an early reference to the seer's freelance mobility. Rebuking the suitor Antinoös for his treatment of the disguised Odysseus, the swineherd Eumaios declares (*Od.* 17.382–85):

τίς γὰρ δὴ ξεῖνον καλεῖ ἄλλοθεν αὐτὸς ἐπελθὼν
ἄλλον γ᾽, εἰ μὴ τῶν οἳ δημιοεργοὶ ἔασι,
μάντιν ἢ ἰητῆρα κακῶν ἢ τέκτονα δούρων,
ἢ καὶ θέσπιν ἀοιδόν, ὅ κεν τέρπῃσιν ἀείδων;

For who, going out himself, summons an utter stranger from elsewhere, unless he is one who works for the people, either a *mantis*, or a healer of sickness, or a skilled workman, or inspired singer, one who can give delight by singing?[49]

The passage situates the seer within a social class of traveling "public workers" (*dēmioergoi*), a category that includes the carpenter, doctor, and bard.[50] By contrast, in the following chapters, we will also encounter numerous seers, both mythical and historical, who belong to the elite. We do not possess enough evidence to ascertain the relationship between seers of different social classes. They appear to have coexisted, and distinctions between them were not necessarily well defined. Yet, regardless of status, a persistent and enduring feature accorded to Greek seers from the archaic through the Hellenistic period is the perception that they are "strangers from elsewhere." For instance, even when a historical seer seems to have spent his career closely tied to a given military leader or polis, he is still often characterized as an outsider to the army or population that he serves.[51]

A seer's cultural capital was derived from an indeterminate combination of perceived capabilities. When called upon, the seer could display his technical

---

48. For a comparison between Greek, Roman, and Neo-Assyrian forms of divination, see Beerden 2013.

49. Trans. Lattimore 2007, adapted. "An utter stranger from elsewhere" is Dillery's (2005: 177) translation. See also *Od.* 1.415–16 for another reference to an itinerant seer.

50. Cf. the comparable list from Solon: sea merchant, farmer, craftsman, poet, seer (*mantis*), and physician (Solon 13.43–62 W²). On this passage, see esp. Burkert 1992.

51. E.g., the seers Megistias (from Akarnania) and Teisamenos (from Elis) who served Sparta during the Persian Wars (see Hdt. 7.228 and 9.35.1, respectively; and chapter 1). The notional itinerancy and independence of the seer are bound up in the pervasive Greek cultural belief that travel and wisdom are profoundly connected. For the connection between wandering and knowledge, see esp. Martin 1992; Montiglio 2005; Hunter and Rutherford 2009. On the Greeks and wandering in general, see Garland 2014.

expertise in seercraft, but this more tangible presentation of competence could also operate in conjunction with other claims to authority based on unseen advantages, such as assertions of intuition, inherited mantic ability, personal charisma, or, as we will see in chapter 1, talismanic power.

It is worth surveying briefly the variety of interpretive techniques encompassed by the category of technical divination and addressing the relationship between this category and both intuitive divination and mantic inheritance. Chapter 1 will then consider in detail the relationship between a seer's technical and talismanic competence. The *Odyssey* passage reveals that *manteis* were considered skilled workers alongside other *dēmioergoi*. Fifth-century poets provide an explicit term for this skill: *mantikē technē* (the art of divination). This skill came in a wide range of forms. The author of *Prometheus Bound*, for instance, organizes the spectrum of divinatory methods into five discrete categories. Prometheus declares (*PV* 484–99):

τρόπους τε πολλοὺς μαντικῆς ἐστοίχισα,
κἄκρινα πρῶτος ἐξ ὀνειράτων ἃ χρὴ
ὕπαρ γενέσθαι, κληδόνας τε δυσκρίτους
ἐγνώρισ' αὐτοῖς ἐνοδίους τε συμβόλους,
γαμψωνύχων τε πτῆσιν οἰωνῶν σκεθρῶς
διώρισ', οἵτινές τε δεξιοὶ φύσιν
εὐωνύμους τε, καὶ δίαιταν ἥντινα
ἔχουσ' ἕκαστοι καὶ πρὸς ἀλλήλους τίνες
ἔχθραι τε καὶ στέργηθρα καὶ συνεδρίαι·
σπλάγχνων τε λειότητα, καὶ χροιὰν τίνα
ἔχουσ' ἂν εἴη δαίμοσιν πρὸς ἡδονὴν
χολή, λοβοῦ τε ποικίλην εὐμορφίαν·
κνίσῃ τε κῶλα συγκαλυπτὰ καὶ μακρὰν
ὀσφῦν πυρώσας δυστέκμαρτον εἰς τέχνην
ὥδωσα θνητούς, καὶ φλογωπὰ σήματα
ἐξωμμάτωσα πρόσθεν ὄντ' ἐπάργεμα.

I also systematized many kinds of seer-craft. I was the first to interpret from dreams what actual events were destined to happen; I made known to them the difficult arts of interpreting significant utterances and encounters on journeys; I defined precisely the flight of crook-taloned birds, which of them were favorable and which sinister by nature, the habits of each species and their mutual hatreds, affections and companionships; and the smoothness of internal organs, and what color bile should have if it is to be pleasing to the gods, and the mottled appearance and proper shape of the liver-lobe; I wrapped the thigh-bones and the long chine in fat and burnt them, guiding mortals towards a skill of making difficult inferences, and opening their eyes to the signs the flames gave, which till then had been dark to them.[52]

52. Trans. Sommerstein 2009.

The god's catalogue of *mantikē technē* consists of the interpretation of dreams, chance utterances and occurrences (i.e., "encounters on journeys"), birds, animal entrails, and sacrificial flames. In addition to Prometheus's categories, our ancient sources refer to numerous other types of omens that a seer could interpret, including the divinatory significance of certain animals, weather portents such as thunder and lightning, natural phenomena such as earthquakes and eclipses, and even sneezing.[53] The most common forms of Greek divination were bird augury (also known as ornithomancy, that is, the interpretation of the movement, actions, and sounds of birds) and extispicy (the examination of the entrails of sacrificed animals).

Oiōnos (bird) captures augury's status as the default mode of divination, since the word can signify not only birds of omen but simply omens in general.[54] Bird augury appears frequently in Greek literature, beginning with our earliest texts.[55] Kalchas, the *Iliad*'s seer par excellence, is called "the best of bird interpreters by far" (*Il.* 1.69), and the Homeric epics are replete with augury. An epic poem called the *Ornithomanteia* (Bird Divination) was attributed to Hesiod in antiquity.[56] The ways in which the Greeks performed augury are mostly lost to us, and references to it, like the *Prometheus Bound* passage above, indicate little beyond the belief that the side on which a bird appeared carried interpretive weight: a bird on the right side of the viewer signaled a propitious omen, while a bird on the left brought ominous news (see, e.g., Soph. *Ant.* 998–1004). The type of bird, such as a bird of prey, also shaped the interpretation.[57]

By contrast, the examination of entrails is at best only vaguely referred to in the Homeric epics. By the last quarter of the sixth century, however, representations of extispicy begin to appear with relative frequency on Attic vases.[58] Especially in the form known as hepatoscopy, that is, divination through the inspection of the liver, extispicy seems to have become the preferred divinatory form in actual practice by the classical period. At Olympia, among other sites, *manteis* practiced empyromancy, a technique that possibly required the diviner to interpret the color and motion of flames produced from burning sacrificial animals or even perhaps to interpret the cracks in the victim's burnt skin.[59]

---

53. See Dillon 1996: 100–101; Johnston 2008: 128–32.
54. See LSJ s.v. οἰωνός III; Ar. *Av.* 716–24.
55. On ornithomancy, see Dillon 1996; Flower 2008b: 24–25; Johnston 2008: 128–32.
56. West (1978: 365) attributes Hesiod frr. 312 and 355 M–W to the lost *Ornithomanteia*.
57. See Johnston 2008: 129–30.
58. Flower 2008b: 25. Flower (25) asserts that extispicy does not appear at all in Homeric epic, but Johnston (2008: 125) lists three Homeric passages (*Il.* 24.221; *Od.* 21.145, 22.318–23) that she understands as obliquely referring to sacrificial divination. See also Parker 2000: 300n7. On the vases, see Van Straten 1995: 156–57; Flower 2008b: 53–58.
59. See Parke 1967: 184–85; Flower 2008a: 193; 2008b: 40; Johnston 2008: 98, 128.

From the archaic period on, military *manteis* accompanying Greek armies performed two distinct types of divinatory sacrifice in warfare.[60] While the armies were still encamped, their seers consulted *hiera*, a polyvalent word signifying in this context both the inspected parts of the sacrificed animal as well as the omens derived from them. The omens, often read on the victim's liver, determined whether it was propitious for the army to engage in battle. On the battlefield itself, before the moment of engagement, a seer would perform *sphagia* (from *sphazein*, "to cut the throat"): an animal's throat would be slit, and a seer would interpret the flow of its blood and the movement of the victim as it fell to the ground. Scholars understand the purpose of this second sacrifice to have been propitiatory as well as divinatory in nature, with a positive outcome from the omens permitting the army to proceed.[61] Like certain other forms of Greek divination, extispicy was brought to Greece from the Near East. The memory of this origin, however, was lost to the Greeks of the historical period, who understood divination as a native invention or else as somehow connected to Egypt.[62]

For the Greeks, these forms of technical divination, which relied on inductive methods of interpretation, could operate in tandem with what Flower terms "intuitive divination."[63] Intuitive divination provided the seer with a kind of "second sight" to discern the past, present, and future. Bestowed by a god (most often Apollo), it could subsequently be inherited by a seer's descendants. This form of divination is to be distinguished, in turn, from "possession divination," in which the medium prophesies in an inspired state or becomes the mouthpiece of a god. Yet, as Flower notes, even possession divination could be referred to as a *technē* (e.g., Aesch. *Ag*. 1209).[64] That is to say, these three types of divination—technical, intuitive, and possession—are not always clearly separated from one another, and this is especially true of technical and intuitive divination.[65] The *Iliad's* characterization of the seer Kalchas as "the best of bird interpreters by far" in fact belongs to

---

60. The definitive discussions of divination in warfare remain Pritchett 1971: 109–15; 1979a: 83–90; Jameson 1991. See also Parker 2000; Flower 2008b: 159–65.

61. For a discussion of *sphagia* and its significance, see esp. Jameson 1991.

62. For Greek divination as a Near Eastern import, see, e.g., Burkert 1992: 46–51; West 1997: 46–51; Flower 2008b: 24–25. According to Herodotus (2.49), Melampous learned the art of divination in Egypt and brought it to Greece.

63. Flower 2008b: 88–89; this discussion of the different types of divination relies on 84–91 ("Towards a Typology of Greek Divination").

64. Flower 2008b: 86. On the Pythia's possession, see also Maurizio 1995.

65. As Flower (2008b: 84–87) emphasizes, the strict dichotomy Plato forms between possession ("natural") divination and technical ("artificial") divination is meant to discredit both forms of divination but especially the technical forms practiced by *manteis*. Plato's binary of natural and artificial divination influenced Cicero's own categorization (*De div.* 1.6.11–12; 1.18.34; 2.11.26–27; 2.100), which, in turn, formed the basis of Bouché-Leclercq's (1879: 1.124–245) influential typology of eight technical methods and three inspired methods of divination.

a longer description that captures this blurring of divinatory categories. Kalchas's technical ability at performing augury appears together with the claim that he could intuit what others could not, and, further, that he personally received this gift of seercraft from Apollo (*Il.* 1.68–72):

> τοῖσι δ' ἀνέστη
> Κάλχας Θεστορίδης οἰωνοπόλων ὄχ' ἄριστος,
> ὃς ᾔδη τά τ' ἐόντα τά τ' ἐσσόμενα πρό τ' ἐόντα,
> καὶ νήεσσ' ἡγήσατ' Ἀχαιῶν Ἴλιον εἴσω
> ἣν διὰ μαντοσύνην, τήν οἱ πόρε Φοῖβος Ἀπόλλων.

And among them arose Kalchas the son of Thestor, the best of bird interpreters by far, who knew the things that are, the things that will be, and the things that were before, and led the ships of the Achaians into Ilion through his seercraft, which Phoibos Apollo gave him.

In conjunction with his divinatory abilities, a seer could also claim descent from a mantic clan. There were four major mantic clans, each associated with a mythical seer: the Melampodidai (descendants of the seer Melampous), the Iamidai (descendants of the seer Iamos), the Klytiadai (descendants of the seer Klytios), and the Telliadai (descendants of the seer Tellias). We will have occasion to mention seers from all four of these clans in the coming chapters. The Melampodidai appear most frequently in our ancient sources and include the seers Theoklymenos (chapter 2) and Amphiaraos (chapter 6). Flower argues that the Iamidai only came to prominence in the fifth century B.C.E. after the Iamid seer Teisamenos's role in the Greeks' victory at the battle of Plataia.[66] With the exception of the Melampodidai, all of the mantic clans came from Elis, the polis associated with the Panhellenic sanctuary of Olympia in the northwestern Peloponnese.[67] Greek myth also provides us with plenty of examples of seers who were not tied to one of these four elite clans, such as Kalchas and Teiresias, who received their mantic gifts through divine favor and, in Teiresias's case, in compensation for blindness.[68] How nonelite seers of the historical period came by their profession is unclear. Nevertheless, asserting a connection to a mantic clan was one way of claiming authority, a claim that worked in combination with personal charisma and demonstrations of divinatory skill.[69]

---

66. Flower 2008a. Chapter 1 demonstrates how Herodotus carefully juxtaposes Teisamenos with the seer Hegesistratos, one of the Telliadai, who assisted the Persian leader Mardonios. Chapter 4 focuses on the Iamid Hagesias, seer to the fifth-century Syracusan tyrant Hieron.

67. Iamid and Klytiad seers officiated at Olympia into the third century C.E., according to inscriptions dating between 36 B.C.E. and 265 C.E. (see Weniger 1915; Flower 2008b: 40n50).

68. For Teiresias, see, e.g., Callim. *Hymn* 5 (to Athena); Ugolini 1995; Griffith 2009.

69. The inheritance of divinatory ability is connected to the larger aristocratic ideal of inherited excellence, an issue explored in chapter 6 pp. 170–77. See also Foster 2017.

Healing and purification also fell within the domain of the Greek seer's expertise.[70] The mythical seer Melampous purified the daughters of Proitos.[71] Aeschylus describes Apollo himself as an *iatromantis* (healer-seer) and *katharsios* (purifier) in *Eumenides* 61–63. According to Plato and later authors, the Athenians brought the *mantis* Epimenides from Crete to purify their city during a plague.[72]

Finally, *manteis* are often linked to two other types of religious experts, the *exēgētēs* (expounder) and the *chrēsmologos*.[73] Little is known of the *exēgētai* other than that they interpreted sacred law at Athens.[74] The relationship between the *mantis* and *chrēsmologos*, however, has been much debated.[75] Part of the difficulty lies in knowing exactly what the *chrēsmologoi* did. The *-logos* suffix can denote a "collector" but also a "chanter," and *chrēsmologoi* appear to have engaged in both functions, compiling collections of oracles as well as performing them.[76] Old Comedy has confused matters further: the genre seems to lampoon certain *manteis* by referring to them as *chrēsmologoi*, a conflation that was then taken at face value by much later authors who continued to use the terms synonymously.[77] But, as Flower shows, our earliest sources tend to distinguish between the two professions: *manteis* performed extispicy and augury, while the *chrēsmologoi* recited from their oracle collections.[78]

The Greek seer was a central figure of the archaic and classical periods. His role encompassed a number of functions (interpreter of divine signs, purifier, healer), and the types of divination he could perform came in a wide range of forms. A "stranger from elsewhere," he traveled through a Greek world crowded with

---

70. Flower 2008b: 27 with Burkert 1992: 42–73.

71. See, e.g., Hes. *Catalogue of Women* frr. 37, 131 M-W; Pherekydes *FGrH* 3 F 114; Apollod. *Bibl.* 2.2.2; and chapter 4.

72. Plat. *Leg.* 642d-643, with Arist. *Rh.* 3.17, 1418a23–26; Plut. *Solon* 12.1–4; Diog. Laert. 1.10. Cf. the figure of Diotima of Mantinea in Plat. *Symp.*

73. Our ancient sources also preserve a number of titles that seem roughly equivalent to the term *mantis*. Thus Homer uses the terms *theopropos* and *thuoskoos* (see Beck 2016 for the nuances in meaning between Homer's use of *mantis* and *theopropos*). Both Pindar (*N.* 1.61–62) and Aeschylus (*Sept.* 609–11) pair *mantis* with *prophētēs* as if they were synonyms. Dillery (2005: 171) argues that a *prophētēs* is more often connected with a particular cult site, a kind of "dependent" diviner; also see Dillery (171) for additional synonyms for *mantis*. See also Griffith 2009: 476–79. I do not discuss here the various terms for magician and sorcerer, on which see Eidinow 2007; 26–28; Johnston 2008: 144–82.

74. See Oliver 1950 with Dillery 2005: 170–71; Clinton 1974.

75. For the scholarly debate about the relationship between the two roles as well as earlier bibliography on the issue, see Dillery 2005: 168–72; Flower 2008b: 60–65.

76. Dillery 2005: 169.

77. See Flower 2008b: 60–63.

78. Flower 2008b: 63. See also the discussions of the *chrēsmologos* Onomakritos in Dillery 2005 and Trampedach 2015: 237–39. We know of collections of oracles attributed to legendary figures such as Bakis, Musaios, and Orpheus.

oracles, other independent seers, and an array of religious experts, whose spheres of competence overlapped, intersected, and so competed with one another.

...

The chapters in this book are meant to be read in order. Chapter 1 sets up a foil for the colonial seer by examining the military *mantis*. Chapter 2 explores the pairing of the colonial seer and oikist in the early archaic *Odyssey*. Chapter 3 proposes two principal reasons for why this same pairing is absent from later archaic and early classical colonial discourse and establishes the model for colonial discourse's suppression of the seer. Chapters 4–6, each focusing on a particular seer, present a sequence of epinikian odes that reveal in different ways Bacchylides' and Pindar's manipulations of this model. Chapter 6 presents the book's culmination, since it offers both the fullest realization of colonial discourse's suppression of the seer as well as Pindar's most daring subversion of it.

Chapter 1 considers Herodotus's characterization of the seer Teisamenos as a "leader of wars" (9.33) and uncovers a cultural desire to regard certain military seers as conduits of talismanic power. I demonstrate how seers were recruited for warfare not only because of their ability to interpret omens but also because they could be seen to possess a talismanic power that guaranteed victory. Once we recognize that seers could be viewed in this light, we can examine the ways in which they intersect with other talismanic figures similarly characterized, including oikists. Understanding seers from this new angle sets the stage for thinking about two related issues central to the book. First, since this chapter discusses how seers were fixtures on military campaigns and since scholars compare military and colonial expeditions, the absence of seers from many foundation tales becomes all the more striking. Second, given the equivalence between the talismanic power of seers and oikists, we can begin to understand one source of tension between the seer and the oikist: the talismanic power of the seer could be seen to conflict with the oikist's own comparable claim to it.

Chapter 2 addresses the partnership between Odysseus and the seer Theoklymenos in the *Odyssey*. I argue that the seer and the hero operate as a coherent pair within the framework of colonization and that Theoklymenos aids Odysseus-as-oikist in effecting the metaphorical refoundation of Ithaka. Theoklymenos and Odysseus reveal that the pairing of the seer and oikist is a possible and productive construct. Yet, Homer's presentation of Theoklymenos as a doublet of Odysseus also suggests the potential for an uncomfortable degree of redundancy between the seer and oikist in later post-Homeric foundation tales.

Following Chapter 1's discussion of the conspicuous presence of seers on military campaigns and Chapter 2's presentation of a productive alliance between the seer and the oikist in an early archaic text, Chapter 3 interrogates the startling excision of seers from later archaic and classical colonial discourse. This chapter offers two basic reasons for the missing seer. First, I argue that in post-Homeric colonial narratives the oikist, singled out by Apollo at Delphi, co-opts the religious authority enjoyed elsewhere by the seer. That post-Homeric colonial discourse is still interested in the seer's form of religious authority but assigns it instead to the Delphi-sanctioned oikist reveals a purposeful ideological effort to exclude the seer. Second, I survey a general cultural tendency to regard the seer in the context of the city with suspicion. The stereotype of the seer as a threat to political leaders makes his incorporation in a discourse that valorizes the oikist unwelcome. For this reason then as well, colonial discourse is motivated to suppress the seer.

Chapters 4–6 put to work the model outlined in chapter 3 and present three epinikian case studies that can be seen, in different ways, to respond to colonial discourse's ideological strategy of suppressing the role of the seer. In chapter 4, I read Bacchylides' *Ode* 11 as a specific example of this phenomenon. In his rendition of the myth of the Proitids, Bacchylides deliberately omits the seer Melampous and at the same time casts Proitos's arrival in Tiryns as a foundation, with Proitos himself as its oikist. I conclude with a connection between this strategy within the ode and its tantalizing historical context. The ode appears to be part of the family of the victor's larger effort to resist a virtual refoundation of their city by a seer-like figure.

Chapter 5 turns to the seer Hagesias in Pindar's *Olympian* 6 and discusses the ideological implications of the poet's decision to link the seer explicitly to a colonial agenda. This chapter reveals what happens when a seer is included in a foundation and the delicate maneuvers required to effect this incorporation. I consider both the broader historical and political significance of Pindar's description of the seer Hagesias in *Olympian* 6 as a *sunoikistēr* (cofounder) as well as how Hagesias's double role (as both a seer and a *sunoikistēr*) is handled within Pindar's poetics. By praising Hagesias in the ode as an athletic victor, seer, and *sunoikistēr*, Pindar marks Hagesias as a figure who enjoys enormous ritual power. Insofar as he characterizes the seer as a *sunoikistēr*, however, Pindar also introduces an uneasy element of competition into Hagesias's relationship with his own patron, Hieron, the self-proclaimed oikist of Aitna. After establishing the challenges of this undertaking, I address Pindar's solution. In the ode's two mythic portions, the poet circumscribes Hagesias's position so as to mitigate any threat the seer might present to Hieron's own political authority. Finally, by reading *Olympian* 6 together with *Olympian* 1 and *Nemean* 1, I argue that, despite his subsequent need to establish that Hagesias will not overthrow Hieron, Pindar joins the seemingly incompatible titles of seer and *sunoikistēr* because Hagesias is crucial to Hieron's colonial enterprise: in *Olympian* 6, Hagesias both personifies and symbolically enacts Hieron's fantasy of uniting the Dorian populations of the Peloponnese and Sicily within the tyrant's colonial city of Aitna.

The final chapter of the book demystifies Delphi's "oracular monopoly" within colonial discourse by focusing on the myth of Alkmaion.[79] In what we might call the myth's mainstream tradition, a tradition that includes epic, tragic, and prose variants of the myth, the seer Amphiaraos's son Alkmaion is never tied to seercraft but is instead characterized as an oikist of a Delphi-sanctioned foundation. Yet this tradition does not merely neglect to highlight Alkmaion's inherited status as a seer. Rather, Delphi asserts itself as the only reliable option for assisting Alkmaion, following the hero's matricide, and, importantly, casts Alkmaion's adherence to Amphiaraos as unreliable. In this way, the tradition seems to require a rejection of Amphiaraos as part of its presentation of Delphi's superior claim to authority and of the oracle's transformation of Alkmaion into an oikist. I contrast the mainstream tradition's presentation of Alkmaion with a version of the myth found in Pindar's *Pythian* 8. In this extraordinary ode, Pindar promotes the relationship between Amphiaraos and his son and, uniquely among our extant sources, asserts Alkmaion's own powers of prophecy. Moreover, just as the dominant tradition conjures Amphiaraos even as it dismisses him, Delphi's role in foundations lies under the surface of the ode, evoked but never fully realized. What both the mainstream tradition and *Pythian* 8 seem to share, however, is conceiving of the seer and oikist as mutually exclusive. A similar opposition is detected in chapter 4 for Melampous and Proitos, but in the case of Alkmaion, the conflict between seer and oikist is waged over a single figure. This investigation of the Alkmaion myth exposes the ideological stance of the mainstream tradition that promotes Delphi's active production of colonial founders and its concomitant suppression of the individual seer within colonial discourse.

A conclusion considers how colonial discourse's pattern of suppressing the seer breaks down once we move temporally and spatially beyond the orbit of Delphi's powerful oracular monopoly. Accounts of Hellenistic foundations, such as Epaminondas's refoundation of Messene and Alexander the Great's foundation of Alexandria, reveal seers working in tandem with the oikist. At the same time, foundation oracles from Delphi disappear after the early fourth century B.C.E. This coincidence strongly suggests that colonial discourse accommodates the seer when Delphi's centripetal pull on and control over the oikist wanes. Similarly, a survey of traditions concerning the seer Amphilochos's foundation of Mallos in Cilicia paints a picture of a seer who, by operating in the East, was viewed as out of range of Delphi's control and could, at least for a time, enjoy the paradoxical role of oikist-seer.

---

79. I borrow the term "oracular monopoly" from Kurke 2011: 60.

1

Beyond Entrails and Omens

Herodotus's Teisamenos and the Talismanic Seer at War

I begin with an observation and a paradox. First, the observation. Greek colonial expeditions resembled in certain fundamental ways military ventures. Just as Greek armies could march with their commanders to the site of a distant battlefield, colonial expeditions, guided by their oikist (founder), traveled to a new land in which awaited at least the possibility of a hostile encounter.[1] Several ancient authors confirm that the colonists' initial engagement with native populations could be violent, while Thucydides explicitly compares colonial and military ventures:[2] in his speech on the eve of the Sicilian expedition, Nikias tries to reason with those citizens eager for the undertaking (6.23.2–3):

> πόλιν τε νομίσαι χρὴ ἐν ἀλλοφύλοις καὶ πολεμίοις οἰκιοῦντας ἰέναι, οὓς πρέπει τῇ πρώτῃ ἡμέρᾳ ᾗ ἂν κατάσχωσιν εὐθὺς κρατεῖν τῆς γῆς, ἢ εἰδέναι ὅτι, ἢν σφάλλωνται, πάντα πολέμια ἕξουσιν.

---

1. This general correspondence obtains whether we understand the expedition to be an ad hoc enterprise or a more formal affair orchestrated by a mother city. Osborne (1998) argues that early archaic colonial expeditions were less organized than those of the classical period. Osborne envisions these earlier ventures as under the leadership not of a state-sponsored oikist but of a "charismatic" individual. The degree to which early Greek colonial activity of the eighth century B.C.E. resembled the more organized and often state-led colonial expeditions of the later archaic and classical periods continues to be debated. See Donnellan and Nizzo 2016: 9–20 for an excellent summary of the key contested issues.

2. Archil. frr. 17, 18, 19, 88, 120 Tarditi; Mimn. fr. 9 W² (= Strabo 14.1.4); Thuc. 6.1–5; Diod. Sic. 8.21.3. See also Paus. 3.14.2–3, 6.13.1–2 with Christesen 2010 on Chionis of Sparta's pacification of the Libyans during the foundation of Cyrene.

We must also consider that we go to settle a city among foreign and hostile people and that those of us who do this must either become masters of the country on the very first day they land in it or know that, if they fail to do so, they will encounter hostilities on every side.

Modern scholars have followed Thucydides' lead in comparing colonial and military campaigns. As Malkin observes, "There is no great difference, after all, between the oikist as a leader of a colonial, or a military expedition."[3]

Second, I note a paradox. Whereas seers are frequently paired with military commanders in accounts of late archaic and early classical Greek warfare as well as in myths current in this period, they rarely appear paired with oikists in colonial narratives concerning the same time frame.[4] This paradox captures the central concern of this book—namely, the consideration of why the seer, while conspicuous in military contexts, is absent from comparable and contemporary colonial ones.

In order to address this discrepancy, however, we must first develop a more nuanced understanding of the presence of the Greek seer on campaign. The prominence of military *manteis* in Greek representations of warfare cannot be attributed solely to their expertise in the divinatory requirements for battle. This expertise is crucial, as others have well shown, but it leaves us with an incomplete picture.[5] This chapter will argue that, in addition to their possession of divinatory skill, certain seers could be considered figures of extraordinary talismanic power. Best observed through specific examples, talismanic power can be defined as a divinely guaranteed ability to succeed, especially in the contexts of warfare and athletic competition. An individual believed to possess talismanic power was seen to enjoy an outsize portion of divine favor that enabled him to win, sometimes against all odds and occasionally in a manner defying rationalization. Put another

---

3. Malkin 1987: 103. See also Malkin 1987: 5. On this same Thucydides passage, Dougherty (1993: 40) writes: "Founding a colony can be as dangerous and violent as war. . . . Each means a dangerous confrontation with hostile peoples and requires a large demonstration of force."

4. Seers accompanying military commanders are found in our ancient sources from Homer to Arrian. Mythical and historical pairs alike are well known: Agamemnon and Kalchas (*Il.* 1); Adrastos and Amphiaraos (Pi. *O.* 6 and *N.* 9); Leonidas and Megistias (Hdt. 7.221); Tolmides and Theainetos (Paus. 1.27.5); Eupompides and Theainetos (Thuc. 3.20.1); Aristomenes and Theoklos and their sons, Gorgos and Mantiklos (Paus. 4.21.2); Kimon and Astyphilos of Poseidonia (Plut. *Kim.* 18.3); Nicias and Stilbiades (Plut. *Nic.* 23.5); Pelopidas and Theokritos (Plut. *Pel.* 21–22); Alexander and Aristander (Plut. *Alex.* 2.3, 14.5, and 25.1–2). See also Flower 2008b: 176–83 on the partnership between Greek military generals and their seers. For the few seers who are mentioned in a colonial context in the late archaic and early classical periods and the problematic nature of these references, see chapters 3, 5, and the conclusion.

5. For the duties of the military *mantis*, see Pritchett 1971: 109–15; 1979a: 83–90; Jameson 1991. See also Parker 2000; Flower 2008b: 159–65. For a brief summary of the evidence, see the introduction under "The Greek Seer: An Overview."

way, we might define talismanic power as a potent, culturally specific, and more narrowly defined form of the general concept of charisma.[6]

A belief in talismanic power flourished during the archaic and classical periods, especially in the late sixth to early fifth century B.C.E. Inherited from earlier generations, the concept of talismanic power was particularly suited to the late archaic and early classical zeitgeist.[7] During this time frame, the perceived existence of talismanic figures and the polis's desire to harness their efficacy dovetailed with a range of analogous phenomena. Anecdotes associated with this period report the assistance of epiphanic heroes and gods in battle, such as Theseus and the Dioskouroi, as well as accounts of athletes who performed extraordinary deeds beyond the limits of normal human capability.[8] A corresponding array of cults sought to incorporate these larger-than-life figures into the framework of the polis with a view to capitalizing on their ritual power. Cults for heroized athletes, for the archaic Seven Sages, for oikists, and for local heroes populated the religious landscape at this time.[9] Herodotus's report of the Spartans' relocation of the bones of Orestes from Tegea to Sparta also belongs to this milieu (1.66–68). Herodotus concludes his story by noting that ever since the bones of Orestes have resided in Sparta, the Spartans themselves have been invincible.[10] Fittingly, archaic and classical literary texts (e.g., epinikia), oral traditions (e.g., hero-athlete narratives), and visual media (e.g., victory statues) that presented expressions of talismanic power accommodated these other beliefs and experiences as well.[11]

Internal and external pressures converged on the late archaic and early classical Greek polis to create an environment especially receptive to these related phenomena. Assertions of talismanic status, especially in connection with athletic victory,

---

6. For the contours and operations of charisma in general, see the canonical study of Weber (1978: 1111–1300).

7. On evidence for talismanic power in the Homeric poems, see Benveniste 1973: 346–56; Kurke 1993; and below.

8. On epiphanies in battle, see below. See Nicholson 2016: 21–49 for numerous examples of hero-athlete narratives and athlete heroization. As Nicholson shows, these phenomena thrived especially in the first half of the fifth century B.C.E.

9. For athlete cults, see Bohringer 1979; Christesen 2010; Currie 2005: 120–23; Nicholson 2016: 40–41. Cults of the Seven Sages: Pittakos (Diog. Laert. 1.175) and Bias (Diog. Laert. 1.88). Hall (2008: 405–11) cautions against exaggerating the prevalence of oikist cults. But the existence of certain oikist cults, such as that of Antiphemos of Gela and, most notably, of Battos of Cyrene, is incontrovertible. For the oikist cult of Antiphemos, see Malkin 1987: 259–60; for Battos, see Pi. *P.* 5.93–98 with Malkin 1987: 204–12.

10. On Herodotus's account of the bones of Orestes, see Boedeker 1993. See also the bones of Theseus (Paus. 3.3.7). Note the general statement of Wallace (2009: 425) in his discussion of charismatic leaders of the archaic period: "A hero was a mortal deemed so great that his bones forever possessed magic powers."

11. For the genre of hero-athlete narrative and its ideological opposition to epinikion, see Nicholson 2016. See Nicholson 2016: 272–76 for the ways in which even the poses of victory statues can align with one or the other of these two different ideological positions. For the connection between victory statues and talismanic power, see Kurke 1993.

seem to have functioned as a strategic way for elites to counter the dilution of their traditional forms of ritual power.[12] At the same time, these elite assertions were offset by the polis's interest in co-opting a variety of powerful talismans for its own use. The looming threat of Persia and its subsequent extraordinary defeat also encouraged the desire for and claims of heroic or numinous assistance.[13]

In this era of internal upheaval and foreign invasion, the Greek seer thrived. Nevertheless, modern scholarship has yet to explain the seer's importance by relating it sufficiently to the phenomena discussed above and especially to the concept of talismanic authority. To uncover the seer's own claim to talismanic power, however, it is necessary first to come to grips more generally with this cultural belief by surveying its most conspicuous recipients, namely, athletic victors of the so-called crown games.[14] To this end, part 1 of this chapter will provide an overview of talismanic athletic victors in the late archaic and early classical periods. Part 1 will emphasize that what distinguishes talismanic power in this period from its manifestations in Homeric poetry is the polis's interest in its regenerative powers. As we will see, a belief in the regenerative or enduring potential of talismanic power helps account for instances of athletic victors who are subsequently recruited by their cities to ensure military victory or to lead successful colonial expeditions as oikists.

In part 2, Herodotus's characterization of the Greeks' seer at Plataia, Teisamenos, as a "leader of wars" will serve as the primary case study for understanding how military seers could also be perceived as talismanic. Herodotus's extended comparison of Teisamenos and the *mantis* serving the Persians, Hegesistratos, further underscores the talismanic nature of the seers at Plataia. Part 3 then integrates seers into a larger cultural nexus of talismanic figures. For, once we recognize that seers could be viewed as talismanic themselves, we can examine how they converge and intersect with other figures similarly depicted, including athletic victors and oikists. That seers are analogous in the context of warfare with other types of talismanic figures anticipates chapters 3–6: since talismanic oikists and athletes prominently appear in colonial contexts, the seer's erasure from these same contexts proves all the more striking. Put another way, the military seer explored in this chapter will serve as a foil for the colonial seer explored in the remainder of the book.

---

12. See Kurke 1993: 153 with Davies 1981: 88–161. For the increasing democratization of Athenian religion in the fifth century, see Ostwald 1986: 137–71; Ober 1989: 57–58.

13. This divine and heroic assistance frequently took the form of epiphany, as we will see below. For the wave of epiphanies of local heroes and gods during the Persian Wars, see Petridou 2016: 113–22.

14. See esp. Kurke 1993; Nicholson 2016. The crown games, also called the games of the *periodos*, are the Panhellenic Olympian, Pythian, Isthmian, and Nemean games.

I. CROWN VICTORS AND THE CONCEPT OF TALISMANIC POWER

In Diodorus Siculus's account of the late sixth-century war between Kroton and Sybaris, the outnumbered Krotoniates manage to defeat the Sybarites. The Krotoniates themselves credit the athlete Milo with the surprise upset (12.9.5–6):

> ... Μίλωνος τοῦ ἀθλητοῦ ἡγουμένου καὶ διὰ τὴν ὑπερβολὴν τῆς τοῦ σώματος ῥώμης πρώτου τρεψαμένου τοὺς καθ' αὑτὸν τεταγμένους. ὁ γὰρ ἀνὴρ οὗτος, ἑξάκις Ὀλύμπια νενικηκὼς καὶ τὴν ἀλκὴν ἀκόλουθον ἔχων τῇ κατὰ τὸ σῶμα φύσει, λέγεται πρὸς τὴν μάχην ἀπαντῆσαι κατεστεφανωμένος μὲν τοῖς Ὀλυμπικοῖς στεφάνοις, διεσκευασμένος δὲ εἰς Ἡρακλέους σκευὴν λεοντῇ καὶ ῥοπάλῳ· αἴτιον δὲ γενόμενον τῆς νίκης θαυμασθῆναι παρὰ τοῖς πολίταις.

> ... with Milo the athlete leading and, due to the superiority of his bodily strength, the first to put to flight those marshaled against him. For this man, who had won an Olympic victory six times and had courage to match his physical nature, is said to have come into battle decked with his Olympic crowns and dressed in Herakles' gear with lion skin and club. And [they say] that he was an object of wonder in the eyes of his fellow citizens because he was the reason for their victory.

In this extraordinary scene, Milo, decked with crowns and the lion skin and club of Herakles, routs the Sybarites. Diodorus at first seems to attribute the feat to Milo's superior strength, but this initial explanation gives way to his description of Milo's striking costume and the Krotoniates' estimation of the Olympic victor as a *thauma* (object of wonder). The effect of the entire passage, culminating in the Krotoniates' astonishment, suggests that physical prowess alone does not tell the whole story.

Leslie Kurke illuminates the strangeness of this passage by connecting it to a cluster of recurring dictional features in agonistic inscriptions and epinikia for athletic victors.[15] As she perceives, a number of agonistic inscriptions and epinikia valorize the victor's crown and, at the same time, formulate an equivalence between the crown and the term *kudos*. This equivalence between the victor's crown and *kudos* introduces a further element in these contexts, the polis. For the crown itself can transform into the *kudos* the victor bestows upon his city, as in Bacchylides' Ode 10 (15–18):[16]

> ὁσσά<-> Νίκας ἕκατι
> ἄνθεσιν ξανθὰν ἀναδησάμενος κεφαλὰν
> κῦδος εὐρείαις Ἀθάναις
>   θῆκας Οἰνείδαις τε δόξαν

---

15. Kurke 1993.
16. For further examples of this equation, see Pi. *O.* 4.8–12, *O.* 5.1–8, *I.* 1.10–12; Bacch. 1.155–65, 13.58–60 with Kurke 1993.

however many times, because of Victory, binding your golden head with flowers, you have established *kudos* for spacious Athens and glory for the Oineidai.

In like manner, Herodotus records a dedicatory epigram that, mirroring the language of agonistic inscriptions, again links a (metaphorical) crown to a polis's *kudos* (4.88.2):

Βόσπορον ἰχθυόεντα γεφυρώσας ἀνέθηκε
  Μανδροκλέης Ἥρῃ μνημόσυνον σχεδίης,
αὑτῷ μὲν στέφανον περιθείς, Σαμίοισι δὲ κῦδος,
  Δαρείου βασιλέος ἐκτελέσας κατὰ νοῦν.

Having bridged the fishy Bosphorus, Mandrokles dedicated to Hera a memorial of the bridge of boats, placing a crown on himself and *kudos* on the Samians, having accomplished it by Darius's design.

Surveying the appearances of *kudos* in Homeric epic, Émile Benveniste observed that the word can signal a hero's talismanic power.[17] In the *Iliad*, a god can bestow *kudos* upon a hero and thereby instantaneously provide him with an "irresistible advantage" for victory. Athena sees to it that Diomedes can win the chariot race: ἐν γὰρ Ἀθήνη / ἵπποις ἧκε μένος καὶ ἐπ' αὐτῷ κῦδος ἔθηκε (For Athena placed strength in his horses and gave *kudos* to him, *Il.* 23.399–400). The hero Antilochos makes clear that he knows full well the cause of Diomedes' victory as he urges his own horses on: ἤτοι μὲν κείνοισιν ἐριζέμεν οὔ τι κελεύω / Τυδεΐδεω ἵπποισι δαΐφρονος, οἷσιν Ἀθήνη / νῦν ὤρεξε τάχος καὶ ἐπ' αὐτῷ κῦδος ἔθηκεν (I am not ordering you in any way to contend with those horses of the valiant son of Tydeus, to whom now Athena has granted swiftness and to [Diomedes] has given *kudos*, *Il.* 23.404–406). As Benveniste observes, in these and other instances in the epic poems, *kudos* appears to operate as a "talisman of supremacy" for the hero to whom it is granted.[18] Building on Benveniste's understanding of the term in Homeric poetry, Kurke argues that the *kudos* referred to in epinikia and agonistic inscriptions continues to operate in this sense in the sixth and fifth centuries. That is to say, athletic victors of the crown games become the primary inheritors in the archaic and classical periods of this "talismanic potency."[19]

---

17. Benveniste 1973: 348.

18. Benveniste 1973: 348; also note Benveniste's (348) observation: "The gift of *kudos* ensures the triumph of the man who receives it." On the definition of the formula *kudos aresthai*, see Benveniste (346): "*Kûdos aresthai*, used of a warrior, properly means 'to seize (from the gods) the *kûdos*,' and consequently, strengthened by this talisman, to cover oneself with glory."

19. Kurke 1993: 136. As noted in this chapter's introduction, this "inheritance" of talismanic power by athletic victors speaks to an attempt by aristocratic families to maintain authority within the archaic and classical polis.

Since post-Homeric texts equate *kudos* with the victor's crown, the crown itself can be understood on its own to signify the talismanic power an athlete receives at his moment of victory. Pindar's *Isthmian* 1 provides a clear instance of the equation between crowns and *kudos* when the poet places them in apposition as he announces his intention to praise the Isthmus (10–12):

ἐπεὶ στεφάνους
ἓξ ὤπασεν Κάδμου στρατῷ ἐξ ἀέθλων,
καλλίνικον πατρίδι κῦδος.

since it gave the people of Kadmos six crowns from contests, triumphant *kudos* for the fatherland.

The merging of the two terms in both epinikia and inscriptions also suggests that the crown becomes more than just a sign of the victor's *kudos*.[20] It can become the physical manifestation of it. As such, the crown itself seems to have served as an expedient vehicle for transferring talismanic power between the victor and his city.[21] The crown's ability to embody the victor's talismanic power accounts for the crown's prominence in certain reentry rituals that attended a victor's return from the games.[22] The *technicus terminus* for the entire reentry ritual was the εἰσάγειν τὸν στέφανον (to bring in the crown), and its culminating moment was the victor's public dedication of the crown at a local shrine.[23] This focus on the crown again implies that more than functioning as a token of prestige the crown brought with it a perceived power that the city desired to incorporate within its walls.

Thus Kurke's important insight into the meaning and internal dynamics of this grouping of recurring terms (athletic victor, crown, *kudos*, and polis) yields results beyond the scope of the texts themselves and makes sense of a number of related cultural practices. Claims of talismanic power are not the genre-bound assertions of epinikion or the boasts of agonistic inscriptions but are in keeping with purported manifestations and declarations of it elsewhere in the late archaic and early classical periods, a point relevant to our encounter with the seer Teisamenos in part 2.

It is necessary to pause and acknowledge that the concept of talismanic power is contested in modern scholarship. Discussions of talismanic power have

---

20. As Kurke (1993: 139) notices, occasionally the verb *kudainō* (to bestow *kudos*) replaces the verb *stephanoō* (to crown). See also Kurke passim for agonistic inscriptions that formulate the same connection between crowns and *kudos*.

21. Pindar refers a number of times to the victor's dedication of the crown: *O.* 9.110–12; *N.* 5.50–54, 8.13–16 (*mitra* [headband]). See also *O.* 5.1–8 with Kurke 1993: 138.

22. See Versnel (1970: 155–62) on the Roman ritual of reentry that Versnel views as an attempt to contain a victor's talismanic power (which Versnel calls *mana*). See also Kurke 1993: 134.

23. See Robert 1967: 17–18; Pleket 1975: 62–64. For the extravagant reentry ritual of a fifth-century Akragantine victor, see Diod. Sic. 13.82.7–8.

encountered resistance over the course of the last century, often because of the larger theoretical frameworks with which the concept has been linked. In the early twentieth century, the so-called Cambridge ritualists were interested in the Greeks' belief in talismanic power, but when this interest became associated with the Cambridge school's discredited and more notorious treatments of topics such as weather magic, their consideration of talismanic power was dismissed as well. The work of a later generation of scholars, such as Émile Benveniste, Hermann Fränkel, and H. S. Versnel, revived the subject, suggesting that one could read together the concepts of talismanic power, *kudos*, and, through a comparative anthropological lens, *mana*. In response, Poulheria Kyriakou and David Pritchard take issue with relating *kudos* to *mana*, with understanding *kudos* as signaling talismanic power, and, by extension, with the concept of talismanic power itself.[24] For Kyriakou and Pritchard, athletic victory brought political capital and prestige.

To my mind, understanding the figures explored in this chapter as endowed with talismanic power as much as with political capital and prestige, which they also certainly enjoyed, more fully explains the way in which these figures are represented by our sources. The concept also helps to account for why ancient authors, as we will see below, repeatedly equate these human figures with numinous phenomena, such as the epiphanies of cult heroes and gods. *Kudos*, as others have shown, is a polyvalent word whose exact meaning in a given context is often difficult to discern.[25] But, as in the examples presented here, the word does seem to have been for some ancient authors one way to attempt to name and articulate talismanic power, whose potential the Greeks were especially keen to recruit in the late archaic and early classical periods.

To return to Milo, we can now see that the athlete heading into battle bedecked with his six Olympic crowns is an image teeming with talismanic power. As Diodorus Siculus presents it, the athlete's talismanic power accounts for his ability to rout the enemy and to appear as an object of wonder, a *thauma*, in the eyes of his fellow Krotoniates. Even Milo's Herakles costume relates to his talismanic status insofar as it announces that his performance in battle will exceed the bounds of normal human capability.[26] What is more, Herakles himself can be viewed as a paradigm of talismanic power, especially given his close identification with both warfare and athletic competition, that is, the two spheres in which *kudos* predominately operates.[27] Finally, the episode reminds us that while *kudos* can denote talismanic power, it remains but one way to define or capture the phenomenon, and our ancient

---

24. Kyriakou 2007, closely followed by Pritchard 2012.
25. See esp. Race 2014.
26. See Nicholson 2016: 27 for further connections between Milo and Herakles.
27. Kurke 1993: 156–57n13. On Herakles' pronounced connection to talismanic hero-athletes, see Nicholson 2016 passim.

evidence can present manifestations of talismanic power without relying on the use of the word *kudos* to signal its appearance. Milo's talismanic power, for instance, receives concrete expression in his six Olympic crowns, while the "proof" of its existence rests in the athlete's ability to deliver victory single-handedly to Kroton.

We might think of Milo as an extreme realization of the talismanic capability of all crown victors. For, although not as dramatically rendered or as overdetermined as Milo, crown victors are frequently mentioned in the context of war. Like the dedication of a returning victor's crown at a local sanctuary, the inclusion of crown victors in battle seems to have been one way for the polis to capitalize on the talismanic power of its athletes. Indeed, I would stress that our archaic and classical sources express a greater interest in the polis's later reuse of a crown victor's talismanic power than on the moment of victory itself. This interest seems to signal a shift from the Homeric material with its focus on the oscillation of *kudos* between heroes. In the *Iliad*, a god delivers *kudos* to an individual warrior at a critical point in battle in order to ensure his victory before bestowing it in turn upon another.[28] By contrast, archaic and classical evidence points toward a belief in talismanic power's enduring potential and a desire to recontextualize it for the benefit of a larger community. As with all benefits associated with their unpredictable gods, the Greeks could never be certain how long this power would last, but the possibility of its persistence explains the cultural motivation to enclose the victor's crown with the city walls and to co-opt the very victors themselves for battle or for the successful foundation of a new city.

Thus a number of archaic and classical crown victors appear to have been put to later use in the contexts of warfare and colonization. These victors, to whom I now turn, anticipate and make sense of the seer Teisamenos in the battle of Plataia, his characterization as a would-be crown victor, and his own talismanic status. These figures will also prepare us for part 3 and its consideration of the homology that obtains between different talismanic individuals.

Particularly in accounts of the Persian Wars, ancient authors repeatedly emphasize the athletic history of *stratēgoi* (military commanders). One such figure is Eurybates, who led a company of Argive volunteers to assist Aegina against Athens in the early fifth century: ἦγε δὲ αὐτοὺς στρατηγὸς [ἀνὴρ ᾧ οὔνομα] Εὐρυβάτης, <ἀνὴρ> πεντάεθλον ἐπασκήσας (The military commander named Eurybates, who had practiced the pentathlon, led them, Hdt. 6.92.2–3).[29] Since the nineteenth century, commentators have preferred to insert an ἀνήρ into the

---

28. See Benveniste 1973: 349–50 for examples. As Benveniste (350) observes, "The effect of the *kudos* is temporary." See also Currie (2005: 151) on the "athlete's aura."

29. I reproduce here Macan's 1908 text. Macan brackets ἀνὴρ ᾧ οὔνομα because the words are absent in two of the major MSS. See Vannicelli 2005: 267 on the way in which Eurybates' military performance replicates his performance as a pentathlete.

second half of the clause, but the emendation dilutes the starkness of a simpler image: the military commander named Eurybates practiced the pentathlon. As Pausanias's version of this same event reveals, Eurybates did not merely enter the pentathlon but also won it at Nemea (1.29.5).

Like Eurybates, Eualkides, an Eretrian *stratēgos* at the time of the Ionian Revolt, was also a former crown victor (Hdt. 5.102). From among the many "men of renown" routed and killed by the Persians at Ephesus, Eualkides is the only one whom Herodotus chooses to identify.[30] The historian records that Eualkides, in addition to being a *stratēgos*, had won στεφανηφόρους ἀγῶνας (contests in which the prize is a crown, 5.102.3).

Kroton produced other victors who became military commanders. Philippos son of Boutakides was "an Olympic victor and the most beautiful man of his time" (Hdt. 5.47).[31] Philippos contributed a trireme at his own expense to the oikist Dorieus's colonial venture and fought together with him in the fatal confrontation against the Phoenicians and the Egestaeans over the settlement's site, presumably leading the force with which he had manned his ship (Hdt. 5.46.1).[32] A second Krotoniate, Phayllos, was a three-time Pythian victor, who, according to Herodotus, was alone among the western Greeks in lending his support at Salamis (8.47).[33] An inscribed epigram dedicated by Phayllos himself on the Athenian acropolis also merges his athletic and military successes:[34]

[...]σι Φάϋλ[λος ἔθεκε
ὁ νι]κῶν τρὶς [τὸν ἀγῶνα]
[τὸμ] Πυθοῖ κα[ὶ νέας ἑλ-
ὸν h]ὰς Ἄσις ἵ[ελεν]

Phayllos made this dedication, the one who won the games at Pytho three times and destroyed the ships sent by Asia.

It is tempting to read the list as a progression, and thus the relationship between these achievements as causal rather than merely paratactic: because Phayllos won a Pythian victory three times, he destroyed the ships of Asia. Visually, "at Pytho," "ships," and the opening syllables of "destroyed" all share a line of the inscription, announcing the key terms and the inextricable connection between them. Without

---

30. Herodotus presumably knows the names of these other men as well but chooses to reveal only that of Eualkides.

31. On Philippos as a central figure of an oral narrative that originated in the 470s B.C.E., see Nicholson 2016: 161–78.

32. One tradition also suggests that Philippos played a role in Kroton's war against Sybaris (see Hdt. 5.42–48, discussed in part 3 of this chapter).

33. On Phayllos, see Nicholson 2016: 196–201. Nicholson exposes a number of crucial distinctions between the ostensibly comparable figures of Phayllos and Philippos.

34. Moretti 1953: no. 11. See also Nicholson 2016: 198.

the talismanic authority of a Pythian victory, the inscription seems to be saying, there would be no military success.[35]

A number of archaic and classical athletic victors appear to have enjoyed second careers as the oikists of colonial expeditions.[36] This correlation suggests that it was important for colonial founders, too, to be seen to possess talismanic power. It also serves as further evidence of the desire to extend beyond his moment of victory an athlete's divinely guaranteed ability to succeed. According to Pausanias, the seventh-century sprinter Chionis of Sparta, with three Olympic victories under his belt, accompanied Battos and helped him found Cyrene (3.14.3). In the 470s Chionis was heroized and received monuments at both Olympia and Sparta.[37] Chionis's monument at Sparta stood beside the tombs of the Agiad kings, and there, at least, Chionis received cult honors.[38] Like the inscription of Phayllos and its merging of athletic and military success, Chionis's Spartan stele at his cult site advertised both his athletic victory and his role as founder. Another Olympic victor by the name of Phrynon led an Athenian colonial expedition to Sigeum around 600 B.C.E. (Diog. Laert. 1.4.74; Strabo 599–600).[39] Herodotus records that the Athenian Miltiades, the son of Kypselos, was first an Olympic victor before leading the Dolonkoi to the Thracian Chersonese (6.36).[40]

In Pindar's and Bacchylides' epinikia, legendary founders serve as the paradigms for victors on a number of occasions: in *Olympian* 7, Pindar pairs the oikist Tlepolemos and the victor Diagoras; in *Pythian* 4 and 5, the oikist Battos and the victor Arkesilas; in Bacchlyides' *Ode* 11, the oikist Proitos and the victor Alexidamos.[41] In *Pythian* 1, Pindar praises Hieron by asserting that "the renowned founder bestowed *kudos* on his city" (κλεινὸς οἰκιστὴρ ἐκύδανεν πόλιν, *P.* 1.31). While other epinikia proclaim that an athlete bestows *kudos* on his city, Pindar can switch out the title of athlete for oikist in this formulaic phrase precisely because of the

---

35. See also the Olympic victor Phanas of Messenia, who reportedly served as a commander with Aristomenes in the Second Messenian War (Paus 4.17.9).

36. As Currie (2005: 151) observes, "Analogous to the important role played by athletes in warfare is their appointment as leaders of colonizing ventures." See also Hodkinson 1999: 170.

37. On the heroization of Chionis of Sparta, see Christesen 2010; Nicholson 2016: 35–36.

38. Christesen 2010: 31–45. On the talismanic power of Spartan kings, see below.

39. Kurke (1993: 156n19) suggests that Phrynon's duel with the tyrant and sage Pittakos is a further sign of his talismanic power.

40. Kurke (1993: 136) calls attention to the way in which Herodotus seems to delay mentioning Miltiades' Olympic victory when he initially introduces him in the narrative in order to pair closely Miltiades' status as an Olympic victor with his role as an oikist. I cannot agree with Kyriakou (2007: 146) that Herodotus's mention of Miltiades' victory here is because the historian "often provides information piecemeal."

41. See also Bacch. *Ode* 1.

analogous talismanic power that obtains between the crown victor and the colonial founder.[42]

An athletic victory was one conspicuous way for an oikist to assert the credential of *kudos*.[43] It was not, however, the only available derivation of an oikist's talismanic power. In chapter 3, I discuss colonial discourse's interest in the role that the Delphic oracle played in providing the oikist with the necessary talismanic authority for the venture.[44] Athletic victory and oracular sanction, both demonstrations of conspicuous divine favoritism and endorsement, were analogous ways for an oikist to claim *kudos*.

Thus in the contexts of warfare and foundations, a crown victor could be enlisted as a leader on account of his perceived talismanic authority and not merely for his physical prowess, for his political clout, or for the prestige accorded the position, however much these other credentials also mattered. The perceived regenerative capability of *kudos*, and the polis's interest in laying claim to it for its own benefit, appear to be a defining constituent of archaic and classical expressions of talismanic power. Pausanias records a story of the victor Oibotas that encapsulates both of these conclusions (7.17.13): The eighth-century athlete was Achaia's first victor in the Olympic games, but the Achaians did not grant him the honor he deserved.[45] Oibotas cursed them for their mistreatment, and for the next three hundred years, the Achaians did not win at Olympia. When they finally consulted Delphi about their centuries of athletic disappointment, the Pythia advised them to erect a statue of Oibotas. Upon doing so, an Achaian claimed victory in the stade race in 460 B.C.E. Pausanias concludes by noting that even in his own time the Achaians who compete at Olympia first make offerings to Oibotas and, if they win, crown his statue at Olympia (7.17.14). The abiding efficacy of Oibotas's statue in the eyes of the Achaians suggests that his talismanic power was felt to endure.[46] Pausanias mentions one further anecdote concerning Oibotas. He reports that, according to some, Oibotas, despite having lived in the eighth century, fought on the Greek side during the battle of Plataia (6.3.8). The late archaic and early classical periods' obsession with the supernatural assistance of cult heroes in battle as well as with the talismanic power of athletic victors and its civic

---

42. Dougherty 1993: 97; see also Dougherty (128) for the comparable *kudos* of the victor Diagoras and the mythical founder Tlepolemos in *Olympian 7*.

43. See Kurke 1993: 136–37 for examples of athletes who become oikists. Kurke (137) suggests that crown victors were chosen as oikists for this very reason, that is, for their perceived talismanic power, and that this power was thought to facilitate the favorable outcome of a colonial enterprise.

44. See also Dougherty 1993: 18–21.

45. See Nicholson 2016: 38–39 on Oibotas and his statue, which Nicholson compares to that of Chionis of Sparta.

46. Kurke 1993: 153.

recontextualization for warfare thus all converge on the figure of Oibotas. Let us turn now to another example of a talismanic figure at Plataia, the seer Teisamenos.

II. TEISAMENOS AND THE TALISMANIC AUTHORITY OF SEERS

The importance of seers for warfare extends beyond their ability to attend to the customary divinatory sacrifices for an army on campaign.[47] In addition to their vital expertise in *mantikē* (the art of divination), certain seers could also be considered figures of extraordinary talismanic power. Seers reputed to be talismanic were critical to military enterprises because, as talismans, they were believed to guarantee victory for the army that enlisted them. Herodotus's presentation of Teisamenos, the seer who accompanied the Greek army at the battle of Plataia (9.33–36), reveals how seers could be recruited for their talismanic potency as much as for their divinatory expertise.

A close reading of Teisamenos's strange biography (9.33) suggests that Herodotus uses it to signal the seer's talismanic status. A second close reading of the episode exposes the ways in which the historian plays with Teisamenos's characterization as a would-be crown victor. This characterization further highlights Teisamenos's talismanic status, even though his *kudos* is ultimately directed toward winning battles as a *mantis* and not as crown victor. Herodotus's oscillation between Teisamenos's potential as a crown victor and as a seer points more generally to the homology that obtains between these two forms of talismanic authority. The relationship between Teisamenos and his mantic nemesis at Plataia, the seer Hegesistratos, who serves the Persians, further illuminates the talismanic nature of seers in warfare. Part 2 concludes with readings of two inscriptions, including one for Teisamenos himself, that suggest that seers actively advertised their claims of talismanic authority.

Teisamenos, the Accidental Seer

On the eve of the battle of Plataia, the Greeks and Persians stand eyeing each other across the Asopos, stalled by the same omen: on both sides, the signs are propitious for remaining in place but unfavorable for an offensive attack. As if to pass the time during this stalemate and also to capture its length, Herodotus delivers protracted stories about the two seers overseeing these sacrificial omens, balancing them, like the two sides of the river and their waiting armies, with a *men/de* construction.[48] The historian first turns to the *mantis* who accompanies the Greek army (9.33.1):

---

47. For the duties of military seers on campaign, see Pritchett 1979a: 47–153; Jameson 1991; Flower 2008b: 153–87; and the introduction.

48. On the "disproportionate" length of these two digressions, see Flower and Marincola 2002: 164.

Ἕλλησι μὲν Τεισαμενὸς Ἀντιόχου ἦν ὁ θυόμενος· οὗτος γὰρ δὴ εἵπετο τῷ στρατεύματι τούτῳ μάντις· τὸν ἐόντα Ἠλεῖον καὶ γένεος τοῦ Ἰαμιδέων [Κλυτιάδην] Λακεδαιμόνιοι ἐποιήσαντο λεωσφέτερον.

For the Greeks it was Teisamenos son of Antiochos who was sacrificing. For he was accompanying this campaign as a *mantis*. He was an Elean [and a Klytiad] of the clan of the Iamidai and the Lakedaimonians made him a fellow-citizen.

Herodotus joins Teisamenos to two different poleis, Elis and Sparta, as well as two different mantic clans, the Iamidai and the Klytiadai.[49] The following *logos* (story) slowly unwinds this dense coil of identity as it takes a seemingly circuitous route through the events that led to Teisamenos's presence at Plataia (9.33–35). Consulting the oracle at Delphi about offspring, Teisamenos receives instead the unsolicited news that he will win the five greatest contests. Misinterpreting the Pythia as referring to the five events of the pentathlon, Teisamenos begins to train as an athlete and nearly wins at Olympia. Enter the Spartans, who, having correctly understood the oracular pronouncement to signify not athletic competitions but "contests of Ares," approach Teisamenos and attempt to make him a "leader of their wars" together with the Heraklid kings: μισθῷ ἐπειρῶντο πείσαντες Τεισαμενὸν ποιέεσθαι ἅμα Ἡρακλειδέων τοῖσι βασιλεῦσι ἡγεμόνα τῶν πολέμων (They were attempting to persuade Teisamenos through payment to be made a leader of wars together with the Heraklid kings, 9.33.3). Teisamenos declines the proffered wage and insists upon being made a citizen with full privileges. Offended by this unheard-of proposal, the Spartans depart, only to return, terrified by the looming threat of Persia. Teisamenos counters with a still higher price—that his brother, Hegias, also be made a Spartan citizen. By behaving in this way, Herodotus informs us, Teisamenos was imitating the mythical seer Melampous who demanded a share of the kingdom of Argos for both himself and his brother, Bias. Like the Argives before them, the Spartans finally agree to the seer's terms, and, according to Herodotus, Teisamenos and Hegias become the first and only foreigners ever to be made citizens of Sparta.[50]

In evaluating the episode, we might first note that Herodotus casts the Spartans as desperate for Teisamenos. No other seer will do. Although they are indignant at Teisamenos's bold demand for citizenship, the xenophobic Spartans do not resort to hiring another seer. That option does not appear to exist. Teisamenos alone must possess something that makes the Spartans so eager to have him on their side. Yet Herodotus's exposition of events does not indicate that the Spartans seek Teisamenos's expertise in divination. In fact, the historian's decision to begin his story

49. For Teisamenos's unusual connection to two mantic clans, see Flower and Marincola 2002: 166–67, 320–22; and below.

50. On the seer Melampous, see chapter 4. Taita (2001) argues that this award of Spartan citizenship may not have been as unique as Herodotus claims it is.

with the seer botching his own oracle has the effect of undercutting any assumed mantic credentials we might have initially accorded him.[51] As Michael Flower perceives, the "internal logic" of the story implies that Teisamenos had not performed as a seer before Plataia. If he had, he might have known that he was meant to be a military *mantis* and not an athlete. Instead, as Flower writes, "We are ... expected to imagine something that might seem unlikely on the face of it—that the Spartans hired someone who had no previous experience in his craft and was completely untested."[52] What this opening encounter between Teisamenos and the Spartans does indicate, however, is that Teisamenos possesses the conspicuous endorsement of Delphi. The oracle has told him he will win the five greatest contests. This divine approval makes him completely irresistible for Sparta. After all, once the Spartans are in possession of him, they are guaranteed victory. In other words, the Spartans believe that the gods have granted Teisamenos talismanic power.[53]

The Spartans confirm that Apollo has indeed conferred this power when they seek to enlist Teisamenos as "a leader of wars together with the Heraklid kings" (Τεισαμενὸν ποιέεσθαι ἅμα Ἡρακλειδέων τοῖσι βασιλεῦσι ἡγεμόνα τῶν πολέμων, 9.33.3).[54] The striking phrase drove earlier scholars to the point of emendation, since it seems unimaginable that the Spartans would want a foreign seer as their commander. How and Wells understand the phrase to indicate Teisamenos's role as a diviner and sacrificial expert for the army.[55] It is true that Teisamenos does perform these functions for the Spartans, but we must understand his divinatory expertise as operating in conjunction with his reputation as a Delphi-sanctioned talismanic figure. In this respect, we might compare Teisamenos to a later classical seer, Agias, who served the Spartan commander Lysander during the battle of Aigospotamoi in 405 B.C.E. (Paus. 3.11.5):

---

51. On Teisamenos's misinterpretation, Flower (2008a: 198) writes, "Herodotus does not explain here how an Iamid could be so stupid or Lacedaemonians so uncharacteristically intelligent."

52. Flower 2008a: 199.

53. Thus I cannot agree with Pritchard (2012: 212) that the Spartans desire Teisamenos partly because he is from a "famous family of military seers." Such a reading does not attend sufficiently to the logic of the narrative and the details of Herodotus's passage, including the historian's attention to Teisamenos's own misreading of the oracle and his insistent characterization of Teisamenos as a would-be crown victor (on this second point, see below). I note here Flower's (2008a) argument that the Iamidai became famous only after Teisamenos's own victory at Plataia.

54. Kurke (1993: 135–36) has discussed Teisamenos as a figure of *kudos* in reference to his athletic activity. I examine the ways in which Teisamenos is characterized as an athlete below.

55. For example, note the remark of How and Wells (2002 *ad* 9.33.3) on ἡγεμόνα τῶν πολέμων: "This cannot mean that the seer was to share the actual command in war, for in comparison with this the grant of citizenship would be nothing. It seems to refer to the position of the kings as priests, since they offered sacrifice before all important undertakings (Xen. *Rep. Lac.* 13). Tisamenus was to act with them in this."

τοῦτον τὸν Ἀγίαν μαντευσάμενόν φασι Λυσάνδρῳ τὸ Ἀθηναίων ἑλεῖν ναυτικὸν περὶ Αἰγὸς ποταμοὺς πλὴν τριήρων δέκα·

They say that this Agias, having provided his services as a seer to Lysander on this occasion, captured the Athenian navy at Aigospotamoi except for ten triremes.

Pausanias attributes the remarkable destruction of the Athenian navy to a seer, an assertion in keeping with claims of other remarkable upsets by other talismanic figures examined in part 1.[56] While Pausanias credits Agias, Lysander's seer, with capturing all but ten ships of the Athenian navy at Aigospotamoi, Plutarch records for the same battle that the Dioskouroi were reportedly seen in the form of stars gleaming upon the tillers of Lysander's ship as he sailed out against the enemy (*Lys.* 12.1). We might read Pausanias's and Plutarch's accounts, therefore, as two versions of a single impulse, namely, to attribute Sparta's incredible defeat of the Athenian navy to talismanic agency.[57] It is worth noting that both Agias and the Dioskouroi are represented on the so-called Navarchs monument, the victory monument at Delphi that Lysander dedicated after the battle (Paus. 10.9.7). According to Pausanias, this statue group also depicted Poseidon crowning Lysander. I would contend, then, that the Navarch's monument overwhelms its viewers with talismans: epiphanic heroes, a Spartan commander crowned by a god, and a talismanic seer credited with destroying most of the Athenian navy.[58] This talismanic Agias, as it happens, was the grandson of Teisamenos.[59]

To return to Teisamenos himself, the Spartans' desire to make him "a leader of wars together with the Heraklid kings" signals that, in the eyes of the Spartans, the seer is a talismanic figure.[60] Teisamenos's talismanic capability places him on the same level as the Spartan kings and accounts for his partnership with them. That

---

56. Other seers characterized as leading armies include Kalchas (Kalchas "led the ships of the Achaians into Ilion through his seercraft, which Phoibos Apollo gave him," *Il.* 1.71–72) and Tellias (Pausanias [10.13.7] describes a statue the Phokians dedicated at Delphi when Tellias led [ἡγήσατο] them against the Thessalians. Herodotus [8.27] identifies this Tellias as a seer).

57. Similarly, Pausanias and Diodorus relate two different accounts of the battle of Sagra. Pausanias preserves the tradition that the hero Aias fought in the front lines of the Lokrians (3.19.12), while Diodorus emphasizes the role of the Dioskouroi (8.32). What both reports agree on, however, is that the Lokrians were helped by the presence of talismanically potent heroes. On the battle of Sagra and its significance in the "athlopolitics" of the Greek West, see Nicholson 2016: 135–39.

58. For crowns as a sign of talismanic power, see Kurke 1993; and part 1 above.

59. See Flower 2008a: 205. Pausanias also mentions a bronze statue of Agias in the agora at Sparta (3.11.5).

60. Vannicelli (2005: 261) intriguingly suggests that the Spartans' negotiations with and eventual hiring of Teisamenos occurred after the death of Megistias at Thermopylai and not beforehand as others have argued. Vannicelli's dating implies that Teisamenos is the replacement seer for Megistias. If Teisamenos is indeed filling the mantic shoes of Megistias, then there is a real possibility that we are meant to think of Megistias as a talismanic "leader of wars" for Sparta as well.

Teisamenos is aligned with the Heraklid rulers in this way is consistent with the kings' own status as talismans. Scholars have long noted that the Spartan kings themselves seem to have been viewed as possessing charismatic authority.[61] In this context, we would do well to remember another pairing of Spartan talismans in war: Herodotus reports a Spartan tradition in which one of the kings and one of the Dioskouroi accompanied the Spartan army on campaign (5.75).[62]

Teisamenos, the Would-Be Crown Victor

Teisamenos's characterization as a potential crown victor amplifies his talismanic status even though this potency is ultimately directed toward winning battles as a *mantis* and not as an athlete. The opening and concluding statements that frame the seer's *logos* capture Herodotus's purposeful interplay between Teisamenos's roles of *mantis* and athlete. After introducing Teisamenos, Herodotus begins the seer's story at Delphi (9.33.1–2):

> Ἕλλησι μὲν Τεισαμενὸς Ἀντιόχου ἦν ὁ θυόμενος· οὗτος γὰρ δὴ εἵπετο τῷ στρατεύματι τούτῳ μάντις· τὸν ἐόντα Ἠλεῖον καὶ γένεος τοῦ Ἰαμιδέων [Κλυτιάδην] Λακεδαιμόνιοι ἐποιήσαντο λεωσφέτερον. Τεισαμενῷ γὰρ μαντευομένῳ ἐν Δελφοῖσι περὶ γόνου ἀνεῖλε ἡ Πυθίη ἀγῶνας τοὺς μεγίστους ἀναιρήσεσθαι πέντε.

> The Greeks had Teisamenos son of Antiochos as the one who was sacrificing. For this man was accompanying the army as its *mantis*. He was an Elean [and a Klytiad] of the clan of the Iamidai, and the Lakedaimonians made him a fellow-citizen. For when Teisamenos was consulting the oracle at Delphi about offspring the Pythia gave the response that he would win the five greatest contests.

At first glance, the participial phrase Τεισαμενῷ γὰρ μαντευομένῳ appears to continue the topic of the preceding sentence, οὗτος γὰρ δὴ εἵπετο τῷ στρατεύματι τούτῳ μάντις (For this man was accompanying the army as its *mantis*, 9.33.1), thereby tempting us to understand the phrase as "when Teisamenos was acting as a *mantis*." Yet, the reference to the Pythia at Delphi brings with it the realization that μαντεύομαι must mean in this context "to consult an oracle." In this way, wordplay pushes Teisamenos the seer aside. In his place, Teisamenos the athlete emerges as the Pythia utters a prophecy composed in the language of athletic competition (ἀγῶνας τοὺς μεγίστους ἀναιρήσεσθαι πέντε).[63] By the sentence's end, it

---

61. As noted above, I treat talismanic authority as a culturally specific Greek form of the more general concept of charismatic authority. Weber (1978: 1285) refers to the "family-charismatic kingship" of Sparta. Versnel (1970: 158) describes the Spartan king as "the *mana*-bearer *par excellence*." See also Carlier 1984: 292–301; Cartledge 1987: 109–10.

62. For this tradition and the possible form the Dioskouroi take, see Hornblower 2001: 140–47.

63. This sentence contains a number of puns, as others have noticed (e.g., Flower and Marincola 2002 ad loc.). In addition to μαντεύομαι, the two meanings of ἀναιρέω are also both present in the sentence (that is, both its active sense of "to give an oracular response" and its middle sense of "to

is as if we ourselves are ready to follow Teisamenos in believing that the Pythia refers to the crown games, until the Spartans approach the pentathlon-practicing seer and apprise him, and us, of the oracle's true meaning. This initial sentence of Teisamenos's story can be compared to the one that concludes it (9.35.1):

συγχωρησάντων δὲ καὶ ταῦτα τῶν Σπαρτιητέων, οὕτω δὴ πέντε σφι μαντευόμενος ἀγῶνας τοὺς μεγίστους Τεισαμενὸς ὁ Ἠλεῖος, γενόμενος Σπαρτιήτης, συγκαταιρέει.

When the Spartans granted him also these things, that is how, acting as a *mantis* for them, Teisamenos the Elean, having become a Spartan, helped them to win the five greatest contests.

Although the same words resurface (Τεισαμενὸς, μαντευόμενος, πέντε ἀγῶνας τοὺς μεγίστους, [συγκατ]αιρέει), the opacity and punning have vanished. The sentence has righted itself, as the explanatory οὕτω δὴ (that is how) signals. In this iteration of these terms, Teisamenos qua *mantis* has returned. As this final instance of μαντευόμενος (acting as a *mantis*) now confirms, his divinatory abilities have replaced his athletic ones. This substitution or switching out of meaning is reflected in the change of word order as well. In contrast to the arrangement of the first sentence, μαντευόμενος is here ensconced within the phrase πέντε σφι μαντευόμενος ἀγῶνας τοὺς μεγίστους as if to attach even at the level of the word order Teisamenos's five victorious "contests" to his performance as a seer.

Both the opening and closing statements of his *logos* assert that Teisamenos is guaranteed five victories, but whereas the riddle of the first sentence suggests that this success will come in the athletic arena, the second links it to Teisamenos's role as a military *mantis*. Put another way, the talismanic power of the seer displaces his talismanic promise as a would-be crown victor. And yet, Teisamenos cannot quite shed his athletic reputation. Both Reginald Macan and Leslie Kurke see in the wording and particular shape this concluding statement takes an evocation of a herald's traditional victory announcement at the games.[64] Even in this culminating

---

win"). Another pun emerges between the Pythia's response about ἀγῶνας (contests) and Teisamenos's question about γόνου (offspring). To Macan's ears, this sounds like a "bad pun" (Macan 1908 ad loc.). In the case of both of these puns (i.e., ἀνεῖλε/ἀναιρήσεσθαι and γόνου/ἀγῶνας) the correct meanings of the words are those associated with athletic competition, and, furthermore, these definitions occur at the expense of the words' association with the language of oracles and divination. Thus, for ἀναιρέω, the definition "to consult an oracle" is replaced by the meaning "to win (athletic competitions or wars)." Likewise, because asking about offspring is a question commonly found in oracular consultation (see Flower and Marincola 2002: 167), the Delphic connotations of this word (γόνου) are displaced by a pun on the athletic connotations of ἀγῶνας. I point to these other puns as additional evidence that Teisamenos's initial connection to divination when we first encounter the participle μαντευομένῳ is displaced by the language of athletic games and crown victors as the sentence progresses.

64. Macan (1908 ad loc.) notes, "It marks the solemnity of the occasion with a quasi-heraldic flourish." Kurke (1993: 136) adds, "Herodotus' diction in this context bears striking similarities to the official victory announcement at the games." On the form of the victory announcement, see Kurke, 142–44.

declaration of his extraordinary achievements as a seer, the specter of Teisamenos's athletic potential endures.

Pitting Talisman against Talisman: Teisamenos and Hegesistratos

The concept of talismanic power provides a new perspective on the relationship between Teisamenos and the seer serving the Persians at Plataia, Hegesistratos. Herodotus meticulously charts the points of contact between the two seers of this decisive battle. I suggest that Herodotus does so in order both to underscore Hegesistratos's own status as a talisman and to imply that the Persians hire him specifically to counteract Teisamenos's talismanic power.

After Herodotus concludes Teisamenos's *logos*, he crosses to the Persian side of the Asopos, to Mardonios, and to his *mantis*, Hegesistratos. Here at last we find the answering *de*, counterbalancing the *men* that introduced Teisamenos three chapters earlier (9.37.1):

Μαρδονίῳ δὲ προθυμεομένῳ μάχης ἄρχειν οὐκ ἐπιτήδεα ἐγίνετο τὰ ἱρά, ἀμυνομένῳ δὲ καὶ τούτῳ καλά. καὶ γὰρ οὗτος Ἑλληνικοῖσι ἱροῖσι ἐχρᾶτο, μάντιν ἔχων Ἡγησίστρατον, ἄνδρα Ἠλεῖόν τε καὶ τῶν Τελλιαδέων ἐόντα λογιμώτατον.

But for Mardonios, who was eager to begin battle, the omens were not favorable to begin battle but were also [i.e., like those of the Greek side] propitious if he should fight in self-defense. For in fact he was also using Greek sacrifices, because he had as a *mantis* Hegesistratos, an Elean man and the most famous of the Telliadai.

Herodotus's estimation of Hegesistratos as the most famous of the Telliadai is soon explained by the historian's assertion that the seer "performed a deed beyond description" (ἔργον ἐργάσατο μέζον λόγου, 9.37.2):[65] The Spartans had imprisoned this Hegesistratos in the belief that they had suffered many horrors at his hands. Fearing for his life, Hegesistratos somehow got hold of a knife and sliced off just enough of his foot to free it from the prison stock. This audacious act of disfigurement precipitated a series of intrepid stunts: giving his guards the slip, digging through a wall, and hiding in the woods, Hegesistratos finally limped his way to Tegea, a distance of some thirty miles. Discovering the abandoned appendage, his astonished captors searched in vain for Hegesistratos. Meanwhile, the seer, recovered from his wound, constructed a wooden prosthetic and, as good as new, applied himself to being "openly hostile towards Sparta" (9.37.4). Hegesistratos was eventually seized by the Spartans and put to death, but Herodotus backtracks from this later event in order to conclude the *logos* with Hegesistratos's role at Plataia. According to Herodotus, the seer was motivated to medize "out of his hatred of the

---

65. The Telliadai are usually classed as one of the four main clans of seers, but little is known of them. The seer Tellias appears at Hdt. 8.27, and Philostratus refers to the clan at *Vita Apollonii* 5.25.

Spartans and his love of profit" (κατά τε τὸ ἔχθος τὸ Λακεδαιμονίων καὶ κατὰ τὸ κέρδος, 9.38.1).

At first glance, Hegesistratos's death-defying tale of escape seems to have little in common with Teisamenos's story of athletic competition and Spartan citizenship. Nevertheless, thematic juxtapositions and verbal parallels abound between the two seers so that Teisamenos and Hegesistratos vividly form a pair for reasons beyond their linking *men/de* construction.[66] Thus both seers perform a kind of intricate duet with Sparta in their respective accounts, although the Sparta that assumes the leading role is markedly different in each. The Spartans shrewdly provide Teisamenos with the correct interpretation to his own oracle, whereas they play the fool to Hegesistratos and his disappearing act. The Spartans hunt down and assassinate Hegesistratos, but they make Teisamenos and his brother citizens. The seers are also described in similar terms. Both seers, for example, are characterized as exceptional. Teisamenos and his brother Hegias are "the only ones out of all mankind to become Spartan citizens" (μοῦνοι δὲ δὴ πάντων ἀνθρώπων ἐγένοντο οὗτοι Σπαρτιήτῃσι πολιῆται, 9.35.1). Hegesistratos is the most noteworthy of the Telliadai clan (τῶν Τελλιαδέων ἐόντα λογιμώτατον, 9.37.1), and his singular escape from the Spartan prison is the "bravest deed of all we know" (ἀνδρηιότατον ἔργον πάντων τῶν ἡμεῖς ἴδμεν, 9.37.2). Moreover, both figures are rendered in ways that refer to or conjure the epic past.[67] Herodotus likens Teisamenos to the mythical seer Melampous, and Hegesistratos's self-inflicted amputation is rendered in the manner of a "heroic accomplishment."[68] As if by some sort of onomastic reversal, the names of Teisamenos and Hegesistratos each evoke an attribute more salient in the other. That is, the Greeks' seer enlisted to be a "leader of wars" is named "Avenger" (Teisamenos), while "Leader of Armies"' (Hegesistratos) medizes out of his hatred for Sparta, an act that looks a lot like vengeance.[69] One effect of these "swapped" names is that they draw the two seers into closer alignment. It is hard not to think about Teisamenos as a "leader of wars" without simultaneously thinking "Hegesistratos."

Herodotus further establishes Teisamenos and Hegesistratos as an oppositional pair by gauging their contradictory reactions to the notion of being hired for a wage by their respective armies. *Misthos* (wage) appears in both *logoi* but is evaluated differently by each seer. The Spartans attempt to persuade Teisamenos through

---

66. Note also Dillery's (2005: 208) observation: "But even more than the formal connection, they are united by a common theme: the independent diviner who advances his private interests while serving a non-native power."

67. Dillery 2005: 208.

68. Dillery 2005: 208.

69. Teisamenos and Hegesistratos are both "speaking names." See Harrison 2000: 263n48; Immerwahr 1986: 294–95 (on Teisamenos's and Hegesistratos's names specifically). To the best of my knowledge, no one has noted that their respective names evoke each other.

payment (μισθῷ ἐπειρῶντο πείσαντες), but the seer demands instead that they make him a citizen with full privileges (9.33.3–4). By rejecting the proffered wage, Teisamenos simultaneously rejects the status of a foreign seer-for-hire such a transaction implies. The seer, in his request for citizenship, aspires instead to become a member of Spartan society and to have access to all the benefits that that civic contract implies. Herodotus's subsequent comparison of Teisamenos to the seer Melampous, who exacted a share of the kingdom of Argos for curing its women of madness, is therefore apt. Scholars have been troubled by the fact that Herodotus equates Teisamenos's request for citizenship with Melampous's demand for the throne, since citizenship seems to be a more modest demand than kingship.[70] Yet, from a certain angle, the mythical and historical *manteis* essentially desire the same thing, the assurance of complete inclusion within a new polis.[71] Both Teisamenos and Melampous insist on enduring forms of compensation in their respective demands for citizenship and kingship. At the same time, the comparison suggests that Teisamenos may be after more than citizenship: he may want to be a "leader together with the Spartan kings" within the city and not just on the battlefield.[72]

By contrast, Herodotus concludes Hegesistratos's *logos* with the following characterization (9.38.1):

τότε δὲ ἐπὶ τῷ Ἀσωπῷ Μαρδονίῳ μεμισθωμένος οὐκ ὀλίγου ἐθύετό τε καὶ προεθυμέετο κατά τε τὸ ἔχθος τὸ Λακεδαιμονίων καὶ κατὰ τὸ κέρδος.

At that time, on the banks of the Asopos, having been hired for not a small price by Mardonios, he was sacrificing and exerting himself zealously both on account of his hatred for the Lakedaimonians and on account of profit.

While Teisamenos desires a permanent form of compensation, Hegesistratos's tale comes to a (incriminating) halt upon the word *kerdos* (profit). Hegesistratos not only allows himself to be hired for a handsome price but also welcomes the opportunity.

---

70. See Vannicelli 2005: 270–76 for a summary of the scholarship on this point. For Herodotus's juxtaposition of Teisamenos and Melampous, see also chapter 3.

71. Melampous, too, rejects the Argives' initial attempt to hire him (ἐμισθοῦντο) and counters with his own idea of a proper *misthos*: half of their kingdom (Hdt. 9.34.). That both Teisamenos and Melampous insist on bringing their brothers along with them adds to what seems like their desire to strike up networks of kinship within their new poleis. Teisamenos's plan seems to have worked beyond Herodotus's narrative, since his descendants remained active as Spartan seers for at least several generations (see Flower 2008a: 205). There is also reason to believe that Teisamenos and his family were settled in the Spartan village of Pitana (see Flower 2008a: 201–2).

72. I discuss in chapter 3 the significance of this request and why a seer as a permanent resident within a given community is a terrifying prospect for both cities (both Argos and Sparta acquiesce only out of utter desperation).

We must account for these scrupulously orchestrated parallels between Teisamenos and Hegesistratos. Hegesistratos clearly functions as a foil to Teisamenos, but his significance as a negative paradigm is more than simply a literary device. Herodotus's entire digression into the biographies of Teisamenos and Hegesistratos begins in the following way: Ὡς δὲ ἄρα πάντες οἱ ἐτετάχατο κατὰ [τε] ἔθνεα καὶ κατὰ τέλεα, ἐνθαῦτα τῇ δευτέρῃ ἡμέρῃ ἐθύοντο καὶ ἀμφότεροι (When they had all been drawn up by nation and by unit, thereupon on the second day both sides were sacrificing, Hdt. 9.33.1). As Michael Flower and John Marincola observe,

> The καί here is emphatic, but there is no reason to suppose (with Macan 664) that one would not have expected the Persians to sacrifice; though their gods were not those of the Greeks, they did sacrifice (1.131–132); what was odd, and what is delayed by Herodotus until it is most appropriate (37.1), is that the Persians were using a *Greek* seer. The Magi, who always preside at a Persian sacrifice (1.132.3), presumably returned with Xerxes to Persia.[73]

Regardless of where the Magi actually are, it is noteworthy that Herodotus emphatically announces that both sides were sacrificing with Greek seers and, further, that this stands in blatant contradiction to Herodotus's earlier statement that the Magi are always present at a Persian sacrifice (1.132.3). More striking still is Mardonios's subsequent behavior. Although at first he abides by the omens Hegesistratos delivers, the Persian commander eventually rejects the portents outright: τά τε σφάγια τὰ Ἡγησιστράτου ἐᾶν χαίρειν μηδὲ βιάζεσθαι, ἀλλὰ νόμῳ τῷ Περσέων χρεωμένους συμβάλλειν (With respect to the sacrifices of Hegesistratos, [Mardonios said] to disregard them and not to force them, but rather to engage in battle using the custom of the Persians, 9.41.4). In short, Mardonios hires a Greek seer when the Magi could have done the job and then ultimately ignores Hegesistratos's predictions. It would seem, then, that Mardonios is not interested in divination as much as he is interested in Hegesistratos himself. I would suggest that, in Herodotus's rendering, the Persians recruit Hegesistratos in order to counteract Teisamenos's talismanic potency with that of another. Like Teisamenos, Hegesistratos seems to enjoy at least temporarily an outsize portion of supernatural assistance and favor. That, at any rate, is one of the conclusions to be drawn from his *logos*: Hegesistratos's biography and the nature of his daring escape from Sparta signal a privileged connection with the gods. Thus Hegesistratos somehow (κως) gets hold of a knife in prison, escapes the notice of his guards, and miraculously recovers from a severed foot despite a thirty-mile nocturnal trek to Tegea (9.37.2–3). In Herodotus's presentation, which resists the clarity of logical explanation, these achievements appear superhuman, as if Hegesistratos were in some way under the guidance and protection of the divine. In short, we might understand the seer's

---

73. Flower and Marincola 2002: 165, emphasis in original.

extraordinary feats and success as indicating that Hegesistratos himself is in possession of talismanic power.⁷⁴

Hegesistratos and Teisamenos are meticulously pitted against one other. What is more, this extensive juxtaposition reveals that both *manteis* are present at Plataia not only in order to perform divinatory sacrifices and interpret omens but also as carefully opposed talismanic seers who form part of an arsenal of combative tactics both armies roll out against the enemy. Herodotus's focus on the talismanic nature rather than the *mantikē* of the seers is reflected in the composition of their *logoi*, both of which have little to do with divination. In fact, reading large swaths of the two accounts, one would be at a loss to uncover Teisamenos's and Hegesistratos's ostensible professions. Instead, we hear of Teisamenos's pentathlon and citizenship and Hegesistratos's severed foot and flight from Sparta.

Two Mantic Inscriptions

I conclude part 2 by considering two dedicatory inscriptions that suggest that seers, beyond being perceived as talismanic, could even proclaim or assert their talismanic authority themselves. First, in *De falsa legatione* (78), Aeschines praises his own uncle for contributing to the defeat of a Spartan admiral in a sea battle during the fourth-century Corinthian War:⁷⁵

καὶ ὁ τῆς μητρὸς τῆς ἡμετέρας ἀδελφός, θεῖος δὲ ἡμέτερος, Κλεόβουλος ὁ Γλαύκου τοῦ Ἀχαρνέως υἱός, μετὰ Δημαινέτου τοῦ Βουζύγου συγκατεναυμάχησε Χείλωνα τὸν Λακεδαιμονίων ναύαρχον·

And the brother of my mother, my uncle, Kleoboulos, the son of Glaukos of Acharnai together with Demainetos of the clan of the Bouzygai assisted in conquering at sea Cheilon the navarch of the Lakedaimonians.

We might assume that Aeschines' uncle was an Athenian naval commander were it not for an inscription on a grave stele dated to the second quarter of the fourth century B.C.E. from Menidi (ancient Acharnai) (*SEG* 16.193). Atop the stele above a relief of an eagle clutching a serpent in its talons the inscription reads:

Κλεόβολος Ἀχα[ρνεὺς]
μάντις.

---

74. Nigel Nicholson points out to me that Hegesistratos's talismanic status seems also to be signaled by his foot and not just his daring escape. For his deformed foot puts him in a category with other talismanic and divine figures such as Oidipous and Hephaistos, and his disability more generally can be seen as comparable to the talismanic oikist Battos and his stutter (see, e.g., Hdt. 4.155). I also note here that the different characterizations of the would-be victor Teisamenos and the extraordinary Hegesistratos conform well to the ideological oppositions Nicholson (2016) sees between the ways in which epinikion and the hero-athlete narrative characterize their respective protagonists.

75. For the possible battle to which Aeschines refers (and the orator's likely exaggeration of the significance of this event), see Harris 1995: 23–24.

An epigram in hexameters is inscribed below the eagle and serpent:

Γλαύκο παῖ Κλεόβολε θανόντα σε γαῖα καλ[ύπτει]
ἀμφότερον μάντιν τε ἀγαθὸν καὶ δορὶ μα[χητήν],
ὅν ποτ᾽Ἐρεχθέως μεγαλήτορος ἐστεφά[νωσε]
δῆμος ἀριστεύσαντα καθ᾽Ἑλλάδα κῦδος ἀρ[έσθαι].[76]

Son of Glaukos, Kleoboulos, having died the earth covers you
both a *mantis* and a good fighter with the spear,
whom once the people of great-hearted Erectheus crowned
since you were the best throughout Greece to win *kudos*.

As the patronymic and demotic reveal, this Kleoboulos is the uncle of Aeschines whom the orator credits with a naval victory. That he is identified as both a good *mantis* and a good fighter suggests that Kleoboulos was a military seer and helps to explain his presence at the battle against the Spartan Cheilon.[77] More important, if we accept *SEG*'s restorations, the epigram contains two prominent tokens of talismanic power. First, the image of the *dēmos* crowning Kleoboulos signals his talismanic power, since, as we saw in part 1, crowns can signify a victor's *kudos*.[78] Second, the inscription's final claim contains the phrase *kudos aresthai* (to win *kudos* for oneself), a formula found in Homer to designate a warrior's talismanic status.[79] The attribution of talismanic power to the seer Kleoboulos thus appears to be overdetermined in this inscription. Yet even if we do not accept the restoration of *kudos aresthai* in the final line, the slightly more secure restoration of *estephanōse* (crowned) is in and of itself a signal of talismanic power.[80]

The epigram allows us to return to Aeschines' statement with a new understanding of the significance of the seer's role in the naval battle. Kleoboulos's assistance there comprised not only his divinatory services as a seer but also the *kudos* his presence was seen to provide.[81] Aeschines' assertion that his uncle helped to

---

76. This is the text printed in *SEG*. For a slightly different version of the third line, see Papademetriou 1957. Daux (1958) brackets both ἐστεφά[νωσε] and κῦδος ἀρ[έσθαι] in their entirety.

77. The second line of the epigram has a pedigree extending back through Aeschylus's *Seven against Thebes* and Pindar's *Olympian* 6 to the *Thebaid*. Papademetriou (1957: 160) first observed that the inscription paraphrases Adrastos's estimation of Amphiaraos as ἀμφότερον μάντιν τ᾽ ἀγαθὸν καὶ δουρὶ μάρνασθαι (good both as a seer and at fighting with the spear) at *O*. 6.17. For the inscription's connections to Aeschylus and the *Thebaid*, see Flower 2008b: 96–97.

78. See also Kurke 1993.

79. In the *Iliad*, for instance, Hektor proclaims, "The son of Kronos gave to me to win *kudos* (κῦδος ἀρέσθ᾽) beside the ships and to pen the Achaians by the sea" (*Il*. 18.293–94).

80. It is interesting that the direction of the crowning is reversed from the usual progression in agonistic inscriptions: in contrast to agonistic inscriptions in which the victor crowns the city, here the city crowns the seer.

81. I thank Matthew Christ for calling my attention to the fact that Demainetos, whom Aeschines pairs with Kleoboulos, is himself from a priestly clan, the Bouzygai. On the Bouzygai, see Parker 2005: 57, 286–87. Aeschines thus credits two religious figures with assisting in Athens' naval victory.

bring about Athens' victory makes specific, then, the grave stele's general boast that Kleoboulos wielded talismanic power.

Finally, a suggested reading of a second inscription returns us to Teisamenos. The inscription (*IG* VII.1670 [= *SEG* 16.304 = *CEG* 328, with Addenda, *CEG* II, p. 302]) appears on a fragment of a marble base found below Mt. Kithairon in Boiotia. Approximately twenty-five meters away lie the probable remains of the sanctuary of Demeter, beside which the final engagement between the Greeks and Persians at the battle of Plataia took place (Hdt. 9.62). Flower and Marincola believe that the dedication originally stood in this nearby sanctuary and date the inscription to the early fifth century based on its letterforms.[82] I reproduce Flower and Marincola's text:

[Δ]άματρο[ς] τόδ' ἄγαλμα [⌣ – ⎯⎯ – ⌣⌣ – ×]
[ἐ]νθάδε γ'[ε]ἰςοράοντι σε[– ⎯⎯ – ⌣⌣ – ×]
[Τ]εισαμενὸς Ϙυδάδας καὶ [– ⎯⎯ – ⌣⌣ – ×]

This is the statue of Demeter . . .
Here for one looking upon . . .
Teisamenos of the family Kudadai and . . .

The provenance and date of the dedication increase the likelihood that this inscription refers to the very Teisamenos who became a "leader of wars" and claimed his first victory at Plataia.[83] Scholars disagree over the meaning of Ϙυδάδας, and it is variously taken as a separate proper name (i.e., "Teisamenos, Kudadas, and . . ."), a patronymic (i.e., "Teisamenos, son of Kudas, and . . ."), or as the name of a family (i.e., "Teisamenos of the family of the Kudadai [of the Iamidai clan] and . . ."). I follow Albert Schachter's proposal that Ϙυδάδας refers to a particular family of seers, and I draw attention to the hitherto-unnoticed detail that Ϙυδάδας seems to have a connection with *kudos*.[84] Schachter makes the intriguing suggestion that this name was perhaps emended to Κλυτιάδην in Herodotus's introduction to Teisamenos at 9.33.1, quoted on page 36. As the text stands now, Herodotus's identification of Teisamenos as being from both the Iamid and the Klytiad clans is highly unusual. Whether or not Herodotus himself used the name found in the inscription, this reading of the inscription itself suggests that Teisamenos and his family

---

82. Flower and Marincola 2002: 320, following Pritchett 1979b.

83. For a commentary on this inscription as well as a bibliography, see Flower and Marincola 2002: 320–22.

84. Schachter 2000. See Flower and Marincola 2002: 231–32. Regardless of whether the name is a proper name, a patronymic, or a family name, all three possible translations of Ϙυδάδας provide further evidence of a general link between seers and *kudos*. "Son of Kudas," however, does contradict Herodotus's assertion that Teisamenos was the son of Antiochos (9.33.1). Although the upsilon scans short instead of the expected long vowel for *kudos,* Nikolaos Papazarkadas reminds me that this type of metrical inconsistency is not unusual in epigrams.

sought to advertise their reputed ability to guarantee victory by going so far as to bear a name associated with *kudos*.[85] Herodotus is not alone in calling attention to Teisamenos's talismanic potency.

III. ANALOGOUS TALISMANS: THE SEER, THE ATHLETE, AND THE OIKIST

Just like athletes and oikists, then, seers can be viewed as bearers of talismanic power. To corroborate this conclusion and to demonstrate that the talismanic power belonging to each of these three types of figures was seen as analogous, I offer a solution to a unexplained discrepancy between three versions of the late sixth-century B.C.E. war between Kroton and Sybaris. The versions diverge in whom they credit as the cause of Kroton's victory.

Herodotus provides two accounts of the war (5.44–45), while Diodorus Siculus offers a third (12.9). In each version, Sybaris is the aggressor and Kroton the unlikely victor, and each version singles out an individual whose participation in the battle was crucial for Kroton. Yet, who that individual is differs in each account. In Herodotus's account, the Sybarites claim that the Spartan oikist Dorieus interrupted his colonial expedition to Sicilian Eryx to come to the aid of Kroton, whereas the Krotoniates assert that the only foreigner to support them was the Iamid *mantis* Kallias of Elis. In Diodorus Siculus's account, the athlete Milo, decked in all six of his Olympic crowns, led the outnumbered Krotoniates. An oikist, a seer, and a crown victor fill the same role in three different renditions of the story. The absence of Milo from the Herodotean variations cannot be explained by the historian's ignorance of this figure because Herodotus refers to Milo elsewhere in his work (3.37).[86] Likewise, Diodorus Siculus knows of Dorieus's colonizing attempt but makes no mention of this earlier stage in his journey (4.23).

All three figures are viewed as the reason for the remarkable upset of Sybaris in their respective versions. In the case of Milo, Diodorus records that he was marvel to the Krotoniates because he was the reason for their victory (αἴτιον δὲ γενόμενον τῆς νίκης θαυμασθῆναι παρὰ τοῖς πολίταις, 12.9.6). As evidence for the veracity of their version, the Sybarites point to a precinct and temple beside the river Krathis that they say Dorieus founded in honor of Athena Krathis after he had helped to capture their city (5.45.1). Conversely, the Krotoniates cite as evidence of their own competing claim the vast amounts of land in Kroton given to Kallias and upon which the seer's descendants continued to live in Herodotus's day (5.45.2). Kallias's

---

85. We can compare this strategy to other military seers, such as Hegesistratos, "Leader of the Army" (Hdt. 9.37), and Hagesias, "Leader" (Pi. *O.* 6.12), whose names also declare their capabilities.

86. At 3.37, Democedes of Kroton sends a message to Darius informing him of his betrothal to the daughter of Milo, "for Darius thought very highly of Milo the wrestler."

reward of land and Dorieus's dedication suggest that both outsiders were seen as a, if not *the*, deciding factor in Sybaris's unlikely defeat.

Rather than privileging one account over the others to get at "what really happened," I propose that we read these different versions together. What we are seeing are actually variations on a common template: the Krotoniates defeated the Sybarites with the aid of a talismanic figure. We have met Milo and his six crowns before. He is the figure par excellence for the talismanic potency of athletic victors.[87] The talismanic status of oikists was presented in part 1 above and will also be discussed in chapter 3. As a would-be king, who leaves Sparta when that title goes to his half brother, and as a colonial founder who is twice given a band of settlers to lead on an expedition, Dorieus seems to have been perceived, at least in some Lakedaimonian circles, as vested with his own talismanic authority.[88] Yet Dorieus's conduct as an oikist is unusual. Herodotus implies that Dorieus's first attempt at founding a settlement in Libya ends in disaster because the oikist did not follow protocol. Dorieus departed from Sparta "having neither consulted the oracle at Delphi as to what land he was to found nor having done any of the customary things" (οὔτε τῷ ἐν Δελφοῖσι χρηστηρίῳ χρησάμενος ἐς ἥντινα γῆν κτίσων ἴῃ, οὔτε ποιήσας οὐδὲν τῶν νομιζομένων, 5.42.2).[89]

Kallias the seer is briefly described at 5.44.2:

> ταῦτα μέν νυν Συβαρῖται λέγουσι ποιῆσαι Δωριέα τε καὶ τοὺς μετ' αὐτοῦ, Κροτωνιῆται δὲ οὐδένα σφίσι φασὶ ξεῖνον προσεπιλαβέσθαι τοῦ πρὸς Συβαρίτας πολέμου εἰ μὴ Καλλίην τῶν Ἰαμιδέων μάντιν Ἠλεῖον μοῦνον, καὶ τοῦτον τρόπῳ τοιῷδε· παρὰ Τήλυος τοῦ Συβαριτέων τυράννου ἀποδράντα ἀπικέσθαι παρὰ σφέας, ἐπείτε οἱ τὰ ἱρὰ οὐ προεχώρεε χρηστὰ θυομένῳ ἐπὶ Κρότωνα.
>
> Now these are the things the Sybarites say Dorieus and the men with him did, but the Krotoniates hold that no foreigner took a hand in the war against the Sybarites except for Kallias alone, an Elean *mantis* of the Iamid clan, and that this man took part in the following way: he came to them having run away from Telys, the tyrant of the Sybarites, since the omens were not turning out favorably when he was sacrificing against Kroton.

This passage reveals little about the Iamid except that he went over to Kroton after giving the Sybarites and their tyrant Telys the slip. Like Dorieus's attempt to side-

---

87. See also Kurke 1993: 134–35.

88. See Carlier 1984: 292–301; Cartledge 1987: 109–10 for the talismanic authority of the Spartan kings.

89. Dorieus's behavior in his second colonial attempt (to found Herakleia in Sicily) is hardly better. Harrison (2000: 155), followed by Hornblower (2007: 169), argues that although he consults Delphi this time, Dorieus wastes the Pythia's positive reply (that he would seize the land he was sent against [Hdt. 5.43]) by getting sidetracked and coming to Kroton's aid. In other words, he "uses up" the oracle's sanction and his own divine favor on the wrong location.

step Delphi's involvement, Kallias's behavior is presented as highly unusual. Seers are never represented as abandoning their armies.[90] Kallias's deviant performance seems best explained in relation to that of Dorieus. As Herodotus presents them, both seer and oikist act outside the cultural norms associated with their professions. Seers do not switch sides, nor do oikists neglect to consult the Delphic oracle before commencing an expedition.[91]

Herodotus not only makes Dorieus and Kallias compatible by calling attention to the transgressive actions of both men but also, in doing so, allows for Dorieus and Kallias to be substituted for each other in the two competing versions of the same story. That Herodotus places both variations side by side without endorsing either claim further adds to their compatibility. In fact, we can refine the template slightly when considering only Herodotus's two renditions of the battle and observe that the Herodotean template might look something like "the Krotoniates defeated the Sybarites with the aid of a talismanic exile."

Let us bring Diodorus Siculus back into the picture. The difference in the three accounts can be explained by the fact that Milo, Dorieus, and Kallias are all transposable with one another because of their analogous forms of talismanic power. Each version had different interests that led to either a crown victor, an oikist, or a seer as the respective focus of the individual accounts. But what all versions could agree on was that a talismanic figure came to Kroton's aid.

The Greeks envisioned the importance of seers in battle to extend beyond their ability to attend to the customary rites of an army on campaign. Teisamenos and other mantic "leaders of war" were enlisted for their talismanic power as much as for their ability to interpret omens and conduct sacrifices. Talismanic potency accounts for the references to seers commanding armies and winning battles. Further, because seers could be viewed as bearers of *kudos,* we can examine how they converge and intersect with other talismanic figures, namely, athletic victors and oikists. In chapter 5, we will turn to Hagesias, the *laudandus* in Pindar's *Olympian* 6 and discuss how these three talismanic categories—crown victor, seer, and oikist—all converge on the same individual to create a figure of overwhelming talismanic potency. But Hagesias is unusual. More frequently, as we will see in chapter 3, the seer is eclipsed as a talismanic figure in colonial discourse and in his place the oikist, a competing recipient of Apollo's divine favor, claims the spotlight instead.

90. Flower 2008a: 195.

91. That an oikist must consult Delphi in order for his expedition to be successful is likely an argument endorsed by Delphi as a way of claiming superiority over other competing oracles and seers. To be sure, there are plenty of foundation traditions that do not mention a connection to Delphi (Hall 2008), but we should nevertheless understand Delphi's centrality to colonization as an argument that Delphi itself wished to promote. See chapter 6 for the ways in which Delphi leverages its oracular monopoly in foundation discourses. For the implications of Dorieus's deviant behavior and its significance vis-à-vis some of the larger thematic concerns of the *Histories,* see Hornblower 2007.

2

Sailing to Sicily

Theoklymenos and Odysseus in the Odyssey

In chapter 1, we established that seers could be enlisted by armies on campaign for their perceived talismanic power and not only for their divinatory expertise. In these military contexts, the seer and the *stratēgos* form a productive and conspicuous pair.[1] We turn now to another type of partnership and another type of context: the partnership between the seer Theoklymenos and Odysseus in the *Odyssey*. In this chapter we will see that the seer and poem's eponymous hero operate as a coherent pair: within the framework of colonial discourse, Theoklymenos aids Odysseus-as-oikist in effecting the metaphorical refoundation of Ithaka. I will argue that Theoklymenos and Odysseus reveal that the seer-oikist relationship is a possible social construct. Acknowledging this construct will not only make sense of the role of Theoklymenos in the *Odyssey*, which scholars have traditionally viewed as suspect, but will also put us in a position to explore the issues addressed in chapters 3–6. For, as we will see in these subsequent chapters, later colonial narratives are ideologically motivated to elide or suppress this pairing. This chapter, then, will set a baseline for the seer-oikist relationship that will allow us to examine the ways in which later archaic and early classical instantiations of colonial discourse deviate from this Homeric paradigm.

The chapter is divided into three main parts. Part 1 assembles previous assessments of Theoklymenos in relation to Odysseus and establishes that the figure of Theoklymenos is rendered in the poem as a doublet of Odysseus. Part 2, drawing on Carol Dougherty's work, charts the colonial resonance of the *Odyssey* and how Odysseus himself is characterized as an oikist. Part 3 joins these two previous parts

---

1. For futher discussion on the pairing of the seer and *stratēgos*, see chapter 3.

together. It first exposes the colonial resonance of Theoklymenos and Odysseus's "meeting" and then traces how this seer-oikist pairing works as a productive partnership in the second half of the poem when Odysseus at last returns to Ithaka. Yet we will also see that the two figures are so closely construed in certain fundamental ways as to appear redundant. This redundancy, I will argue, becomes one of the driving forces behind the seer's excision from later post-Homeric colonial discourse.

THE PALIMPSEST OF THEOKLYMENOS

Theoklymenos has chafed against the sensibilities of previous generations of scholars of the *Odyssey*. The narrative ellipses and inconsistencies that cluster around the seer were, for Denys Page, "not the work of a man who has gone far in his profession."[2] His arrival in the poem seems abrupt, his interpretation of an omen incorrect, his ecstatic vision of the suitors' destruction eerie.[3] As a result, Theoklymenos became the object of Analytic attempts at unraveling the filaments of interpolation.[4] Representative of this approach is Erich Bethe, who saw Theoklymenos as an illustration of the work of a redactor skilled at introducing self-contained elements into the poem without disturbing the surrounding story.[5] But later scholars, responding to Theoklymenos's relegation to secondary status, reclaimed the seer and argued for his relevance to the unfolding of the second half of the *Odyssey*. Bernard Fenik in particular defends each of Theoklymenos's appearances over the course of books 15–20 as "genuine" examples of Odyssean style.[6] Others focus on Theoklymenos's prophecy (*Od.* 20.351–57), including Daniel Levine, who examines the ways in which the vision pulls together a number of crucial motifs in the final moments before Odysseus's revenge.[7]

Yet while Page's view of Theoklymenos as "wonderfully unimportant" has since been discredited, scholars who defend the seer's thematic significance have not fully accounted for his lacunose strangeness in the poem. Theoklymenos's speeches may be stylistically sound, but nothing in the plot seems to hinge on their content.

---

2. Page 1955: 85. Kirk (1962: 240), noting the abruptness of Theoklymenos's entrance into the poem, granted him the distinction of being the "only character in the *Iliad* or *Odyssey*—with the exception of Phoinix—whom one feels to have arrived there almost by mistake."

3. Such are the complaints leveled against Theoklymenos by Page, Kirk, and others. See Fenik (1974: 233–34) for a list of all of Theoklymenos's supposed infractions, which Fenik methodically defends. On Theoklymenos's interpretation of the omen (*Od.* 15.531–34), Kirk (1962: 241) writes, "Now Homeric omens normally have some detectable relation to the interpretation offered for them; this one has none, and the interpretation is in addition both weak and vague."

4. E.g., Wilamowitz-Moellendorff 1927: 148–50; Merkelbach 1951: 69.

5. Bethe 1922: 40.

6. Fenik 1974: 233–44. See also Beye 1966: 168; Thornton 1970: 58–62; Erbse 1972: 42–54; Hansen 1972: 34–47; Race 1993: 98–99; Reece 1994; de Jong 2001: 372–73.

7. Levine 1983. See also Amory 1963: 109–12; Austin 1975: 246, 250; Broggiato 2003.

Further, the issue of why Theoklymenos suddenly appears for the completion of Odysseus's *nostos* remains a mystery. In this chapter I will argue that while Theoklymenos is in fact wonderfully important to the *Odyssey*, his mantic abilities, on which previous scholarly discussion has tended to focus, do not tell us very much about his presence in the poem. Progress can be made in understanding Theoklymenos, however, by exploring him in relation to Odysseus.

Despite his low opinion of Theoklymenos, Page offers a productive starting point for this undertaking. Page posits that the seer must have belonged to another instantiation of the story in which he performed a more satisfyingly plausible and coherent role: Theoklymenos's presence would be more relevant if, in this alternate version, he were in fact "Odysseus himself in disguise."[8] In a different approach to the poem, Albert Lord supports this suggestion. Lord also views the seer as a possible doublet for Odysseus, his existence a relic of a variant in which Telemachos met his father not within Eumaios's hut but at Pylos.[9] In this way, both Page and Lord discern what might be thought of as a palimpsest of a Theoklymenos-as-Odysseus.

Let us consider the implications of this hypothesis. In doing so, I do not wish to reconstruct a lost variant of the *Odyssey* but rather to consider how our extant version of the poem continues to think about these two figures in tandem. Without dismissing the possibility of an alternate version featuring Odysseus as Theoklymenos, I will demonstrate how Theoklymenos and Odysseus even as discrete characters generate some of the same salient motifs and patterns. Page's insight illuminates a muted but nevertheless discernible alignment that is still being played out between the two characters in our *Odyssey*. Part 1 explores this alignment more fully and establishes that a homology between a seer of allegedly little consequence and the epic's eponymous hero manifests in the second half of the *Odyssey*. After part 1 tracks how Theoklymenos and Odysseus converge, parts 2 and 3 will consider why they do so.

I. THEOKLYMENOS AS ODYSSEUS, ODYSSEUS AS THEOKLYMENOS

Scholars have noticed a number of thematic and dictional parallels between Theoklymenos and Odysseus. Below I list nine of these repetitions in sequential order

---

8. Page 1955: 88.

9. Lord 2000: 174. As Lord (174) argues, "[These two versions] have been put together in oral tradition as we have it in this song of Homer's. The result is duplication often with one element in the duplication being vestigial or partial, and hence an apparent postponement and suspense, or an inconsistency." See also Reece (1994), who makes the compelling argument that our version reflects a variant of the poem in which Telemachos met Odysseus in Crete. Reece suggests that in this version Odysseus decided to return to Ithaka disguised as a seer.

as they occur in books 13–20 (i.e., from the time Odysseus returns to Ithaka to Theoklymenos's exit from the poem):[10] (1) Odysseus, on his arrival to Ithaka, tells a disguised Athena that he is a fugitive homicide from Crete (*Od.* 13.256–86). In like manner, Theoklymenos enters the *Odyssey* on the run for murder (*Od.* 15.223–25).[11] (2) Telemachos's initial encounter with the seer at Pylos has been seen as an "anticipatory doublet" of his reunion with Odysseus at the home of Eumaios (*Od.* 15.256–78 and 16.42–48, respectively).[12] (3) As part of these two encounters, Theoklymenos and Odysseus both cast themselves as suppliants of Telemachos, who is consequently placed in the position of host to these unforeseen *xenoi* (guest friends).[13] (4) Both Theoklymenos and Odysseus are steered toward trusted allies on Ithaka. In book 13, Athena tells Odysseus to go first to Eumaios before venturing home to Penelope (*Od.* 13.404–6). Telemachos abruptly reroutes Theoklymenos away from the clutches of the suitor Eurymachos, where he initially intends to send the seer, and directs him to his companion Peiraios instead (*Od.* 15.512–43). (5) Theoklymenos's and Odysseus's respective departures from these locations with Peiraios and Eumaios and their subsequent arrivals at the palace frame the events of book 17.[14] (6) When Theoklymenos and Odysseus find themselves in the presence of Penelope, each takes the opportunity to inform her of Odysseus's impending return.[15] (7) Carolyn Higbie shows that while the suitors address Penelope as if she were unwed or widowed by referring to her as the daughter of Ikarios (e.g., *Od.* 16.435), only the disguised Odysseus and Theoklymenos call her by her proper title: ὦ γύναι αἰδοίη Λαερτιάδεω Ὀδυσῆος (chaste wife of Odysseus, son of Laertes, *Od.* 17.152 [Theoklymenos] = *Od.* 19.165, 262, 336, 583

---

10. Reece (1994) includes many of these parallels in his own discussion of the similarities between the seer and Odysseus.

11. For a discussion of this Cretan lie, see below.

12. Higbie 1995: 73. As mentioned above, this idea was first suggested by Lord (2000: 174). De Jong notes the *Odyssey*'s several other character doublets: Euryklea and Eurynome (2001: 42–43 at *Od.* 1.428–35, 431 at *Od.* 17.492–506); Circe and Calypso (2001: 129–30 at *Od.* 5.89–91; cf. West 2014: 127); Melanthios and Melantho (2001: 416–17 at *Od.* 17.212–14); Philoetius and Eumaios (2001: 494 at *Od.* 20.185–240); and Leodes and Amphinomos (2001: 512 at *Od.* 21.144–48). Theoklymenos, then, is one of a number of doublets in the poem.

13. See Fenik 1974: 238. Eumaios tells Telemachos that the stranger who has come to his farmstead claims to be his suppliant (*Od.* 16.67). Theoklymenos also presents himself as a suppliant to Telemachos (*Od.* 15.277).

14. These respective arrivals roughly begin and conclude book 17: Theoklymenos reaches the palace at *Od.* 17.84, Odysseus at 17.336. There is also a parallel between Eumaios's escorting Odysseus here in book 17 and Peiraios's escorting Theoklymenos in book 15 when he first disembarks on Ithaka (*Od.* 15.542–43). In both cases, Telemachos orders a friend to accompany his guest into the city. On this particular parallel, Lord (2000: 170) writes, "These two scenes look like multiforms of the same theme."

15. Theoklymenos tells Penelope that Odysseus is already on Ithaka (*Od.* 17.157–59); the disguised Odysseus tells her that Odysseus will return "at this very *lykabas*" (*Od.* 19.306). On the meaning of *lykabas* (often translated as "month" or "year"), see Austin 1975: 244–47.

[Odysseus]).¹⁶ (8) Although Theoklymenos and Odysseus swear that Odysseus's return is imminent, they are met with the verbatim skepticism of Penelope, who replies to both that she will bestow upon them many gifts if only what they say is true (*Od.* 17.163–65 [to Theoklymenos] = *Od.* 19.309–11 [to Odysseus]).¹⁷ (9) Lastly, Theoklymenos and Odysseus both become the targets of the suitors' abuse in book 20 and thus help to showcase the suitors' blind depravity as they feast in Odysseus's hall for a final time. The suitors' insults provoke Theoklymenos's exit, but only after he has delivered his vision of their impending destruction (*Od.* 20.351–57), a prophetic draft of the actual slaughter upon which Odysseus is about to embark.¹⁸

Thus, generally speaking, and with greater detail necessarily given to the epic's main protagonist, the itineraries of seer and hero on Ithaka duplicate one another as the plot slides back and forth between them, staggering their comparable narrative arcs. Their interactions with Penelope are especially aligned, insofar as their conversations with her prompt some of the same diction in the narrator-text. Before considering why Odysseus is shadowed by a seer in this way as he carries out the completion of his *nostos*, I wish to examine one further and hitherto unnoticed correspondence between the two characters. The parallel concerns Theoklymenos's entrance in *Odyssey* 15.

Hidden Identities

As Telemachos sacrifices to Athena before departing from Pylos, he is suddenly approached by a stranger: σχεδόθεν δέ οἱ ἤλυθεν ἀνὴρ / τηλεδαπός, φεύγων ἐξ Ἄργεος ἄνδρα κατακτάς, / μάντις· (A man came near him from a far-off country, fleeing from Argos for killing a man, and he was a *mantis*, *Od.* 15.223–25). This introduction triggers the fugitive seer's genealogy, an extended, thirty-two-line circuit through the preceding generations of his mantic clan, the Melampodidai: Homer recounts the myths of Melampous and his escape from Pylos, of Amphiaraos and his death in Thebes, and of the seer Polypheides who immigrated to Hyperesia out of anger toward his father.¹⁹ Along the way, the poet catalogues

---

16. Higbie 1995: 130. Higbie (130) notes, "Although I would not want to push this point too far, as married women can be identified by their father's name, the consistency of usage for Penelope may be a subtle reminder of others' desires and views." Whatever the implications of the address, the fact remains that it is only Theoklymenos and Odysseus who refer to Penelope as the wife of Odysseus.

17. The oaths that Theoklymenos and Odysseus swear in these comparable contexts are also similar (compare *Od.* 17.155–56 to 19.303–4). Furthermore, Theoklymenos's version of this oath is identical to an oath Odysseus swears to Eumaios at *Od.* 14.158–59.

18. Amory (1963: 112–13) argues that Theoklymenos's prophecy motivates Penelope to initiate the contest of the bow.

19. Theoklymenos's own imminent escape from Pylos with Telemachos thus echoes Melampous's escape from Pylos recorded in the genealogy. For Melampous, see chapter 3. According to Homer, Amphiaraos died at Thebes, in contrast to other versions of the myth in which Amphiaraos is swallowed alive by the earth (e.g., Pi. *N.* 9.24–27). For Amphiaraos, see chapter 6.

other descendants of Melampous, including Amphiaraos's sons Alkmaion and Amphilochos (*Od.* 15.248). But it is not until the ring composition at last circles back to the present that the poet finally reveals the current Melampodid standing before Telemachos to be Theoklymenos: Τοῦ μὲν ἄρ' υἱὸς ἐπῆλθε, Θεοκλύμενος δ' ὄνομ' ἦεν, /ὅς τότε Τηλεμάχου πέλας ἵστατο· (It was [Polypheides'] son, Theoklymenos was his name, who then approached and stood near Telemachos, *Od.* 15.256–57).

Page describes Theoklymenos's entrance into the poem as "by far the longest and most elaborate preparation of its kind in the *Odyssey*."[20] It is true that the arrivals of most Homeric characters into the narrative are not accompanied by such lengthy excursions into their family histories. Nevertheless, in terms of its genre, Theoklymenos's introduction is a genealogy and but one of several equally expansive examples of this form in Homeric poetry, including those of Glaukos (*Il.* 6.145–211) and Aeneas (*Il.* 20.213–41).[21] What is particularly noteworthy about this introduction, however, is not so much its length or degree of specificity, although these are significant, but that Homer does not initially make clear to whom the genealogy belongs. Despite plotting the seer's entire pedigree, the poet strangely suspends the revelation of Theoklymenos's own name until the final line of the ring composition directs the spotlight back to the setting at Pylos.

This delayed identification of the seer seems to make the account of Theoklymenos's origins unique among Homeric genealogies. Because the name of a character often activates his or her genealogy in Homeric poetry, its absence at the outset of Theoklymenos's own genealogy is all the more striking. Athena's description of Arete's royal lineage serves as a representative example of this convention (*Od.* 7.53–59):

δέσποιναν μὲν πρῶτα κιχήσεαι ἐν μεγάροισιν·
Ἀρήτη δ' ὄνομ' ἐστὶν ἐπώνυμον, ἐκ δὲ τοκήων
τῶν αὐτῶν, οἵ περ τέκον Ἀλκίνοον βασιλῆα.
Ναυσίθοον μὲν πρῶτα Ποσειδάων ἐνοσίχθων
γείνατο καὶ Περίβοια, γυναικῶν εἶδος ἀρίστη,
ὁπλοτάτη θυγάτηρ μεγαλήτορος Εὐρυμέδοντος,
ὅς ποθ' ὑπερθύμοισι Γιγάντεσσιν βασίλευεν.

First you will come upon the mistress in her halls. Arete is her given name, and she is from the same forebears who bore King Alkinoös. Poseidon the earth-shaker begot Nausithoos with Periboia, most outstanding of women in appearance, the youngest daughter of great-hearted Eurymedon, who, once upon a time, used to rule over the bold Giants.

---

20. Page 1955: 83.
21. For the genre of genealogy, see Martin 1989: 85–86.

Arete's proper name initiates her history. In like manner, Polyphemos's name also precedes the story of the Cyclops's birth and the identification of his parents (*Od.* 1.68–73):

ἀλλὰ Ποσειδάων γαιήοχος ἀσκελὲς αἰὲν
Κύκλωπος κεχόλωται, ὃν ὀφθαλμοῦ ἀλάωσεν,
ἀντίθεον Πολύφημον, ὅου κράτος ἐστὶ μέγιστον
πᾶσιν Κυκλώπεσσι· Θόωσα δέ μιν τέκε νύμφη,
Φόρκυνος θυγάτηρ, ἁλὸς ἀτρυγέτοιο μέδοντος,
ἐν σπέσσι γλαφυροῖσι Ποσειδάωνι μιγεῖσα.

But earth-embracing Poseidon is ever unrelenting in his anger because of the Cyclops, whose eye he [Odysseus] blinded, god-like Polyphemos, whose might is greatest among all the Cyclopes. Thoösa the nymph bore him, daughter of Phorkys, ruler of the barren sea, having lain with Poseidon in hollow caves.

Similarly, in the *Iliad*, in the so-called obituaries of heroes killed in battle, the dead warrior's name typically prompts an excursus on his ancestry.[22]

Not all genealogies begin this way. As Leonard Muellner observes, characters reciting their own lineages never state their names but only those of their forebears.[23] Yet prior to a character's performance, the narrator-text always identifies who the speaker is. That is to say, the name of the hero who is presenting his genealogy is always known to the audience even when the speaker himself does not offer it.[24] Genealogies aside, Egbert Bakker demonstrates that Homer goes to great lengths to mark out with dictional cues which character is in focus at any given time.[25] It is thus exceedingly unusual for Homer to withhold the identity of a character, no matter what the genre.[26]

Although exceptional, the deferment of Theoklymenos's name is not without precedent. In fact, it is a well-known feature of another introduction in the poem: the proem to the *Odyssey*. Indeed, I would contend that the entrance of Theoklymenos mimics the notorious delay of Odysseus's own name in the opening to the epic poem.

In order to appreciate this correspondence, we must first look briefly at the proem itself. That Odysseus enters the poem anonymously is an observation at least as old as Eustathius.[27] The postponement of Odysseus's name for a full

---

22. See Stoevesandt 2004: 128 for a useful list of the nineteen obituaries for dead warriors in the *Iliad*.

23. Muellner 1976: 74n9.

24. E.g., Glaukos is named at *Il.* 6.119 before reciting his own genealogy at 6.145.

25. Bakker 1997: 54–85.

26. On the importance of naming in Homeric poetry in general, see Higbie 1995. For naming in the *Odyssey*, see Goldhill 1991: 24–36 with bibliography.

27. Eust. p. 1381, 20–25 with Clay 1983: 26.

twenty-one lines at the beginning of his epic clearly stands in contrast to Achilles' forceful claim on *Iliad* 1.1.[28] At the same time, as Simon Goldhill observes, the *Odyssey*'s opening periphrasis *andra polutropon* (man of many ways) says as much about Odysseus as the proper name whose place it has hijacked:

> *Andra* . . . announces the concealment and revealing of the name that plays a crucial role in the *kleos* of Odysseus' return. Yet, as Pucci also notes, the name is displaced by an adjective, *polutropon*, that itself expresses the very quality of deceptive wiliness that is seen most strikingly in Odysseus' constant disguises, which, precisely, withhold the proper name. *Polutropon*, in other words, both marks Odysseus' capability to manipulate language's power to conceal and reveal, and, at the same time, *enacts* such a revealing and a concealing.[29]

Goldhill compares the resulting configuration of the proem to "a *griphos*, a riddle, and enigma, where a series of expressions (of which *polutropon* is the first) successively qualifies the term *andra* as the name 'Odysseus' is approached."[30]

Enlisting Goldhill's observations on the proem, I suggest that the presentation of Theoklymenos is also organized, both thematically and formally, as a *griphos* (riddle). Like the proem, the introduction of Theoklymenos "enacts" the Odyssean motif of concealing and revealing names. By deferring Theoklymenos's proper name until the end of the genealogy, Homer presents an anonymous seer whose identity must be puzzled out (at least notionally) by an audience removed from its customary position of omniscience. Because the seer's introduction involves the poem's audience in this way, and not just its characters, the riddle of Theoklymenos's introduction aligns itself specifically with the proem of the *Odyssey* itself.

The proem may even be slyly evoked in Theoklymenos's own entrance: σχεδόθεν δέ οἱ ἤλυθεν ἀνήρ / τηλεδαπός, φεύγων ἐξ Ἄργεος ἄνδρα κατακτάς, / μάντις· (A man came near him from a far-off country, fleeing from Argos for killing a man, and he was a *mantis*, *Od.* 15.223–25). Like the *Odyssey*'s opening *andra* (= *anēr* in the accusative case), Theoklymenos himself is at first identified only as an *anēr*. In fact, *mantis* has been delayed to achieve this effect, waiting two lines away in clarifying apposition at the end of the clause. What is more, in keeping with its allusion to *Odyssey* 1.1, the proper name of this *anēr* is not revealed for the first thirty-two lines of his genealogy.[31]

---

28. Clay 1983: 26. See also de Jong 2001: 7: "The suppression of Odysseus' name is a common Odyssean motif. . . . By inserting this motif into his proem, the narrator signals his story's preoccupation with (the concealing of) names."

29. Goldhill 1991: 4.

30. Goldhill 1991: 4.

31. We might also think of the second line of Theoklymenos's introduction as organized in a manner similar to that of the proem. In the proem, the *polutropos anēr* is "driven far astray after he had sacked the sacred citadel of Troy" (*Od.* 1.2). So too, in the second line of Theoklymenos's

Finally, when the audience is at last rewarded with Theoklymenos's name, I would suggest that the name itself works as a deliberate pun to recall further Odysseus and the thematic importance of its protagonist's concealed identity in the *Odyssey*. For the revelation "Theoklymenos" (whose etymology includes *theos* [god] and *kleos* [fame]) seems to pun on a moment that is itself the revelation of a name after a prolonged delay: Odysseus's famous characterization of his identity to the Phaiakians (9.19–20):

εἴμ' Ὀδυσεὺς Λαερτιάδης, ὅς πᾶσι δόλοισιν
ἀνθρώποισι μέλω, καί μευ κλέος οὐρανὸν ἵκει.

I am Odysseus the son of Laertes, who troubles all mankind with my contrivances, and my *kleos* goes up to heaven.

"Theoklymenos" thus mimics in the form of a single name Odysseus's own claim, at his own moment of revelation, that his *kleos* reaches the gods.

Although Theoklymenos's name is eventually revealed to the audience, the characters themselves never learn it, and he remains an anonymous outsider, even to his host Telemachos, until his departure in book 20.[32] We might consider, then, the delay of Theoklymenos's name in his opening genealogy to be as programmatic for the seer as the postponement of Odysseus's name in the proem is for the hero. This possibility suggests that the structure of Theoklymenos's introduction does not merely serve the purpose of imitating Odysseus's proem but rather points to a fundamental quality shared by the seer and hero.[33] Part 3 will address these deeper cultural connections between Odysseus and Theoklymenos within the poem's colonial framework.

II. THE *ODYSSEY* AS A COLONIAL NARRATIVE

Before we can turn to the alliance of Theoklymenos and Odysseus, we must first understand the ways in which the *Odyssey* itself can be understood as an example of colonial discourse. To do so, I will build on the work of Carol Dougherty and her analysis of the *Odyssey* as a colonial narrative. After reviewing Dougherty's own argument, I will further develop her claim that Odysseus is characterized as

---

description, the seer "[came] from afar fleeing from Argos because he killed a man" (*Od.* 15.224). There are then, generally speaking, the same ingredients in the same order: involuntary travel (much wandering vs. fleeing from afar) brought on by bloodshed (the sacking of Troy vs. murder) located in a specific city (Troy vs. Argos). It is also tempting to view the opening of Theoklymenos's "proem" as having the ability to spin off into another epic (e.g., a *Melampodeia*).

32. See Benardete 1997: 119.

33. That is, Odysseus is not the only figure in the poem with the ability to withhold his identity. Of course, if Theoklymenos is the vestige of Odysseus in disguise from another version of the story, then Theoklymenos's delayed name would be another instance of Odysseus delaying his identity.

an oikist. Once we have established the poem's colonial nature and Odysseus's role as an oikist, we will then be in a position to consider how the pairing of Theoklymenos and Odysseus functions in this colonial context.

The *Odyssey* has long invited ethnographic approaches to its characters and plot, but, as Dougherty argues, we should view the poem itself as an ethnographic text. As Dougherty emphasizes, the *Odyssey* is a cultural product of a period, the late eighth century B.C.E., when the Greek world was highly unstable and in flux, a period whose new challenges the Greeks tried to understand through the lens of their myths.[34] The Greek colonial movement contributed to the volatile nature of the archaic period and is thus a major theme explored in the poem.[35] Dougherty sees the poem's construal of Odysseus's travels as its way of coming to terms with the dangers and the benefits of colonial ventures in the "New World." For example, she observes that by exploiting the "prominent motifs and strategies of colonial discourse" Homer figures both the hypocivilized Cyclopes and the hypercivilized Phaiakians as (extreme versions of) the indigenous inhabitants who awaited Greeks exploring distant lands.[36] The diametrically opposed receptions of Odysseus by Polyphemos and Alkinoös (cannibalism vs. the offer of marriage and assimilation) can be read as ethnographic formulations and mystifications of the potential outcomes, both bad and good, of colonial contact with non-Greeks.[37]

Dougherty is not the first to have approached the *Odyssey* from a colonial perspective, but, generally speaking, earlier discussions on this issue have mainly centered on the poem's descriptions of the foundation of Scheria and the island off the coast of the Cylcopes.[38] By contrast, one of Dougherty's important contributions is her consideration of how the challenges of colonization manifest themselves also in the poem's construction of Odysseus's return. For Dougherty, Odysseus's experience with the exotic places encountered in his adventures is directly brought to bear on his reunion with Penelope and the restoration of his power on Ithaka. That is, Odysseus's homecoming is orchestrated as a kind of "re-foundation" of Ithaka, and this refoundation operates as a culmination to and application of the colonial crash-course the hero has undergone in the preceding episodes of the epic.[39] Fur-

---

34. Dougherty 2001: 9.
35. Dougherty 2001: 112.
36. Dougherty 2001: 162.
37. Dougherty 2001: 122–42.
38. Other scholars who see the *Odyssey* engaged with the colonization movement include Finley (1978: 61–63); Clay (1980); Vidal-Naquet (1986: 26); Rose (1992: 134–40); Crielaard (1995: 236–39); Dench (1995: 36–38).
39. Dougherty 2001: 169. Dougherty (169) clarifies her statement: "By this I don't mean to say that Odysseus literally re-founds Ithaka; rather, the themes and issues of colonial discourse articulate the terms of his return to represent it as a kind of re-foundation." Redfield (1983: 222) calls Odysseus the "refounder" of his house.

ther, since it is Odysseus who effects this refoundation, Dougherty rightly emphasizes that Odysseus necessarily performs the role of Ithaka's oikist. Before expanding on Dougherty's argument, I note her key insights into how Odysseus undertakes the metaphorical refoundation of Ithaka.

Dougherty tracks the ways in which certain elements from Odysseus's earlier travels resurface on Ithaka. She exposes, for example, how the imagery of book 9 appears again in the second half of the poem to align the gluttonous suitors with the Cyclopes. The reunion of Odysseus and Penelope, in turn, is laden with allusions to the temptingly marriageable Nausikaa in book 6 and that former enticement for Odysseus to settle on Scheria forever.[40] Dougherty demonstrates that the challenges to Odysseus's return (i.e., overthrowing the suitors, reuniting with Penelope) not only recall these earlier episodes of the poem but also correspond to recurring motifs of colonial discourse in general.[41] In non-Homeric examples of colonial discourse, the successful oikist can subdue the local population or marry into the royal family. So, too, Odysseus must now overpower the suitors, transformed into uncivilized brutes, as well as win the hand of Penelope, the native queen, in order to gain control of the territory.[42]

Odysseus's mounting colonial claim to Ithaka is also registered at the level of the island's landscape over the course of the second half of the poem. Initially characterized by Athena as a site of raw possibility in book 13, Ithaka metamorphoses and becomes, in the verbal parallels drawn between Laertes' orchard and Scheria in book 24, a place that teems with cultivated and civilized prosperity. Dougherty, however, is careful to call attention to the distinction the poem simultaneously marks between the Golden Age gardens of the Phaiakians and those of Laertes: the latter, in contrast to the former, are clearly the result of agricultural skill and human toil. Viewed through the lens of the eighth century, in other words, Ithaka is transformed from a land awaiting colonization in book 13 to a model of a thriving colony in book 24. Thus Odysseus, back from his travels in the New World, metaphorically becomes Ithaka's oikist, lifting it out of the heroic past and introducing it to the archaic present.[43]

---

40. Dougherty 2001: 167–69.

41. On the metaphor of marriage in colonial discourse, see Dougherty 1993: 61–80; on violence and colonial discourse, see 40–41.

42. As Dougherty (2001: 167) observes, "Cannibals function rhetorically as a marker of the violence of colonial settlement. Once the *Odyssey* assimilates the suitors' greed to the cannibal behavior of Polyphemus, it projects this colonial framework onto the slaughter of the suitors at Ithaca. By doing so, it recasts the problematic violence of Odysseus' revenge as a positive act of foundation."

43. Dougherty 2001: 162, 169–72. Other scholars have noted that Odysseus's qualities are of the sort required for this age of exploration. See, e.g., Rose 1992: 120: "Odysseus' heroic characteristics, his psychological profile, and his cultural role evoke the energetic and aggressive elements in the late eighth-century Greek society—elements that were the force behind the extraordinary burst of colonization into the western Mediterranean, northern Aegean, and Black seas." See also Redfield 1983: 221–22.

I would like to build on this image of Odysseus as (re)founder of Ithaka. For Odysseus not only metaphorically occupies the position of oikist in relation to Ithaka but also willingly and explicitly plays this role upon his arrival home.

Odysseus as Oikist

In book 13, Athena delays Odysseus's recognition of Ithaka, and it becomes instead, in the hero's eyes, yet another unknown land. Odysseus's disorientation amid his disguised surroundings resonates with the imagery of his previous travels. His reaction to the unfamiliar environment repeats verbatim his outburst on Scheria (ὤ μοι ἐγώ, τέων αὖτε βροτῶν ἐς γαῖαν ἱκάνω; Alas! Into the land of what mortals have I now come? *Od.* 13.200 = *Od.* 6.119-21; cf. *Od.* 9.174-76). The narrator-text, moreover, is complicit in the goddess's ruse: at the beginning of this episode, Ithaka's harbor and cave of the Nymphs are described as if the poet were introducing his audience to a strange new land (*Od.* 13.96-112). The ethnographic bent of book 13 is then fully realized when Athena, appearing as a young shepherd, catalogues for the bewildered Odysseus the island's natural resources (13.236-47):

> Τὸν δ' αὖτε προσέειπε θεὰ γλαυκῶπις Ἀθήνη·
> "νήπιός εἰς, ὦ ξεῖν', ἢ τηλόθεν εἰλήλουθας,
> εἰ δὴ τήνδε τε γαῖαν ἀνείρεαι. οὐδέ τι λίην
> οὕτω νώνυμός ἐστιν· ἴσασι δέ μιν μάλα πολλοί,
> ἠμὲν ὅσοι ναίουσι πρὸς ἠῶ τ' ἠέλιόν τε,
> ἠδ' ὅσσοι μετόπισθε ποτὶ ζόφον ἠερόεντα.
> ἦ τοι μὲν τρηχεῖα καὶ οὐχ ἱππήλατός ἐστιν,
> οὐδὲ λίην λυπρή, ἀτὰρ οὐδ' εὐρεῖα τέτυκται.
> ἐν μὲν γάρ οἱ σῖτος ἀθέσφατος, ἐν δέ τε οἶνος
> γίνεται· αἰεὶ δ' ὄμβρος ἔχει τεθαλυῖά τ' ἐέρση.
> αἰγίβοτος δ' ἀγαθὴ καὶ βούβοτος· ἔστι μὲν ὕλη
> παντοίη, ἐν δ' ἀρδμοὶ ἐπηετανοὶ παρέασι."

The grey-eyed goddess Athena addressed him in turn: "You are a fool, stranger, or else you have come from far away, if you inquire about this land. For it is not so very obscure (as you suggest), but many people know it, both as many as dwell toward the dawn and the sun as well as those who dwell where the day ends toward the dusky gloom. To be sure, it is rugged and is not good for driving horses, but neither is it very poor, even though it is not spacious. For it has an unlimited amount of food and there is wine here too, and there is always rain and copious dew. It is also good for browsing goats and grazing cattle, and there are all kinds of timber and watering-places in abundance."

As Dougherty notices, many of Ithaka's traits listed in the goddess's description, such as its wine, goats, and plentiful rain, coincide with those applied to the land of the Cyclopes and its neighboring island, locations that were themselves evaluated in the poem as though they were potential sites for Greeks to settle.[44] Athena mischievously depicts Ithaka as if it, too, were another place suitable for founding a viable settlement.

Dougherty's own argument for this episode stops here, but I would push it further and refine our view of both Athena's address and Odysseus's subsequent response. In her topographical overview of Ithaka, Athena does not merely suggest that this land could accommodate a Greek colony. Rather, the goddess departs from the generic register of epic and formulates her speech as a colonial narrative. The detailed appraisal of a land's physical features that Athena offers here is a motif of colonial discourse. What is more, as noted above, Athena's exposition of Ithaka directly parallels the description of the Cyclopes' land (*Od.* 9.116–24), a description that Dougherty classifies elsewhere as a typological component of foundation tales.[45]

Athena's speech is also a trick, and waiting at the end of her description is the true identity of this strange new land: τῷ τοι, ξεῖν', Ἰθάκης γε καὶ ἐς Τροίην ὄνομ' ἵκει, /τήν περ τηλοῦ φασὶν Ἀχαιΐδος ἔμμεναι αἴης (Accordingly, stranger, the name of Ithaka reaches even to Troy, which they say is very far from Achaian land, 13.248–49). As Jenny Strauss Clay argues, Athena's surprise finish is meant to catch Odysseus off guard and lure him into prematurely disclosing his own identity. But in place of openly rejoicing at his good fortune, Odysseus famously and carefully holds back before the stranger (*Od.* 13.254–55).[46] Refusing to buckle to temptation, Odysseus assumes instead the role of a fugitive from Crete and recounts the reason for his exile, namely, his murder of Idomeneus's son, Orsilochos, for attempting to seize his Trojan spoils (*Od.* 13.256–86). The standard reading of this Cretan tale maintains that the details of Odysseus's lie not only offer an explanation to the young shepherd as to why Odysseus has been found alone amid the gifts of the Phaiakians but also contain a veiled threat: in describing his ambush of Orsilochos, the Cretan Odysseus makes it clear to the spear-carrying youth that he is capable of defending himself against someone who might attempt to seize his possessions.[47] Without dismissing this interpretation, I would add another reason for Odysseus's particular choice of casting himself as a fugitive homicide. Odysseus's volleying trick counters Athena specifically by taking over from the goddess

---

44. Dougherty 2001: 163–64. See also de Jong (2001: 325–26), who notes the unusual length and detail of this particular description of Ithaka.

45. See Dougherty 1993: 21. Other examples of such descriptions in colonial narratives include Plat. *Leg.* 704 and Archilochus frr. 17 and 18 Tarditi.

46. On this passage Clay (1983: 196n19) notes, "These two lines intervene between the ἔπεα πτερόεντα προσηύδα and the actual speech which normally follows immediately. This interruption of the normal formulaic sequence vividly illustrates Odysseus' suppression of his immediate impulse."

47. See the discussions of this scene by Clay (1983: 195–98) and de Jong (2001: 326–29).

her colonial narrative. He does so by implying, in his concocted persona, that he is a figure capable of laying claim to the colonial landscape she has just evaluated. For, in the narrative trajectory of a number of foundation tales, it is the murderer in exile who assumes the role of oikist. For instance, Archias, forced to leave Corinth for killing the king's son, founded the city of Syracuse (Plut. *Mor.* 772e–773b). Strabo records that Orestes founded a city, Argos Orestikon, during his wanderings after his matricide (7.7.8). Aeolos killed his stepmother, left his native city of Metapontion, and founded Lipara (Diod. Sic. 4.67.4–6).[48] But we need not go so far afield. The Homeric poems also show an awareness of the fugitive homicide turned founder paradigm. The *Iliad* tells of Tlepolemos's flight from his homeland for murdering his father's uncle Licymnios and concludes with his settlement of Rhodes (*Il.* 2.661–69).

This paradigm of the oikist as fugitive homicide within foundation stories motivates Odysseus's decision to portray himself as exiled from his homeland for murder. Athena presents Ithaka as a new land, and Odysseus answers by suggesting that he, as a murderer in exile, fits the mold of this land's oikist. In taking up the colonial narrative initiated by the disguised Athena, Odysseus casts himself as the potential oikist of the country she has just defined. As a result, Odysseus's response also contains an undercurrent of intimidation against the young shepherd who has discovered a stranger alone and surrounded by treasure. Within the narrative scenario of foundation tales, a stranger in a foreign land is not a victim but an invading aggressor. By countering with his own motif of colonial discourse, Odysseus reorganizes the situation to his own advantage and reimagines the native shepherd as the local population that he, as conquering oikist, will subdue.

The roles of oikist and fugitive homicide continue to intersect beyond this initial episode in book 13. Let us track these intersections now, since they become relevant to the characterizations of both Odysseus and Theoklymenos at the end of the poem. Odysseus's Cretan tale in book 13 is followed by two other references to fugitive homicides. As noted above, Homer describes Theoklymenos as a murderer in exile, a designation reiterated in the seer's own self-description (*Od.* 15.223–25 and 15.271–78, respectively). In the following book, Eumaios, recounting a visit from an Aitolian stranger, remembers his anonymous guest as "one who had murdered a man and having wandered over much of the earth had come to his house" (*Od.* 14.379–85). As Irad Malkin observes, taken together, these three instantiations of the murderer in exile form a crescendo as the narrative approaches the climax of the epic.[49] For the poem's climax, Odysseus's slaughtering of the suitors, brings with it the real possibility of exile, a consequence of his revenge that

---

48. For the progression from murderer in exile to oikist and for more examples, see Dougherty 1993: 45–60.

49. Malkin 1998: 124n17.

Odysseus himself anticipates.⁵⁰ His acknowledgment of this looming repercussion appears, for example, in book 23 when Odysseus offers Telemachos the following assessment of their situation (23.118–22):

> "καὶ γάρ τίς θ' ἕνα φῶτα κατακτείνας ἐνὶ δήμῳ,
> ᾧ μὴ πολλοὶ ἔωσιν ἀοσσητῆρες ὀπίσσω,
> φεύγει πηούς τε προλιπὼν καὶ πατρίδα γαῖαν·
> ἡμεῖς δ' ἕρμα πόληος ἀπέκταμεν, οἳ μέγ' ἄριστοι
> κούρων εἰν Ἰθάκῃ· τὰ δέ σε φράζεσθαι ἄνωγα."

> "For in fact the man who has killed one person in a community for whom there are not many supporters left behind goes into exile and leaves behind his kinsmen and fatherland. But we have killed the mainstays of the city who were far and away the best youths in Ithaka. These things I exhort you to ponder."

The *Odyssey* ultimately circumvents the possibility of Odysseus's being driven from Ithaka for having killed the suitors. Yet expulsion from Ithaka seems to have been the default outcome for Odysseus in traditions outside the *Odyssey*.⁵¹ A fragment of Aristotle's *Constitution of the Ithakans* preserves a clear instance of Odysseus as fugitive (fr. 507 Rose):⁵²

> τῷ Ὀδυσσεῖ μετὰ τὴν μνηστηροφονίαν οἱ ἐπιτήδειοι τῶν τεθνηκότων ἐπανέστησαν, μεταπεμφθεὶς δ' ὑπ' ἀμφοτέρων διαιτητὴς Νεοπτόλεμος ἐδικαίωσε τὸν μὲν Ὀδυσσέα μεταναστῆναι καὶ φεύγειν ἐκ τῆς Κεφαλληνίας καὶ Ζακύνθου καὶ Ἰθάκης ἐφ' αἵματι, τοὺς δὲ τῶν μνηστήρων ἑταίρους καὶ οἰκείους ἀποφέρειν ποινὴν Ὀδυσσεῖ τῶν εἰς τὸν οἶκον ἀδικημάτων καθ' ἕκαστον ἐνιαυτόν. αὐτὸς μὲν οὖν εἰς Ἰταλίαν μετέστη, τὴν δὲ ποινὴν τῷ υἱῷ καθιερώσας ἀποφέρειν ἐκέλευσε τοὺς Ἰθακησίους·

> After the slaughtering of the suitors, the friends of the dead men rose up against Odysseus. Neoptolemos was sent for by both sides as an arbitrator, and his judgment was, on the one hand, for Odysseus to leave the country and to be banished for homicide from Kephallenia and Zakynthos and Ithaka, and, on the other hand, for the companions and relatives of the suitors to pay an annual recompense for their injustices against his house. Therefore, Odysseus himself withdrew to Italy, but having established the recompense as sacred, he ordered the Ithakans to pay it to his son.

Many of these alternate traditions also reveal that Odysseus is not idle in his exile. Instead, he makes use of his time fathering royal lines and founding cities. Thus, for instance, Odysseus is credited with settling the poleis of Bouneima in Thesprotia and Crotona in Etruria, and, according to Hellanikos, even accompanied

---

50. See Malkin's (1998: 120–34) discussion of Odysseus and exile.
51. See Malkin 1998 for these "post-Ithaca" stories.
52. Fr. 507 Rose = Plut. *Quest. Graec.* 14.

Aeneas when he founded Rome.⁵³ These diverse post-*Odyssey* accounts demonstrate that the part of oikist was a familiar role played by Odysseus in Greek culture.⁵⁴ Seeing Odysseus as a founder of cities beyond the *Odyssey* allows for such a characterization to appear less strange within it: if Odysseus can slip easily into this role in other traditions, we should be amenable to viewing him in this capacity in the *Odyssey* as well. Moreover, given the general cultural reflex to pair fugitive homicides and oikists, the motif of the fugitive homicide that permeates the end of the epic bolsters our reading of Odysseus as the oikist of Ithaka in the second half of the poem. The *Odyssey* does stand in contrast to other stories of Odysseus and to other colonial narratives, however, insofar as the expected progression (in which murder and exile precede foundation) has been folded in on itself: in reclaiming his house and power from the suitors, Odysseus avoids exile and instead becomes both a homicide and oikist simultaneously.⁵⁵

With the help of Dougherty, we have seen that the *Odyssey* articulates many of the challenges of Odysseus's homecoming through the framework of colonial discourse. In particular, Odysseus himself, in numerous ways, is characterized as the founder of his native land. But we must not forget that at the same time as he is portrayed as an oikist, Odysseus is also closely aligned with a seer. As the first portion of this chapter revealed, in many ways Odysseus and Theoklymenos are constructed as doublets of one another. Turning now to the final part of the chapter, I will join the two preceding parts together to explore the notion that the mirroring, doubling presence of Theoklymenos in the poem can be explained by his involvement in and even facilitation of Odysseus's refoundation of Ithaka.

III. TRAVELING TO SICILY

As part 1 demonstrated, Theoklymenos and Odysseus not only generate the same motifs and diction but also follow complementary courses on Ithaka as they interact with the same characters in quick succession. If not literally Odysseus in

---

53. Thesprotia: schol. *ad* Lycoph. *Alex.* 800; schol. *ad Od.* 11.121; Steph. Byz. s.v. Βούνειμα. Etruria: Theopompus *FGrH* 115 F 354 = schol. *ad* Lycoph. *Alex.* 806. Rome: Dion. Hal. 1.72.2 = Hellanicus *FGrH* 4 F 84; Damastes *FGrH* 5 F 3. For Odysseus as progenitor, see, e.g., Apollod. *Epit.* 7.40 (and Eust. p. 1796, 51) where Apollodorus reports that Odysseus immigrated to Aitolia and married the daughter of Thoas, a Calydonian king. He never returns to Ithaka but dies there, having fathered a son, Leontophonos. Many other *Nostoi* poems featured the hero founding a city (see Malkin 1998 passim).

54. I follow Malkin (1998: 190) in taking "post-*Odyssey*" and "post-Ithaka" to mean "not composed later but concerning what happened to Odysseus after his return to Ithaca."

55. Further, we might note that the *Odyssey* itself accepts that its hero must depart from home again, a position that surfaces in Teiresias's instructions to Odysseus to travel to a place so far inland that the oar he carries will be thought to be a winnowing fan and to make sacrifices to Poseidon there (*Od.* 11.119–37). According to Malkin (1998: 122), Teiresias's prophecy "implies an awareness of post-Ithaca stories."

disguise in our extant version, Theoklymenos is still in certain fundamental ways his figurative substitute. Why is Odysseus shadowed by a seer upon his return to Ithaka? In part 3 we will see that Theoklymenos and Odysseus can be understood as a coherent pair and that this pair operates in a colonial context. To do so, I will concentrate not on Theoklymenos's prophetic abilities, the focus of previous studies, but on his movements to and from Ithaka vis-à-vis Odysseus's own activities. For, by attending to Theoklymenos's entrance and exit in the poem, we can begin to understand not only the pairing of Theoklymenos and Odysseus but also how the Greeks conceived of the relationship between seers and colonial founders. What is more, we will be able to detect a possible source of tension within this relationship.

Theoklymenos and Odysseus chart comparable itineraries on Ithaka, but their paths never actually intersect. Even in book 20, in which they both occupy the same physical space as they sit among the feasting suitors in Odysseus's hall, the seer and the hero still do not acknowledge one another's presence. During this episode it is especially difficult not to see the two as different variations of a disguised Odysseus that were never fully synthesized in our version of the poem.[56] Yet, a small fissure in the narrative partition that divides them does appear in book 20, and for a moment the segregated stories of Theoklymenos and Odysseus fleetingly collide. This fissure takes the form of an insult that the suitors hurl at Telemachos, and it is within the space of this insult that seer and hero finally meet.

At the end of book 20, Athena drives the suitors mad, and Theoklymenos foresees their impending annihilation (*Od.* 20.351–57).[57] When his prophecy goes unheeded and is met only with ridicule, Theoklymenos takes himself away from Odysseus's hall and out of the poem. After his departure, the suitors turn to mock Telemachos by laughing at his guests. Their collective criticism of Telemachos takes the following form (20.376–83):

"Τηλέμαχ', οὔ τις σεῖο κακοξεινώτερος ἄλλος·
οἷον μέν τινα τοῦτον ἔχεις ἐπίμαστον ἀλήτην,
σίτου καὶ οἴνου κεχρημένον, οὐδέ τι ἔργων
ἔμπαιον οὐδὲ βίης, ἀλλ' αὔτως ἄχθος ἀρούρης.
ἄλλος δ' αὖτέ τις οὗτος ἀνέστη μαντεύεσθαι.
ἀλλ' εἴ μοί τι πίθοιο, τό κεν πολὺ κέρδιον εἴη·
τοὺς ξείνους ἐν νηῒ πολυκληῗδι βαλόντες

---

56. This scene contributes to the argument by some scholars that Theoklymenos does not quite fit in the poem. E.g., discussing this episode and Theoklymenos's prophecy in book 20, Benardete (1997: 120) writes that Theoklymenos "belongs to another story."

57. For the prophecy itself, see Amory 1963: 109–12; Austin 1975: 246, 250; Levine 1983; Broggiato 2003.

ἐς Σικελοὺς πέμψωμεν, ὅθεν κέ τοι ἄξιον ἄλφοι."
Ὣς ἔφασαν μνηστῆρες·

"Telemachos, no one is more unlucky in his guest friends than you. Like this wanderer you have whom someone has brought in, longing for food and wine, who is not skilled at anything, and who is not even strong, but is just a burden on the land. And, again, this other one stood up and began to utter a prophecy. But if you should take my advice, it would be very profitable: Let us throw the guest-friends in a many-oarlocked ship and send them to the Sikels, where it would fetch a worthy price."[58] Thus spoke the suitors.

The suitors tauntingly recommend that Telemachos, since no one is more unlucky in guest friends than he, send these men to the Sikels. Because Theoklymenos exits before the insult is delivered, this fantasized departure of the seer is the last reference to him in the poem.[59] The final image of Theoklymenos with which the audience is left, then, is not of the seer walking out on the suitors but rather of his being placed aboard a ship and sailing with Odysseus to Sicily.

After avoiding any acknowledgment that Theoklymenos and Odysseus exist in the same poem, the *Odyssey* suddenly envisions the two traveling west together.[60] I suggest that we read the suitors' insult as a distillation of the way the pair operates more generally in the colonial context of the second half of the *Odyssey*. In order to view the moment as an embodiment of this larger dynamic, however, we must parse some of the components of this imagined scenario.

First, the suitors advise that Telemachos send Theoklymenos and Odysseus to Sicily. We can be fairly certain that to mention Sicily in the *Odyssey* necessarily implies an awareness of Greek colonies there. The earliest Greek settlements on the island date to the eighth century B.C.E. and are thus contemporary with our version of the poem.[61] In the *Odyssey*, then, travel to Sicily evokes the colonial pos-

---

58. This final clause ("it would fetch a worthy price") is adapted from Stanford's (2000: 356) translation. The clause is problematic because the subject of ἄλφοι is unclear. I would simply note that the subject of the verb is single and yet seems to have to refer to both Theoklymenos and Odysseus. The singular verb thus seems to collapse or merge Theoklymenos and Odysseus even further by thinking of them as a single unit. Although the sense of the line has been traditionally taken to mean that the pair will be sold into slavery, the line's vagueness leaves room for other interpretations and other reasons for their usefulness in Sicily for Telemachos.

59. See Russo et al. 1992: 126: "Theoklymenos, recently departed, is vividly evoked as if present."

60. Odysseus's inclusion in the insult seems especially marked given that the events of the episode leading up to the insult (i.e., the seer's prophecy and the suitors' dismissive reaction to it) have concerned only Theoklymenos. Odysseus's sudden presence in the insult is jarring, but, I would argue, necessary in order for the image's colonial resonance to work.

61. For the earliest Greek settlements on Sicily, see De Angelis 2016: 28–61. For the *Odyssey* as representing the concerns of eighth-century Greece, see esp. Dougherty 2001.

sibilities of journeys made in this westward direction. Odysseus and Theoklymenos are to be sent to the same place to which Greek colonists also sail.[62]

Second, commentators often link the suitors' insult against Theoklymenos and Odysseus to a threat delivered to the beggar Iros by the suitor Antinoös. Antinoös taunts Iros as the beggar nervously prepares for his boxing match with Odysseus in book 18 (84–87):

> "αἴ κέν σ' οὗτος νικήσῃ κρείσσων τε γένηται.
> πέμψω σ' ἤπειρόνδε, βαλὼν ἐν νηΐ μελαίνῃ,
> εἰς Ἔχετον βασιλῆα, βροτῶν δηλήμονα πάντων,
> ὅς κ' ἀπὸ ῥῖνα τάμῃσι καὶ οὔατα νηλέϊ χαλκῷ
> μήδεά τ' ἐξερύσας δώῃ κυσὶν ὠμὰ δάσασθαι."

> "If this man beats you and proves himself the stronger, I will send you toward the mainland, having thrown you on a black ship, to King Echetos, a scourge for all men, who will cut off your nose and ears with pitiless bronze and, tearing off your genitals, give them raw to the dogs to divide among themselves."

Likewise, in a similar passage, Antinoös warns a disguised Odysseus that he will be sent to this same Echetos if he dares to touch Odysseus's bow (*Od.* 21.307–9). Yet such cross-referencing between our insult in book 20 and Antinoös's warnings obscures the different directional cues embedded in these punishments. The baneful King Echetos is reached by sailing back ἤπειρόνδε (toward the mainland, *Od.* 18.85).[63] Moreover, the suitor's scare tactics target Odysseus and Iros individually: each is to travel to King Echetos alone. The examples stand in contrast, then, to the insult of the suitors in book 20. It is only the pair, Theoklymenos and Odysseus, who are sent west. Put another way, I would contend that it is only the seer and the oikist who activate the colonial image of traveling out from Greece to Sicily.

Finally, the pairing of Theoklymenos and Odysseus in the image can be understood further by examining the associations each figure elicits on his own in being figuratively placed aboard this ship. We can begin by teasing out how Odysseus belongs in this context. In post-Ithaka traditions, Odysseus has strong ties to the West, and these ties are frequently connected with the founding of cities or *ethnē* (people). The *Constitution of the Ithakans*, quoted on page 65, claims that Odysseus went to Italy after killing the suitors (fr. 507 Rose). Other traditions, one at least as early as Hesiod, credit Odysseus with fathering various lines across the Italian peninsula. In the

---

62. In book 24, a redisguised Odysseus burdens his father with an invented tale of his attempt to reach Sicily from his hometown of Alybas (24.304–307). It is interesting that once he has "refounded" Ithaka by killing the suitors and remarrying Penelope, Odysseus sheds his Cretan persona and, in his final lying tale, presents himself instead as being from the colonial West. For the city of Alybas, see Montiglio 2005: 11.

63. I agree with Malkin (1998: 153) that the "mainland" here must refer to mainland Greece.

Theogony, Agrios and Latinos, both eponymous heroes of Italic peoples, are the sons of Odysseus and Circe (1011-13). This passage in the *Theogony* immediately follows a reference to the birth of Aeneas, a suggestive collocation, since Hellanikos claims that Odysseus joined Aeneas to found Rome.[64] According to the second-century B.C.E. historian Xenagoras, Odysseus fathers by Circe Rhomos, Anteias, and Ardeias, who give their names to the cities of Rome, Antium, and Ardea, respectively (*FGrH* 240 F 29). Finally, from Theopompos we learn that Odysseus not only founded the city of Cortona but even seems to have received an oikist cult there after his death. Cortona is here called Gortynaia (Theopompus *FGrH* 115 F 354 = schol. *ad* Lycoph. *Alex.* 806):[65]

> Θεόπομπός φησιν ὅτι παραγενόμενος ὁ Ὀδυσσεὺς καὶ τὰ περὶ τὴν Πηνελόπην ἐγνωκὼς ἀπῆρεν εἰς Τυρσηνίαν καὶ ἐλθὼν ᾤκησε τὴν Γορτυναίαν, ἔνθα καὶ τελευτᾷ ὑπ' αὐτῶν μεγάλως τιμώμενος.
>
> Theopompos says that Odysseus, having arrived [in Ithaka] and having realized the affairs concerning Penelope, sailed away to Tyrsenia and went and settled Gortynaia, where he reached the end of his life, greatly honored by them.

The *Odyssey* in general is cognizant of the range of available options for Odysseus's *nostos* that are played out in other versions of the story, and the poem frequently alludes to or directly cites these other traditions.[66] The shape of the suitors' insult seems to allude to Odysseus's rich and numerous connections with the West observable elsewhere. Yet we can be more specific in what these alternate versions reveal and thus what association the image of Odysseus sailing to Sicily in our poem might elicit: not only is Odysseus linked to the West, but he is frequently linked to it as an oikist and progenitor.[67]

It is culturally appropriate, then, to envision Odysseus sailing to Sicily, but how are we to understand Theoklymenos's presence aboard the ship? Theoklymenos's

---

64. See Malkin 1998: 194 for this point. Dionysius of Halicarnassus also credits Odysseus and Aeneas with the foundation of Rome: ὁ δὲ τὰς ἱερείας τὰς ἐν Ἄργει καὶ τὰ καθ' ἑκάστην πραχθέντα συναγαγὼν Αἰνείαν φησὶν ἐκ Μολοττῶν εἰς Ἰταλίαν ἐλθόντα μετ' Ὀδυσσέα οἰκιστὴν γενέσθαι τῆς πόλεως, ὀνομάσαι δ' αὐτὴν ἀπὸ μιᾶς τῶν Ἰλιάδων Ῥώμης, But the author of the history of the priestesses at Argos and of what happened in the days of each of them says that Aeneas came into Italy from the land of the Molossians with Odysseus and became the founder of the city, which he named after Romē, one of the Trojan women (*Rom. Ant.* 1.72.2, trans. Carey 1937). As noted on pp. 65-66, Odysseus is also connected with Etruria and Thesprotia.

65. See Malkin 1998: 174 for this reading of the passage.

66. On the issue of these alternate versions, Malkin (1998: 35) writes, "The *Odyssey* also indicates awareness of its own alternatives: its sequels or alternative returns are either alluded to or expressly attested. By "allusion" I mean not specfic verse allusions—a contested question among Homerists—but the more basic plot elements."

67. Other heroes are also linked to the West in this way, although not in such a pervasive and wide-ranging manner as Odysseus; see, e.g., Malkin 1998: 210-33 on Nestor and Philoktetes.

arrival in the epic proves to be a helpful parallel. Just as Theoklymenos exits the poem (figuratively) traveling with Odysseus, so too does he enter the *Odyssey* accompanying Telemachos. In book 15, as Telemachos sacrifices to Athena before departing from Pylos, he is suddenly approached by the seer, who appeals to Odysseus's son (15.271–78):

> Τὸν δ' αὖτε προσέειπε Θεοκλύμενος θεοειδής·
> "οὕτω τοι καὶ ἐγὼν ἐκ πατρίδος, ἄνδρα κατακτὰς
> ἔμφυλον· πολλοὶ δὲ κασίγνητοί τε ἔται τε
> Ἄργος ἀν' ἱππόβοτον, μέγα δὲ κρατέουσιν Ἀχαιῶν·
> τῶν ὑπαλευάμενος θάνατον καὶ κῆρα μέλαιναν
> φεύγω, ἐπεί νύ μοι αἶσα κατ' ἀνθρώπους ἀλάλησθαι.
> ἀλλά με νηὸς ἔφεσσαι, ἐπεί σε φυγὼν ἱκέτευσα,
> μή με κατακτείνωσι· διωκέμεναι γὰρ ὀΐω."

Then godlike Theoklymenos addressed him: "I too am out of my fatherland, having killed a man from my own tribe. And he has many brothers and kinsmen in horse-grazing Argos, and they wield great power over the Achaians. Escaping death and black doom from these men I flee, since it is my fate to wander among men. But place me upon your ship, since I supplicate you as a fugitive, in order that they not kill me. For I think they are chasing me."

Theoklymenos beseeches Telemachos to aid him in fleeing his pursuers, and Telemachos grants the seer passage aboard his ship. The timing of Theoklymenos's sudden entrance deserves serious consideration. Theoklymenos materializes at the very moment at which Telemachos is about to sail back to Ithaka. The voyage for which Theoklymenos appears is a perilous one: off the coast of Ithaka, the suitors are on the lookout, hoping to intercept Telemachos's ship and murder him. In fact, the suitors are amazed when Telemachos manages to slip past their ambush and return safely home. Antinoös details the near impossibility of Telemachos's feat (16.364–70):

> ὦ πόποι, ὡς τόνδ' ἄνδρα θεοὶ κακότητος ἔλυσαν.
> ἤματα μὲν σκοποὶ ἷζον ἐπ' ἄκριας ἠνεμοέσσας
> αἰὲν ἐπασσύτεροι· ἅμα δ' ἠελίῳ καταδύντι
> οὔ ποτ' ἐπ' ἠπείρου νύκτ' ἄσαμεν, ἀλλ' ἐνὶ πόντῳ
> νηΐ θοῇ πλείοντες ἐμίμνομεν Ἠῶ δῖαν,
> Τηλέμαχον λοχόωντες, ἵνα φθείσωμεν ἑλόντες
> αὐτόν· τὸν δ' ἄρα τεῖος ἀπήγαγεν οἴκαδε δαίμων.

Ah! How the gods rescued that man from destruction. During the day we sat as lookouts upon windy hilltops always in shifts. And with the setting sun not once did we spend the night on land, but sailing the sea in a swift ship we were watching for divine Dawn, lying in wait for Telemachos, in order that we might anticipate and seize him. But meanwhile a *daimon* led him home.

Antinoös's conviction of divine assistance for Telemachos's return home (τὸν δ' ἄρα τεῖος ἀπ ἤγαγεν οἴκαδε δαίμων, But meanwhile a *daimon* led him home, *Od.* 16.370) seems to signal that Theoklymenos's position aboard the ship is more than one of a dependent suppliant. This possibility gains ground with an inevitable comparison. Theoklymenos in effect replaces the one figure, now absent, who had clearly played the role of escort on the outbound leg of Telemachos's journey, namely, Athena.

Telemachos's surprising journey home and Antinoös's interpretation of it imply that Theoklymenos's abilities lie not only in accessing divine knowledge (through interpreting omens and delivering prophecies) but also in reaching physically remote or challenging locations. As such, the seer conforms well to the model formulated by the ethnographer Mary Helms.[68] In her comprehensive survey of preindustrial cultures, Helms formulates the following connection: "In traditional cosmologies geographical distance and space/time are accorded political and ideological qualities virtually identical to those associated with vertical (heavens-underworld) distance and space/time."[69] Helms's study reveals that, in addition to the concordance between the vertical and horizontal axes of distance, a homology obtains between figures who are adept at long-distance travel (e.g., sailors and traders) and those who mediate supernatural distance (e.g., shamans and other religious experts). I would argue that Theoklymenos offers another instantiation of the homology that obtains between experts who mediate supernatural distance and those adept at long-distance travel.[70] When Theoklymenos travels with Telemachos, it is not as a suppliant but as a guide.[71]

---

68. Helms 1988 and 1993.

69. Helms 1993: 44.

70. See also Helms 1988: 80–81: "Geographical distance can again be seen to offer political-ideological challenges not unlike those posed by other dimensions of dangerous and powerful supernatural distance. Consequently, experts in the control and exploitation of geographical distance may be equated with experts who control and exploit other forms of distance as political-religious elites." While Helms tends to be more concerned with long-distance travelers who are accorded the qualities of religious experts, I would focus here on the reverse but equally true phenomenon: the religious expert Theoklymenos is a skillful long-distance traveler.

71. Page found fault with Theoklymenos's apparent rudeness in the way the seer initially approaches Telemachos and demands that he identify himself (*Od.* 15.260–64). Theoklymenos's questioning stands in contrast to other episodes in which it is the newly arrived stranger who is interrogated about his origins (e.g., Nestor questions Telemachos [*Od.* 3.69–74]; Penelope questions Odysseus [*Od.* 19.104–5]). Of Theoklymenos in this episode Page (1955: 86) writes, "Great is the descent from the moderately sublime; all the more offensive since ancient custom would frown upon a suppliant who began his prayer by asking the name and address of his protector; it is for Telemachos to ask Theoklymenos, not vice versa." In the seer's defense, Fenik (1974: 235) attributes the fugitive's questioning to the urgency of his situation. But the perceived "rudeness" of Theoklymenos that vexed Page stemmed from his assumption that Telemachos plays host to a suppliant Theoklymenos. If, however, it is actually Theoklymenos who safely leads Telemachos back to Ithaka, then this apparent "breach of etiquette" disappears (Fenik, 233). We might even say that Homer is actually signaling that Theoklymenos is really the one in charge by putting in his mouth a formula traditionally reserved for hosts.

Telemachos and Theoklymenos's journey from Pylos to Ithaka presents new implications for the suitors' insult and the relationship of Odysseus and Theoklymenos within it: Odysseus's own presence on this ship is enmeshed in colonial possibilities, and Theoklymenos's presence is that of his guide who ensures that they will reach their western destination safely. To be clear, I am not making any claim about how the suitors themselves conceive of the relationship between Theoklymenos and Odysseus when they deliver their insult. Their suggestion seems to be for Theoklymenos and Odysseus to be sold into slavery, not to found a colony.[72] But the coalescence of elements within their threat (i.e., Odysseus and Theoklymenos as a pair and the direction of their journey) seems driven by a cultural reflex within the poem itself to pair these figures in this way. As noted above, Odysseus's presence in the insult seems especially marked given that the events of the episode leading up to the insult have only concerned Theoklymenos (i.e., the seer's prophecy and the suitors' dismissive reaction to it). I would contend that Odysseus is co-opted into the insult because his presence is necessary for its particular construction to work. The image of sailing west makes better cultural sense if Theoklymenos and Odysseus are present in it together.

I have focused on the suitors' insult not only to draw attention to the pairing of seer and oikist and its occurrence in conjunction with the colonial direction of their journey, but, more importantly, because I think that the insult itself functions as a kind of distillation of the dynamics of Theoklymenos's and Odysseus's relationship more generally in the second half of the *Odyssey*. Theoklymenos's appearance in the suitors' imagined scenario repeats in miniature the seer's accompanying presence during Odysseus's homecoming to Ithaka. For in both instances Theoklymenos, skilled in traveling both the horizontal and the vertical axes of distance, can be seen to assist Odysseus in a foundation, whether it be a potential one off in Sicily or the metaphorical refoundation of Ithaka. Thus it is not just the characters of Theoklymenos and Odysseus who finally cross paths in the suitors' insult, but, based on the motifs and qualities that have been accorded these characters leading up to this moment, it would perhaps be better to say that it is Theoklymenos as seer-navigator and Odysseus as oikist who are placed together aboard the ship.

The extensive doubling of Theoklymenos and Odysseus explored in part 1 is thus the result of the *Odyssey*'s conceptualization of the seer and oikist as a meaningful alliance within the framework of colonial discourse. In chapters 3–6, I will explore the convergence of seers and oikists in the late archaic and early classical periods and consider the fraught nature of this collocation. The primary ideological strategy that we will attend to in these chapters is colonial discourse's privileging of the

---

72. For a discussion of the reference to slavery in the insult, see Crielaard 1995: 232–33; see also n.58 above for the passage's ambiguity.

oikist at the specific expense of the seer. The *Odyssey* does not seek to suppress the role of the seer in the same way as these other later archaic and classical instantiations of colonial discourse. I would argue that one crucial difference between the *Odyssey* and these later texts is the absence of Delphi in the *Odyssey* as a powerful presence in colonial contexts. As Barbara Kowalzig observes of the many foundations associated with the *Nostoi*, Delphi does not generally seem to be a source of authority for these returning Greek heroes.[73]

Theoklymenos replicates and so implicitly accompanies Odysseus's own movements on Ithaka. But one consequence of Theoklymenos's visible presence on Ithaka is the redundant nature of his characterization vis-à-vis Odysseus. As we explored in part 1, Theoklymenos and Odysseus do and say many of the same things over the course of books 13–20. This redundancy suggests that a fundamental similarity inheres in the way in which these two figures have been constructed. When we look beyond the limits of the *Odyssey* itself, as I will do below, the correspondence between their attributes increases. That is to say, both figures have the ability to perform the role of the other.

I will conclude, then, by considering how Theoklymenos-as-seer and Odysseus-as-oikist are not only doublets of each other within the poem but also have the potential to absorb the salient characteristic (i.e., of seer and oikist, respectively) of the other. This complementarity is at the heart of their alliance but, at the same time, seems to point to an undercurrent of competition. By recognizing this competition, we begin to see part of the motivation for why later archaic and classcial texts manage this pairing by eliding the presence of the seer. Theoklymenos and Odysseus themselves embody the permeability between these two types of figures. First, the intricate genealogy that announces Theoklymenos's entrance in book 15 mentions the preceding members of his family in some detail. According to the genealogy, stasis and subsequent exile follow the clan as persistently as their inherited prophetic abilities. Generation after generation, the seers are forced out of their native cities and settle somewhere new. Bookending the list of the nine Melampodidai are the stories of Melampous himself and Theoklymenos's father, Polypheides, both of whom flee from their homes before going to live among other people: Melampous came to rule over Argos (*Od.* 15.239–40), and Polypheides settled in Hypersia where he prophesied for all men (*Od.* 15.254–55).[74] In addition to these ancestors, Amphiaraos's two sons, Alkmaion and Amphilochos, are mentioned (*Od.* 15.248). Their names, I would argue, signpost their own colonial legends that lie beyond the scope of the *Odyssey*. According to a tradition that goes back to the Theban epics,

---

73. Kowalzig 2007: 240 with Malkin 1998.
74. The portion of the myth of Melampous mentioned here can be contrasted to the one told in *Od.* 11.288–97. There, the focus is on Pero, whereas here the story is one of exile and resettlement—fitting in a genealogy with other similar stories. On the seer Melampous, see chapter 4.

Alkmaion, wandering throughout Greece as a fugitive homicide after killing his mother, eventually founds Akarnania.[75] Thucydides tells us that Amphilochos founded Argos Amphilochikon, while Strabo says that he founded the city and oracle of Mallos in Asia Minor together with the seer Mopsos.[76] Theoklymenos's genealogy, then, invokes a whole family of seers who double as oikists, settling and founding cities throughout the Greek world.[77] The nature of this pedigree leaves open the possibility that Theoklymenos, on the run from his own native land for murder, will leave the *Odyssey* only to become an oikist and found a city himself.

Second, out of the many post-Ithaka traditions that refer to Odysseus establishing cities and fathering royal lines, the following fragment presents a different kind of foundation (Aristotle, *Constitution of the Ithakans*, fr. 508 Rose):

> Ἀριστοτέλης φησὶν ἐν Ἰθακησίων πολιτείᾳ Εὐρυτᾶνας ἔθνος εἶναι τῆς Αἰτωλίας ὀνομασθὲν ἀπὸ Εὐρύτονος, παρ' οἷς εἶναι μαντεῖον Ὀδυσσέως.
>
> Aristotle says in the *Constitution of the Ithakans* that the Eurytanes are a people in Aitolia, named after Euryton, and that among them there is an oracle of Odysseus.

I close with the image of Odysseus's oracle because it crystallizes what I have sought to explore in this chapter, namely, the convergence of the oikist and the seer, a pair so in counterpoint to each other that Denys Page was, in his own way, right to suggest that sometimes these two figures can become one.

---

75. See, e.g., Thuc. 2.102.5–6. For Alkmaion's role as an oikist, see chapter 6.

76. Mallos: Strabo 14.5.16. Notice that Mallos is founded by a pair, both of whom are simultaneously a seer and an oikist. Argos Amphilochikon: Thuc. 2.68. For Amphilochos and Mallos, see the conclusion.

77. Although Melampous does not found Argos, he does co-opt a portion of the kingdom and becomes its ruler.

3

Suppressing the Seer in Colonial Discourse

Delphic Consultations and the Seer in the City

Chapter 1 explored the conspicuous presence of the seer on military campaigns and the comparable talismanic power of the seer and oikist. Chapter 2 uncovered the productive alliance between the seer and the oikist in the *Odyssey*'s metaphorical refoundation of Ithaka. This chapter will consider why a similar pairing of the seer and the oikist in late archaic and early classical colonial discourse is markedly absent even as the seer enjoys a visible role in Greek warfare during the same time frame.[1] Before the second half of the fifth century B.C.E., only one historical seer is explicitly linked to a foundation, Hagesias, the *laudandus* of *Olympian* 6. But, as chapter 5 will show, his inclusion in a foundation requires an enormous degree of finessing on Pindar's part.[2] This chapter, then, attempts to account for the missing seer in the colonial discourse of this period, a period in which both colonial activity and the seer himself flourished.[3]

In contrast to the book's other chapters that center on a particular seer and text, the present chapter takes a broader view and discusses the ideological motivations for the seer's suppression in colonial discourse in general terms. Doing so establishes a model or blueprint for the following three chapters. This model of colonial ideology and its motivations is not meant to be monolithic but rather offers a point of entry into a more nuanced understanding of this cultural phenomenon. Chapters 4–6, then, put this model to work, with each chapter presenting an early clas-

---

1. For the various cultural factors that made colonial discourse of the late archaic and early classical period especially charged, see the introduction.

2. Pindar's *Olympian* 6 is traditionally dated to between 472 and 468 B.C.E.

3. The heyday of the Greek colonial movement was the eighth to sixth century, but colonial activity continues into the fifth century.

sical epinikian ode in which, in different ways, we are able to catch sight of the ideological clashes and tensions between the seer and oikist in action. Before we can turn to these case studies, however, I will propose in this chapter two principal reasons for the missing seer in colonial discourse. To be sure, these are not the only reasons, but, as I hope to show, they shape the contours of colonial ideology in certain fundamental ways. First, by highlighting the oikist's privileged relationship with Delphic Apollo, colonial discourse establishes the oikist as a figure who wields not only political but also religious authority.[4] The religious authority Delphi grants the oikist is not unlike that enjoyed by the seer in other contexts. As a result, in colonial discourse, the Delphi-sanctioned oikist is characterized in such a way that the seer himself is virtually sidelined and made redundant. Yet the seer is not simply viewed as a neutral figure whose disappearance can be treated as collateral damage for colonial discourse's greater interest in Delphi and the oikist. Rather, a second principal reason, working in tandem with the first, generates the seer's elision from foundation tales. In the context of the Greek city in general, the seer is often cast as a threat to political leaders and an instigator of stasis within the community. This deeply rooted cultural antagonism between mantic and political authority also exposes the ideological incompatibility of the seer within the framework of colonial discourse. Traditionally perceived as a potential menace to a polis's leaders, the seer does not belong in a discourse that valorizes the oikist's successful foundation of a notionally stable community and political order.

I. THE OIKIST AS EXEGETE

From the perspective of modern historiography, accounts of archaic and classical colonization tend to be woefully unconcerned with the accurate chronicling of the Greek foundation process. Instead, as Carol Dougherty shows, these foundation tales adhere to a formulaic pattern and often relate the events that comprise a foundation in a highly metaphorical manner. For example, the oikist can be characterized as a murderer or the new land can be characterized as its eponymous nymph.[5] The formulaic pattern itself runs as follows. A crisis in the mother city triggers a Delphic consultation. At Delphi, Apollo prescribes a foundation as the solution to

---

4. While we will never know how many colonies really did consult Delphi, Delphi's position in the Greek cultural imaginary as the leading colonial oracle is firmly established by the late archaic and early classical periods, as our literary evidence demonstrates. Herodotus's Dorieus episode, for instance, makes Delphi's centrality clear (5.42–43). According to Herodotus, Dorieus fails as an oikist precisely because he attempts to found a colony without first seeking Delphi's approval. I also note in this context Apollo's cult title Archegetas (Founder), a title associated with the colonial West as well as Cyrene. On Apollo Archegetas, see esp. Malkin 1986 and Donnellan 2015.

5. For oikist as murderer, see Dougherty 1993: 31–44; for characterization of new land as a nymph, Dougherty, 61–80.

the crisis and singles out an oikist to lead the expedition. Resolution is then achieved by establishing a new, independent polis.[6] Rather than accord each of these events equal weight, however, colonial narratives tend to emphasize the first two stages of the process, that is, the crisis itself (often rendered in symbolic terms) and the subsequent Delphic consultation. Depictions of the third stage, the actual foundation of the new city and what exactly that entailed, are exceedingly rare.[7]

Given the narrative economy of these tales, their highly elliptical language, and their tendency to report certain events while passing over others in silence, we might conclude that the role of the seer was simply deemed inconsequential. Certainly ancient authors recount military campaigns without always naming the seers who accompanied armies and whose presence, required for the necessary divinatory sacrifices, can only be assumed in these instances.[8] And it is true that we can make a similar assumption for the presence of seers on colonial expeditions and at the site of the new foundation. By analogy with his role as a military *mantis*, the seer of the late archaic and early classical periods likely did accompany colonial expeditions as a member of the oikist's retinue.[9] Further, once we move into the later classical and Hellenistic periods, we do find seers mentioned in conjunction with oikists.[10] The participation of seers in these later colonial ventures also strongly suggests that they accompanied the expeditions of earlier periods. It is thus highly probable that colonial seers, like military ones, were required for their divinatory expertise during the various stages of founding a city. Yet although many, if not the majority, of military *manteis* remain anonymous and their presence is only implied by our ancient sources, we still receive numerous accounts in which they are named and acknowledged.[11] By contrast, as noted in the introduction, seers are almost completely absent from accounts narrating foundations that occurred before the mid-fifth century B.C.E. It cannot be the case that they were all deemed so insignificant and unworthy of mention. Rather, I will argue that, far

---

6. For the various components of this pattern, see Dougherty 1993: 3–80.

7. Dougherty 1993: 21. See Malkin 1987: 135–86; 2003; 2009; 2011: 189–97 (on *nomima* [customary institutions]) for important discussions of the array of religious duties and requirements that awaited the inhabitants of a new colony, from the siting of precincts for their gods to the organization of religious festivals and sacred laws.

8. Note Flower 2008b: 2: "We know the names of about seventy 'historical' seers (as opposed to mythical/legendary ones), some of whom were individuals of considerable influence. Many more seers are left anonymous by our sources, even when their presence and contribution were crucial to the matters at hand."

9. See, e.g., Malkin 1987: 112: "It is probable ... (although we possess no explicit evidence) that a *mantis* had been present in most colonial expeditions from early times, accompanying the oikist in his capacity as a military leader." See also Malkin 2011: 30. See Parker (1985: 307) for the reference to omens in Brea's foundation decree and the implication of this reference for the presence of seers at Brea's foundation.

10. See the conclusion for a discussion of these seers.

11. For examples, see chapter 1.

from a sign of narrative indifference, this suspiciously pervasive absence is the product of an ideological strategy. Colonial ideology, like ideologies in general, emphasizes certain elements by necessarily suppressing others.[12] What exactly colonial ideology makes explicit and how it makes it explicit will help us to account for the missing seer.

A number of narratives associated with archaic foundations highlight the oikist's consultation at Delphi and the foundation oracle he receives there.[13] We should take seriously this emphasis and try to see if it can tell us something about colonial discourse's suppression of the seer. I will first consider the significance of the consultation and then the nature of the foundation oracle itself.

In these episodes, the oikist both enters into a privileged relationship with Apollo and, relatedly, is endowed with religious authority. Consider, for example, Diodorus Siculus's account of Myskellos of Rhype, the oikist of Kroton (8.17.1):[14]

ἡ δὲ Πυθία ἀνεῖλεν οὕτως·
Μύσκελλε βραχύνωτε, φιλεῖ σ' ἑκάεργος Ἀπόλλων,
καὶ γενεὰν δώσει· τόδε δὲ πρότερόν σε κελεύει,
οἰκῆσαί σε Κρότωνα μέγαν καλαῖς ἐν ἀρούραις.

The Pythia answered thus: "Short-backed Myskellos, Apollo the Far-Darter loves you and will give you offspring. But this thing he commands for you first, to settle in mighty Kroton among the beautiful plowlands."

In this passage, the Pythia not only marks Myskellos out as the future oikist of Kroton but also underscores his superabundance of divine favor: φιλεῖ σ' ἑκάεργος Ἀπόλλων (Apollo the Far-Darter loves you). This divine favor brings with it religious authority. Irad Malkin rightly observes that the consultation stage of the colonial process is crucial not only because it provides the oikist with oracular instructions concerning his new site but also because it calls attention to the moment when Delphic Apollo personally supplies the oikist with the necessary divine mandate for the undertaking.[15] We might also think of this consultation as

---

12. See the introduction for this point.

13. On the oikist's consultation at Delphi and foundation oracles, see Defradas 1954; Leschhorn 1984: 105–9; Malkin 1987: 17–91; Morgan 1990: 172–78; Londey 1990; Dougherty 1993: 3–80; Rosenberger 2001: 69–78. For general statements from ancient authors about the need to consult oracles, including in colonization, see Plat. *Leg.* 738b ff.; Plut. *De Pyth. or.* 398d, 407f-408a; Cic. *Div.* 1.3; Vitr. 4.1.4. For further ancient references to foundation oracles, see Pease 1917; Parke and Wormell 1956: 1.79n4; Lombardo 1972; Miller 1997.

14. It is not clear when particular foundation tales associated with archaic colonies were composed. The examples cited here seem to have been in circulation by the fifth century B.C.E., if not earlier: a version of the oracle for Myskellos is found in the fifth-century historian Antiochus of Syracuse (Antiochus *FGrH* 555 F 10 = Strabo 6.1.12; see also Hippys *FGrH* 553 F 1). The second example concerning Battos's consultation, cited below on p. 80, was in circulation in the fifth century since it is preserved by Herodotus.

15. For the divinely appointed oikist, see, e.g., Malkin 1987: 27, 51, 142–43, 185.

signaling the conferral of talismanic power.[16] At this moment, Apollo singles the oikist out and guarantees his successful completion of the colonial venture. For Apollo, only one person fits the bill for a given foundation, a point underscored by colonial narratives that feature the "surprised oikist" motif. In these stories, an individual consults the oracle about a personal matter and is instead unexpectedly told to found a city.[17] Herodotus records that when Battos consulted the oracle about his speech impediment, he was told instead to found Cyrene (4.155.3):

> Ἐπείτε γὰρ ἠνδρώθη οὗτος, ἦλθε ἐς Δελφοὺς περὶ τῆς φωνῆς· ἐπειρωτῶντι δέ οἱ χρᾷ ἡ Πυθίη τάδε·
>
> Βάττ', ἐπὶ φωνὴν ἦλθες· ἄναξ δέ σε Φοῖβος Ἀπόλλων
> ἐς Λιβύην πέμπει μηλοτρόφον οἰκιστῆρα.
>
> When he had reached adulthood, he [Battos] went to Delphi to ask about his voice. And Pythia answered him with the following prophecy:
>
> "Battos, you have come for a voice. But Lord Phoibos Apollo sends you to Libya, nurse of sheep, as an oikist."

As Herodotus goes on to relate, Battos's initial resistance to this injunction is in vain. His inescapable fate is to be Apollo's choice for oikist of Cyrene (Hdt. 4.155–58). This episode corresponds to Teisamenos's own experience at Delphi, explored in chapter 1, in which the seer consulted Delphi about childlessness and was told instead that he would win the five greatest contests (Hdt. 9.33.1–2). As the Spartans who hire him rightly perceive, Teisamenos—and only Teisamenos—possesses the ability to win these contests. Accordingly, this divine guarantee of victory transforms Teisamenos into a talismanic figure, and, as Herodotus underscores, the Spartans are willing to pay any price to retain him, including Spartan citizenship. In like manner, we might understand Delphi's choice of a particular oikist as another transformative moment in which the oikist becomes the talisman whose presence will guarantee the successful foundation of the new city. In this context as well, we would do well to recall the connection between talismanic athletes and oikists, also discussed in chapter 1: talismanic crown victors can go on to become oikists. But another opportunity for an oikist to receive such a superabundance of divine favor occurs when Delphic Apollo himself selects him for this role through an oracle, as he does with Battos.

The consultation at Delphi is transformative for the oikist in another way as well. For, in this moment, the oikist also becomes an interpreter of divine will. In colonial narratives, the oikist's interpretive skill is especially emphasized when the geographical directions embedded in a foundation oracle take the form of a riddle.

---

16. Note that Malkin (1987: 5) describes the oikist after his consultation as now possessing a "religious aura."

17. See Malkin 1987: 27–28, 65 with Parke and Wormell 1956: 1.50 for other examples of this motif.

In these instances, it falls to the oikist to construe the riddle's correct meaning and thus the correct site for the colony. In a passage from Diodorus Siculus, the Pythia rejects a certain Phalanthos's request to settle the land between Sikyon and Corinth (8.21.3):

Σατύριον φράζου σὺ Τάραντός τ' ἀγλαὸν ὕδωρ
καὶ λιμένα σκαιὸν καὶ ὅπου τράγος ἁλμυρὸν οἶδμα
ἀμφαγαπᾷ τέγγων ἄκρον πολιοῖο γενείου·
ἔνθα Τάραντα ποιοῦ ἐπὶ Σατυρίου βεβαῶτα.

Heed Satyrion and the shining water of Taras and a harbor on the left and [the place] where a goat warmly greets the salty swell of the sea, moistening the tip of his grey beard. There erect Taras, mounted upon Satyrion.

Phalanthos is able to decipher this enigmatic oracular response and thus discovers the correct location for Taras when he realizes that *tragos* does not refer to a literal goat but is rather a metaphor for a wild fig tree dipping its branches into a stream.[18]

In *De Pythiae oraculis*, Plutarch notes the interpretive abilities of famous oikists of the past, including Phalanthos (407f-408a):

ἴστε γὰρ τὸ † χῖον καὶ Κρητίνην καὶ Γνησίοχον καὶ Φάλανθον ἄλλους τε
πολλοὺς ἡγεμόνας στόλων ὅσοις ἔδει τεκμηρίοις ἀνευρεῖν τὴν δεδομένην
ἑκάστῳ καὶ προσήκουσαν ἵδρυσιν·

For you all know about . . . and Kretines and Gnesiochos and Phalanthos and many other leaders of expeditions who had to discover by means of signs the proper place for foundation given to each.

The act of deciphering an oracular riddle in order to find the divinely sanctioned site for the new foundation is an act of interpreting the will of the gods not unlike the process of divination itself, which also relies on the interpretation of signs.[19]

I would argue, therefore, that in colonial discourse, the amalgam of religious authority and talismanic power conferred on the oikist as well as his consequent ability to interpret Apollo's riddling commands accord him qualities reserved for the seer in other contexts. Both seer and oikist are endowed with the same combination of attributes insofar as both are cast as talismanic expounders and interpreters of the divine. Further, just as an oikist leads a colonial expedition, the seer, too, can guide others safely across geographical distance. In the *Iliad*, Kalchas leads the ships of the Achaians to Troy through his seercraft (*Il* 1.71–72). Theoklymenos's presence aboard Telemachos's ship appears to help their stealthy return to Ithaka, a feat characterized by the suitor Antinoös as the work of a *daimon* (*Od.*

---

18. For foundation oracles containing riddles, including this one, see Dougherty 1993: 44–60.
19. Note Malkin's (1987: 51) formulation: "To the colonists, then, their oikist would appear to be translating the god's own command into physical terms of the site."

16.364–70). Military seers steer the course of armies on campaign, as when Teisamenos advises the Greek army not to cross the Asopos River (Hdt. 9.36).

Viewed from this angle, both the seer and the oikist conform well to the ethnographer Mary Helms's model of the homology between vertical and horizontal axes of distance and between the figures who traverse them:

> Geographical distance can again be seen to offer political-ideological challenges not unlike those posed by other dimensions of dangerous and powerful supernatural distance. Consequently, experts in the control and exploitation of geographical distance may be equated with experts who control and exploit other forms of distance as political-religious elites.[20]

Helms's model elucidates why the oikist and seer share the ability to guide others across both supernatural and geographical distance. Yet, through the lens of colonial discourse, this homology between the oikist and the seer is not acknowledged but rather actively suppressed. The emphasis placed on the consultation stage of the colonial process suggests that colonial discourse is ideologically invested in foregrounding the oikist and his relationship with Delphi and, in so doing, of granting the oikist religious and talismanic authority. This characterization produces an oikist who assumes attributes strikingly similar to those of the seer. That colonial discourse is still interested in religious authority, talismanic power, and interpreting divine will but assigns these qualities to the oikist suggests a purposeful effort to occlude the seer. In colonial discourse, the oikist co-opts the functions of the seer and simultaneously, with the help of Delphi, writes the seer out of the picture.

II. THE SEER IN THE CITY

It is possible to discern a second fundamental reason for the seer's disappearance from foundation stories that operates in conjunction with colonial discourse's valorization of the Delphi-oikist bond. In addition to their religious authority, oikists wielded political power within their new communities.[21] As we have seen, ancient authors generally do not reveal the dynamics of the seer-oikist relationship, but they do tell us about the seer's relationship to political leaders more generally.[22] When we survey these instances, we find that the seer's presence within the polis

---

20. Helms 1988: 80–81. See also Helms 1993: 44, quoted on p. 72 n. 70.

21. On the political authority of oikists, see Morgan 1990: 174; Miller 1997: 193–99. See Rosenberger 2001: 69–74 for Delphi's legitimation of foundations. See Malkin 1989 for a comparison between oikists and other political leaders, such as lawgivers and tyrants.

22. See chapter 2 on Odysseus and the seer Theoklymenos for an instance in which we do see the seer aiding the oikist in a metaphorical foundation. See also the conclusion for examples of later seers involved in foundations.

is a flashpoint for crisis, with the seer himself frequently cast as a fomenter of stasis. This cultural stereotype of the seer makes his inclusion in a colonial context that favors the oikist an undesirable prospect.

The Greek seer enjoyed a relatively adaptable and flexible profession, especially in comparison with his counterparts in neighboring civilizations to the East.[23] Seers were independent, itinerant, and, collectively speaking, could claim expertise in a wide range of different divinatory techniques (augury, extispicy, empyromancy, and many others) as well as in purification and healing.[24] Despite this catholic mixture of attributes, the seer's reputation within the polis remains relatively consistent across the archaic and classical periods. First, as scholars have noted, Greek *manteis* could enjoy extaordinary cultural capital within a given sociopolitical sphere.[25] I would argue that part of this cultural capital derived from their perceived talismanic authority. Second, in part because of their access to and influence over the "exercise of power," seers are frequently characterized in our extant literary sources as figures capable of threatening or contesting with figures who enjoy political authority.[26] Numerous seers, both legendary and historical, upset a city's ruling elite or otherwise disrupt the current status quo. The seer Melampous exacts a portion of Proitos's kingdom in return for curing the king's daughters and thereby diminishes Proitos's own domain.[27] Mythical generations later, Telemachos encounters the Melampodid Theoklymenos, on the run for murdering a man whose male relatives "wield great power over the Achaians" (*Od.* 15.271–78). In his four extant appearances in Attic tragedy, Teiresias finds himself at odds with the reigning king, be it Kreon, Oidipous, Pentheus, or Eteokles.[28] Oidipous's outburst at the seer in *Oidipous Tyrannos* captures this tension: ὃν δὴ σὺ πειρᾷς ἐκβαλεῖν, δοκῶν θρόνοις / παραστατήσειν τοῖς Κρεοντείοις πέλας ([And I am the one] whom you are attempting to cast out, thinking that you will stand close to Kreon's throne, 399–400). The form Oidipous's unsubstantiated accusation takes is noteworthy because it reveals his assumption that Teiresias's motives stem from his desire to overthrow the king in order to increase his own political clout.

---

23. For an extended comparison between Greek seers and the Neo-Assyrian diviners of Mesopotamia, see Beerden 2013.

24. On the different types of divinatory practices of the seer, see the introduction.

25. For the cultural capital of seers, see Bremmer 1996; Griffith 2009.

26. Bremmer 1996: 97. Note Bremmer's (109) conclusion: "In ancient Greece the position of seers seems to have depended on the quality of the kings: the weaker the kings, the stronger the seers." Dillery (2005: 209) writes that "the seer contests with the polis for supreme authority." Of fundamental importance to this idea is Vernant 1991. For examples of mythical seer-kings, see Bremmer 1996: 100–101. See Trampedach 2008 for the seer's contested authority in Homeric poetry.

27. See chapter 4 for a detailed account of the myth of Melampous.

28. For Teiresias's relationship with the Theban royal families and his involvement in their rises to and falls from power, see esp. Griffith 2009.

Historical *manteis* also conform to this stereotype insofar as they are occasionally implicated in uprisings and coups and depicted as catalysts of stasis. Herodotus tells of the seer Kleander, who convinces the slaves of Tiryns to wage war against their former Argive owners (6.83). To take two slightly later examples, the Spartans arrest the seer Teisamenos, the grandson of the Teisamenos at Plataia, after accusing him of participating in the conspiracy of Kinadon in 399 (Xen. *Hell.* 3.3.11). Theokritos, also a seer, reportedly helped Pelopidas overthrow the Theban oligarchy in 379 B.C.E. (Plut. *Mor.* 575b-598f).[29]

Herodotus alludes to the possibility of a power struggle between the earlier Teisamenos and the Spartan kings in 9.33–35.[30] When the Spartans initially approach Teisamenos and offer to make him a "leader of wars together with the Heraklid kings" (9.33), Teisamenos insists that he and his brother Hagias must first be made full citizens of Sparta. Herodotus compares Teisamenos's behavior to that of Melampous, who demanded portions of Argos for himself and his brother, Bias. The Spartans follow the Argives in eventually conceding out of desperation to the seer's terms. I would contend, then, that part of the Spartans' extreme trepidation in granting the seer's request derives not merely from Sparta's general penchant for excluding outsiders but also from an underlying anxiety that Teisamenos will not be satisfied with being merely a "leader of wars" and will also, like Melampous, want a share of the Spartan leadership within the polis itself.[31] This trepidation accounts in part for Herodotus's juxtaposition of the two seers in this context. To be sure, seers can also assist political rulers. The *chrēsmologos* Onomakritos was associated with the Peisistratidai, while the *mantis* Lampon is repeatedly linked to Perikles. Yet, although these figures seem to have enjoyed close ties to the politicians they served, Onomakritos is vilified by Herodotus, and Lampon by Aristophanes.[32] The negative portrayal of Lampon appears to stem from Old Comedy's generally critical view of divination.[33] Nevertheless, the result is that, at least from these perspectives, both the *chrēsmologos* and the seer are characterized as problematic for the well-being of Athens itself, even as they assist its political leaders.

The seer's uneasy position within the polis framework comes into greater focus when compared to the military *mantis* on the battlefield. In this space beyond the bounds of the polis, the seer collaborates with his *stratēgos* (military commander). *Stratēgoi* accompanied by their military *manteis* are found from the archaic to

---

29. A late fourth-century gold amphora discovered in Bulgaria in 1949 may depict this story; see Flower 2008b: 157–58.
30. For the seer Teisamenos, see chapter 1.
31. This is perhaps why it is significant that Teisamenos's brother, Hagias, is also made a citizen: the two brothers are viewed as a threat to the two kings of Sparta.
32. On Onomakritos, see Shapiro 1990; Dillery 2005. On Lampon, see chapter 6, pp. 136–37.
33. See Smith 1989.

Hellenistic periods.[34] To take one famous example, Megistias, the Spartans' seer at Thermopylai, is closely joined to Leonidas in his epitaph. Herodotus records the inscription, attributing it to Simonides (7.228.3):

Μνῆμα τόδε κλεινοῖο Μεγιστία, ὅν ποτε Μῆδοι
Σπερχειὸν ποταμὸν κτεῖναν ἀμειψάμενοι,
μάντιος, ὅς τότε Κῆρας ἐπερχομένας σάφα εἰδὼς
οὐκ ἔτλη Σπάρτης ἡγεμόνας προλιπεῖν.

This is the memorial of glorious Megistias whom once upon a time the Medes killed when they crossed the river Spercheios, a seer, who, although clearly aware that the goddesses of doom were approaching then, did not suffer to abandon the *hēgemōn* (leader) of Sparta.

As we might expect, the inscription honors the seer's ability to predict the future and to foresee his own approaching death. Yet, as the second couplet continues, we realize that Megistias's skill as a diviner accompanies another great achievement: the seer did not abandon his Spartan *hēgemōn* (leader). The ringing conclusion of the dedication is Megistias's abiding connection on the battlefield with the king and *stratēgos* of Sparta.

The partnership of the commander and seer is not always a harmonious one, but our sources tend not to represent disputes between the pair as evidence of the seer's desire to challenge his commander's authority over the army. Rather, reports of dissent emphasize how a commander's refusal to heed the omens of his seer leads to disastrous consequences for himself and/or the army.[35] By contrast, within the polis, seers can be cast as troublemakers, and this tendency seems to be tied to their reputation as figures who compete for political authority with those already in power.

---

34. Pairs of generals and seers include Leonidas and Megistias (Hdt. 7.221); Tolmides and Theainetos (Paus. 1.27.5; cf. Thuc. 3.20.1 for the seer Theainetos, son of Tolmides, and the general Eupompides); Aristomenes and Theoklos and their sons, Gorgos and Mantiklos (Paus. 4.21.2); Kimon and Astyphilos of Poseidonia (Plut. *Kim.* 18); Nicias and Stilibiades (Plut. *Nic.* 23.5); Aristander and Alexander (Plut. *Alex.* 2.3, 14.5, and 25.1–2).

35. The doomed Tydeus berates Amphiaraos for refusing to let him cross the Ismenos River (Aesch. *Sept.* 377–83); Mardonios decides to ignore his Greek seer Hegesistratos's interpretation of the omens and to engage in battle with the Greeks at Plataia, where he is ultimately killed (Hdt. 9.41–42); Alexander falls ill after disregarding Aristander's reading of an omen (Arr. 4.4). See also Xen. *Hell.* 3.1.17–19 and 4.8.35–39 for two Spartans who disobey omens and are wounded or killed as a result. As a counterexample, in the *Iliad,* Agamemnon insults Kalchas but ultimately agrees to follow his advice to return Chryseis to her father (*Il.* 1.106–17). Agamemnon specifically says that he obeys Kalchas because he does not wish for his army to be destroyed (i.e., he knows that if he acts contrary to Kalchas's pronouncements he will only bring disaster upon his men). Concerning historical military *manteis,* Flower (2008b: 159) notices that "our historical sources do not report heated confrontations" between seers and their generals.

The contrast that arises from the rapport between a seer and his military commander on campaign and the tensions between a seer and political rulers within the city is neatly encapsulated in the different ways in which Pindar depicts the relationship of Amphiaraos and Adrastos in *Olympian* 6 and *Nemean* 9, respectively. In *Olympian* 6, after Amphiaraos has disappeared under the earth, Adrastos laments (16–17):

> 'Ποθέω στρατιᾶς ὀφθαλμὸν ἐμᾶς
> ἀμφότερον μάντιν τ' ἀγαθὸν καὶ
> δουρὶ μάρνασθαι.'

"I yearn for the eye of my army, good both as a *mantis* and at fighting with the spear."

On the battlefield, Amphiaraos is an indispensable member of Adrastos's army.[36] Conversely, in *Nemean* 9, Amphiaraos forces the king out of his own city of Argos and temporarily assumes the throne himself while Adrastos escapes to Sicyon (13–14):

> φεῦγε γὰρ Ἀμφιαρῆ
> ποτε θρασυμήδεα καὶ δεινὰν στάσιν
> πατρίων οἴκων ἀπό τ' Ἄργεος· ἀρχοὶ
> δ' οὐκ ἔτ' ἔσαν Ταλαοῦ παῖδες, βιασθέντες λύᾳ.

For once he [Adrastos] escaped intrepid Amphiaraos and dread stasis by fleeing his ancestral home and Argos; and the children of Talaos were rulers no longer, having been overcome by civil strife.

In a polis setting, these two heroes of the Seven against Thebes regard one another as enemies, and Amphiaraos, who overthrows Adrastos to take control of Argos, is singled out as the instigator of political conflict.

If the seer is indeed perceived as a destabilizing presence within the polis and as one who prompts contestations over power when he remains in one location for long, we can perhaps understand why colonial discourse avoids acknowledging the presence of seers in the foundation process. Colonial narratives commemorate the oikist's creation of a new polis. As a traditional threat to a polis's leaders, the seer does not belong in a context that proclaims the oikist's own political hegemony.[37]

If the salient pair in warfare is the *mantis* and the military commander, then its counterpart in colonial discourse is Delphi and the oikist. Colonial discourse's ideological stance benefited the oracle and founder alike. Colonies legitimized their identity by envisioning their communities as the direct result of Delphic

---

36. For a more detailed discussion of this passage, see chapter 5, pp. 117–18.
37. Dillery (2005: 208–9) also discusses how seers around the time of the Persian Wars especially "demonstrate how a tension exists between the *polis*-framework and the individual specialist from outside."

Apollo's own divine initiatives.³⁸ The assertion of such a connection, promoted especially in the Greek West, is neatly captured by archaic Kroton's decision to place an image of the Delphic oracle's tripod on its coinage.³⁹ Delphi not only legitimized the wider colonial community but also the political authority of the oikist himself. As I argued in part 1, colonial narratives foreground the oikist as a recipient of religious and talismanic authority from the oracle. We should view these various strains of authority as inextricably related to one another. In their totality, they produced the outsize figure of the oikist, who, with Apollo's backing, successfully founds a colony and, at least in some cases, goes on to receive cult himself.

George Forrest once famously argued that colonization did more for Delphi than Delphi did for colonization.⁴⁰ While this stance may be extreme, it serves as a reminder that Delphi also benefited to a fantastic degree from this arrangement, both materially and in the place it occupied in the Greek cultural imaginary. Delphi was successful in maintaining its "oracular monopoly."⁴¹ If other oracles were consulted for foundations during this time, no evidence for this remains.⁴² Yet we should not take this monopoly at face value. In chapter 6 we will discuss some of the signs indicating that Delphi in fact had to work hard to assert its primacy.

Colonial discourse's ideological strategy advanced the agendas of both Delphi and the oikist. Scholars have taken different positions on the origin of these narratives and whether they emerged from Delphi or the colonies.⁴³ For our purposes here, I would stress instead the mutually beneficial nature of this discourse for both parties and imagine an ongoing circulation of these narratives between Delphi and the colonies, looping out and back as the colonists themselves continued to travel between the sanctuary and their cities. I have argued in this chapter that one of the essential tactics of colonial discourse's ideological program was to elide the seer by casting the oikist as a seer-like figure who possessed both the necessary religious and talismanic authority and the interpretive expertise to render the seer himself redundant. That colonial discourse was able to successfully perform this excision was in part due to a more widespread cultural suspicion that the seer could not be trusted within the context of the city and posed a threat to those in power. I turn now to one such seer, Melampous, and his erasure from the colonial context of Bacchylides' *Ode* 11.

---

38. D'Agostino 2000: 82–85; Giangiulio 2001: 117–18; Aurigny 2011; Nicholson 2016: 82.
39. For this coin issue, which dates from ca. 530–510 B.C.E., see Morgan 1990: 176; Nicholson 2016: 82. For Kroton's close connection with Pythian Apollo in general, see Giangiulio 1989: 131–53.
40. Forrest 1957.
41. I borrow this term from Kurke 2011: 60.
42. Malkin 1987: 17. Later sources do mention other oracles: see Pease 1917; Lombardo 1972.
43. See Giangiulio 2010.

4

The Disappearance of Melampous in Bacchylides' *Ode* 11

This chapter is the first of three that put to work the general theory posited in the preceding chapter for why the seer goes missing in colonial discourse. In chapter 3, I proposed two fundamental reasons for colonial discourse's suppression of the role of the seer in Greek foundations. First, colonial discourse promotes the religious authority and talismanic power of the Delphi-sanctioned oikist and does so at the expense of the seer. Second, this ideological strategy takes advantage of a more endemic cultural suspicion and negative portrayal of the seer within the framework of the polis. As I noted, this model of colonial ideology and its motivations is not meant to be rigid or monolithic. Colonial ideology itself, like any ideology, is volatile and complex and coexists with other current, vestigial, and incipient ideologies.[1] Rather, the model represents a point of entry to a more nuanced understanding of the ideological operations of colonial discourse. Indeed, the following case studies in chapters 4–6 will reveal a number of permutations of the model outlined in chapter 3. At the same time, even as we explore the variety and complexity inherent in these idiosyncratic manifestations of colonial discourse, I would contend that these case studies ultimately validate the general conclusions reached in chapter 3.

Chapters 4–6 center on extended close readings of three epinikian odes, Bacchylides' *Ode* 11, Pindar's *Olympian* 6, and Pindar's *Pythian* 8, respectively. Epinikion, the genre of choral poetry that celebrates athletic victors, offers an especially productive generic laboratory in which to observe colonial ideology's suppression of the seer in the late archaic and early classical periods. The heyday of this relatively short-lived genre falls squarely within this time frame, and its concerns

---

1. See the introduction for this point.

coincide with the major cultural phenomena examined in this study. For instance, epinikion displays a general interest in talismanic victors and, more specifically, repeatedly links *kudos* and crowns.[2] Colonial imagery is also a persistent feature of the genre, not surprisingly since many of its patrons came from colonial cities.[3] Delphi, too, plays a prominent role, with twelve odes of Pindar and at least two odes of Bacchylides composed for victors in the Pythian games.[4] Individual seers also populate the odes, appearing especially in the mythic portions.[5]

In addition to epinikion's interest in the necessary constituents for tracking the ideology of colonial discourse (talismanic power, oikists, Delphi, and seers), the genre lends itself well to symptomatic readings of literary texts.[6] One of epinikion's principal tasks was to reintegrate the homecoming athletic victor into his community. To carry out this reintegration, the epinikian poet deployed a variety of rhetorical tactics to stave off potential tensions and enmities effected by the return of a talismanic crown victor to his awaiting polis and its citizen body.[7] An ode's resulting anomalies and omissions, often elicited through intertextual juxtapositions, can point to the poet's finessing or negotiating elements of ideological contestation within the victor's community. For these reasons, epinikion is a productive medium for exploring colonial discourse's ideological suppression of the seer.

To turn, then, to our first ode, the contestatory dynamics between the seer and oikist generate a curious version of the myth of the daughters of Proitos found in Bacchylides' *Ode* 11. There have been a number of excellent studies of this epinikion, and my own reading will build on several of them in order to propose a new reading attuned to the ode's colonial ideology.[8] Part 1 will argue that in *Ode* 11's version of the Proitid myth, Bacchylides intentionally excises the seer Melampous

---

2. For a discussion of this link, see chapter 1.

3. Pindar's greatest patron, Hieron of Syracuse, founded the city of Aitna (see chapter 5). *Pythian* 1 especially celebrates Hieron in the role of oikist of Aitna. Two Pindaric odes, *Nemean* 1 and 9, were composed for Hieron's lieutenant, Chromios, who became the regent of Aitna. See chapter 5 for the colonial ideology of *Olympian* 6. *Pythian* 4, 5, and 9 were composed for patrons from the colonial city of Cyrene. For a discussion of these odes, see esp. Calame 2003; Neer and Kurke, forthcoming. See Nicholson 2016: 280 for Bacchylides' much more tenuous ties both to epinikion and to patrons in the Greek colonial West. See Hornblower (2004: 26–27), who posits a possible colonial origin for the genre as a whole.

4. Pi. *P.* 1–12; Bacch. 4 and 11.

5. See, e.g., the four appearances of the seer Amphiaraos (*O.* 6.13, 17; *P.* 8.56; *N.* 9.13; *N.* 10.9). Other seers include Iamos (*O.* 6.50); Kassandra (*P.* 11.33); Mopsos (*P.* 4.190); Polyidos (*O.* 13.74).

6. For symptomatic reading, see the introduction.

7. For this general point about epinikion, see Kurke 1991. Pindar's odes, for example, demonstrate a persistent concern with warding off *phthonos* (jealousy).

8. See, e.g., Burnett 1985: 101–13; Montepaone 1986; Garner 1992a; Dougherty 1993: 120–35; De Siena 1998; Seaford 1988; Hall 2002: 58–65; Cairns 2005; Kowalzig 2007: 267–327; Currie 2010; Nicholson 2016: 277–307. See Nicholson 2016: 277n1 for further bibliography.

at the same time as he transforms the myth into a foundation tale. A shorter part 2 will conclude the chapter by turning to Antonio De Siena's reconstruction of religious and political changes within early fifth-century Metapontion and to Nigel Nicholson's reading of the ode in relation to this context. As I will argue, the promotion of the oikist Proitos and the concomitant silencing of the seer Melampous that I trace in the ode's mythic portion constitute a rejection of the refoundation of the colonial polis's religious and political order during this period.

I. THE MISSING *MANTIS* AND THE FOUNDATION OF TIRYNS

Bacchylides' *Ode* 11 celebrates a certain Alexidamos of Metapontion, victor in the boys' wrestling event at the Pythian games. The ode's date falls between 470 and Bacchylides' death in the 430s.[9] The patron of the ode was the youth's father, Phaiskos, a member of the local Metapontine aristocracy.[10] The family of Phaiskos and Alexidamos seems to have controlled a sanctuary of Artemis near the river Kasas (the modern Basento) that has been excavated at San Biagio della Venella.[11] In this extraurban sanctuary, located roughly eight kilometers outside of the civic center of Metapontion, Zeus Aglaos was worshipped in conjunction with Artemis. Both cults from the sanctuary, especially the cult of Artemis Hemera, prominently feature in *Ode* 11, and it is for this reason that scholars have argued for a strong connection between the sanctuary at San Biagio and the local aristocratic family of Phaiskos and Alexidamos.[12] I will revisit this connection and its relevance for *Ode* 11 at the end of the chapter. For now, let us turn to the epinikion itself and, more precisely, to its mythic portion.

After celebrating Alexidamos and acknowledging Artemis in the youth's present success, the ode enters into an extended aetiological myth from which it never fully resurfaces. Our focus here will be on Bacchylides' rendering of this mythic portion of the ode, which features not only the foundation of Artemis's Metapontine cult but also the madness of the daughters of Proitos (the Proitids) and Proitos's own foundation of Tiryns.

The myth of *Ode* 11 takes the shape of an elaborate, double ring composition in which the outer ring recounts the madness of the Proitids before spiraling into an inner, chronologically earlier account of the quarrel between the brothers Akrisios and Proitos of Argos. If we straighten out these narrative loops into a linear

---

9. For the date of the ode as well as the date of Bacchylides' death, see Nicholson 2016: 293n45.

10. On Phaiskos's unusual decision to commission an epinikian ode for his son and the ideological implications of this decision, see Nicholson 2016: 277–307.

11. Montepaone 1986: 234; Nicholson 2016: 303.

12. Burnett 1985: 187–88n8; De Siena 1998: 168–70; Cairns 2005: 37–38; Kowalzig 2007: 291–97; Nicholson 2016: 302 with further bibliography.

sequence, the myth of *Ode* 11 runs as follows. The brothers' quarrel is introduced in medias res, at the point where it threatens the entire population with stasis (64–68).[13] In response, the people of Argos collectively beseech their leaders to divide their land (69–72). Their plea is successful, and the younger brother, Proitos, departs and settles nearby Tiryns, whose walls the Cyclopes come and build for the city's new inhabitants (77–81). Misfortune strikes again in the tenth year after the foundation of Tiryns when Proitos's daughters insult Hera within the goddess's *temenos* (sanctuary) by unfavorably comparing her wealth (i.e., the wealth of her temple) to that of their father (47–52). An enraged and vengeful Hera places "backturning thinking" (παλίντροπον νόημα, 57) in their breasts, and, as if "back-turning" were a directional cue, the maidens head for the hills, leaving Tiryns behind (53–58).[14] The daughters wander for thirteen months until Proitos, after temporarily losing his own wits and attempting suicide, prays to Artemis to lead his daughters out of their madness (85–88, 104–5). Artemis accomplishes this request, and the maidens, their sanity restored, establish a *temenos*, altar, and choruses of women for the goddess at Lousoi (106–12). The myth concludes with this altar at Lousoi as the hook back into the present. Artemis followed the Achaians from this Arkadian precinct to Metapontion where she now also dwells beside the river Kasas (113–23).

This is the tale Bacchylides offers to the Metapontian youth Alexidamos, a tale of wandering wits and physical migration punctuated by the architecture of altars and Cyclopean masonry. The maidens' madness appears as an extremely odd choice for an epinikion honoring an athletic victory in wrestling. The curious choice of myth, in addition to Bacchylides' reference to Alexidamos's former defeat at Olympia (22–36), seemingly an epinikian gaffe, inspired Anne Pippin Burnett to note that "we are apt to find the whole song somewhat insane."[15]

But scholars, including Burnett herself, have worked out much of *Ode* 11's inscrutability. The ode has been interpreted, for instance, as a reflection of girls' maturation rites: the Proitids' movements within the myth trace an initiatory arc that begins with their rejection of Hera, the goddess of marriage, and culminates in their institution of women's choruses at Lousoi. This conclusion signals their

---

13. Bacchylides avoids identifying the cause of the dispute, but other authors such as Pindar (fr. 284) and Apollodorus (*Bibl*. 2.4.1) do provide an explanation for the quarrel, namely, that Proitos was accused of raping his niece, Danaë. On the more detailed versions of the quarrel, see Seaford 1988: 132–33.

14. On the spatial connotations of παλίντροπον here, see Seaford 1988: 119.

15. Burnett 1985: 107. Garner (1992a: 523) amusingly captures this earlier stage of scholarship on the ode: "There was a time when the detractors of Bacchylides singled out his eleventh ode as inept even by Bacchylidean standards: it was like the unfortunate tenor who was so stupid that even the other tenors noticed."

readiness for marriage and reintegration into society.[16] Taking another approach, Carol Dougherty and Douglas Cairns both explore the ways in which Tiryns and Proitos operate as paradigms for the colonial city of Metapontion and its victor.[17] Barbara Kowalzig shows that *Ode* 11 participates in the contested concept of Achaian identity in early to mid-fifth-century southern Italy and charts how Bacchylides implicates Artemis's cult at Metapontion in this negotiation.[18] Recently, Nigel Nicholson has convincingly accounted for the ode's most anomalous features, including the attention Bacchylides' devotes to Alexidamos's defeat at Olympia, by reading these anomalies in relation to recent political and religious developments within Metapontion.[19]

And yet there remains another exceedingly strange feature about the epinikian ode that, although it has been noted, has never been sufficiently resolved. Bacchylides' version of this myth contains a glaring omission: the seer Melampous, who is the central figure in almost all other versions of the Proitid myth, is completely missing from *Ode* 11. To appreciate this absence, let us first examine other instantiations of the Proitid mythographic tradition.

The Mythographic Tradition of Melampous

The mythographic tradition of the seer Melampous is a rich one and encompasses a number of variants that differ in the form of the maidens' transgression as well as in their subsequent punishment.[20] The early fifth-century Argive genealogist Akousilaos, for example, held that Hera's anger was due not to the maidens' declaration of their father's superior wealth but rather to their disparaging the goddess's cult statue (*FGrH* 2 F 28).[21] Both Probus and Servius favor a Hesiodic version in which Hera altered the Proitids' minds in such a way that the maidens believed that they had become cows.[22] Another fleeting glimpse of Hesiod reveals a different

---

16. On the initiatory aspects of the ode, see Burnett (1985: 100–113), who carefully plots the ode's thematic oscillations between nature and culture; Seaford 1988; Dowden 1989; Suarez de la Torre 1992: 3–6; Cairns 2005: 47–48. Kowalzig (2007: 274) is right to point out that while this initiatory element is certainly an important component to the ode, "Bacchylides' myth-telling is highly complex and cannot be reduced to a single local or ritual context."

17. Dougherty 1993: 129–35; Cairns 2005. Both Dougherty's and Cairns's arguments will be discussed below.

18. Kowalzig 2007: 267–327.

19. For other treatments of Bacchylides' unusual reference to Alexidamos's past defeat, see esp. Carey 1980: 229–40; Garner 1992a; MacFarlane 1998.

20. Dowden (1989: 71–95) provides the fullest presentation of the different versions within this tradition, but see also Cairns 2005. On Melampous in general, see Gantz 1993: 185–88.

21. On the relationship between Hera and Artemis in the myth, see Kowalzig (2007: 281), who refers to the myth as containing a "jumble of Heraian and Artemisian imagery."

22. On Hesiod as the source for both Probus and Servius, see Dowden 1989: 94–95; Cairns 2005: 41; see also below.

scene in which the Proitids were found guilty of a more physical offense, lewdness, that produced in turn a more physical punishment, leprosy and hair loss (frr. 132–33 M-W):

εἵνεκα μαχλοσύνης στυγερῆς τέρεν ὤλεσεν ἄνθος
[ ]δε.ọ[
[ ]ἀπείρονα γαῖαν
καὶ γάρ σφιν κεφαλῇσι κατὰ κν̣ύος αἰνὸν ἔχευ̣εν·
ἀλφὸς γὰρ χρόα πάντα κατέσχ<εθ>εν, αἱ δέ νυ χαῖται
ἔρρεον ἐκ κεφαλέων, ψίλωτο δὲ καλὰ κάρηνα.

On account of their loathsome lewdness she destroyed the delicate bloom of their youth ... the boundless earth. For in fact she poured down a terrible itch on their heads: for *alphos* [white leprosy] covered all of their skin, and now their hair fell out of their heads, and their beautiful heads became bald.

The fate of the daughters of Proitos is closely related to that of the women of Argos. In the latter myth, the Argive women are driven mad and sent out of the city by another slighted immortal, Dionysos, for refusing to accept the god's rites. The two stories are in many respects doublets of one another and are eventually merged by Apollodorus (*Bibl.* 2.2.1–2). Apollodorus figures the Bacchic frenzy as a two-stage epidemic in Argos, affecting first the Proitids before spreading to the rest of the adult female population.[23]

Despite these various riffs on the causes and symptoms of the Proitids' demise, and the analogous ruin of the women of Argos, the majority of accounts converge on one essential claim: Melampous played a leading role in the subsequent purification.[24] Melampous appears in the Proitid myth as early as Hesiod and also seems to have been included in the versions offered by two of Bacchylides' contemporaries, Akousilaos of Argos and Pherekydes of Athens.[25] The genealogist Akousilaos

---

23. The stories were originally separate but are so closely construed that the Proitid myth can take on a "Dionysiac colouring" (Cairns 2005: 43). Kowalzig (2007: 276–77) accounts for their similarity: "The resemblences stand a good chance of being the result of shifting emphases in intertwining religious and social structures at Argos, part of the political changes in the Argive Plain towards democratization, and possibly, a newly formulated civic ideology, which also bring about a new role for Dionysos." That Melampous is a prominent figure in both myths may even have aided in the two stories merging into one.

24. Several other ancient authors do not mention Melampous. Callimachus (*In Dianam* 236) agrees with Bacchylides and assigns the cure solely to Artemis. Polyarchos or Polyanthos of Cyrene (*FGrH* 37 F 1) claims Asklepios healed the Proitids.

25. Hesiod fr. 131 M-W = Probus on Virgil's *Eclogue* 6.48: Hesiodus docet ex Proeto et Stheneboea Amphidamantis natas has, quod Iunonis contempserant numen, insania exterritas, quae crederent se boves factas, patriam Argos reliquisse, postea a Melampode Amythaonis filio sanatas ita uti [lacuna] (Hesiod reports that they [the Proitids] were born from Proetus and Stheneboea, Amphidamas's daughter. Because they had despised Hera's divinity, they became terrified by madness, thinking that they had become cows, and

is likely to have mentioned Melampous if he discussed the Proitids' genealogy, since two of the Proitids conventionally go on to marry the seer and his brother Bias.[26] Pherekydes' account, preserved in the scholia to the *Odyssey*, bears a striking resemblance to *Ode* 11, with the significant exception that Pherekydes prominently features Melampous (*FGrH* 3 F 114 = schol. MV *ad Od.* 15.225):

> Μελάμπους ὁ Ἀμυθάονος παῖς, πολλὰ μὲν καὶ ἄλλα διὰ τῆς μαντικῆς τεράστια ἐποίει, οὐχ ἥκιστα δὲ αὐτῷ καὶ οὗτος ἐνδοξότατος ἆθλος ἐγένετο. τῶν γὰρ Προίτου θυγατέρων, τοῦ βασιλέως τῶν Ἀργείων, Λυσίππης καὶ Ἰφιανάσσης, διὰ τὴν ἀκμαιότητος ἀνεπιλογιστίαν ἁμαρτουσῶν εἰς Ἥραν· παραγενόμεναι γὰρ εἰς τὸν τῆς θεοῦ νεών, ἔσκωπτον αὐτόν, λέγουσαι πλουσιώτερον μᾶλλον εἶναι τὸν τοῦ πατρὸς οἶκον. καὶ διὰ τοῦτο μάντις ὢν παραγενόμενος ὁ Μελάμπους, ὑπέσχετο πάσας θεραπεύειν, εἰ λάβοι κατάξιον τῆς θεραπείας μισθόν. ἤδη γὰρ ἡ νόσος δεκαετής, καὶ ὀδύνην φέρουσα οὐ μόνον αὐταῖς ταῖς κόραις, ἀλλὰ καὶ τοῖς γεγεννηκόσιν. ἐπαγγειλαμένου δὲ τοῦ Προίτου τῷ Μελάμποδι καὶ μέρος τῆς βασιλείας, καὶ μίαν τῶν θυγατέρων ἣν ἂν θέλοι εἰς γάμον δώσειν, ἰάσατο τὴν νόσον ὁ Μελάμπους, διά τε ἱκεσιῶν καὶ θυσιῶν τὴν Ἥραν μειλιξάμενος, καὶ λαμβάνει πρὸς γάμον Ἰφιάνασσαν, ἕδνον αὐτὴν τῶν ἰατρειῶν καρπωσάμενος. ἡ δὲ ἱστορία παρὰ Φερεκύδῃ.

> Melampous, the son of Amythaon, did many other wondrous things through his seercraft, and not the least glorious of his labors was the following. For Lysippe and Iphianassa, the daughters of Proitos, the king of the Argives, on account of the thoughtlessness characteristic of youth transgressed against Hera. For when they came to the goddess's temple, they scoffed at it, saying that their father's house was richer. And, on account of this, Melampous, a seer who had newly arrived, promised to treat them all, if he should get a wage worthy of his treatment. For at this point the sickness had lasted for ten years and had brought pain not only to the girls themselves but also to their parents. And after Proitos promised to give Melampous both a portion of his kingdom and one of his daughters to marry, whichever one he wanted, Melampous cured them of their sickness, propitiating Hera through prayers of supplication and sacrifices, and married Iphianassa, reaping her as a reward for the treatments. And that is the story related by Pherekydes.

Because the fragment of Pherekydes is so similar to *Ode* 11 in many other respects, it has been argued that the scholiast who claims to summarize the genealogist was

---

abandoned their homeland Argos; later they were healed by Melampus, Amythaon's son, so that ... [trans. Most 2007]). Cf. Hesiod fr. 37 M-W, where both Melampous and Proitos are again mentioned and where Merkelbach and West (1967: 25), Burkert (1983: 170n12), and Vian (1965: 29) all restore "Proitids." Dowden (1989: 95) defends the assertion that Probus's entire entry is taken from Hesiod: "Our passage is carefully written in indirect speech throughout and it would be out of character if Probus was not, as he purports to be, summarizing Hesiod throughout." Also included in the scholia on *Eclogue* 6.48 is a more detailed account of the Proitids and Melampous by Servius Auctus, although he does not cite Hesiod as his source. The family of scholia to which both Probus and Servius belong are so similar with respect to this line that Dowden (95) contends that Servius is also using Hesiod.

26. Cairns 2005: 41.

in fact primarily citing Bacchylides.[27] Yet this assertion underscores the peculiarity of Bacchylides' omission of Melampous, for it suggests that the scholiast felt Bacchylides' version to be incomplete without the seer and supplemented it with Pherekydes' account. In like manner, Melampous consistently receives credit for securing the psychological and physical return of the women of Argos. Both myths also share the same conclusion, namely, that the seer was awarded a generous swath of Argos for his trouble.[28]

Melampous's prominence within the tradition also appears in a number of renderings of the myth that focus on the Proitids' purification rather than on the grounds for their impiety. A fourth-century inscription from Sikyon, for instance, purports to mark the site where Melampous hid his healing *pharmaka* after restoring the maidens' sanity (*SEG* 15.195):

Ἐνθάδε ὑπὲρ Προίτου παίδων ἔκρυψε Μελάμπους
βλαψίφρονος μανίας φάρμακα λυσίνοσα,
ἥ τ' ἔθανεν παίδων, ὅτε δεῦρ' ἔμολον διὰ μῆνιν
Ἥρας, Ἰφινόην ἥδ' ἀγορὰ κατέχει.

Here for the daughters of Proitos Melampous concealed his sickness-dissolving drugs for the mind-damaging madness, and this agora covers Iphinoe, one of the daughters, who died when they came here on account of the wrath of Hera.

Other variations offer other explanations as to how Melampous cured the Proitids. Stephanus of Byzantium (s.v. Λουσοί) and Strabo (8.3.19) have the seer wash the maidens in a river, while, more dramatically, Apollodorus (*Bibl.* 2.2.2) has Melampous and a band of ephebes pursue them out of the mountains and down into Sicyon "with loud howling and some divinely inspired *khoreia* [choral dancing]."[29] Regardless of technique, however, Melampous is consistently credited with the achievement of releasing the maidens from their madness.

The Proitids are still cured in *Ode* 11, but Artemis is the figure who receives credit for their purification. Yet, Bacchylides' exclusion of Melampous cannot be explained solely by his desire to implicate the goddess in the Proitids' recovery. As other versions of the myth reveal, there was space within the tradition for Melampous to participate even when Artemis herself was present. Pausanias joins the two figures in the following way (8.18.8):

τὰς δ' οὖν θυγατέρας τοῦ Προίτου κατήγαγεν ὁ Μελάμπους ἐς τοὺς Λουσοὺς καὶ ἠκέσατο τῆς μανίας ἐν Ἀρτέμιδος ἱερῷ· καὶ ἀπ' ἐκείνου τὴν Ἄρτεμιν ταύτην Ἡμερασίαν καλοῦσιν οἱ Κλειτόριοι.

27. First proposed by Robert (1917).
28. See also Hdt. 9.34.
29. Trans. Kowalzig 2007: 282. The rivers to which Stephanus of Byzantium and Strabo refer are the Lousos River in Arkadia and the Anigros River in Elis, respectively. While these authors are late, this method of purification may go back to Hesiod (see Kowalzig 2007: 282; and below).

Melampous led the daughters of Proitos to Lousoi and cured them of their madness in the temple of Artemis. And from that time on the Kleitorians call this Artemis "Hemerasia."

Like Bacchylides, Pausanias locates the site of the Proitids' purification at Lousoi and applies the same cult-title to the goddess that Bacchylides uses (Pausanias's "Hemerasia" is thought to be a textual corruption of "Hemera" at Bacch. 11.39).[30] The noticeable difference between Bacchylides' and Pausanias's accounts, then, is the absence of Melampous from *Ode* 11. Similarly, Melampous is the defining feature of Stephanus of Byzantium's entry on Lousoi: Λουσοί, πόλις Ἀρκαδίας, ὅπου Μελάμπους ἔλουσε τὰς Προίτου θυγατέρας καὶ ἔπαυσε τῆς μανίας (Lousoi, a city of Arkadia, where Melampous washed the daughters of Proitos and stopped their madness, s.v. Λουσοί). Although the grammarian does not specifically mention Artemis, she is surely not far off since Lousoi was known primarily as the site of her sanctuary throughout antiquity.[31] Hesychius (s.v. ἀκρουχεῖ) records that Melampous founded a temple to the goddess after the purification. Finally, a South Italian vase painting of the fourth century captures a scene in which Melampous heals the maidens before a temple as Artemis's cult statue looks on.[32] In the myth of the Proitids, then, Melampous and Artemis need not be mutually exclusive but can work in tandem.

As the above discussion reveals, Melampous appears to be inseparably linked to the daughters of Proitos. Before we can claim that the seer's absence from *Ode* 11 was intentional, however, we must address the following concerns.[33] First, we can be fairly certain that Bacchylides does not make use of an earlier, more succinct instantiation of the myth that did not yet contain the seer, since Melampous's role in the story dates back at least to Hesiod.[34] Second, the poet does not seem to draw from a competing epichoric version that eschewed a Melampous-centered perspective: given the pervasiveness of Melampous in the mythographic tradition, there is little evidence to suggest such a competing variant. What is more, Bacchylides seems to adhere to the established template for the tale in other respects, since his Proitids, too, follow the standard sequence of the myth, from their transgression against Hera to their madness to their final purified reintegration. We must conclude, therefore, that Bacchylides was familiar with Melampous's connection with the Proitids and that the absence of the seer from

---

30. See Cairns 2005: 42n47. Hemera as a cult-title for Artemis is attested elsewhere for Lousoi: *IG* V.2 398, 400, and 403; Call. *In Dianam* 236. See Jost 1985: 47–48, 419–20.

31. For an extensive discussion of the site of Lousoi and its significance for Achaian identity, see Kowalzig 2007: 267–90.

32. Lucanian Nestoris, 390–370 B.C.E.; Naples, Mus. Naz. 82125 (H 1760); see *LIMC* 7, no. 445.

33. Here I follow Cairns (2005: 43) closely.

34. See above.

the myth is a calculated exclusion. One further piece of evidence contributes to the argument that Bacchylides intentionally suppressed the role of the seer. In fragments 22 and 4, Bacchylides not only mentions Melampous but also refers to him as coming from Argos (50–51), a signpost for this connection with the Proitids that the poet conceals here.

As Burnett and others observe, by eliminating Melampous, Bacchylides also eliminates the price that Proitos must pay for the seer's services and thus prevents the partition of the kingdom of Argos within this particular unfolding of the tale. Furthermore, Burnett notices that Bacchylides short-circuits the myth's conclusion by freezing the story at the moment when the daughters are cured but before they are married off to the seer and his brother. In this way, Bacchylides circumvents not only the disastrous dismantling of Proitos's domain but also the exogamous dissolution of his kingship.[35] As Burnett concludes, "Proetus can take his daughters back to Tiryns that has lost none of its power, and with the story cut at the moment of salvation, he seems to continue there as an example of god-favored kingliness."[36]

Both Burnett and Cairns rightly argue that Melampous is suppressed and Proitos's power is preserved because this manipulation of the myth allows for Tiryns to become a proper paradigm for Metapontion.[37] With Melampous gone, Tiryns is a peaceful and successful polis whose king is no longer threatened and that enjoys, like the Metapontines generations later, the divine favor of Artemis. Thus, Melampous's absence can be explained in part by Tiryns' and Proitos's significance in the myth as positive examples for Metapontion and its victor, Alexidamos. Yet, although I agree with these conclusions, we cannot overestimate the strangeness of what Bacchylides has done in adjusting the myth in this particular way. That is to say, we must also question why, if Bacchylides' intent with the myth was to present a paradigmatic vision of a properly functioning city and its steadfast king, he chose a story that traditionally emphasized the opposite and, before doing away with Melampous, would have been ill suited as a model for the polis and victor he wished to praise.

We can refine the arguments of Burnett and Cairns by demystifying Bacchylides' choice and subsequent modification of this particular myth. I would contend that part of the point of Bacchylides' reworking of the myth of the Proitids is to call attention to its conspicuous revision in *Ode* 11. I will return to this assertion shortly, but, in order to do so, we must understand this innovative and purposeful

---

35. Proitos's devastation at the collapse of his kingdom and his daughters' marriage to foreigners is registered in the name of his son, born after these events, Megapenthes (Great Suffering) (Eust. ad Hom. p. 1480, 4).

36. Burnett 1985: 109.

37. Burnett 1985: 109; Cairns 2005: 45–46.

omission of Melampous in relation to another significant alteration to the traditional myth.[38]

Bacchylides' Ode 11 as Foundation Tale

Bacchylides manipulates the Proitid myth in a second innovative way by casting the ode as a colonial narrative. At the center of *Ode* 11's mythic portion, the people of Argos negotiate a reconciliation between Proitos and his brother Akrisios by advising that Proitos settle Tiryns (69–81):

λίσσοντο δὲ παῖδας Ἄβαντος
γᾶν πολύκριθον λαχόντας

Τίρυνθα τὸν ὁπλότερον
κτίζειν, πρὶν ἐς ἀργαλέαν πεσεῖν ἀνάγκαν·
Ζεύς τ' ἔθελεν Κρονίδας
τιμῶν Δαναοῦ γενεὰν
  καὶ διωξίπποιο Λυγκέος
παῦσαι στυγερῶν ἀχέων.
  τεῖχος δὲ Κύκλωπες κάμον
ἐλθόντες ὑπερφίαλοι κλεινᾶι π[όλ]ει
κάλλιστον, ἵν' ἀντίθεοι
ναῖον κλυτὸν ἱππόβοτον
Ἄργος ἥρωες περικλειτοὶ λιπόντες.

They beseeched the children of Abas, having inherited the barley-rich land,[39] for the younger one [Proitos] to settle Tiryns before they fell into grievous necessity. And Zeus the son of Kronos, honoring the race of Danaos and horse-driving Lygkeus, was willing to put an end to their hateful distress. The overweening Cyclopes came and built the most beautiful wall for the famous city where the god-like ones were dwelling, the far-famed heroes, having left renowned horse-rearing Argos.

Bacchylides portrays Proitos's migration to Tiryns as a foundation (κτίζειν, 72). The arrival of the Cyclopes to ring Tiryns with walls underscores the newness of

---

38. It is important to note here that Seaford (1988) also argues for the purposeful omission of Melampous in Bacchylides *Ode* 11 but attributes it to a different reason, namely, the suppression of Dionsysiac elements in the ode. For Seaford's argument to work, the amalgamation of the Proitid/Hera myth and the women of Argos/Dionysos myth (see above) needs to have already taken place. An amalgamation of the two myths may be possible at this date, although it is not clear when in the fifth century the integration occurred. Kowalzig (2007: 277) considers the possibility that the amalgamation postdates Herodotus. Kowalzig (277) also notes concerning the two related myths, "Until well into the fifth century, however, the two groups and the language tying them to their deities remain distinct.... When scrutinized in detail, the Proitids have little in common with Dionysiac maenadism to start with, a further indication that the girls acquired Dionysiac language once the two legends mixed in a fifth-century context."

39. Maehler (2004: 150) argues that λαχόντας refers to the brothers' inheritance.

Proitos's settlement (77–79).⁴⁰ By the end of the stanza, a city has been built, fortified, and settled by the king and his heroic companions, who accompany him from Argos. Describing Proitos's migration to Tiryns in these terms differs from the way in which the event is portrayed in other sources.

Apollodorus (*Bibl.* 2.2.1) records that Proitos seized Tiryns (καταλαμβάνει Τίρυνθα), suggesting that in his version the city already existed, since it was able to be captured. Similarly, Strabo (8.6.11) claims that Proitos resolved to use Tiryns as a "headquarters" (ὁρμητηρίῳ) and led an army from Lycia, the home of his father-in-law, to take it. This version, too, implies that Tiryns existed before Proitos assumed power there. Pausanias (2.25.8), surveying the ruins in which Tiryns lay in his day, mentions that the city was named after the hero Tiryns, the son of Argos, presumably the city's eponymous founder.⁴¹ Even if we are meant to understand Bacchylides' Tiryns as already inhabited before it was acquired by Proitos and his men, the poet still chooses to cast the ruler's occupation of the polis in terms of a foundation, a decision that stands in contrast to the way in which other ancient authors represent it.

The colonial resonance of Proitos's move to Tiryns is taken up by another description in the ode's mythic portion when Proitos is said to have founded an altar (β]ωμὸν κατένασσε) at Lousoi (41). Bacchylides' choice of words here is striking, since the verb καταναίω is typically used of settling people in a particular location, not of dedicating altars.⁴² In addition, scholars have proposed the metrically sound emendation κτίσαν / σταθμασάμενοι for the textual corruption at lines 119–20, thus producing the following image: ἄλσος δέ τοι ἱμερόεν / Κάσαν παρ' εὔυδρον κτίσαν / σταθμασάμενοι (And they founded a lovely grove, measuring it out beside the fair-watered Kasas, 118–20).⁴³ If this restoration is correct, it would provide both another instance of the verb κτίζω in the poem as well as another example of a word associated with the founding of cities applied to the establishment of a sacred precinct. The language accorded to Artemis's altar and possibly to her grove thus contributes to a series of colonial images found throughout the ode as a whole, from Proitos's initial exile from Argos (60, 81) to the Achaian colonists' arrival at Metapontum (113–20).⁴⁴

Dougherty also finds a number of colonial motifs at work in *Ode* 11. The quarrel between Proitos and Akrisios that triggers Proitos's departure to Tiryns parallels other instances in which civic strife in the mother city serves as the impetus for a

---

40. Note how the wall (τεῖχος . . . κάλλιστον, 77–79) syntactically rings the city as well (MacFarlane 1998: 48).
41. Hall (2000: 88) considers this Tiryns to be the founder of Tiryns.
42. In fact, this is the only instance in which the verb is used in this manner (Maehler 2004: 145).
43. Emendation proposed by Turyn (1924: 112); see Maehler 2004: 155. Cf. Pi. *O.* 10.45.
44. Cairns 2005: 38.

colonial expedition.[45] Since Dougherty is interested in the ways in which colonization can be represented as "civic purification," she also examines the relationship between the healing of the Proitids and the founding of Tiryns. Drawing on Burnett's demonstration of how these two myths become enmeshed in the ode, Dougherty argues that the conflation of the two myths allows for the settlement itself to be viewed as a "purificatory act."[46] From a different but related angle, Cairns argues that the ode's motif of purification has migrated from its expected position in the narrative arc of foundation tales (that is, as the curative conclusion to an initial crisis) to a later time in the history of Tiryns ("in the tenth year," 59).[47] I would simply say for now that the presence of the motif of purification is by itself further evidence of Bacchylides' interest in imbuing the epinikian ode with colonial overtones through a variety of strategies. Below I will discuss how the maidens' purification and the foundation of Tiryns are joined together in another way that contributes to the mythic portion's colonial theme, namely, through Proitos's characterization as an oikist.

In this part of the chapter we have seen that Bacchylides figures Proitos's settlement of Tiryns as the foundation of a new city. Moreover, the language of colonial discourse is not limited to this particular moment in the ode but rather reappears in the unusual way in which Bacchylides chooses to describe both the dedication of Artemis's altar (β]ωμὸν κατένασσε, 41) and possibly her Metapontine grove (ἄλσος δέ τοι ἱμερόεν / Κάσαν παρ' εὔυδρον κτίσαν, 118–19). In addition, Bacchylides makes use of motifs that are conventional components of colonial narratives, namely, those of stasis in the mother city (i.e., the quarrel between Proitos and Akrisios at Argos) and purification. In *Ode* 11, then, a myth that is ostensibly about the madness of the Proitids comes to take on the qualities of a foundation tale.

That Tiryns is characterized as a colony and that the rest of the mythic portion of the ode brims with colonial imagery make sense insofar as Tiryns functions as a paradigm for Metapontion. Tiryns, with its Zeus-honored leaders (73–74) and its mighty Cyclopean walls (77–78), becomes a positive forerunner for Metapontion, a god-honored polis (12) aware of its status as a colony, even if it could not quite remember by whom it was settled or exactly when it was founded.[48] Yet, we must also challenge Bacchylides' decision to give the story of Proitos and his daughters a colonial inflection, especially when, as far as we can tell, other versions did not treat it in this way. Additionally, in calling into question why Bacchylides constructed a foundation myth out of the Proitid one, we must relate this decision to

---

45. Dougherty (1993: 131), comparing this story to the foundation myths of Cyrene and Elea.
46. Dougherty 1993: 132.
47. Cairns 2005: 39n27.
48. Kowalzig 2007: 298–301. Bacchylides aligns the two cities still further by underscoring their mutual connection with Artemis and assembling a shared Achaian heritage for them.

the other innovation to the tale explored above, namely, the omission of the seer Melampous. For I would contend that these two alterations to the myth, that is, eliminating the seer Melampous and portraying Tiryns as a new foundation, are profoundly connected. Bacchylides has not just taken any myth to transform into a foundation tale. The myth he has chosen is one that conspicuously and famously concerns a seer.

In chapter 3 we found that stories of seers and of the foundations of cities tend to be mutually exclusive. In *Ode* 11, a story of a seer is blatantly replaced by a story about a foundation as Bacchylides excises Melampous while turning the myth into a foundation tale. Given how central Melampous is to the myth elsewhere and therefore how marked his absence is in the ode, I would again assert that this excision must be part of the point. In Part 2 I will offer a reason for this bold excision based on the ode's historical context.

The metamorphosis into colonial narrative of the Proitid myth can also be gauged by the characterization of Proitos himself, who, if Tiryns is cast as a foundation, must necessarily be considered its oikist. As I argued above, seers are elided from colonial discourse not only for political reasons (because they are seen to threaten the stability of a polis and its oikist) but on religious grounds as well, insofar as the oikist himself is cast as a figure of religious authority. We find evidence of both of these reasons in *Ode* 11, and I will close this part of the chapter by examining more closely how Proitos-as-oikist achieves this double erasure of Melampous.

Proitos as Oikist

In *Ode* 11 Bacchylides celebrates the successful foundation of Tiryns by freeing it from the looming threat of a seer who swindles Proitos out of most of his kingdom. But Bacchylides goes further than merely securing Proitos's political hegemony. He also replaces Melampous with Proitos as the figure who negotiates with the gods for the maidens' recovery.

While his daughters head for the hills, Proitos travels to Lousoi (95–109):

ἀλλ' ὅτε δή
Λοῦσον ποτὶ καλλιρόαν πατὴρ ἵκανεν,
ἔνθεν χρόα νιψάμενος φοι-
νικοκ[ραδέμνο]ιο Λατοῦς

κίκλη[σκε θύγατρ]α βοῶπιν,
χεῖρας ἀντείνων πρὸς αὐγάς
ἱππώκεος ἀελίου,
τέκνα δυστάνοιο Λύσσας
πάρφρονος ἐξαγαγεῖν·
"θύσω δέ τοι εἴκοσι βοῦς
ἄζυγας φοινικότριχας."

τοῦ δ' ἔκλυ' ἀριστοπάτρα
θηροσκόπος εὐχομένου· πιθοῦσα δ' Ἥραν
παῦσεν καλυκοστεφάνους
    κούρας μανιᾶν ἀθέων·

But when their father came to the beautifully flowing Lousos, having washed his skin there, he called upon the ox-eyed daughter of Leto of the crimson headdress, extending his hands toward the rays of the charioteer sun, [calling upon her] to deliver his children from their mind-altering terrible madness. "I will sacrifice to you twenty red-haired oxen not yet yoked." And the daughter of the noblest father heard him praying. And, having persuaded Hera, she stopped the godless frenzy for the bud-wreathed girls.

At Lousoi, Proitos calls upon Artemis and arranges a transaction of promised sacrifices in return for his daughters' purification. In so doing, Proitos performs the role of mediator, orchestrating the divine resolution for the maidens' predicament. To be sure, Proitos does not act in the same capacity as Melampous does in other instantiations of the myth. In contrast to the seer, who is credited with healing the maidens either by *pharmaka* or by other means, Proitos does not cure his daughters himself. Yet Proitos's ability to contact the gods effectively, as well as the divine favor he can subsequently lay claim to as Artemis heeds his request, obviates the need for Melampous's presence in the first place.

Proitos supplants the necessity for Melampous's expertise. But, what is more, Proitos does so in a way that allows him to remain the focus of the story even after the mythic portion circles away from the foundation of Tiryns. As Burnett perceives, although the third strophe returns to the subject of the Proitids' madness, the daughters themselves fade from the narrative, and Proitos alone enjoys the narrative spotlight.[49]

The transference of religious authority and narrative attention from seer to oikist is neatly encapsulated in the image of the king bathing in the river Lousos: ἀλλ' ὅτε δὴ /Λοῦσον ποτὶ καλλιρόαν πατὴρ ἵκανεν,/ ἔνθεν χρόα νιψάμενος ... (But when their father came to the beautifully flowing Lousos, there having washed his skin ..., 95–97). Curative bathing in a river is in fact one of the remedies with which Melampous is said to have healed the Proitids. This antidote is connected with certain variations of the myth in which Hera's punishment took the form of a skin disease. Although explicit references to Melampous and purifying river baths are late, Kowalzig argues that this specific restorative treatment is likely to be as early as Hesiod, who, as we saw above, speaks of Hera as afflicting the maidens

---

49. Thus Burnett 1985: 11: "It is Proetus who bathes at Lousoi (97), instead of the afflicted ones; it is he who makes a prayer, he who promises sacrifice; the song makes his actions the only ones that we can perceive."

with *alphos* [white leprosy].⁵⁰ *Ode* 11, however, contains none of the conditions for this particular form of purification. The goddess's revenge is psychological, not physical, torture, and it is Proitos, not his daughters, who washes off his skin. Yet Kowalzig rightly sees that Proitos's bathing must be understood as an allusion to this other rendition of the myth:

> Despite the absence of a full immersion rite in the ode, a puzzling trace of literal cleansing is still there: when the Proitids' father Proitos bathes himself in the "stream at Lousos," he suspiciously washes his skin (χρόα νιψάμενος, l. 97) in a wording too close to Hesiod's not to recall the Proitidean skin-disease.⁵¹ . . . The purificatory bath only makes sense as long as there is a skin-disease to be washed off, but it has no place in the *nosos* [sickness] the Proitids incur here.⁵²

By placing Proitos in the Lousos River, Bacchylides blatantly cites an alternate, Melampous-centered account. But he cites it in order to diverge from it. In other words, it seems that we are being reminded of Melampous's cleansing of the Proitids' *alphos* precisely in order to heighten its contrast with our present version and to underscore the fact that it is now Proitos who will bring about his daughters' purification.

In *Ode* 11, Bacchylides transforms a traditional myth about the seer Melampous into a foundation tale. In the process, the seer is written out of both the political components of the myth (Proitos's kingdom is saved from destruction) and the religious ones (Proitos arranges for his daughters' purification himself). By retaining his political power and absorbing Melampous's religious power, Proitos, the oikist of Tiryns, assumes the functions left vacant by the missing seer.

II. ARISTEAS AND ALEXIDAMOS

I conclude this chapter by considering the ode in relation to its historical context. De Siena's argument that Metapontion underwent a political and religious reorganization in the late archaic to early classical period and Nicholson's reading of *Ode* 11 in light of these events suggest an exciting point of contact between this Metapontine context and Melampous's suppression in the ode's mythic portion.⁵³

We know precious little about late archaic and early classical Metapontion, but De Siena, followed by Nicholson, calls attention to an extraordinary account of the

---

50. Kowalzig 2007: 282. According to Strabo (8.3.19), some say the reason the river Anigros in Elis has a terrible smell and inedible fish is due "to the fact that Melampous used these cleansing waters for the purification of the Proitids. The bathing-water from here cures leprosy, elephantiasis, and scabies" (trans. Jones 1927).
51. See Hesiod frr. 132–33 M-W, quoted on p. 93.
52. Kowalzig 2007: 282–83.
53. See De Siena 1998; Nicholson 2016: 297–307.

colonial polis recorded by Herodotus. The historian preserves the story of Aristeas of Prokonnesos and his mysterious arrival at Metapontion in the first half of the fifth century (4.15.2–4):

> Μεταποντῖνοι γάρ φασι αὐτὸν Ἀριστέην φανέντα σφι ἐς τὴν χώρην κελεῦσαι βωμὸν Ἀπόλλωνος ἱδρύσασθαι καὶ Ἀριστέω τοῦ Προκοννησίου ἐπωνυμίην ἔχοντα ἀνδριάντα παρ' αὐτὸν στῆσαι· φάναι γάρ σφι τὸν Ἀπόλλωνα Ἰταλιωτέων μούνοισι δὴ ἀπικέσθαι ἐς τὴν χώρην, καὶ αὐτός οἱ ἕπεσθαι ὁ νῦν ἐὼν Ἀριστέης· τότε δέ, ὅτε εἵπετο τῷ θεῷ, εἶναι κόραξ. καὶ τὸν μὲν εἰπόντα ταῦτα ἀφανισθῆναι, σφέας δὲ Μεταποντῖνοι λέγουσι ἐς Δελφοὺς πέμψαντας τὸν θεὸν ἐπειρωτᾶν ὅ τι τὸ φάσμα τοῦ ἀνθρώπου εἴη. Τὴν δὲ Πυθίην σφέας κελεύειν πείθεσθαι τῷ φάσματι, πειθομένοισι δὲ ἄμεινον συνοίσεσθαι. καὶ σφέας δεξαμένους ταῦτα ποιῆσαι ἐπιτελέα. καὶ νῦν ἕστηκε ἀνδριὰς ἐπωνυμίην ἔχων Ἀριστέω παρ' αὐτῷ τῷ ἀγάλματι τοῦ Ἀπόλλωνος, πέριξ δὲ αὐτὸν δάφναι ἑστᾶσι· τὸ δὲ ἄγαλμα ἐν τῇ ἀγορῇ ἵδρυται.

The Metapontines say that Aristeas himself appeared to them in their territory and ordered them to erect an altar of Apollo and to set up beside it a statue bearing the name of Aristeas of Prokonnesos. For he said that Apollo had come to their territory and to them alone of all the Italiotes and that he himself, the one who was now Aristeas, had followed him, although at the time when he had followed the god, he had been a crow. And, having said these things, he disappeared. But the Metapontines say that they sent to Delphi to ask the god what the apparition of the man was. The Pythia ordered them to obey the apparition and told them that it would go better for them if they did obey. And when they heard these things, they accomplished them. Now there stands a statue bearing the name of Aristeas next to the actual cult statue of Apollo and around it stands a laurel tree. The cult statue is set up in the agora.

De Siena has identified "Aristeas's" altar of Apollo in the Metapontine agora and dated it to around 450 B.C.E.[54] This altar is in keeping with other large-scale changes to the religious architectural landscape of Metapontion's agora during this period. Around 470 B.C.E., a new temple to Apollo was built with a different orientation from that of the two major temples already there.[55] A smaller sanctuary was also refurbished with a new foundation and façade and set on the new orientation.[56] De Siena suggests that these developments reflect the efforts of a particular faction within the city to promote the new cult of Apollo, a cult that the narrative of the Delphi-backed Aristeas helped to legitimize. This new cult would have pulled religious authority and political power away from the city's elite families, who had previously dominated the political and religious life of the city through control of

---

54. De Siena 1998: 156–58 with Nicholson 2016: 299.

55. This new orientation was actually a return to an older orientation that had been subsequently altered in the mid-sixth century (see Nicholson 2016: 299). The new temple to Apollo is the so-called Temple D; the older temples are Temples A (for Hera) and B (for Apollo Lykeios) (De Siena 1998: 161–66).

56. Nicholson 2016: 299.

Metapontion's traditional cults. These older cults had strong ties to extraurban sanctuaries in the surrounding *chōra* (countryside), and the emergence of the new cult of Apollo signaled the aristocracy's inability to maintain connections between the extraurban and urban religious spaces of the polis.[57] By contrast, De Siena proposes, the new cult located within the city sought to enfranchise a larger swath of the citizen population (recall that Herodotus stresses that Apollo's cult statue was set up in the agora).[58] As De Siena argues, this shift in the religious and political structure of the city by means of the cult of Apollo could have been viewed as a virtual refoundation, with Aristeas in the role of oikist or "quasi-oikist."[59]

Around the same time, another cult was established in the Metapontine agora, the cult of Zeus Aglaos. This is the cult that shared the extraurban sanctuary with Artemis at San Biagio, and De Siena suggests that its transfer to the agora during this period represents an effort by an aristocratic family or group to challenge the new cult of Apollo and to attempt to retain their political and religious hegemony.[60] This cult of Zeus Aglaos is the very same one that appears in *Ode* 11 and that, together with the cult of Artemis at San Biagio, the victor's family presumably administered.

Following De Siena's proposal, Nicholson understands *Ode* 11 as a determined response to the new cult of Apollo and its Aristeas narrative. The ode, that is, can be viewed as a kind of choral counterattack by the victor Alexidamos's family. The choral performance of *Ode* 11 became one way for the family to reinforce the ties between the extraurban sanctuary of San Biagio and the newly relocated cult of Zeus Aglaos in the agora and to assert its control over these connected spaces. While the ode refers to itself as being performed within the city (11.12), it also emphatically conjures the extraurban sanctuary of Artemis. Further, Nicholson demonstrates that, on the level of genre, Bacchylides' epinikion skillfully pits itself against the so-called hero narrative of Aristeas by reconstituing many of its elements in epinikian terms.[61]

I am in complete agreement with this argument and would simply add that we can also witness, on a discursive level, a further form of resistance and opposition to the Aristeas narrative taking place in *Ode* 11. This resistance relates directly to the reading of the ode's mythic portion that I have traced in this chapter. For the Aristeas narrative and its connection with the religious and political refoundation of Metapontion present a compelling motive for Melampous's suppression in *Ode*

---

57. De Siena 1998: 168–70. For the older cults of Metapontion and their extraurban sanctuaries, see Nicholson 2016: 299n63.
58. De Siena 1998: 167–68.
59. De Siena 1998: 167–68. "Quasi-oikist" is Nicholson's (2016: 299) term.
60. De Siena 1998: 168–70; see also Nicholson 2016: 299–300.
61. Nicholson (2016: 301) also convincingly argues that the Aristeas narrative itself would have been dramatically performed, so that we are meant to understand the performance of *Ode* 11 as an attempt to counter the dramatic reenactments of Aristeas's visit to Metapontion.

11. As we have seen, within the ode, the oikist Proitos serves as a paradigm for the victor Alexidamos.[62] When we situate the Proitos–Alexidamos relationship in its historical context, the suppressed Melampous necessarily becomes a paradigm for Aristeas.

Yet Melampous does not just serve as the paradigm for Aristeas by analogy with the pairing of Proitos and Alexidamos. A considerable degree of correspondence actually obtains between the seer and the shaman, making Bacchylides' comparison of them strikingly apt. To be sure, the shaman Aristeas is not strictly a seer. For the Greeks, however, the boundary between shamans and seers was porous, and the two categories of "holy men" shared a number of attributes, including a privileged connection with Apollo and purificatory abilities.[63] Both Melampous and Aristeas can also be viewed as talismanic.[64] Melampous's talismanic power inheres in his status as a legendary seer. Aristeas's talismanic potency is registered by his characterization as a supernatural figure for whom the normal restrictions of time, space, and corporeality do not apply.[65] Parallels between the two run deeper still. Like Melampous in Argos, Aristeas is an outsider who appears in Metapontion from elsewhere. What is more, if we follow De Siena's and Nicholson's reconstructions, Aristeas was viewed as usurping religious and political power from the Metapontine aristocracy, just as Melampous cheated Proitos out of two-thirds of his kingdom.

Reading with a view to its historical context, then, I would suggest that *Ode* 11 conspicuously rejects Melampous in order to reject, beyond the frame of the ode, the narrative of the shaman Aristeas and what that narrative represented. That is, the ode resists the seizure of religious authority within Metapontion from the ruling elite as well as Aristeas's supposed role as the oikist figure in this restructuring and refoundation of the city's religious and political order. In Aristeas-as-Melampous's place, Bacchylides foregrounds Proitos as an oikist who never cedes control of his

---

62. Epinikian convention places the figures of an ode's mythic portion in a paradigmatic relation to the victor. More specifically, the oikist as a paradigm for the athletic victor is found elsewhere in the genre (e.g., Battos and Arkesilas in *Pythian* 4 and 5; Hieron as both the oikist and the victor in *Pythian* 1; cf. the discussion of Hagesias and Iamos in chapter 5). As noted above, both Burnett (1985: 109) and Cairns (2005: 45–46) have noted that Tiryns functions as a model for Metapontion.

63. Epimenides, for example, displays both mantic and shamanistic attributes (Plat. *Leg.* 642d-643 with Arist. *Rh.* 3.17, 1418a23–26; Plut. *Solon* 12.1–4; Diog. Laert. 1.110). The shaman Zalmoxis is often linked to the *manteion* (mantic oracle) of Trophonios (see Bonnechere 2003: 177). On shamans and seers, see Ustinova 2002.

64. For the talismanic power of seers, see chapter 1.

65. Nicholson (2016: 300) also characterizes Aristeas as talismanic. Both Melampous and Aristeas, as part of their superhuman characterizations, are connected with animals. Herodotus (4.15.2–4) speaks of Aristeas's ability to take the form of a crow. Melampous is said to have received the gift of prophecy when snakes licked his ears (Hes. fr. 261 M-W). Once endowed with the gift of second sight, he could apparently understand the language of animals (Apollod. *Bibl.* 1.9.11).

own foundation and who thereby fittingly becomes a paradigm for Alexidamos, his aristocratic family, and their threatened claim to Metapontine hegemony.

The Aristeas narrative itself complicates the general theory of colonial ideology outlined in chapter 3. As Herodotus emphasizes, Aristeas had close ties to Apollo, and Delphi sanctions Aristeas's cultic prescriptions to the Metapontines. In the Aristeas narrative, that is, Delphi aligns itself with a seer-like figure in the context of a foundation. But Delphi's approval of Aristeas-as-oikist is also something that *Ode* 11 implicitly rejects through its own colonial ideology. It rejects the seer element of this scenario, as we have seen, by eliding the Melampous tradition and presenting Proitos as an oikist who possesses both political and religious authority. But it also responds to and dismisses the Aristeas-Delphi bond by foregrounding Alexidamos's own connection with Delphi (15–21):

ἵλεωι [ν]ιν ὁ Δα[λ]ογενὴς υἱὸς βαθυζώνο̣[ιο] Λατοῦς
δέκτ[ο] βλεφ[άρω]ι· πολέες
δ᾽ ἀμφ᾽ Ἀλεξ[ίδα]μον ἀνθέων
ἐν πεδίωι στέφανοι
Κίρρας ἔπεσον κρατερᾶς
ἦρα παννίκοι<ο> πάλας·

The Delos-born son of deep-girded Leto received him with a kindly eye. Many crowns of flowers fell around Alexidamos on the Plain of Kirrha because of his powerful, all-victorious wrestling.

As Bacchylides envisions it, Alexidamos, too, can claim a superabundance of Apollo's favor because he has won a Pythian victory.[66] We might note that in describing Alexidamos at the Pythian games, Bacchylides focuses on the very moment at which Alexidamos becomes a talismanic figure himself, that is, the moment he is crowned. With this image of the crown, Alexidamos implicitly rejects the talismanic Aristeas and his connection with Delphi by asserting his own talismanic status derived from Delphi.[67]

Thus, on two complementary levels, the ode's characterization of Alexidamos spurns the story of Aristeas and the Metapontine faction that promoted it. Alexidamos is celebrated both as a Delphi-sanctioned victor and, through the paradigm of Proitos, as an oikist figure in an ode full of foundations. In his promotion of the oikist and conspicuous suppression of the seer, Bacchylides has composed just the type of ode that a beleaguered aristocratic family needed in order to counter an intruding shaman's attempt to refound their native city.

---

66. For the significance of Apollo's title of Delos-born at this moment and how it too represents an explicit rejection of Aristeas, see Nicholson 2016: 303.

67. For crowns as the physical manifestations of talismanic power, see chapter 1.

5

Hagesias as *Sunoikistēr*

Mantic Authority and Colonial Ideology in Pindar's Olympian 6

In the early fifth century B.C.E., the Deinomenid tyrants of Syracuse, Gelon and Hieron, expended vast amounts of their considerable resources on the Panhellenic sanctuaries of Olympia and Delphi, where they frequently outshone their mainland competitors in athletic competitions and the accompanying apparatus of commemoration. Elaborate chariot groups, statues, votive columns, and other dedications, as well as a treasury at Olympia, resided on site, announcing the incontrovertible success and wealth of the Deinomenid empire to the rest of the Greek world.[1] Hieron also secured his fame through poetry, and the material monuments left behind at Olympia and Delphi found their poetic counterparts in a host of commissioned epinikia. Hieron commissioned seven epinikia to celebrate his Olympic and Pythian equestrian victories, more than any other patron of Pindar and Bacchylides.[2] Two other odes, *Nemean* 1 and 9, celebrate Hieron's brother-in-law and regent of Aitna, Chromios. Pindar composed *Olympian* 6 for another associate of the tyrants, Hagesias, the son of Sostratos, and, as we will see, the ode belongs firmly within this Deinomenid context.

Hagesias was the victor in the mule-cart race at Olympia in 472 or 468 B.C.E.[3] According to the scholia, Hagesias served Gelon and Hieron as their

---

[1]. For recent discussions of the Deinomenidai and their empire, see Bonnano 2010; Morgan 2015: 23–86; Nicholson 2016; Neer and Kurke, forthcoming. See Morgan (2015: 390–412) for a discussion of *Olympian* 6 that addresses a number of the topics included here, especially the ode's relationship to *Olympian* 1.

[2]. The epinikia commissioned by Hieron are Pi. *O.* 1, *P.* 1, 2, 3; Bacch. 3, 4, 5.

[3]. On the date of the ode, see Farnell 1932: 40.

seer.[4] As the ode itself reveals, Hagesias was a member of the Iamidai, the mantic clan to which the Greeks' seer at Plataia, Teisamenos, discussed in chapter 1, also belonged.[5] The ode begins by conferring three titles on its *laudandus* (4–7): the first and expected designation of Olympic victor (4); the status of *tamias* (steward) of Zeus's mantic altar at Olympia (5); and lastly, the honorific "*sunoikistēr* [cofounder] of renowned Syracuse" (6):

> εἰ δ' εἴ-
> η μὲν Ὀλυμπιονίκας,
> βωμῷ τε μαντείῳ ταμίας Διὸς ἐν Πίσᾳ,
> συνοικιστήρ τε τᾶν κλεινᾶν Συρακοσ-
>   σᾶν, τίνα κεν φύγοι ὕμνον
> κεῖνος ἀνήρ, ἐπικύρσαις
> ἀφθόνων ἀστῶν ἐν ἱμερταῖς ἀοιδαῖς;

If he should be an Olympic victor, and a steward of the mantic altar of Zeus in Pisa, and a cofounder of renowned Syracuse, what hymn could that man escape, as he meets with ungrudging townsmen amid lovely songs?

Of Hagesias's three epithets, "*sunoikistēr* of Syracuse" has proved the most inscrutable. For, taken literally, it appears to be nonsensical: the conventional foundation date of Syracuse is some three centuries earlier, and its oikist is said to have been one Archias of Corinth.[6] What is more, Hagesias's status as both a mantic *tamias* and a *sunoikistēr* is the only instance in which a historical seer is explicitly linked to a foundation before the second half of the fifth century.[7] The inscrutability of *sunoikistēr*, I suggest, is tied to the title's being accorded to a seer. Parsing this combination of terms gives rise to a number of broader questions concerning colonial politics and the relationship between mantic and political authority. This chapter will consider both the larger cultural and ideological Deinomenid context

---

4. The scholia record that Hagesias was Hieron's military seer (schol. *ad O.* 6.30c) and that Hagesias was executed after the Deinomenid tyranny collapsed (schol. *ad O.* 6.165). Luraghi (1997: 84–85) questions the reliability of both entries. Yet, as Morgan (2015: 400) observes, since the reference to Hagesias's execution cannot be inferred from the ode itself, it is reasonable to suppose that the scholiasts had information beyond the content of *Olympian* 6 itself for asserting the seer's close connection with Hieron.

5. On the Iamidai, see Flower 2008a. Flower argues that the Iamidai only rose to prominence in the fifth century after Teisamenos's successful participation at Plataia.

6. Thuc. 6.3.2 gives a date of 733 B.C.E. for the foundation of Syracuse. For other eighth-century dates for Syracuse's foundation provided by ancient authors and for the problems of calculating foundation dates using literary sources, see Hall 2008: 402–11. For Archias as the founder of Syracuse, see Thuc. 6.3.2; Plut. *Mor.* 772–773b; Strabo 8.380; see Malkin 1987: 41 for further references.

7. See Dillery 2005: 193; Malkin 1987: 92–113, esp. 93–97. After Hagesias, the next historical seer connected with colonization is the Athenian Lampon, who helped to found Thurii in 444/3 B.C.E. On Lampon and Thurii, see chapter 6, pp. 136–37.

that informs Pindar's pairing of seer and *sunoikistēr* as well as how the poet manages this collocation within *Olympian* 6 itself.

Part 1 of this chapter builds on the conclusions reached in chapter 1 and argues that, by praising Hagesias as an athletic victor, seer, and *sunoikistēr*, Pindar marks Hagesias as a figure who enjoys extraordinary talismanic power. This part of the chapter also addresses the ways in which Pindar, following a convention of epinikion, secures these three prestigious titles to both Hagesias's past and present. This attention to precedent as an essential generic requirement of epinikion will aid us in deciphering the term *sunoikistēr*. Yet, insofar as he characterizes the seer as a *sunoikistēr*, Pindar introduces an element of competition into Hagesias's relationship with his own patron, Hieron, the self-proclaimed oikist of Aitna. Part 2 addresses Pindar's solution to this dilemma. In the ode's two mythic portions, the poet circumscribes Hagesias's position so as to mitigate any threat the seer might present to Hieron's own political authority. Finally, by reading *Olympian* 6 intertextually with *Olympian* 1 and *Nemean* 1, part 3 argues that, despite his subsequent need to establish that Hagesias will not overthrow Hieron, Pindar joins the seemingly incompatible titles of seer and *sunoikistēr* because Hagesias is crucial to Hieron's colonial enterprise: in the ode, Hagesias both personifies and symbolically performs Hieron's fantasy of uniting the Dorian populations of the Peloponnese and Sicily within the tyrant's colonial city of Aitna. In this way, through epinikion, Pindar maximizes the glory not only of Hagesias but also, by extension, of Hieron himself.

I. HAGESIAS'S TALISMANIC POWER AND THE IMPORTANCE OF PRECEDENT

In chapter 1, I offered a solution to an unexplained discrepancy between three versions of the late sixth-century B.C.E. war between Kroton and Sybaris. Herodotus provides two versions of the story, one in which he attributes Kroton's victory to the oikist Dorieus and another in which he credits the seer Kallias with the same success (5.44–45). Diodorus Siculus, in turn, presents the image of the athlete Milo in his six Olympic crowns leading the Krotoniates in battle (12.9). As I argued in chapter 1, the three versions of the story, featuring an oikist, seer, and athletic victor, respectively, all work from a shared template: Kroton's remarkable feat can be attributed to a figure seen to possess talismanic power.

In the extravagant opening address of *Olympian* 6, the same three titles of athletic victor, seer, and oikist intersect as they do in the competing versions of the battle of Kroton and Sybaris. But here, in place of three discrete figures with comparable claims to talismanic power, Pindar has merged the positions of athlete, seer, and oikist in order to conjure a single individual of overwhelming talismanic authority. Other Pindaric odes link the *laudandus* to a polis's founder, and the athlete and seer converge elsewhere in Greek literature.[8] In *Olympian* 6, however, Pindar uniquely joins together all three roles to produce a potent trio of praise, the seer who is not only a crown victor but also a cofounder.

Before turning to the internal dynamics of this grouping, it is necessary to recognize first that Pindar locates all three of these titles within a larger context of familial accomplishment. He does so as a means of praising Hagesias properly and to the fullest extent possible in accordance with the generic conventions of epinikion. In the poetics of Pindar, individual achievement neither exists nor is celebrated as an isolated event. Rather, because the *oikos* (household) as a whole operates as the "minimal social unit," the poet must demonstrate that the *laudandus*'s personal success also crucially replenishes his family's existing supply of *kleos* (fame).[9] The three titles that Hagesias enjoys conform to this essential requirement of praise poetry. Pindar not only foregrounds Hagesias's roles as victor, mantic *tamias*, and *sunoikistēr* in the present but also gestures toward an ancestral precedent for each position. Simply put, Hagesias is shown to continue the family business in all three of his roles. Recognizing this epinikian imperative aids especially in our understanding of Hagesias's designation as a *sunoikistēr* of Syracuse. After noting how Pindar establishes a hereditary basis for the titles of victor and *tamias*, I will turn to a more detailed discussion of the meaning of *sunoikistēr* in this context.

Pindar implies that Hagesias's relatives were accustomed to winning athletic contests, although no external evidence supports this contention.[10] Praising the fame and prosperity of the Iamidai, the poet announces (74–76):

μῶμος ἐξ ἀλ-
λων κρέμαται φθονεόντων
τοῖς, οἷς ποτε πρώτοις περὶ δωδέκατον δρόμον
ἐλαυνόντεσσιν αἰδοία ποτιστά-
ξῃ Χάρις εὐκλέα μορφάν.

Censure looms from others envious of those upon whom, when driving around the twelfth lap in first place, revered Charis showers a glorious form.

According to Nigel Nicholson, in these lines Pindar summons an image of past Iamid victories in four-horse chariot races and, more specifically, in chariot victories at Olympia, the site of Hagesias's own epigonic triumph.[11] Despite the

---

8. See chapter 1 for the connection between athletes and oikists. Teisamenos is the best-known example of an athlete-seer, but Pausanias mentions two others, Satyros (6.4.5 with Kett 1966: 67) and Eperastos (6.17.5–6).

9. Kurke 1991: 8; for this phenomenon as a key concern of epinikion, see Kurke, 15–82.

10. Nicholson 2005: 88.

11. Nicholson 2005: 88. Nicholson (88) argues that the reference to twelve laps must mean that Pindar is describing four-horse chariot races and not mule-cart races.

questionable veracity of the poet's claim, Pindar delivers it in part to assert that Hagesias's victory is but one instantiation of prizewinning Iamid performances at the Olympic games.[12] Pindar also provides a patrilineal origin for Hagesias's status as *tamias* of Zeus's altar. The major mythic portion of *Olympian* 6 culminates in an account of how Apollo initially granted the stewardship to Hagesias's forefather, Iamos (70). This aetiology makes Hagesias the latest recipient of a privilege that stretches back to the founding member of his mantic clan.[13]

The generic conventions of epinikion also direct us toward a better understanding of the term *sunoikistēr* itself. As noted in the introduction, it is not immediately evident why Pindar should choose to call Hagesias the cofounder of Syracuse, since the polis was established in the eighth century B.C.E. The ancient scholiasts themselves found the term strange, as two of their entries on *Olympian* 6 make clear (schol. *ad O*. 6.8a and b):

συνοικιστήρ τε: ὅτι οἱ πρόγονοι αὐτοῦ σὺν Ἀρχίᾳ παρεγένοντο ἐν Συρακούσαις οἱ Ἰαμίδαι, ἀφ' ὧν εἰκὸς παραλαβεῖν τινας.

Cofounder: because his ancestors, the Iamidai, from whom it was reasonable to take some [seers?], came to Syracuse with Archias.

συνοικιστήρ τε: τοῦτο δὲ οὐκ ἀληθῶς· οὐ γὰρ οὗτος συνῴκισε τὰς Συρακούσας. ἀλλὰ πρὸς ἐγκώμιον εἴληφεν· ἀπὸ γὰρ ἐκείνων ὁ Ἁγησίας τῶν συνοικισάντων.

Cofounder: this is not true; for this man did not cofound Syracuse. But he [Pindar] has taken it with a view toward praise; for Hagesias is a descendant of those who did cofound [it].

Whether the scholiasts were privy to information about this title beyond the ode itself is not known, and some scholars treat their statements as guesswork.[14] Simon Hornblower, conversely, is among those less skeptical about this ancient interpretation and suggests that the Iamidai themselves might have promoted the idea that they were involved in Syracuse's original foundation and had accompanied the oikist Archias.[15] *Sunoikistēr*, then, was, or at least was purported to be, an ancestral title handed down through the generations.

---

12. On the implications of attributing horse racing to the Iamidai, see Nicholson 2005: 88.
13. For the possibility that Pindar invented at least portions of the Iamos myth as well, see Flower 2008a; and below.
14. See Malkin 1987: 95–97. See also Luraghi 1994: 292–93; 1997: 77.
15. Hornblower 2004: 185. Farnell (1932: 41) also argues that *sunoikistēr* is a hereditary title. Hutchinson (2001: 378–79) notes that the meaning of the term is unclear but thinks a hereditary title might be possible, comparing it to how the Corinthians continued to be known as the "founders" of Corcyra (Thuc. 1.25.1). See Luraghi 1994: 292n86 for additional bibliography on the interpretation of this phrase as an ancestral title.

In contrast to Hornblower, Irad Malkin argues that the term *sunoikistēr* refers to Hagesias's own activities in early fifth-century Syracuse and to the seer's involvement as a *mantis* in the Deinomenidai's colonial enterprises.[16] Malkin contends that Gelon's restoration in 485 B.C.E. of the Gamoroi (Syracuse's ousted oligarchs), together with his expansion of the city by means of a synoikism, was viewed as a (re)foundation.[17] As he also emphasizes, because both Gelon and Hieron were fixated on the trappings and privileges of oikist cult, the characterization of one of their henchmen as a *sunoikistēr* would not have been out of place in the cultural and political climate of the tyrants' regime.[18]

Malkin's assessment attaches a general Deinomenid relevance to Pindar's "*sunoikistēr* of Syracuse." The phrase, however, becomes pertinent to Hieron's colonial agenda in particular, and thus to the immediate context of *Olympian 6*, when we realize that, elsewhere in his poetry, Pindar's references to Syracuse are frequently paired with those to Aitna. More important, Pindar connects the older city with the new one in such a way that oftentimes it is hard to distinguish Syracuse and Aitna as two discrete poleis. In *Pythian 3*, for example, Pindar unites the two locations through the figure of Hieron by calling the tyrant both the Aitnaian host and the king of Syracuse (68–70):

καί κεν ἐν ναυσὶν μόλον Ἰονίαν τάμνων θάλασσαν
Ἀρέθοισαν ἐπὶ κράναν παρ' Αἰτναῖον ξένον,

ὃς Συρακόσσαισι νέμει βασιλεύς

---

16. Malkin 1987: 93–97. See also Luraghi (1994: 292–93; 1997: esp. 76–77), who understands the title as Pindar's exaggerated, propagandistic way of praising Hagesias for the fact that Gelon simply awarded the seer with Syracusan citizenship during the refoundation of the city in 485 B.C.E.

17. Malkin 1987: 96–97, citing contemporary parallels. Hornblower (2004: 184) also cites several parallels for the use of the title of founder in connection with a refoundation: in the fifth century, the Spartan Brasidas commandeered the title and honors of oikist from the Athenian oikist of Amphipolis, Hagnon, and was honored ὡς οἰκιστῇ (as an oikist, Thuc. 5.11.1); in the fourth century, Euphron was honored as *archēgetēs* of Sikyon (Xen. *Hell.* 7.3.12), and Timoleon of Corinth was honored as the second oikist of Syracuse (Diod. Sic. 16.90; Plut. *Timol.* 39). For the refoundation of Syracuse, see Dunbabin 1948: 416; Luraghi 1994: 288–304; Morgan 2015: 54–56.

18. Malkin 1987: 97. Munson's (2006: 264) summary of the Deinomenid perspective is also helpful here: "They [Gelon and Hieron] advertised their depopulations, refoundations and other feats of social engineering in the light of the colonisation model, even expecting, and receiving, heroic honours as oikists after their deaths." Diodorus Siculus attributes the following motive to Hieron in his founding of Aitna: τοῦτο δ' ἔπραξε σπεύδων ἅμα μὲν ἔχειν βοήθειαν... ἅμα δὲ καὶ ἐκ τῆς γενομένης μυριάνδρου πόλεως τιμὰς ἔχειν ἡρωικάς (And he did this desiring both to have substantial help at the ready for any future need and also, from the recently founded city of ten thousand men, to receive heroic honors, 11.49.2). In *Pythian 1*, Hieron is called κλεινὸς οἰκιστήρ (renowned oikist, 31) (cf. Pi. fr. 105a), while Aristophanes refers to him as κτίστωρ Αἴτνας (founder of Aitna, *Av.* 926). Similarly, Gelon is said to have received hero cult upon his death in 478 B.C.E. (Diod. Sic. 11.38.5). I adopt the term "henchmen" to describe members of Hieron's court from Morgan 2015.

And I would have come, cleaving the Ionian Sea on a ship, to Arethusa's spring and to my Aitnaian host, who keeps watch as king over Syracuse

Similarly, in *Nemean* 1, Pindar joins Aitna to Syracuse by envisioning Ortygia, the island of Syracuse, singing in honor of Zeus Aitnaios, the patron god of Aitna (1–6):[19]

Ἄμπνευμα σεμνὸν Ἀλφεοῦ,
κλεινᾶν Συρακοσσᾶν θάλος Ὀρτυγία,
δέμνιον Ἀρτέμιδος,
Δάλου κασιγνήτα, σέθεν ἁδυεπής
ὕμνος ὁρμᾶται θέμεν
αἶνον ἀελλοπόδων
    μέγαν ἵππων, Ζηνὸς Αἰτναίου χάριν·

Sacred breathing place of the Alpheios, Ortygia, offshoot of renowned Syracuse, couch of Artemis, sister of Delos, from you a sweet-voiced hymn originates to sound high praise of storm-footed horses for the sake of Zeus Aitnaios.

This geographical conflation occurs even within *Olympian* 6 itself when Hieron and Zeus Aitnaios appear in conjunction with Syracuse late in the ode (92–96):

εἶπον δὲ μεμνᾶσθαι Συρα-
    κοσσᾶν τε καὶ Ὀρτυγίας·
τὰν Ἱέρων καθαρῷ σκάπτῳ διέπων,
ἄρτια μηδόμενος, φοινικόπεζαν
ἀμφέπει Δάματρα λευκίπ-
    που τε θυγατρὸς ἑορτάν
καὶ Ζηνὸς Αἰτναίου κράτος.

Bid them call to mind Syracuse and Ortygia which Hieron administers with a pure scepter as he contrives straight counsels and attends to red-footed Demeter and the festival of her daughter of the white horses and to mighty Zeus Aitnaios.

Pindar's repeated synthesis of Syracuse and Aitna is not surprising, since Hieron was tyrant of Syracuse when he founded Aitna in 476 B.C.E. But the poet's tendency to fuse the two locations through his imagery also allows for the possibility that, in praising Hagesias as a "*sunoikistēr* of Syracuse," Pindar is calling to mind the seer's involvement in present-day Aitna as well. Hieron himself shifts easily between the two poleis.[20] As a member of the tyrant's circle, Hagesias need not be

---

19. For a more detailed discussion of this passage, see below.
20. As Neer (2007: 237) observes, "As if to literalize the elitist's claim to transcend the local community, the Deinomenids actually changed cities on more than one occasion, calling themselves Geloans, Syracusans, or Aetnans as the political situation required." For example, in *Pythian* 1.29–33, Pindar says that Hieron had himself announced as Hieron of Aitna at the Pythian games, but Bacchylides in *Ode* 4, composed for the same victory, does not connect the tyrant with Aitna, only with Syracuse.

literally bound to Syracuse alone, especially given the extent to which he is connected with Aitna elsewhere in the ode, as we will see below.

In sum, Malkin makes the case that the appellation "*sunoikistēr* of Syracuse" is consistent with the colonial obsessions of Gelon and Hieron and possibly refers to Hagesias's involvement in a Gelonian refoundation of Syracuse. Pindar's repeated merging of Syracuse and Aitna also supports understanding this title as alluding to Hieron's recent foundation of Aitna. At the same time, it is important to take seriously Hornblower's (and the scholiasts') view that "*sunoikistēr* of Syracuse" may be meant to conjure the tradition of the oikist Archias's initial expedition. In fact, the slippery quality of *sunoikistēr*, which defies scholarly attempts to assign it securely to either the shadowy past of Syracuse's original foundation or the historical, fifth-century present (and to Aitna) is part of the phrase's point.[21] "*Sunoikistēr* of Syracuse" sounds like an ancestral claim, but it is also directly applicable to Hagesias's current situation. In order to solidify a *laudandus*'s *kleos*, an epinikian poet must both commemorate his accomplishments and simultaneously contextualize them by placing them within a broader landscape of familial achievement. Pindar deploys a single phrase, "*sunoikistēr* of Syracuse," to perform this twofold obligation. Pindar's intentionally puzzling and highly allusive phrase is relevant simultaneously to his *laudandus*'s past and present. Pindar links Hagesias's position of co-oikist to the past, regardless of the reality behind the claim that earlier family members were involved in colonization. At the same time, he implicates Hagesias in the colonial agendas of Gelon and, especially, Hieron. Finally, just as the poet cites exempla for Hagesias's inherited roles as Olympic victor and *tamias* within the ode itself, so too he provides a paradigm of a former family member performing the role of cofounder: in part 3, we will see that Hagesias's ancestor Iamos, in addition to becoming the first *tamias* of Zeus's altar, also participates in the foundation of Olympia.

In *Olympian* 6's opening address, Pindar praises Hagesias as a figure who unites the talismanic potential of the athletic victor, the seer, and the oikist, all powerful positions in their own right. At the same time, Hagesias is honored for his ability to replenish his family's acquisition of *kleos* in each of these roles. This trio of titles, however, contains an internal tension in that Hagesias is called both a seer

---

21. That Pindar does not explicitly mention, but merely alludes to, Aitna and Hagesias's involvement in its foundation strongly suggests that Pindar is treading carefully here. As an anonymous reader for *Classical Antiquity* helpfully pointed out for the article version of this chapter, one reason for Pindar's caution may be that to call Hagesias an oikist of Aitna would necessarily imply that the seer also expected to receive a posthumous cult, an expectation that would, in turn, not sit well with Hieron. In the following two sections, I explore some of the other potentially threatening implications for Hieron of Pindar's attaching the title of *sunoikistēr* to Hagesias and the ways in which the poet manages this challenge.

and a cofounder. It is to this historical tension and its repercussions within the ode that I now turn.

II. HAGESIAS AS *MANTIS*

By designating Hagesias as both a seer and a *sunoikistēr*, Pindar joins together two occupations that are not typically found together before the second half of the fifth century.[22] His combination of the terms is unusual, but more striking still is that he speaks of them in a celebratory context. In chapter 3, I argued that we can detect two main reasons for the seer's general exclusion from colonial discourse and for the persistent suppression of those figures who possess *mantikē* in favor of those who become oikists. First, the oikist seems to absorb the religious authority accorded to the seer in other contexts, in part by means of the role Delphi plays in foundation tales. Second, the seer himself is often seen to pose a threat to those in positions of political power, including the oikist, when his attention is turned toward the city and not outward to the battlefield. As we will see, in *Olympian* 6, Pindar's concern appears mostly to be with the latter tension, that is, with the extent to which Hagesias presents a threat to Hieron's tyranny.

A text that brings together an oikist and a seer creates an opportunity for competition and hostility. *Olympian* 6's opening strophe, which endows Hagesias with the ill-fitting titles of seer and co-oikist, thus calls for a certain degree of epinikian delicacy. Pindar works hard within the poem to demonstrate that the seer Hagesias, despite being included in a foundation and receiving a colonial title, will not exhibit the seer's penchant for undermining authority by encroaching upon Hieron's own role as oikist of Aitna. One of the ways in which Pindar goes about mitigating Hagesias's unsettling status as a seer who participates in a foundation is by using the ode's two mythic portions to establish that Hagesias is Hieron's trusted subordinate and is without overt political ambition. In the first brief myth, Pindar co-opts the productive rapport between Amphiaraos and Adrastos on the battlefield for Hagesias and Hieron's own partnership within the polis. The second myth then formulates an even more explicit contrast between mantic and political power.

In the first triad of *Olympian* 6, Pindar compares the acclaim Hagesias will receive to Adrastos's tribute to Amphiaraos, who has just disappeared under the ground at Thebes (12–18):

---

22. As noted above, Hagesias's titles are the only reference to a historical seer's participation in a foundation before the mid-fifth century. For the involvement of seers in foundations of the later classical and Hellenistic eras, see chapter 3; the conclusion; Malkin 1987: 97–108. There are several mythical exceptions to the overall absence of seers from foundation tales. See the conclusion for Amphilochos, the son of Amphiaraos, who is credited with founding Argos Amphilochikon (Thuc. 2.68; Strabo 6.2.4) and (together with the seer Mopsos) Cilician Mallos (Lycoph. 440).

Ἁγησία, τὶν δ' αἶνος ἑτοῖμος, ὃν ἐν δίκᾳ
ἀπὸ γλώσσας Ἄδραστος μάντιν Οἰκλείδαν ποτ' ἐς Ἀμφιάρηον
φθέγξατ', ἐπεὶ κατὰ γαῖ' αὐ-
 τόν τέ νιν καὶ φαιδίμας ἵππους ἔμαρψεν.
ἑπτὰ δ' ἔπειτα πυρᾶν νε-
 κροῖς τελεσθέντων Ταλαϊονίδας
εἶπεν ἐν Θήβαισι τοιοῦτόν τι ἔπος·
 'Ποθέω στρατιᾶς ὀφθαλμὸν ἐμᾶς
ἀμφότερον μάντιν τ' ἀγαθὸν καὶ
 δουρὶ μάρνασθαι.' τὸ καί
ἀνδρὶ κώμου δεσπότᾳ πάρεστι Συρακοσίῳ.

Hagesias, the praise is ready for you that Adrastos once proclaimed from a just tongue about the seer Amphiaraos, the son of Oikles, after the earth engulfed him and his radiant horses. And later on, with the corpses of seven pyres consumed, the son of Talaos spoke a word such as this at Thebes: "I yearn for the eye of my army, good both as a seer and at fighting with the spear." This befits as well the Syracusan man, the master of the victory revel.

In chapter 3, I compared this passage to another interaction between Amphiaraos and Adrastos in *Nemean* 9 (13–14):

φεῦγε γὰρ Ἀμφιαρῆ
 ποτε θρασυμήδεα καὶ δεινὰν στάσιν
πατρίων οἴκων ἀπό τ' Ἄργεος· ἀρχοὶ
 δ' οὐκ ἔτ' ἔσαν Ταλαοῦ παῖδες, βιασθέντες λύᾳ.

For once he [Adrastos] escaped intrepid Amphiaraos and dread stasis by fleeing his ancestral home and Argos; and the children of Talaos were rulers no longer, having been overcome by civil strife.

In *Nemean* 9, Amphiaraos and Adrastos clash at home in Argos. By contrast, in *Olympian* 6, as the "eye" of the army, Amphiaraos is seen as vital to Adrastos, and the Argive leader suffers from the loss of his seer.[23] Thus, in *Olympian* 6, in the shift from mythical past to epinikian present, the poet compares Hagesias to the famous seer in a scene that calls attention to Amphiaraos's role as a warrior-*mantis* and to his alliance with Adrastos on the battlefield.[24] Pindar transfers the camaraderie

---

23. Pindar also formulates a contrast between the Amphiaraos of the polis and the Amphiaraos of the battlefield within *Nemean* 9 itself. In *Nemean* 9's version of the Seven against Thebes, Pindar focuses on Amphiaraos's divinely orchestrated disappearance beneath the earth (21–27). In so doing, the poet creates a contrast between Amphiaraos as a "terrifying and demonic fomentor of discord" at Argos (Hubbard 1992: 102) and a warrior whom Zeus personally protects from a disgraceful death on the battlefield.

24. This comparison is particularly apt if we believe a scholiast's assertion that Hagesias was Hieron's military seer and accompanied him in many battles (schol. *ad O.* 6.30c).

between a military *mantis* and his commander in war to Hagesias and Hieron's own civic collaboration: what is true for Amphiaraos and Adrastos before the walls of Thebes, Pindar says, is also true for this "man from Syracuse" (18) returning home from Olympia to Hieron.[25] Pindar thus discourages the perception of Hagesias as a potential danger to Hieron within the city and enjoins us to apply to him the model of the military seer instead. In this way, the imagined scene at Thebes begins Pindar's project of allaying the possible tension inherent in Hagesias's competing roles as seer and *sunoikistēr*. The poet then continues this effort in the new and more expansive myth that follows.[26]

The main mythic portion of *Olympian* 6 tells the story of Iamos, the progenitor of Hagesias's mantic clan. This genealogical tour de force provides our only independent source for the legend. Unlike seers such as Melampous, Amphiaraos, Mopsos, and Teiresias, who appear first in epic poetry and frequently thereafter, Iamos and the events of his "biography" can only be traced as far back as this ode.[27] Indeed, in his characterization of the seer, Pindar seems to recycle components of Melampous's own mythology and to reattribute them to Iamos.[28]

Given this correspondence between Melampous and Iamos, Michael Flower concludes that Pindar might have invented some or all of the myth of Iamos.[29] If

25. In his role as a *despotas* (18), Hagesias initially sounds like a rival to Hieron, the *despotas* of Syracuse. Yet, as elsewhere in the ode, the threat is staved off: Hagesias turns out to be merely a *despotas* of a *kōmos*. On Hagesias's *kōmos*, see below.

26. Kirkwood (1982: 80) notes that it is highly unusual for the end of the first myth to coincide with the end of the first triad, and Greengard (1980: 80–81) observes that the ode's second triad creates the impression (through the address to Phintis and a second architectural metaphor ["the gates of song"]) that the ode restarts again, as if from a new beginning. Neer and Kurke (forthcoming, chapter 5) notice that the first triad contains all or nearly all of the requirements of an epinikion (victor's name, patronymic, ethnic, site of games) and seems to form a *prooimion* of song. I would simply add that the relationship between the two myths is in keeping with these observations: the stand-alone first myth of Adrastos and Amphiaraos presents the theme of the cooperative seer that the second myth of Iamos reprises in a more fully developed, resounding way. At the same time, the two myths (Adrastos-Amphiaraos and Iamos) present mirror images of each other: the first highlighting the death of Amphiaraos, the second the birth of Iamos (see also n. 29 below).

27. Flower 2008a: 200. There are also no known artistic representations of the seer, although some scholars have wondered whether the old man on the east pediment of the temple of Zeus at Olympia is not Iamos (see *LIMC* 5.1: 614–15). This supposition, however, is based solely on *Olympian* 6.

28. As Flower (2008a: 201n44) observes, both Melampous and Iamos are given the gift of seercraft after they come upon or pray to Apollo in the Alpheios River (compare Melampous at Apollod. *Bibl.* 1.9.11 with Iamos at O. 6.57–63). Snakes also figure prominently in both stories. Hesiod (fr. 261 M-W) says that snakes licked Melampous's ears and thereby gave him the ability to prophesy. Pindar has snakes feed the infant Iamos honey at *O.* 6.45–47.

29. Flower 2008a: 201. Flower argues that the Iamidai rose to prominence only in the fifth century after Teisamenos's successful participation at Plataia. We might say that the Iamidai at this moment also replace the Melampodidai by co-opting their mythic material. This usurpation may even be registered figuratively in the relationship between the two mythic portions: as noted above, the myth

Pindar fashions, or mostly fashions, a past for the Iamidai in *Olympian* 6, we must be especially sensitive to how these invented ancestral exploits dovetail with Pindar's portrayal of Hagesias himself within the ode. What we will find is that the myth of Iamos repeatedly considers the seer's claim to political power, a claim that has implications for Hagesias's own relationship with Hieron.

At two key moments in the myth, the possibility that Iamos will become king surfaces only to be abruptly suppressed. Pindar begins his account of Iamos by traveling back two generations before the birth of the seer. Pitana, the eponymous nymph of the Spartan village, bore a daughter by Poseidon, Euadne (29–30).[30] Euadne was entrusted to Aipytos, the ruler of Arcadian Phaisana, but, like her mother, could not escape the notice of the gods. Seduced by Apollo, she gave birth to Iamos (31–41).[31] Aipytos's reaction upon discovering Euadne's pregnancy offers the first instance of the future seer's thwarted potential as a king. Pindar recounts the progression of Aipytos's emotions from outrage to relief at the birth of the child (36–51):

οὐδ' ἔλαθ' Αἴπυτον ἐν παν-
  τὶ χρόνῳ κλέπτοισα θεοῖο γόνον.
ἀλλ' ὁ μὲν Πυθῶνάδ', ἐν θυμῷ πιέσαις
  χόλον οὐ φατὸν ὀξείᾳ μελέτᾳ,
ᾤχετ' ἰὼν μαντευσόμενος ταύ-
  τας περ' ἀτλάτου πάθας. . . .

      . . . βασιλεὺς δ' ἐπεί
πετραέσσας ἐλαύνων ἵκετ' ἐκ Πυθῶνος, ἅπαντας ἐν οἴκῳ
εἴρετο παῖδα, τὸν Εὐά-
  δνα τέκοι· Φοίβου γὰρ αὐτὸν φᾶ γεγάκειν
πατρός, περὶ θνατῶν δ' ἔσεσθαι μάντιν ἐπιχθονίοις
ἔξοχον, οὐδέ ποτ' ἐκλείψειν γενεάν.

Nor did she [Euadne] in the end keep hidden from Aipytos the offspring of the god. But he went to Pytho, suppressing unutterable anger in his heart with keen resolve, to consult the oracle about that unbearable misfortune. . . . But when the king, driving from rugged Pytho, returned, he asked everyone in the house about the child whom Euadne bore; for he said that his father was Phoibos and that he would become for mankind a seer supreme among mortals and that his race would never fail.

Aipytos's initial hostility conforms to the traditional story pattern of the ruler whose fear of being supplanted causes him to view an unforeseen newcomer (often

---

of the Melampodid Amphiaraos focuses on his death at Thebes, while the second myth emphasizes the birth of the first Iamid seer.

30. On the Iamid seer Teisamenos's connection with the Spartan village of Pitana as the reason why Pindar features the nymph Pitana in this myth, see Flower 2008a: 201.

31. On the multiple etymologies of Iamos's name and their significance, see Segal 1998: 118–19.

a younger male relative) as an adversary.[32] Pindar activates this established storyline, however, only to curtail its expected narrative trajectory and take his tale in a different direction.[33] The "unutterable anger" that Iamos's birth initially elicits in Aipytos is, by the end of the epode, transformed. The king returns from consulting Delphi about the "unbearable misfortune" with the surprising announcement that Euadne's son will be a renowned seer. He thereupon proceeds to search for the whereabouts of the child whom he now prizes. This marked reversal in Aipytos's behavior can only mean that he believes that his throne is no longer in jeopardy. In this passage, then, Pindar appears to set Iamos on a path toward kingship only to cut short this option soon after. He lures his audience into expecting a certain outcome: like Aipytos at the birth of Iamos, we anticipate the child's eventual seizure of his grandfather's throne. Aipytos's own relief instructs us to interpret the oracle that Iamos is to become a seer as evidence that he no longer poses a threat to the king.

The second instance of Pindar's suppression of the seer's claim to kingship comes in Iamos's own realization of his intended fate. As the myth's opening genealogy establishes, Iamos is twice descended from the gods and can boast of possessing both Apollo and Poseidon as his forebears. Fittingly, as soon as he comes of age, Iamos turns to this pair for guidance and is subsequently led by Apollo to Olympia (57–70):

τερ-
πνᾶς δ' ἐπεὶ χρυσοστεφάνοιο λάβεν
καρπὸν Ἥβας, Ἀλφεῷ μέσσῳ καταβαὶς
   ἐκάλεσσε Ποσειδᾶν' εὐρυβίαν,
ὃν πρόγονον, καὶ τοξοφόρον Δάλου θεοδμάτας σκοπόν,
αἰτέων λαοτρόφον τιμάν τιν' ἑᾷ κεφαλᾷ,
νυκτὸς ὑπαίθριος. ἀντεφθέγξατο δ' ἀρτιεπὴς
πατρία ὄσσα, μετάλλασέν τέ νιν· Ὄρσο, τέκνον,
δεῦρο πάγκοινον ἐς χώ-
   ραν ἴμεν φάμας ὄπισθεν.'

ἵκοντο δ' ὑψηλοῖο πέ-
   τραν ἀλίβατον Κρονίου
ἔνθα οἱ ὤπασε θησαυρὸν δίδυμον
μαντοσύνας, τόκα μὲν φωνὰν ἀκούειν
ψευδέων ἄγνωτον, εὖτ' ἂν
   δὲ θρασυμάχανος ἐλθὼν
Ἡρακλέης, σεμνὸν θάλος Ἀλκαϊδᾶν, πατρί
ἑορτάν τε κτίσῃ πλειστόμβροτον τε-

---

32. Stern 1970: 333; Goldhill 1991: 152–53.

33. Stern (1970: 333) and Goldhill (1991: 152–53) both point out that Pindar aborts this traditional narrative arc but do not discuss the implications of this tactic.

θυμόν τε μέγιστον ἀέθλων,
Ζηνὸς ἐπ' ἀκροτάτῳ βω-
μῷ τότ' αὖ χρηστήριον θέσθαι κέλευσεν.

And after he took the fruit of pleasant golden-crowned Hebe, descending into the middle of the Alpheios, he called upon his ancestor Poseidon whose power extends far and wide and upon the bow-bearing watcher of god-built Delos, asking for himself, in the open air of night, for some honor of rearing a people.[34] And the clear-speaking prophetic voice of his father answered and sought him out: "Rise up and come this way, child, following my voice, to the place that is open to all. And they came to the steep rock of Kronos's high hill where he bestowed on him a double treasury of seercraft, to hear at that time the voice ignorant of lies, and whenever Herakles, bold and resourceful, revered offshoot of the Alkaidai, came and founded for his father a festival crowded with people and the greatest institution of contests, at that time in turn he ordered him to establish an oracular seat on the highest altar of Zeus.

First, we might observe that although Iamos calls upon both his immortal father and grandfather as he wades into the Alpheios, only Apollo answers the youth. Poseidon remains silent and unresponsive to Iamos's prayer and is never heard from again in the myth.[35] Let us simply note Poseidon's reticence for now. Its significance will become clearer below in part 3 when this moment is compared to a passage in *Olympian* 1. Second, the ambiguous nature of Iamos's request in asking for λαοτρόφον τιμάν τιν' (some honor of rearing a people, 60) suggests that what Iamos seeks to obtain with the help of his divine forefathers is kingship, perhaps even Aipytos's own throne. Yet, when Apollo answers his son, he grants him something else entirely. In place of sovereignty, Apollo bestows on Iamos a "double treasury of seercraft." Pindar's maneuver here is similar to his orchestration of the earlier scene concerning Aipytos and the birth of Iamos. Once again, the poet initially raises the specter of Iamos's becoming king only to withdraw this opportunity and, simultaneously, to call attention to Apollo's different gift of *mantosunē* (seercraft).

As the myth of Iamos unfolds, the seer emerges as the counterexample of a figure bent on seizing power, the antithesis to *Nemean* 9's Amphiaraos, who expels Adrastos from Argos. Although Pindar may appropriate elements of Melampodid mythology for the Iamidai, he also departs from that established mantic mode of behavior. That is to say, his Iamidai neither incite stasis nor seize power, as certain

---

34. "The honour of rearing a people" is Farnell's (1932: 45) translation. Slater (1969 ad loc.) translates λαοτρόφον as "consisting in care of the people."

35. I owe this observation to Leslie Kurke. *Contra* Segal (1998: 118), who writes of this scene that "both divine father-figures, Poseidon and Apollo, are present to usher him into the realm of masculine success, achievement, and honor."

mythical Melampodidai were famously known for doing.[36] In *Olympian* 6, Pindar instead positions mantic and political forms of authority as mutually exclusive undertakings in which the presence of the former does not imperil the latter. He suggests that the Iamidai, beginning with their progenitor Iamos and extending by implication to their latest member Hagesias, are not interested in political upheaval. They only pursue and are destined for *mantosunē*. I wish now to return to the politically loaded term *sunoikistēr* that Pindar applies to this purportedly apolitical Iamid and to consider the impetus that propels the poet to go to such lengths to accommodate the incongruous roles of seer and *sunoikistēr*.

III. HAGESIAS AS *SUNOIKISTĒR*

It is not immediately evident why Pindar should desire to praise Hagesias by applying to him a title that is culturally at odds with his position as seer and that subsequently forces him to account for the pairing of these terms throughout the rest of the ode. I would contend that the seer is called a *sunoikistēr*, despite the resulting risk this claim seems to pose for Hieron, in part because Hagesias both embodies and metaphorically enacts the tyrant's synoikism of Aitna. As we will see, Hagesias is cast as one who possesses the ability to unite the Peloponnese with Aitna. Since Pindar also carefully establishes that Hagesias will not undermine Hieron, the poet can present Hagesias as a figure who is in the service of the tyrant and, what is more, is a profoundly appropriate collaborator for his colonial project.

The main mythic portion of *Olympian* 6 is again paradigmatic for the contours of Hagesias's own characterization in the ode. Before turning to Hagesias himself, I will first offer an intertextual reading of the myth of Iamos and the myth of Pelops in *Olympian* 1.[37] This intertextual juxtaposition makes clear that Iamos provides a model for Hagesias not only as a seer who is without political ambition more generally (and so can perform the role of a trustworthy subordinate within the polis setting) but also as a desirable ally in a foundation. For part of the epinikion's way of asserting that Hagesias can contribute to a foundation is to claim that his ancestor has already successfully performed this task. I then take up Pindar's depiction of Hagesias himself. Hagesias's idiosyncratic representation as a Syracusan who is nevertheless rooted in the Peloponnese seems to align closely with Hieron's designs for Aitna's new population. Finally, a second intertexual reading of *Olympian* 6

---

36. In addition to Amphiaraos's characterization in *Nemean* 9, Melampous presents a threat to the automony of Proitos of Argos, as chapter 4 discussed. Recall also that the Melampodid Theoklymenos, discussed in chapter 2, was on the run for murdering a man and causing stasis in Argos.

37. I thank G. B. D'Alessio for alerting me to the idea that the story of Iamos is engaged in a dialogue with the mythic portion of *Olympian* 1. Morrison (2007: 76, citing Kirkwood 1982: 90 and Carey 1993: 106–7) notes that *O.* 6.58–63 and *O.*1.71–87 are similar scenes.

with *Nemean* 1 helps us to see how Hagesias symbolically performs his role of *sunoikistēr* within *Olympian* 6 through the image of the *kōmos* (victory revel) he leads "from home to home" (99).

Whether *Olympian* 6 was composed in 472 or 468, it follows *Olympian* 1's own performance date of 476, and we can therefore speak of Hagesias's ode as possessing an intertexual awareness of Hieron's.[38] Like *Olympian* 6, *Olympian* 1 contains an entreaty to Poseidon. Pelops, Poseidon's beloved, appeals to the god for help in winning Oinomaos's deadly chariot race and the hand of Hippodameia (67–87):

πρὸς εὐάνθεμον δ' ὅτε φυάν
λάχναι νιν μέλαν γένειον ἔρεφον,
ἑτοῖμον ἀνεφρόντισεν γάμον
Πισάτα παρὰ πατρὸς εὔδοξον Ἱπποδάμειαν
σχεθέμεν. ἐγγὺς {δ'} ἐλθὼν πολιᾶς ἁλὸς οἶος ἐν ὄρφνᾳ
ἄπυεν βαρύκτυπον
Εὐτρίαιναν· ὁ δ' αὐτῷ
πὰρ ποδὶ σχεδὸν φάνη.
τῷ μὲν εἶπε· 'Φίλια δῶρα Κυπρίας
   ἄγ' εἴ τι, Ποσείδαον, ἐς χάριν
τέλλεται, πέδασον ἔγχος Οἰνομάου χάλκεον,
ἐμὲ δ' ἐπὶ ταχυτάτων πόρευσον ἁρμάτων
ἐς Ἆλιν, κράτει δὲ πέλασον.
ἐπεὶ τρεῖς τε καὶ δέκ' ἄνδρας ὀλέσαις
μναστῆρας ἀναβάλλεται γάμον
θυγατρός. . . .
            ἀλλ' ἐμοὶ
   μὲν οὗτος ἄεθλος
ὑποκείσεται· τὺ δὲ πρᾶξιν φίλαν δίδοι.'
ὣς ἔννεπεν· οὐδ' ἀκράντοις ἐφάψατο
ἔπεσι. τὸν μὲν ἀγάλλων θεός
ἔδωκεν δίφρον τε χρύσεον πτεροῖ-
   σίν τ' ἀκάμαντας ἵππους.

And toward the blooming age of youth when soft hair began to darken his cheek, he contemplated a marriage that was ready at hand: to take renowned Hippodameia from her Pisan father. And going alone to the gray sea in the darkness of night he was calling upon the loud-thundering Trident-Bearer, who appeared to him, right at his feet. He said to him, "Come! If the lovely gifts of Kypris count at all in my favor, shackle the bronze spear of Oinomaos and convey me upon the swiftest of chariots to Elis and bring power within my reach. Since, having killed thirteen suitors, he

---

38. Most Pindarists accept the date of 476 for *Olympian* 1, and *P. Oxy.* 222 lists a victory for Hieron in the horse race for that year (see Morrison 2007: 57n117).

postpones the marriage of his daughter.... For my part, that contest lies before me; but you, grant me lovely achievement." Thus he spoke, nor did he touch on unfulfilled words. The god honored him and granted him a golden chariot and tireless, winged horses.

Pelops by the sea recalls Iamos at the Alpheios River. In both scenes, the suppliant, upon reaching manhood, goes alone to a body of water at night to petition Poseidon (Pelops) or Poseidon and Apollo (Iamos). Yet the parallel scenes also exhibit a striking difference. In contrast to Iamos's request, Pelops's appeal is heard by the god, who provides him straightaway with a golden chariot and magic horses. Pelops will go on to use these horses to win not only Hippodameia's hand in marriage but also Oinomaos's throne.[39] Whereas Poseidon offers Pelops a means of acquiring kingship, in ignoring Iamos, he takes no steps to grant the seer-to-be this same privilege. Juxtaposing the two scenes in this way corroborates the conclusion reached in part 2, namely, that Iamos becomes a seer specifically instead of becoming a king.[40] Because Iamos operates as a paradigm for Hagesias, this intertextual reading thus throws into greater relief Hagesias's own portrayal as a seer who does not threaten Hieron's regime.

The points of contact between the myths of *Olympian* 1 and *Olympian* 6 also assist us in viewing Iamos as a seer who cooperates specifically in an act of foundation. After their nocturnal invocations, both Pelops and Iamos travel to Olympia. In *Olympian* 1, Pindar identifies the Panhellenic sanctuary as "the *apoikia* [settlement] of Lydian Pelops" (24). According to Lucia Athanassaki, the poet here designates Olympia as an *apoikia* and, by implication, Pelops as its founding hero in order to evoke Aitna and Hieron, respectively.[41] By rendering the peaceful and divinely sanctioned founding of Olympia as a mythological predecessor for Hieron's colonial enterprise, Pindar glosses over the tyrant's reportedly brutal program of forced relocation back in Sicily.[42] I would suggest that, in addition to the Peloponnese's characterization as an *apoikia*, the myth's account of the hero's abduction by Poseidon (*O.* 1.40–45), which the poet conspicuously privileges in the epinikion over a competing version of the myth of Pelops, brings to mind the foundation of

---

39. As Nagy (1986: 84) observes, Pelops's horses lead directly to political power: "It is with this chariot-team that Pelops wins his race against Oinomaos and the hand of Hippodameia, thereby inaugurating a kingship that serves as a foundation for the royal Peloponnesian dynasties of Argos, Sparta, and Messene."

40. For the audience of *Olympian* 6, some of whose members (including Hieron himself) were likely also present at the performance of *Olympian* 1, there was perhaps a real expectation that Poseidon would answer Iamos. Poseidon's silence in *Olympian* 6 may have formed a strikingly pointed and specific contrast to his response to Pelops in *Olympian* 1's analogous scene. See Morrison (2007: 64) for the ways in which the Pelops-Poseidon scene in *Olympian* 1 is already a moment of great suspense.

41. Athanassaki 2003: 121.

42. On the violent nature of Hieron's colonial program, see Diod. Sic. 11.49; Asheri 1992.

Aitna.[43] For vase paintings reveal that the foundation of Aitna was rendered mythologically as an abduction as well.[44] One vase in particular, a neck amphora from Paestum dated to 330–10 B.C.E., captures the critical scene: Zeus in the form of an eagle snatches the nymph Thalia up from the ground, clutching her by the waist with his talons.[45] Other sources report that the subsequent rape of this local nymph Thalia produced the region of Aitna.[46]

The close parallels between the scenes of Pelops and Iamos, in which the youths both invoke Poseidon (and, for Iamos, also Apollo) and subsequently travel to Olympia, encourage us to associate the Panhellenic sanctuary in *Olympian* 6 with Pindar's designation of Olympia as Pelops's *apoikia* in *Olympian* 1. Apollo escorts Iamos to Olympia with the promise that he will receive a "double treasury of seercraft," namely, the ability to hear "the voice ignorant of lies" and, when Herakles comes to found the games, the right "to establish an oracular seat on the highest altar of Zeus" (64–70). In this way, Pindar portrays Olympia as a cofoundation: Apollo instructs Iamos to establish (θέσθαι, 70) an oracle when Herakles founds (κτίσῃ, 69) the festival and games.[47] This collaboration shows the seer peacefully lending Herakles a hand in the creation of Pelops's sanctuary. In so doing, it provides us with the model for how we are meant to imagine Hagesias assisting in Hieron's foundation of Aitna. Just as Pelops and Olympia correspond to Hieron and Aitna, respectively, in *Olympian* 1, so too does *Olympian* 6's Iamos at Olympia have a counterpart in the *sunoikistēr* Hagesias.

In the myth of Iamos, Pindar creates a means for Hagesias to register symbolically his subordination to Hieron in a colonial context. Pindar grants Hagesias the com-

---

43. In the myth of *Olympian* 1, the poet rejects the story of the gods' dismembering and devouring of Pelops and replaces it with an account of how Poseidon, falling in love with the youth, whisked him away to Mt. Olympos. For one interpretation of the significance of these two myths and their incorporation in the ode, see Nagy 1986. See also Köhnken 1974; Krummen 1990: 168–211. See Athanassaki (2003: 121–22) for the intriguing possibility that Pindar used the foundation tale of Syracuse as a template for the abduction of Pelops. If Athanassaki is correct, this would mean that Pindar evokes the foundation tales of both Aitna and Syracuse in the myth of *Olympian* 1.

44. Marriage, abduction, and rape are motifs of Greek colonial discourse. For discussion and further examples of this motif, see Dougherty 1993: 61–80.

45. For this vase, see Kossatz-Deissmann 1978: 36–37; Dougherty 1993: 85–86.

46. See Kossatz-Deissmann 1978: 33–44.

47. The founding of games at Olympia may be especially pertinent to Aitna, since, according to the scholiasts, Hieron established athletic contests, the so-called Aitnaia, to mark the occasion of the city's founding (schol. *ad O.* 6.86). We might also note here that Apollo, and specifically Delphic Apollo, aids Iamos twice in this mythic portion (Delphic Apollo reveals the identity of Iamos to Aipytos; Apollo leads Iamos to Olympia). Delphic Apollo's assistance of a seer involved in a foundation is thus another striking moment in *Olympian* 6 and stands in contrast to the model of colonial discourse discussed in chapter 3 and the seers discussed in chapter 6. In *Olympian* 6, Apollo's approval and support of Iamos, and by extension Hagesias, further mitigates the seers' potential danger in their respective colonial contexts. At the same time, Delphi plays a minor role in the ode, as if content to stand mostly offstage while the seer assumes the spotlight.

bined talismanic authority of the seer and *sunoikistēr* but, by analogy with Iamos, simultaneously suggests that his position as cofounder will be shaped by his position as a seer—that is, just as Iamos's participation at Olympia is to found the mantic altar of Zeus, so Hagesias's participation in a foundation will be defined in religious, and not political, terms.[48] Yet, although Iamos may prove that the seer-as-*sunoikistēr* is a possible construct, we are still left wondering why Pindar should seek to accord Hagesias this position at all. I will consider this question now by turning to Hagesias's connections with both Sicily and the Peloponnese and exploring how Pindar makes the seer's ties to these multiple locations crucial for his distinctive relationship with Hieron. As part of this endeavor, I will discuss the way in which the two metaphors that frame the ode contribute to Hagesias's idiosyncratic characterization.

Hagesias's ability to claim the title of *tamias* of Olympia's mantic altar brought with it significant cultural capital.[49] Moreover, throughout *Olympian* 6 Pindar emphasizes that Hagesias has roots in the Greek mainland that stretch beyond the Panhellenic sanctuary. Pindar not only traces the Iamid clan back to Arcadian Phaisana and Sparta in the myth of Iamos but also dedicates an epode to the seer's maternal relatives in Stymphalos, yet another polis in the Peloponnese (77–81). He may be called a Syracusan man (ἀνδρὶ Συρακοσίῳ, 18), but Hagesias's Peloponnesian origins are also firmly established in the ode. This sense of belonging to two places at once is encapsulated in the image of the seer's *kōmos* moving from home to home (92–100):

εἶπον δὲ μεμνᾶσθαι Συρα-
κοσσᾶν τε καὶ Ὀρτυγίας·

---

48. In addition to Iamos's characterization in the ode's mythic paradigm, another major way in which Pindar registers Hagesias's subordination to Hieron is through the seer's choice of athletic event, namely, mule-cart racing. As Nicholson (2005: 82–94) shows, Hagesias's participation in the mule-cart race and Pindar's conspicuous treatment of this event within the ode foreground Hagesias's secondary position to Hieron. Griffith's (2006) work on the disputed meaning of mules within the Greek cultural imaginary directs us to another way in which Pindar exploits Hagesias's connection with these hybrid equids (insofar as a mule is the offspring of a horse and a donkey) throughout the ode (see esp. 336–55). Griffith demonstrates that the mule exhibits a kind of double nature: on the one hand, the animal can be characterized as a dependable, trusty comrade; on the other, it can be deployed as a metaphor for figures of mixed race or dubious origin and status who threaten political upheaval (see, e.g., Herodotus's depiction of Kyros in 1.55 with Griffith 342). I would contend that Pindar activates and closely aligns Hagesias with the cultural ambiguity of the mule as part of his larger endeavor both to point toward Hagesias's own potential ability to unseat Hieron and, ultimately, to cast the seer as the tyrant's reliable lieutenant. See also Griffith (341n101) for how Pindar constructs a close connection between the seer and his mules by means of a pun on Hagesias's own name.

49. In lieu of establishing Panhellenic or even regional Pansikeliote ritual centers of their own, the Western Greek elite focused on the mainland arenas of Delphi and Olympia. For the relationship between Magna Graecia and Delphi and Olympia, see, e.g., Morgan 1993; Philipp 1994; Bell 1995; Antonaccio 2007; Neer 2007; Morgan 2015; Nicholson 2016; Neer and Kurke, forthcoming.

τὰν Ἱέρων καθαρῷ σκάπτῳ διέπων,
ἄρτια μηδόμενος, φοινικόπεζαν
ἀμφέπει Δάματρα λευκίπ-
   που τε θυγατρὸς ἑορτάν
καὶ Ζηνὸς Αἰτναίου κράτος. ἀδύλογοι δέ νιν
λύραι μολπαί τε γινώσκοντι. μὴ θράσ-
   σοι χρόνος ὄλβον ἐφέρπων,
σὺν δὲ φιλοφροσύναις εὐ-
   ηράτοις Ἁγησία δέξαιτο κῶμον
οἴκοθεν οἴκαδ' ἀπὸ Στυμ-
   φαλίων τειχέων ποτινισόμενον,
ματέρ' εὐμήλοιο λείποντ' Ἀρκαδίας.

Bid them call to mind Syracuse and Ortygia, which Hieron administers with a pure scepter as he contrives straight counsels and attends to red-footed Demeter and the festival of her daughter of the white horses and to mighty Zeus Aitnaios. Sweetly speaking lyres and songs know him. May time not steal up and shatter his happiness, but with lovely acts of friendship may he receive the victory revel of Hagesias as it comes from home to home, leaving the walls of Stymphalos, the mother of Arcadia, rich in flocks.

Pindar's emphasis on Hagesias's ties to both the Peloponnese and Sicily accords well with Hieron's plans for stocking the recently founded Aitna with Dorian settlers. In his account of the foundation, Diodorus Siculus states that Hieron had specific ideas about who was to live in his city (11.49.1):

Ἱέρων δὲ τούς τε Ναξίους καὶ τοὺς Καταναίους ἐκ τῶν πόλεων ἀναστήσας, ἰδίους οἰκήτορας ἀπέστειλεν, ἐκ μὲν Πελοποννήσου πεντακισχιλίους ἀθροίσας, ἐκ δὲ Συρακουσῶν ἄλλους τοσούτους προσθείς· καὶ τὴν μὲν Κατάνην μετωνόμασεν Αἴτνην.

Hieron removed the Naxians and Katanians from their cities and dispatched there his own personal settlers, having collected five thousand from the Peloponnese and having added just as many others from Syracuse. And he changed the name of Katana to Aitna.

According to Diodorus, Hieron sought a Dorian polis composed of Peloponnesians and Syracusans in equal number.[50] Mercenaries and citizens from Syracuse, along with mercenaries from the Peloponnese, perhaps particularly from Arcadia, were recruited to settle the new city.[51] The hybridity of Hagesias, a Syracusan man

---

50. For the foundation of Aitna, see Luraghi 1994: 335–46; Bonanno 2010: 127–39. In Burton's (1962: 91) words, Pindar "sees the foundation of Etna as the establishment of a fresh outpost of the Dorian way of life."

51. Bonanno 2010: 136.

who was also from Arcadian Stymphalos and Olympia, is thus the individual articulation of that ambitious synoikism.[52]

Hagesias's ability to embody Hieron's synoikism and the importance Pindar places on this ability, even as it forces him to finesse his pairing of the contradictory roles of seer and *sunoikistēr*, also elucidate the two prominent metaphors that bookend the ode. These metaphors, ostensibly incongruous, in fact brilliantly intersect in the way in which they both capture precisely this critical component of Hagesias's character, his spatial hybridity. *Olympian* 6 begins by enjoining its audience to assemble a figurative edifice (1–7):

Χρυσέας ὑποστάσαντες εὐ-
　　τειχεῖ προθύρῳ θαλάμου
κίονας ὡς ὅτε θαητὸν μέγαρον
πάξομεν· ἀρχομένου δ' ἔργου πρόσωπον
χρὴ θέμεν τηλαυγές. εἰ δ' εἴ-
　　η μὲν Ὀλυμπιονίκας,
βωμῷ τε μαντείῳ ταμίας Διὸς ἐν Πίσᾳ,
συνοικιστὴρ τε τᾶν κλεινᾶν Συρακοσ-
　　σᾶν, τίνα κεν φύγοι ὕμνον
κεῖνος ἀνήρ, ἐπικύρσαις
　　ἀφθόνων ἀστῶν ἐν ἱμερταῖς ἀοιδαῖς;

Setting golden columns beneath the strong-walled porch of a storeroom as when we build a splendid hall, let us build. For at the beginning of our work it is necessary to make the façade radiant from afar. If he should be an Olympic victor, and a steward of the mantic altar of Zeus in Pisa, and a cofounder of renowned Syracuse, what hymn could that man escape, as he meets with ungrudging townsmen amid lovely songs?

In typical fashion, Pindar concretizes the experience of song making by depicting it as the creation of a physical structure, but the exact nature of this structure has proved difficult to identify in these compressed and elliptical opening lines.[53] Scholars have proposed a range of options, including a palace, a house, a temple, or a treasury.

Anna Bonifazi and Kathryn Morgan, resisting such specificity, argue that the conjured structure is purposefully ambiguous.[54] The vagueness of the image, as Morgan notes, allows it to be associated with a number of different buildings

---

52. Hubbard (1992: 80) posits that the recruitment of settlers for Aitna may have continued after the city's official foundation date of 476. If Aitna's synoikism were still taking place when *Olympian* 6 was first performed, it would have endowed Hagesias's characterization as the embodiment of the unification of Dorian Sicily and the Peloponnese with an even greater relevance for the audience of the ode.

53. See Steiner 1993 for how Pindar deploys images of victory monuments (including stelai and statues) to articulate the work he claims his poetry performs.

54. Bonifazi 2001: 104–12; Morgan 2015: 402–4.

simultaneously.⁵⁵ This kind of ambiguity is in keeping with other moments of intentional imprecision in the ode, including the blurring of spatial boundaries between Aitna and Syracuse in connection with the title of *sunoikister* noted above. Without discounting this reading, I also call attention to a new interpretation by Richard Neer and Leslie Kurke.⁵⁶ *Olympian 6*'s opening strophe refers to a *thalamos* with a well-built porch (1) and the ash altar of Zeus at Olympia (βωμῷ μαντείῳ, 5). As Neer and Kurke point out, the combination of *thalamos* and Olympia calls to mind a treasure-house, of the type found in relative abundance in the Altis. One stumbling block for this argument appears to be that treasuries do not have porches with multiple columns as the structure described in *Olympian 6* does. Yet, as Neer and Kurke show, there is one—and *only* one—treasury that did have such a configuration at the time of *Olympian 6*'s performance: the Treasury of Gela, whose hexastyle prostyle porch stood out prominently from the rest of the surrounding treasuries at Olympia.⁵⁷ The contours of *Olympian 6*'s opening structure may metamorphose, as Bonifazi and Morgan suggest, calling to mind other buildings as the poem progresses and as the performance venue of the ode itself changes.⁵⁸ Yet we should also understand the opening image as powerfully conjuring at the outset the Deinomenid Treasury of Gela as its material counterpart.⁵⁹

This interpretation finds a close parallel in *Pythian 6*, whose initial strophe declares that a "treasure-house of hymns has been built" for its victor (ὕμνων θησαυρὸς ... / τετείχισται, 7–9). As in Hagesias's ode, *Pythian 6*'s *thēsauros*, too, has a *prosōpon* (façade) (14). More important, the image of a *thēsauros* appears in *Olympian 6*'s own mythic portion when Pindar describes Apollo's gift to Iamos as a "double treasury of prophecy" (θησαυρὸν δίδυμον / μαντοσύνας, 65–66).⁶⁰ By

---

55. See Morgan 2015: 403 for the possible buildings evoked.
56. Neer and Kurke, forthcoming, chapter 5.
57. For the dating of the porch, see Neer and Kurke, forthcoming (chapter 5 and appendix on the dating of the Geloan porch).
58. For the multiple performance venues of *Olympian 6*, see esp. Morrison 2007: 71–79 (on the location of the ode's first performance); Stamatopoulou 2014.
59. Of the other architectural elements enumerated, all can be components of treasuries (columns, storeroom, and façade [*prosōpon*]), and *thalamos* is the name given to the storeroom of a treasury. See, e.g., Paus. 6.19: ἐν δὲ τῷ θησαυρῷ καὶ θαλάμους δύο ἐποίησε, τὸν μὲν Δώριον, τὸν δὲ ἐργασίας τῆς Ἰώνων (And in this treasury, he made two storerooms, one Dorian, the other Ionic). Hutchinson (2001: 376), who sees θαλάμου as referring to the room of a house, suggests that the word be changed to the plural θαλάμων because "one should not have a προθύρον [porch] to only a room or part of a house, and this one is to be a πρόσωπον ... τηλαυγές [radiant façade]." He also points out that the plural "rooms, halls" can be used to signify a house, but not the singular (i.e., θαλάμου cannot mean "rooms"). The word θαλάμος usually denotes the inner room of a house (LSJ s.v. θαλάμος). These issues are resolved if we understand the word to mean the storeroom of a treasury and not an (inner) room of a house.
60. For the importance of the image of the *thēsauros* in Pindar's poetics, see Kurke 1991: 156–58, 189–90; Steiner 1993. On the architecture of treasuries in general, see Partida 2000. On the politics of treasuries, see Neer 2001, 2003, and 2007.

associating both Hagesias and Iamos with a metaphorical *thēsauros* in this way, Pindar establishes another link between the victor and his ancestral exemplum.[61]

Pindar's choice of metaphor becomes clear once we understand the symbolic work that actual treasuries performed at Panhellenic sanctuaries. As Neer perceives,

> [A] treasury's purpose is not just to store votives but to nationalize them, and with them a dedicant's privileged relationship to the gods. When placed on view in a treasury, the individual dedication—say, a golden bowl—is recontextualized: it still reflects well on its dedicant, to be sure, but it also glorifies the polis.... A *thēsauros* is not just a storeroom: it is a frame for costly dedications, a way of diverting elite display in the interest of the city-state.[62]

Hagesias's "privileged relationship to the gods" is "nationalized" and shared with Hieron and his fellow Syracusans through the way in which Pindar enshrines Hagesias's talismanic titles in a treasury of song. With this one image, he straightaway assures his audience that the seer will not hoard his talismanic power but will readily share it with the tyrant's city. This assurance is then confirmed through litotes: none of his fellow citizens will begrudge him praise for these achievements ("what hymn could that man escape, as he meets with ungrudging townsmen amid lovely songs?" 7)

The metaphor of the treasury captures an essential aspect of Hagesias's idiosyncratic character. Observing how Greek poleis went to great lengths to build treasuries at Delphi and Olympia out of native stone hauled all the way from home, Neer concludes, "The treasury ... is a little bit of the polis in the heart of a Panhellenic sanctuary, so that when it is placed in a treasury a dedication never really leaves home at all."[63] A treasury, that is, has the unique capacity to be in two places at once. It is physically located in a distant sanctuary, but it also (symbolically) transports the votives that enter it back to the home polis. This feature of the *thēsauros* helps to explain its occurrence in *Olympian 6*. After all, Pindar's characterization of the seer represents Hagesias in exactly this way, as someone who belongs in both Olympia and Syracuse at the same time (cf. οἴκοθεν οἴκαδ', 99). Pindar asks his audience to envision the construction of a *thēsauros* because it is a profoundly appropriate image for Hagesias.

---

61. Scholars have long understood Hagesias's titles as forming the figurative pillars of this structure. See, e.g., Gildersleeve 1890: ad loc.; Luraghi 1997: 74. Alternatively, these titles may be equivalent to inscriptions written on the façades of treasuries that announce the victor and his victory (since they appear at the beginning, the "façade," of the ode). This possibility merits attention because the list of Hagesias's titles follows upon Pindar's reference to the building's *prosōpon*. Cf. *P.* 6.15 (with Steiner 1993: 170) where the metaphorical façade of the "treasure house of hymns" proclaims Thrasyboulos's victory in the chariot race.

62. Neer 2003: 129.

63. Neer 2003: 129.

Olympian 6 opens with the building of a treasury but ends at sea aboard a ship with two anchors (101-5):

ἀγαθαὶ δὲ πέλοντ' ἐν χειμερίᾳ
νυκτὶ θοᾶς ἐκ ναὸς ἀπεσκίμ-
   φθαι δύ' ἄγκυραι. θεός
τῶνδε κείνων τε κλυτὰν αἶσαν παρέχοι φιλέων.
δέσποτα ποντόμεδον, εὐθὺν δὲ πλόον καμάτων
ἐκτὸς ἐόντα δίδοι, χρυσαλακάτοιο πόσις
   Ἀμφιτρίτας, ἐμῶν δ' ὕ-
   μνων ἄεξ' εὐτερπὲς ἄνθος.

On a winter's night, it is good to have two anchors to drop down from a swift ship. May a god out of love furnish a glorious fortune for these men and for those. Master of the sea, grant a straight voyage free from troubles, and, husband of Amphitrite of the golden distaff, cause the lovely blossom of my hymns to flower.

The two anchors represent the two homes, Syracuse and Stymphalos, between which Hagesias travels.[64] This final reference to a ship recalls the initial image of the treasury. For, like the treasury, the double-anchored vessel captures in metaphorical terms Hagesias's ability to straddle two distinct locations, to belong simultaneously in Sicily and in the Peloponnese, and to be able to travel paradoxically "from home to home" (99).

Beyond embodying Hieron's fantasy for Aitna in the way I have traced above, Hagesias also symbolically enacts this synoikism in *Olympian* 6. Hagesias's *kōmos*, which appears late in the ode, leads a group of revelers from Peloponnesian Stymphalos to Sicily and, in so doing, takes the form of a colonial expedition. In this respect, Hagesias's *kōmos* fulfills a similar function to that of *Nemean* 9, which declares in its opening lines, Κωμάσομεν παρ' Ἀπόλλωνος Σικυωνόθε, Μοῖσαι, / τὰν νεοκτίσταν ἐς Αἴτναν (Let us proceed in a victory revel from Apollo at Sicyon, Muses, to newly founded Aitna, *N.* 9.1-2). *Nemean* 9 commemorates a victory in the Sicyonian games of another Deinomenid henchman, Chromios, the governor (*epitropos*) of Aitna.[65] As Thomas Hubbard notes, *Nemean* 9's *kōmos* both mimics the path of Peloponnesian settlers to the new Sicilian city and depicts this westward

---

64. On the metaphor of the double anchor, see Norwood 1945: 129; Goldhill 1991: 164; Hubbard 1992: 80n7; Hutchinson 2001: 422; Hornblower 2004: 85. I follow Hubbard, Hutchinson, and Hornblower in taking the anchors to represent Hagesias's two homes. The two pairings of Stymphalos and Syracuse in the same epode as the ship reinforce our understanding of the two anchors as signifying these two locations: the poet hopes that Hagesias's *kōmos* may be welcomed home to Syracuse from his home in Stymphalos (97-100) and utters a wish "for these men and for those," meaning the Syracusans and Stymphalians (101-2).

65. For another comparison between *Olympian* 6 and *Nemean* 9, see Morgan 2015: 390-412. For *Nemean* 9, see esp. Hubbard 1992; Braswell 1998.

revel (and therefore the relocation of actual settlers it evokes) as a celebratory event. For Hubbard, this characterization of the *kōmos* is part of the way in which *Nemean* 9 serves as an "advertisement" for Aitna and a justification for Hieron's course of action vis-à-vis its foundation.[66] A comparable strategy is at work in Pindar's representation of the *kōmos* in *Olympian* 6.

In addition to *Nemean* 9, we can also look to *Nemean* 1 to elucidate *Olympian* 6's *kōmos*. *Nemean* 1's Alpheios River plays an analogous role to Hagesias's *kōmos*, since it, too, conspicuously joins the Peloponnese to Syracuse in its ode. Although *Nemean* 9's *kōmos* may have a closer, more literal fit with Hagesias's own victory revel, understanding the cultural work that the Alpheios performs in *Nemean* 1 will help us discern further what precisely Hagesias achieves in *Olympian* 6.

Nemean 1, like *Nemean* 9, was written for Chromios.[67] The ode opens with an address to the island of Ortygia, the "old quarter" of Syracuse (1–7):[68]

Ἄμπνευμα σεμνὸν Ἀλφεοῦ,
κλεινᾶν Συρακοσσᾶν θάλος Ὀρτυγία,
δέμνιον Ἀρτέμιδος,
Δάλου κασιγνήτα, σέθεν ἁδυεπής
ὕμνος ὁρμᾶται θέμεν
αἶνον ἀελλοπόδων
   μέγαν ἵππων, Ζηνὸς Αἰτναίου χάριν·
ἅρμα δ' ὀτρύνει Χρομίου Νεμέα
   τ' ἔργμασιν νικαφόροις ἐγκώμιον ζεῦξαι μέλος.

Sacred breathing place of the Alpheios, Ortygia, offshoot of renowned Syracuse, couch of Artemis, sister of Delos, from you a sweet-voiced hymn originates to sound high praise of storm-footed horses for the sake of Zeus Aitnaios. And the chariot of Chromios and Nemea spur me to yoke a song of praise for victorious achievements.

By identifying Ortygia as "the sacred breathing place of Alpheios," Pindar refers to the myth of Arethousa and Alpheios. Pausanias provides the fullest version of the

---

66. Hubbard 1992: 80–82. Hubbard (80) suggests that Chromios's participation in the local Sicyonian games may have been part of a Deinomenid attempt to recruit Dorian settlers from this region.

67. Schol. *ad N.* 9. inscr. Morrison (2007: 76–79) charts the striking degree of thematic and dictional parallels between *Nemean* 1 and *Olympian* 6. I follow Morrison in taking *Nemean* 1 as the earlier of the two odes. In light of the correspondence between them and the fact that Herakles is the mythic paradigm for Chromios in *Nemean* 1, I wonder if the Herakles in *Olympian* 6's myth of Iamos is not meant to evoke Chromios. Chromios, like Hagesias himself, is both a henchman of Hieron and an accomplice in the tyrant's colonial program. The myth of Iamos would then provide us with the model for how we are meant to imagine Hagesias, *together with Chromios*, assisting in Hieron's foundation of Aitna. On the dating of *Nemean* 1, see Carey 1981: 104; Braswell 1992: 25–27; Luraghi 1994: 339–40; Morrison 2007: 24.

68. According to Thucydides (6.3.2), Ortygia was the first part of the city to be settled.

tale of the hunter Alpheios's love for the huntress Arethousa (5.7.2–4).[69] Arethousa, the story goes, rejected Alpheios and fled from the Greek mainland to the island of Ortygia where she was turned into a spring. In response, Alpheios changed into a river and, flowing under the sea from Greece, emerged from the fountain of Arethousa, mixing his water with her own. According to Pausanias, the legend of Alpheios and Arethousa played a central role in the foundation oracle delivered to Archias, the oikist of Syracuse (5.7.3):

> ὃς Ἀρχίαν τὸν Κορίνθιον ἐς τὸν Συρακουσῶν ἀποστέλλων οἰκισμὸν καὶ τάδε εἶπε τὰ ἔπη·
> Ὀρτυγίη τις κεῖται ἐν ἠεροειδέι πόντῳ,
> Θρινακίης καθύπερθεν, ἵν᾽ Ἀλφειοῦ στόμα βλύζει
> μισγόμενον πηγαῖσιν εὐρρείτης Ἀρεθούσης.

[It was the god at Delphi] who, when he was sending Archias the Corinthian off to found Syracuse, also uttered the following oracle:

"An island, Ortygia, lies in the misty ocean above Thrinacia where the mouth of the Alpheios bubbles forth mixing with the springs of fair-flowing Arethousa."

The Pythia's description of Arethousa as the "mouth of the Alpheios" intriguingly recalls Pindar's image of Ortygia as the "breathing place of the Alpheios" (N. 1.1). We cannot be certain whether Pindar knew of this foundation oracle associated with the original migration to Syracuse and incorporated it in this image in Nemean 1, although this remains an exciting possibility.[70] What we can do, however, is recognize that the image of the comingling waters of Alpheios and Arethousa is not merely tied to Syracuse's colonial past but is also productive for the city's fifth-century present. As Nemean 1's first line implies, the Alpheios continues to tether Syracuse to Olympia and to the rest of the Peloponnese beyond. Arethousa and Alpheios remain pertinent to Pindar's audience because they symbolize Syracuse's ongoing unbroken tie to the Greek mainland by means of the trans-Adriatic river that (supposedly) still flowed to Sicily.[71] That the Syracusans placed the nymph Arethousa on their coins during this period epitomizes the story's relevance to their civic identity.[72]

---

69. Ibykos (PMG 323) offers the earliest extant instance of the myth.
70. On attempts to date this oracle, see Braswell 1992: 33–34.
71. For Antonaccio (2007: 284), Pindar's references to the Alpheios River assert the "intimate link" between Olympia and Syracuse. As Hornblower (2004: 185) notes, "The direction of the flow corresponds to the original direction of human migration." See also Dougherty 1993: 69 for a similar point.
72. For these coins, see Kraay 1976: 210 and pl. 47, no. 800. See also Rutter 1998, 2000. Rutter (2000: 80) notes how Pindaric imagery often corresponds to iconography found on contemporary coins (cf. Dougherty 1993: 86).

Yet, the Alpheios and the spring of Arethousa were valuable emblems not only for Syracuse more generally but also for Hieron's colonial program in particular. First, the Alpheios, a river that originates deep within Arcadia before crossing the Adriatic, reaching Ortygia, and mixing with Arethousa, symbolically captures the synoikism of Peloponnesians and Syracusans that Hieron hoped to engineer at Aitna.[73] Second, I would suggest that the reference to Zeus Aitnaios in the same strophe as the Alpheios in *Nemean* 1 relates this myth explicitly to Hieron's vision for Aitna. Pindar declares that from Ortygia a sweet-voiced hymn originates for the sake of Zeus Aitnaios (Ζηνὸς Αἰτναίου χάριν, 6). Zeus Aitnaios was the patron deity of the city of Aitna and appears both on coins contemporary with *Nemean* 1 and in vase paintings representing its foundation.[74] By envisioning Ortygia, the mouth of the Alpheios, as singing in honor of Zeus Aitnaios, Pindar draws Aitna within the ambit of Syracuse's own ties to the Greek mainland and thereby implies that this myth of mingling Peloponnesian and Ortygian waters suits Hieron's newly founded city as well.[75]

As noted above, *Olympian* 6 also features Ortygia (92–100). The "sweetly speaking (ἁδύλογοι) lyres and songs" that "know Ortygia" (96–97) recall *Nemean* 1's "sweet-voiced hymn" (ἁδυεπής ὕμνος, 4–5) issuing forth from Ortygia. Both passages also refer to Zeus Aitnaios. In fact, *Nemean* 1 and *Olympian* 6 are the only odes to name Aitna's patron deity in this way.[76] These analogous passages, however, also exhibit an instructive difference. In *Olympian* 6, the work of joining Sicily to the Peloponnese remains a salient feature of the scene, but, in place of the absent Alpheios, Hagesias performs the task as the *despotas* of his returning *kōmos*. As a substitute for the Alpheios, the *sunoikistēr* Hagesias assumes the symbolic work the river achieves in uniting the Peloponnese not only with Syracuse but with Aitna as well.

I end by calling attention to how the specific point of Hagesias's departure from the mainland makes even more explicit the colonial overtones of the seer's *kōmos*. To return to the relevant passage (98–100):

σὺν δὲ φιλοφροσύναις εὐ-
 ηράτοις Ἁγησία δέξαιτο κῶμον
οἴκοθεν οἴκαδ' ἀπὸ Στυμ-

---

73. See Diod. Sic. 11.49.1, quoted on p. 127.

74. See Dougherty 1993: 85–88. For these coins, see Kraay 1976: 212, 317, and pl. 49, nos. 837 and 838.

75. This reading assumes a terminus post quem of 476 B.C.E. for *Nemean* 1. The Pindaric sleight of hand through which Ortygia sings in honor of Zeus Aitnaios instantiates yet again the poet's blurring of the line between these two locations (Syracuse proper and Hieron's Aitna).

76. The later *Olympian* 4 refers to Zeus as Κρόνου παῖ, ὃς Αἴτναν ἔχεις (Child of Kronos, you who hold Aitna, 6). In the case of *Olympian* 6, Hieron links the two locations himself by ruling Syracuse and Ortygia (92–93) and simultaneously being devoted to Zeus Aitnaios (95–96). Cf. P. 3.68–70 (quoted on p. 113), wherein Hieron as both king of Syracuse and *Aitnaios xenos* again links Syracuse to Aitna.

φαλίων τειχέων ποτινισόμενον,
ματέρ' εὐμήλοιο λείποντ' Ἀρκαδίας.

but with lovely acts of friendship may he receive the victory revel of Hagesias as it comes from home to home, leaving the walls of Stymphalos, the mother of Arcadia, rich in flocks.

The choice of Stymphalos as the starting location of the *kōmos* is unusual. When other epinikian *kōmoi* appear in Pindar's poetry, they commence from a more expected site, that is, the site of the athletic victory.[77] By contrast, the *kōmos* at the end of *Olympian* 6 leaves from a polis in the Peloponnese, not Olympia. As a result, Hagesias, in guiding his revel "from home to home," from mainland Stymphalos to Syracuse and Aitna, moves in the direction of a western migration and mimics a colonial expedition that departs from a polis. Pindar's assertion that the *kōmos* is "leaving the mother of Arcadia, rich in flocks" (100) reinforces the colonial resonance of the epode. Although the phrase ostensibly means that Stymphalos is the mother of Arcadia, "leaving the mother" is what colonists do when they leave their metropolis, and the expression momentarily turns Hagesias's band of revelers into a group of settlers.[78]

Olympian 6 celebrates Hagesias as a talismanic figure whose talismanic power stems from his positions as athletic victor, seer, and *sunoikistēr*. As part of this trio, Pindar creates a paradoxical pairing of titles by according Hagesias the potentially jarring roles of seer and co-oikist. Yet, with the aid of the ode's two mythic portions, the poet presents the Iamidai as seers without political ambition who can thus successfully assist in foundations. Pindar's praise takes the form it does, despite the ensuing need to downplay the seer as a threat to Hieron's power, in part because Hagesias is invaluable to the tyrant. I would also suggest here that Hagesias can be given free rein to operate as a seer-oikist because of the minor role Delphi itself plays only in the ode. Within the ode, the talismanic and hybrid Hagesias alone both personifies and successfully carries out Hieron's vision for Aitna.

Olympian 6 ends with an entreaty to Poseidon, the very god who failed to answer Iamos's bid for kingship mythical generations before, to grant a safe voyage for Hagesias's returning *kōmos*. In these closing lines, Pindar seems to be saying, it is only as a traveler between two homes, without the desire to rule either, that this seer and *sunoikistēr* can hope for Poseidon to hear his prayer.

---

77. See, e.g., *N.* 9.1. Morrison (2007: 72) observes that the "starting-point [of the *kōmos*] is usually the place of victory." One could assert that all returning Syracusan victors retrace the path of the Sicily-bound Alpheios River. For example, Antonaccio (2007: 284) notes that the athletes mentioned in *Nemean* 1 take this route. What sets Hagesias apart, however, is that, unlike other athletes, he leaves from his Peloponnesian polis and not from the site of the games.

78. For another Pindaric example of the image of the mother (city) in a colonial context, see *Pa.* 2.28–30.

6

Amphiaraos, Alkmaion, and Delphi's Oracular Monopoly

The foundation of Thurii in 444/43 B.C.E. was an Athenian-sponsored enterprise on the site of the older colony of Sybaris in Italy. Of the various figures associated with the foundation, the Athenian seer Lampon is the one most consistently linked with leading the expedition. A scholion to Aristophanes' *Birds* records the following entry (schol. *ad* Ar. *Av.* 521):

> ἐξέπεμψαν δὲ ἐπὶ τὴν κτίσιν αὐτῶν Ἀθηναῖοι δέκα ἄνδρας, ὧν καὶ Λάμπων ἦν ὁ μάντις ἐξηγητὴς ἐσόμενος τῆς κτίσεως τῆς πόλεως.
>
> And the Athenians sent out ten men for its founding, among whom was also Lampon the *mantis* to be an exegete of the founding of the city.

Plutarch even identifies Lampon as Thurii's oikist (*Prae. ger. reip.* 812d):

> Λάμπωνα δὲ Θουρίων οἰκιστὴν ἐξέπεμψεν.
>
> And he [Perikles] sent out Lampon as an oikist of Thurii.

Diodorus Siculus names the seer Lampon as one of two oikists: κτιστῶν γενομένων Λάμπωνος καὶ Ξενοκρίτου (its founders being Lampon and Xenocritus, 12.10.3). Diodorus also provides the most extensive account of Thurii.[1] As part of his discussion of the early history of the colony he relates the following dispute that arose in the aftermath of its foundation (12.35.2–3):

> οἵ τε γὰρ Ἀθηναῖοι τῆς ἀποικίας ταύτης ἠμφισβήτουν, ἀποφαινόμενοι πλείστους οἰκήτορας ἐξ Ἀθηνῶν ἐληλυθέναι, οἵ τε Πελοποννήσιοι, πόλεις οὐκ ὀλίγας

---

1. On Diodorus Siculus's account of Thurii, see Rutter 1973.

παρεσχημέναι παρ' αὐτῶν εἰς τὴν κτίσιν τῶν Θουρίων, τὴν ἐπιγραφὴν τῆς ἀποικίας ἑαυτοῖς ἔφησαν δεῖν προσάπτεσθαι.... τέλος δὲ τῶν Θουρίων πεμψάντων εἰς Δελφοὺς τοὺς ἐπερωτήσοντας τίνα χρὴ τῆς πόλεως οἰκιστὴν ἀγορεύειν, ὁ θεὸς ἔχρησεν αὐτὸν δεῖν κτίστην νομίζεσθαι. τούτῳ τῷ τρόπῳ λυθείσης τῆς ἀμφισβητήσεως τὸν Ἀπόλλω κτίστην τῶν Θουρίων ἀπέδειξαν, καὶ τὸ πλῆθος τῆς στάσεως ἀπολυθὲν εἰς τὴν προϋπάρχουσαν ὁμόνοιαν ἀποκατέστη.

The situation was that the Athenians were laying claim to this colony on the grounds, as they alleged, that the majority of its colonists had come from Athens; and, besides, the cities of the Peloponnese, which had provided from their people not a few to the founding of Thurii, maintained that the colonization of the city should be ascribed to them.... In the end the Thurians sent a delegation to Delphi to inquire what man they should call the founder of their city, and the god replied that he himself should be considered to be its founder. After the dispute had been settled in this manner, they declared Apollo to have been the founder of Thurii, and the people, being now freed from the civil discord, returned to the state of harmony which they had previously enjoyed.[2]

According to Diodorus, once the foundation was established, the new colony descended into stasis. Diodorus attributes the crisis in part to a disagreement over what political faction should receive credit for the city's foundation. A delegation was sent to Delphi, whereupon Apollo resolved the issue by claiming the title of oikist for himself.

Delphic Apollo's maneuver to claim the title of oikist can be read in conjunction with our sources', including Diodorus's, repeated identification of the seer Lampon as one of the leaders or the leader of the colonial expedition. Rather than giving the Athenian faction credit and, by extension, honoring the seer Lampon as an oikist of Thurii, Delphic Apollo decides to adopt the position of oikist himself.[3]

Chapters 3–5 exposed an ideological incompatibility between the figures of the oikist and seer and the resulting exclusion of the seer from most examples of late archaic and early classical colonial discourse. As chapter 3 discussed, while the seer goes missing in these contexts, the oracle at Delphi enjoys a prominent role in the foundation process by serving as the oracular source on which the oikist often relies in order to ensure the successful foundation of his new polis. The prominence of the Delphic oracle and the pairing of Delphi and the oikist are still mostly taken for granted in modern scholarship. While chapters 2–5 focused on the seer-oikist relationship, this chapter turns to Delphi's contestatory relationship with the seer in order to uncover the oracle's own participation in the seer's absence from colonial discourse.

2. Trans. Oldfather 1946.
3. Apollo here seems to enact his cult title of Archegetas (Founder). On the cult of Apollo Archegetas, see esp. Malkin 1986; Donnellan 2015.

The Thurii episode represents a single manifestation of the broader cultural issue of Delphi's monopoly in colonial discourse and the way in which Delphi's promotion of its own oracular authority occurs at the expense of the seer. This chapter will focus on the figures of Amphiaraos and his son Alkmaion to provide a more productive and wide-ranging case study for witnessing Delphi's stance toward individual seers and Delphi's consequential use of colonial discourse to assert its primacy. Part 1 of this chapter establishes that a competitive relationship between Delphi and Amphiaraos existed beyond the parameters of colonial discourse. Herodotus's presentation and juxtaposition of these two forms of religious authority in his Kroisos *logos* in book 1 expose this more diffuse dynamic. Part 2 turns to the myth of Alkmaion. In what I term the "mainstream" or "dominant" tradition of the myth, our sources regularly detach Alkmaion from any claims to inheriting his father's *mantikē* and simultaneously promote him as an oikist with close ties to Delphi. That is, the tradition seems to require a rejection of Amphiaraos as part of its presentation of Alkmaion as a Delphi-sanctioned oikist. Part 3 reads Pindar's *Pythian* 8 as "Amphiaraos's revenge" with respect to this dominant tradition. In the ode, Pindar, uniquely among our extant sources, emphasizes Alkmaion's powers of prophecy and asserts that these powers are inherited from Amphiaraos. Moreover, just as the dominant tradition conjures Amphiaraos even as it dismisses him, Delphi's role in foundations is evoked but ultimately silenced. Through this investigation of the Alkmaion myth, then, this chapter seeks to expose Delphi's active production of colonial founders and its concomitant suppression of the individual seer within colonial discourse.

I. DELPHI, AMPHIARAOS, AND THE KROISOS *LOGOS*

I begin by stepping away from colonial discourse and seers temporarily to examine a more widespread rivalry between Delphi and the oracle of the seer Amphiaraos. Our evidence suggests that Delphi competed with a number of oracles. Catherine Morgan, for instance, detects a rivalry between Delphi and Dodona emerging in the late archaic period in which Dodona distanced itself from Delphi by aligning with the oracle of Zeus at Ammon. In so doing, Morgan argues, Dodona sought to resist the dominance of Delphi.[4] Albert Schachter interprets the sudden increase in dedications at the Ptoion, the oracular sanctuary of Apollo Ptoieus in Boiotia, in the mid-sixth century B.C.E. as evidence that the local sanctuary benefited from Delphi's temporary inaccessibility and decline during the same period.[5] This inverse relationship between Delphi's and the Ptoion's prosperity suggests a motivation for competition between oracles: the sites vied for patrons and dedicants. We might

---

4. Morgan 1990: 148–49, 222.
5. Schachter 1994.

also think of Aristophanes' *chrēsmologos* in *Birds* and how his oracle of Bakis is pitted against Peisetairos's own Delphic oracle (*Av.* 981–91).[6] Finally, Roland Crahay has argued that, in Herodotus's Kroisos *logos*, the oracles subjected to Kroisos's test represent Delphi's fifth-century rivals.[7] In this part of the chapter, I would like to consider in detail an oracular rival of Delphi found in the Kroisos *logos*. When we return to colonial discourse in part 2, we will then be able to perceive colonial discourse's own ideological strategies as part of a larger effort by Delphi to assert its primacy throughout the Greek world.

Herodotus's Kroisos *logos* in book 1 offers a good starting point for tracing an ongoing current of competition between Delphi and the oracle of Amphiaraos, the so-called Amphiareion.[8] Leslie Kurke's analysis of Herodotus's treatment of Kroisos and his interactions with the Delphic oracle provides a crucial framework for understanding this dynamic. I will summarize Kurke's argument first before turning to consider how the Amphiareion fits into Herodotus's presentation of Delphi.

In Herodotus's extended account of the downfall of the Lydian king (1.46–92), Kroisos assumes that by bestowing extravagant dedications on Delphi, among other oracular sites, he will receive as compensation for this munificence straightforward oracular responses to his inquiries. What he does not realize, as Kurke demonstrates, is that his dedications to Apollo and the god's responses to his inquiries in fact denote two "discrete and incommensurable 'economies,'" an economy of gift exchange and an economy of oracles.[9] Kroisos believes that his fabulous wealth is evidence of a privileged relationship with the divine. As long as he continues to compensate the gods materially, thinks Kroisos, divine favor, together with his power and prosperity, will endure. Accordingly, Kroisos assumes that the obligations of reciprocity inherent in this system of human-divine gift exchange should join Apollo to him in a reliable way. Yet, much to Kroisos's surprise, the god's oracles turn out not to conform to this gift-exchange model of reciprocity but rather to signify an entirely different system of interaction, one in which pronouncements from the gods are unreliable and unknowable.

Further, Kurke demonstrates that at the same time as Apollo's utterances are revealed as performing differently from Kroisos's dedicatory practices and expectations, they can also be seen to coincide with another system of exchange, namely, the civic economy. As we learn especially from the earlier story of Kroisos and the

---

6. For this passage, see the introduction.
7. Crahay 1956: 195 on Hdt. 1.46.2–3, discussed below.
8. Kindt (2016: 20–28) rightly emphasizes the prominence and sheer number of oracles and prophesies in the Kroisos *logos*. For an exhaustive survey of representations of Amphiaraos throughout the ancient Mediterranean world, including Etruria and Rome, see Terranova 2013.
9. Kurke 1999: 152.

Athenian lawgiver Solon (1.30–35), the civic economy also operates with the understanding that divine favor is erratic and incomprehensible.[10] The dialectic between the gift-exchange model and the oracular-civic model culminates in the story's scene of Kroisos on the pyre. As Kurke shows, Kroisos receives two epiphanies on the pyre, and these two epiphanies correspond to the oracular and gift-exchange economies, respectively. The defeated king, placed on the pyre, first realizes the divinely inspired truth of Solon's former injunction (i.e., that no man should be considered blessed until the end of his life) and calls out the lawgiver's name three times (1.86.3–4). The invocation of Solon, carefully construed in epiphanic language, successfully checks Kyros's desire to immolate Kroisos. But, since the fire has already been lit and the Persians cannot extinguish it, Kroisos calls out a second time, praying to Apollo that the god rescue him from his present misfortune, if any of his former gifts ever pleased him (1.87.1). In response, a rain storm suddenly appears from a cloudless sky and quenches the pyre's flames. In this second epiphany, Apollo acts out of *charis* (divine favor linked to reciprocity): Apollo comes to Kroisos's aid because of Kroisos's own previous generosity to him.

Apollo's epiphany instantiates the gift-exchange model. But this epiphany is "preempted" by that of Solon.[11] Solon's epiphany signals Kroisos's acknowledgment of divine incomprehensibility and changeability, an acknowledgment operative in the oracular and civic systems of exchange alike. Solon's epiphany, then, marks a convergence of these oracular and civic models of exchange. At the same time, although Solon and the civic economy he exemplifies coincide with the oracular economy, they ultimately outperform it. For Solon not only acts on the basis that the gods are indecipherable but also simultaneously offers a solution to that incomprehensibility. As Kurke concludes,

> Solon (like the oracle) represents a cosmos of inscrutable gods and unstable fortune, whose only defense is the mediating rationality of civic order. We might say it is the ultimate presumption of the civic appropriation of the long-term transactional order to replace the saving divinity with the saving lawgiver, whose wisdom structures and makes sense of an unintelligible cosmos.[12]

Kurke's conclusions have an important corollary implication that pertains directly to our present study, for they expose one important way in which Delphic Apollo's authority can be challenged. The civic model, however, whose preeminence Solon's epiphany confirms, enters at a particular point in the story of Kroisos. When the

---

10. Thus Kurke 1999: 152: "The 'economy of oracles' turns out to have more in common with the civic ecomony than the model of gift exchange Kroisos thinks to impose upon it." On the civic economy and Solon as its representative, see Kurke 1999: 142–51. On the junctures between Delphic oracles and civic debate, see also Maurizio 1997; Kurke 2009.
11. Kurke 1999: 159.
12. Kurke 1999: 159.

story begins in 1.46, it is not yet Solon with whom Delphi must share the narrative spotlight. What Kurke's analysis also allows us to see is that the oracle of Amphiaraos in many ways anticipates and performs the same role of undercutting Delphi's uncontested authority that Solon himself eventually (and more effectively) performs. Let us turn, then, to the earlier portions of the story of Kroisos in order to attend to the role of the oracle of Amphiaraos and its own relationship to Delphi.

Earlier in book 1, Kroisos, wary of Persia's expanding power, decides to test oracles throughout the Greek world as the first stage of an elaborate justification for confronting Kyros (1.46.3). The nature of the test is outrageous. The oracles are asked to reveal what Kroisos is up to on a given day, and on that day, Kroisos boils a tortoise and lamb in a bronze cauldron, an act impossible to determine by guesswork (1.48). Herodotus lists seven oracles subjected to the test: Delphi, Abai in Phokis, Dodona, the oracles of Amphiaraos (the Amphiareion) and Trophonios, the oracle of the Branchidai in Milesia, and the oracle of Zeus Ammon in Libya (1.46.2–3).[13]

Despite the range of oracles included in this initial list, Herodotus proceeds to focus almost exclusively on Delphi in relating the consequences of Kroisos's scheme. In fact, the degree of narrative attention devoted to Delphi throughout the entire account strongly suggests that Herodotus receives much of this story from the sanctuary itself.[14] Thus Herodotus asserts that none of the oracles' responses were recorded save Delphi's, whose hexameter answer he includes (1.47). He also reports Kroisos's reaction to the Pythia's reply, a reaction that highlights Delphi's superiority over the other oracular contenders (1.48.1):

ὡς δὲ καὶ ὧλλοι οἱ περιπεμφθέντες παρῆσαν φέροντες τοὺς χρησμούς, ἐνθαῦτα ὁ Κροῖσος ἕκαστα ἀναπτύσσων ἐπώρα τῶν συγγραμμάτων. τῶν μὲν δὴ οὐδὲν προσίετό μιν· ὁ δὲ ὡς τὸ ἐκ Δελφῶν ἤκουσε, αὐτίκα προσεύχετό τε καὶ προσεδέξατο, νομίσας μοῦνον εἶναι μαντήιον τὸ ἐν Δελφοῖσι, ὅτι οἱ ἐξευρήκεε τὰ αὐτὸς ἐποίησε.

And when the others who had been sent round arrived, bringing the oracular responses, then Kroisos unfolded and looked at each of the written documents, none of which pleased him. But when he heard the response from Delphi, at once he offered prayers and accepted it, believing that Delphi was the only true oracle, because it had discovered the things that he himself had done.

Delphi reigns supreme in this passage. Yet, through a series of narrative fissures in Herodotus's account of Kroisos's consultations, the Amphiareion repeatedly surfaces to contest the notion of Delphic Apollo's status as the one true oracle. Thus in a coda to his explanation of Kroisos's test and the Pythia's accurate reply,

---

13. See Asheri (2011: 108–9) for a number of oracles Herodotus excludes here, including that of Zeus at Olympia. Asheri notes that seven is a symbolic number.

14. See Flower 2013: 131.

Herodotus contradicts the previous assertion that Delphi alone is the only reliable oracle (1.49):

> τὰ μὲν δὴ ἐκ Δελφῶν οὕτω τῷ Κροίσῳ ἐχρήσθη· κατὰ δὲ τὴν Ἀμφιάρεω τοῦ μαντηίου ὑπόκρισιν οὐκ ἔχω εἰπεῖν ὅ τι τοῖσι Λυδοῖσι ἔχρησε ποιήσασι περὶ τὸ ἱρὸν τὰ νομιζόμενα (οὐ γὰρ ὦν οὐδὲ τοῦτο λέγεται) ἄλλο γε ἢ ὅτι καὶ τοῦτον ἐνόμισε μαντήιον ἀψευδὲς ἐκτῆσθαι.

> Such things were proclaimed by Delphi to Kroisos: but concerning the answer from the oracle of Amphiaraos, I am not able to say what it foretold to the Lydians who had carried out the customary procedures at the temple (for indeed this is not even recorded), other than that he believed that he had found in that one too a truthful oracle.

Out of all the other oracular contenders, the Amphiareion, like Delphi, seems to have passed the test of the boiled tortoise and lamb.

The following chapters (1.50–52) follow a similar pattern. Herodotus enumerates at length Kroisos's sacrifices to Delphic Apollo and catalogues his extravagant dedications at the sanctuary. By way of a conclusion, however, he turns again to the Amphiareion (1.52):

> ταῦτα μὲν ἐς Δελφοὺς ἀπέπεμψε, τῷ δὲ Ἀμφιάρεῳ, πυθόμενος αὐτοῦ τήν τε ἀρετὴν καὶ τὴν πάθην, ἀνέθηκε σάκος τε χρύσεον πᾶν ὁμοίως καὶ αἰχμὴν στερεὴν πᾶσαν χρυσέην, τὸ ξυστὸν τῇσι λόγχῃσι ἐὸν ὁμοίως χρύσεον· τὰ ἔτι καὶ ἀμφότερα ἐς ἐμὲ ἦν κείμενα ἐν Θήβῃσι καὶ Θηβέων ἐν τῷ νηῷ τοῦ Ἰσμηνίου Ἀπόλλωνος.

> These offerings, then, he sent off to Delphi, but to the Amphiareion, having learned of his military valor [*aretē*] and his suffering [*pathē*], he dedicated a shield made entirely of gold and likewise a solid gold spear, the shaft being gold in the same way as the point: both of these were still in Thebes in my day, in the Theban temple of Apollo Ismenios.[15]

We hear of these gifts once more. At the conclusion of the story of Kroisos, Herodotus identifies several other Greek sanctuaries to which the king had sent offerings. He organizes these dedications into two groups: the gifts he dedicated at Delphi and the Amphiareion were the first-fruits of all the wealth he had received from his father; the dedications sent to all the other oracles came from the fortune of a conspirator whom Kroisos had brutally punished (92.2).[16] This particular distribution of gifts again links Delphi to the Amphiareion, since their gifts alone derive from Kroisos's personal estate. In the eyes of Kroisos, it seems, the modest sanctuary merits an honor equal to that of the Panhellenic Delphic oracle.

Kroisos performs two further oracular consultations in this portion of the narrative. After his initial test of the boiled tortoise and lamb, Kroisos sends envoys to

---

15. *Aretē* in this passage refers to military valor, as elsewhere in Herodotus (Asheri 2011: 113).
16. On the significance of Kroisos's brutal treatment of his opponent, see Kurke 1999: 163–65.

the "winners," Delphi and the Amphiareion, in order to present his dedications as well as to pose a second question (1.53.2–3):

Κροῖσος ὁ Λυδῶν τε καὶ ἄλλων ἐθνέων βασιλεύς, νομίσας τάδε μαντήια εἶναι μοῦνα ἐν ἀνθρώποισι, ὑμῖν τε ἄξια δῶρα ἔδωκε τῶν ἐξευρημάτων, καὶ νῦν ὑμέας ἐπειρωτᾷ εἰ στρατεύηται ἐπὶ Πέρσας καὶ εἴ τινα στρατὸν ἀνδρῶν προσθέοιτο σύμμαχον. οἱ μὲν ταῦτα ἐπειρώτων, τῶν δὲ μαντηίων ἀμφοτέρων ἐς τὠυτὸ αἱ γνῶμαι συνέδραμον, προλέγουσαι Κροίσῳ, ἢν στρατεύηται ἐπὶ Πέρσας, μεγάλην ἀρχήν μιν καταλύσειν· τοὺς δὲ Ἑλλήνων δυνατωτάτους συνεβούλευόν οἱ ἐξευρόντα φίλους προσθέσθαι.

Kroisos, the king of the Lydians and other nations, believing that these are the only true oracles among mankind, has given to both of you gifts worthy of your discoveries and now asks you both whether he is to march against Persia and whether he should take an army of allies. Such things the emissaries asked, and the judgments of both oracles agreed on the same thing, foretelling to Kroisos that if he were to march against Persia, he would destroy a great empire. And they advised him to discover the most powerful of the Greeks and to make them his friends.

The formulation of the question not only pairs Delphi with the Amphiareion but also does so by closely imitating the praise previously reserved for Delphi alone. That original evaluation, νομίσας μοῦνον εἶναι μαντήιον τὸ ἐν Δελφοῖσι (believing that Delphi was the only true oracle, 1.48.1), now acknowledges the Amphiareion's comparable claim: νομίσας τάδε μαντήια εἶναι μοῦνα ἐν ἀνθρώποισι (believing that these are the only true oracles among mankind, 1.53.2). Delphi must share with Amphiaraos the title of the "only true oracle among men," a phrase that generates the paradoxically plural μοῦνα. Indeed, for the rest of chapter 53, Delphi and the Amphiareion are indistinguishable. Their answers to Kroisos's second consultation are the same (τὠυτό), that Kroisos will destroy a great empire, as is their specific advice for the Lydian to find Greek allies.

Yet after matching Delphi in oracular competence and authority in these two successive inquiries, the Amphiareion suddenly drops out of the narrative. Kroisos has one final question to ask in this round of questioning but consults only the Pythia. This final consultation, however, is preceded by a shift in the recipients of Kroisos's largess. When Kroisos learns that he will destroy a great empire, he once again sends gifts to Delphi. These gifts are different in nature from his previous dedications: Kroisos now offers the Delphians two staters each. The Delphians counter by giving Kroisos extraordinary privileges at the sanctuary, including awarding Kroisos and the rest of the Lydians, if they wish, with the right of Delphic citizenship for all time (1.54). Only after this exchange between Kroisos and the Delphians do we learn that Kroisos has one final question to ask (whether his rule will be a long one) and that he asks it of the Delphic oracle alone (1.55.1). This sequence is suggestive, for it implies that the perks lavished by the Delphians on Kroisos, and not Apollo's superior oracular abilities, ultimately divert Kroisos's focus and Herodotus's narrative onto Delphi exclusively. Put another way, the Amphiareion is never proven to be qualitatively inferior to Delphi in terms of its oracular pronouncements. Rather, it is after the human-human gift exchange between Kroisos and the citizens of Delphi that the Amphiareion fades from view.

The list of Delphic privileges given to Kroisos is striking: the Delphians offer *promanteia* (the right to consult the oracle first), *ateleia* (exemption from taxes associated with consulting the oracle), *prohedria* (the right to front-row seats at the Pythian festivals and games), and, finally, the award of honorary citizenship (1.54.2). Kurke notes how the nature of these gifts embraces all aspects of Delphi: they represent access to Delphic Apollo himself (*promanteia*), his oracle and sanctuary (*ateleia* and *prohedria*), and the polis of Delphians (citizenship).[17] The range of gifts marks a convergence of oracular and civic elements, a fitting combination given how these two systems, as discussed above, come to intersect in other ways in the story and eventually culminate in Solon's epiphany. What is more, this exchange of gifts also signals the moment at which a civic register or framework first becomes activated in the narrative. For, as if triggered by Kroisos's own honorary Greek citizenship, an extended story-within-a-story of the sixth-century history of two Greek poleis, Athens and Sparta, immediately follows in chapters 56–68.

I suggest that we read these two narrative features together, that is, the point at which the disappearance of the Amphiareion allows Delphi to enjoy the oracular spotlight alone and the point at which a civic dimension enters the picture. For both the oracular Amphiareion and the civic register, whose final expression is the epiphany of its representative, Solon, serve a similar function insofar as both undercut Delphi's status as an uncontested source of authority for Kroisos. Yet these constraints on Delphi's monopoly vis-à-vis Kroisos are not in play at the same time. The progression traced above suggests that Herodotus substitutes the ultimately more effective civic authority of the Greek polis for the oracular authority of the Amphiareion. The hinge or changeover between these two sources of competition for Delphi occurs in the human-human gift exchange between Kroisos and the citizens of Delphi.

With the Amphiareion out of the way, Delphi becomes the only oracle to which Kroisos and others turn for the remainder of the narrative of the Lydian king. Thus we learn of a further response by the Pythia concerning Kroisos's mute son (1.85) and, following his downfall, how Kroisos sent envoys to Delphi for one final exchange (1.90–91). Delphi also plays a crucial part in the overview of Spartan history that Herodotus provides in his subnarrative of Athens and Sparta. In this account, the Spartans receive three oracles from the Pythia, all of which Herodotus

---

17. Kurke 2011: 58.

directly quotes (1.65.3, 1.66.2, and 1.67.4) and all of which become crucial for Sparta's development as a properly functioning polis.[18]

The one instance in which Delphi does not serve as the default oracular authority in the remainder of this narrative occurs during Herodotus's discussion of Athens and his account of Peisistratos's repeated attempts to become its tyrant. On the eve of his third attempt to take the city, Peisistratos is met by an Akarnanian *chrēsmologos*, Amphilytos, who delivers a prophecy in hexameters (1.62.4). As Michael Flower observes, Amphilytos is the only known "historical" figure who utters a prophecy under inspiration (ἐνθεάζων, 1.63.1) instead of interpreting, for example, an omen, oracle, or entrails.[19] For Flower, Amphilytos creates the possibility that "seers sometimes did deliver prophecies in real life, and like the Pythia, they perhaps did so in a state of altered consciousness."[20] Whether or not we take Amphilytos as evidence for real-life seers, Flower's comparison between this otherwise unknown figure and the Pythia is revealing. Herodotus's paired accounts of Athens and Sparta within this subnarrative are clear counterparts to each other.[21] I would argue that the more pervasive correlation between the two poleis in this section prepares us to see Amphilytos's hexameter prophecy, especially given its anomalous nature, as corresponding directly to the Pythia's own hexameter oracles in the following account of Sparta. In other words, like the oracle of the seer Amphiaraos in the Kroisos story, the seer Amphilytos proves capable of performing the same function as Delphi, and just as effectively.[22]

Finally, a passage from the first-century B.C.E. Greek historian Nicolaus of Damascus also helps to make sense of the contestation between Amphiaraos and Delphic Apollo. In his *Universal History*, Nicolaus includes his own version of the famous downfall of Kroisos, including the Lydian king's narrow escape from immolation on a pyre. One of the Sibyls appears in Nicolaus's account of the dramatic scene (*FGrH* 90 F 68.11–15):

> Κροίσου δ' ἐπιβαίνοντος αὐτῇ, ἡ Σίβυλλα ὤφθη ἀπό τινος
> ὑψηλοῦ χωρίου καταβαίνουσα, ἵνα καὶ αὐτὴ ἴδῃ
> τὰ γινόμενα. Ταχὺ δὲ θροῦς διῆλθε διὰ τοῦ ὁμίλου,
> ὅτι ἡ χρησμῳδὸς ἥκει, καὶ ἐν προσδοκίᾳ πάντες ἐγέ-
> νοντο, εἴ τι πρὸς τὰ παρόντα θειάσειε. Καὶ μετ' οὐ
> πολὺ ἔντονόν τι φθεγξαμένη βοᾷ·

---

18. See Kurke (1999: 152–56) for the way in which the oracular and civic economies again intersect in this narrative and how this intersection serves as a paradigm for Kroisos.

19. Flower 2008b: 64 and 79. The verb ἐνθεάζω itself is a *hapax legomenon* in Herodotus.

20. Flower 2008b: 79.

21. See Boedeker 1993.

22. In this context it is interesting to note that, while visiting the sanctuary of Amphiaraos at Oropos, Pausanias claims to have seen hexameter verses that Amphiaraos supposedly delivered to the Argives during the Seven against Thebes (1.34.4).

Ὦ μέλεοι, τί σπεύδεθ' ἃ μὴ θέμις; οὐ γὰρ ἐάσει
Ζεὺς ὕπατος Φοῖβός τε καὶ ὁ κλυτὸς Ἀμφιάραος·
Ἀλλά γ' ἐμῶν ἐπέων πείθεσθ' ἀψευδέσι χρησμοῖς,
Μὴ κακὸν οἶτον ὄλοισθε παρὲκ θεοῦ ἀφραίνοντες.
Κῦρος δ' ἀκούσας ἐκέλευσε τὸν χρησμὸν διεξενεγκεῖν
τοῖς Πέρσαις, ὡς ἐξευλαβηθεῖεν ἁμαρτάνειν.

When Kroisos was mounting the pyre, the Sibyl was seen to come down from a height in order that she herself might see what was happening. Soon a murmur passed through the crowd that the singer of oracles had come, and all wanted to see if she would be inspired about the present situation. After a brief pause she cried out:

> Foolish men, why do you seek what is unlawful? Neither highest Zeus nor Phoibos nor famous Amphiaraos will allow it. But obey the truthful oracles of my words, in order that you may not be destroyed by an evil doom because of your foolishness against god.

Kyros, upon hearing this, ordered them to deliver the oracle to the Persians in order that they might be on guard against their error.

Nicolaus drew on a number of ancient sources, most notably Herodotus and the mid-fifth-century historian Xanthus the Lydian, importing virtually wholesale certain passages from earlier works and embellishing others for his own melodramatic ends.[23] It is not clear whether Nicolaus takes the Sibyl's outcry from an earlier source. The Sibyl does appear elsewhere in his work in connection with Kyros, and this connection possibly derives from Xanthus.[24] At the same time, Nicolaus mines the *Histories* for material elsewhere in this scene.[25] Yet whether derived from another source or embellished from Herodotus, Nicolaus's pyre scene illuminates not only the double epiphany of Herodotus's Kroisos on the pyre but also Herodotus's larger Kroisos narrative. In the Sibyl's account, Amphiaraos appears as yet another divine figure willing to come to Kroisos's aid, together with Apollo and Zeus. Zeus, we might note, was another oracular competitor of Apollo.[26] I would suggest, then, that Nicolaus's version crystallizes in the single utterance of the Sibyl the cumulative effect of the Amphiareion's successive appearances in Herodotus's Kroisos narrative. The Sibyl's invocation of "Zeus, Phoibos, and famous Amphiaraos" makes explicit the comparability of these figures in connection with Kroisos,

---

23. Parke 1984: 226.
24. Parke 1984: 227.
25. Thus Nicolaus follows Herodotus closely in his rendering of Kroisos's invocations on the pyre. As in Herodotus's account, Kroisos himself first calls upon Solon and then, when the Persians are unable to extinguish the pyre's flames, upon Apollo (*FGrH* 90 F 68.16–17).
26. See p. 138 above with Morgan 1990: 148–49, 222. Recall that Zeus Ammon is a contender in Kroisos' testing of the oracles (Hdt. 1.46.2–3 with Crahay 1956: 195).

a comparability that also emerges between Apollo and Amphiaraos during the Herodotean Kroisos's testing of the oracles.

We might also briefly compare both Nicolaus's and Herodotus's pyre scenes to that of Bacchylides' *Ode* 3. In *Ode* 3 we receive a perfect epinikian vision of human-divine *charis:* placed on the pyre, Kroisos calls upon Apollo alone and Apollo reliably comes to his aid. In the epinikian version of these events, Apollo enjoys an uncontested, although still not unproblematic, hold on Kroisos.[27] Bacchylides' Apollo does not have to contend with the intruding and comparable authority of Amphiaraos or Solon or even Zeus as he does for Herodotus and Nicolaus.

Kurke demonstrates how the historian explores the problematic nature of Kroisos's human-divine gift exchange with Delphic Apollo and the Lydian king's failure to comprehend the workings of the oracular economy. I would argue that, at the same time as this interplay and its consequences unfold, a second dynamic develops in tandem, one that situates Delphi in relation to other, comparable sources of authority that repeatedly undercut Delphi's own oracular monopoly. The undermining of Delphi is carried out first by the Amphiareion, a local Theban oracle, and then, more successfully, by the Athenian lawgiver Solon, and this substitution of Amphiaraos for Solon is triggered by Kroisos's gifts to the Delphians. As I have argued here, that gesture gives the narrative a civic dimension and shifts its attention away from oracles and onto the Greek polis.

Delphi's Revenge

We have just observed how the *Histories* can be deployed as a site for tracing the way in which Delphi contests with other sources of authority, including the oracular authority of the Amphiareion. I would now like to examine an instance of a possible Delphi-supported rejoinder to this oracular rival. A recently discovered inscription supports evidence found in the *Histories* for what appears to be an effort to disenfranchise the oracle of Amphiaraos.

Let us return first to Herodotus's account of Kroisos's offerings to Amphiaraos after his initial testing of the oracles. According to Herodotus, Kroisos rewards Amphiaraos for passing the test of the boiled tortoise and lamb with the dedications of a golden shield and spear, which Herodotus himself saw stored in the Theban Ismenion (1.52, quoted on p. 142). Some modern scholars argue that the oracle of Amphiaraos was only ever located at the site of Oropos in the border region between Attica and Boiotia.[28] But the ancient sources themselves strongly suggest that an earlier Amphiareion existed in the vicinity of Thebes and that it was to this sanctuary that Kroisos sent the golden shield and spear. When Herodotus describes the Persian Mys's consultation of the Amphiareion, Mys is clearly visiting Thebes

---

27. On Bacchylides' version of Kroisos on the pyre, see Carson 1984; Kurke 1999: 130–42.
28. See Schachter 1981: 21–23; Parke 1984: 212n7; Travlos 1988: 301–18.

(8.134). Plutarch also supports a Theban location for Mys's visit to the Amphiareion (*De def. or.* 411f-412b).²⁹ Strabo states that the oracle marked the site of Amphiaraos's disappearance underground during the battle of the Seven against Thebes (9.1.22). Pausanias places it along the road from Thebes to Potniai (9.8.3).³⁰ At some point before Herodotus's time, however, the Theban Amphiareion fell out of use, and the contents of the defunct sanctuary wer transferred to the Theban Ismenion, where the historian saw them. In the 420s B.C.E., the sanctuary at Oropos was built on virgin soil.³¹

An epigram recently published by Nikolaos Papazarkadas strikingly matches Herodotus's description both of Kroisos's dedication to Amphiaraos and its placement in the Theban Ismenion. The epigram is actually a synthesis of two texts inscribed on the same column drum, one written in Boiotian script, the other in Ionic. The Boiotian text on this column drum can be dated to the late sixth–early fifth century B.C.E. The Ionic script suggests a date of the early to mid-fourth century B.C.E.³² The inscriptions are not identical but overlap significantly. Papazarkadas was able to collate the two inscriptions with the following results:³³

[σοὶ] χάριν ἐνθάδ' Ἀπολο[ν, ⌣ | – ⌣⌣ | – ⌣⌣ | – ⌣]
[κὲ]πιστὰς ιαρο στᾶσε κατ[ευχσά]μενος
[μα]ντοσύναις εὑρον ὑπὸ ΤΑ[. . .]ΟΙΟ φαενὰν
[ἀσπ]ίδα τὰν Ϙροῖσος κα[λϜ]ὸν ἄγαλ[μα θέτο?]
[Ἀμ]φιαρέοι μνᾶμ' ἀρετ[άς τε πάθας τε ⌣ | – ⌣]
[..]μεν³⁴ ἅ ἐκλέφθε ΦΟ[⌣⌣ | – ⌣⌣ | ⌣]
[Θε]βαίοισι δὲ θάμβος Ε[– ⌣⌣ | – ⌣⌣ | – ⌣]
[..]πιδα δαιμονίος ‖ ΔΕ [⌣⌣ | – ⌣⌣ | ⌣]

As a gift of recompense for you, Apoll[o, . . .] the priest of the sanctuary set [this] up here as he had vowed. Th rough divination, he found the shining shield which Kroi-sos [dedicated] as a beautiful gift to Amphiaraos, a memorial of his virt[ue (*aretē*) and . . .] was stolen . . . a marvel to the Th ebans . . . [the sh]ield, miraculous . . .³⁵

---

29. See Hubbard 1993: 196n16 for a brief but helpful discussion of this passage.
30. On attempts to locate the site of the sanctuary, see Hubbard 1993: 196n14.
31. Ogden 2001: 85n28. This Oropian site became a healing sanctuary that thrived into the third century C.E. On Amphiaraos's oracle at Oropos, see esp. Sineux 2007: 91–109; 119–86.
32. For the phenomenon of rewriting in Ionic script at a later date an earlier Boiotian text, see Papazarkadas 2014: 246. As Papazarkadas notes, the impetus for a reinscription still holds even if there were two sanctuaries to Amphiaraos (see below).
33. The underlined words represent the overlapping sections of the two inscriptions.
34. Papazarkadas (2014: 244) proposes [αἰχ]μέν (spear) as a possible restoration. If he is correct, then the epigram, like Herodotus, lists both a shield and a spear as Amphiaraos's gifts.
35. Cf. Thonemann 2016.

As in Herodotus's passage, the epigram refers to Kroisos's gift of a shield (and possibly a spear in line 6) for Amphiaraos. Both Herodotus and the epigram also assert that Kroisos bestowed these gifts on account of Amphiaraos's military valor (*aretē*) and suffering (*pathē*).[36] In addition, the epigram contains a fascinating new detail: the shield, it claims, was stolen and recovered by a supervisor (possibly a priest) of the shrine through divination. Based on these references to divination and a priest of Apollo as well as the location in which the inscription was found, Papazarkadas argues that this shrine must be the Theban Ismenion.[37]

Papazarkadas suggests that the reason Apollo, and not Amphiaraos, was enlisted to recover the stolen dedication was because, as Herodotus tells us in 8.134, Thebans were barred from consulting the oracle of Amphiaraos on account of having chosen him as their *summachos* (military ally) instead.[38] Further, Papazarkadas conjectures that the dedications were possibly stolen as the result of a rivalry between Athens and Thebes over the Amphiareion. This theory assumes that there was only ever one sanctuary of Amphiaraos, located at Oropos, over which, at least at a later date, the Thebans and Athenians did repeatedly vie for control.[39] In this scenario, the Thebans, forced to cede control over the sanctuary to the Athenians, took the shield and set it up in the Theban Ismenion instead.[40] Papazarkadas's interest primarily lies in the inscription itself, and he merely suggests this theory as a possible explanation for the theft of the shield. Yet, taking together the compelling evidence for an earlier Amphiareion located in Thebes, and the above discussion of Herodotus's Kroisos narrative, it is possible to discern an alternative reason for Amphiaraos's stolen gifts.

We might begin by considering anew two related questions—namely, why it is Apollo Ismenios who receives credit for locating the missing objects, and why the Ismenion comes to display Amphiaraos's gifts. The Ismenion was an oracular center particularly linked to Theban civic identity.[41] But it was also a sanctuary with close cultic ties to Delphi.[42] These ties are manifest in several ways: both sanctuaries, for instance, feature an oracle of Apollo with an accompanying cult of

---

36. Papazarkadas (2014: 243) convincingly recruits Hdt. 1.52 to restore this line of the epigram.

37. For the shrine in line 2 referring to the Theban Ismenion, see Papazarkadas 2014: 240; on the relationship between the epigram and Hdt. 1.52, see Papazarkadas, 246–47.

38. Papazarkadas 2014: 246. See Hdt. 8.134, quoted on p. 151.

39. On Oropos's shifting allegiance between Athens and Boiotia, see Mackil 2013: 357–58.

40. This theory seems to account well for the epigram's reinscription in Ionic script in the fourth century when the Thebans-Athens rivalry over Oropos persisted, but, as Papazarkadas (2014: 246) points out, a reinscription could have occurred even if there had been two sanctuaries of Amphiaraos (i.e., first the Theban and then the Oropian).

41. On the Ismenion in its Boiotian and Theban context, see Mackil 2013: 167–71; see also Kowalzig 2007: 371–82.

42. Defradas 1954: 61; Schachter 1967; 1981: 1.59–60, 80–85; Kurke 2013: 136–37.

Athena Pronaia. The Ismenion's principal ritual, the Daphnephoria (Carrying of the Laurel), also points to the influence of Delphi.[43]

The impetus for Amphiaraos's stolen shield, then, may be evidence not of a power struggle over the Amphiareion itself but rather of a contestation between local oracles, one of which closely identified with Delphi. That the shield disappeared and was "miraculously" (recall the epigram's references to *thambos* [marvel] and *daimonios* [miraculous]) discovered by the personnel of the Ismenion suggests an active attempt to disenfranchise the Amphiareion, an attempt, we might note, that was ultimately successful, since the Amphiareion at Thebes became defunct. Furthermore, in light of this possibility, it is worth calling attention to the justification for Kroisos's gifts that both Herodotus and the epigram provide: the Lydian dedicated the shield and spear on account of Amphiaraos's military valor and suffering (*aretē* and *pathē*). That is to say, both texts claim that Kroisos's admiration of Amphiaraos had nothing to do with his status as an oracle or with his mantic abilities. The omission is striking, and, in fact, we can contrast this formulation of Amphiaraos's exceptional qualities to what seems to have been the paradigmatic summation of the seer. This assessment, found in Pindar's *Olympian* 6 and Aeschylus's *Seven against Thebes* and likely deriving from the Theban epics, praises Amphiaraos as "both a good *mantis* and good at fighting with the spear."[44] Herodotus 1.52 and the epigram replace Amphiaraos's seercraft with his suffering (*pathē*). Moreover, Kroisos's regard for Amphiaraos's *aretē* and *pathē* in 1.52 suspiciously contradicts the conclusion reached in the surrounding narrative, namely, that the Lydian king rewards the Amphiareion because it was able to pass his test and become, together with Delphi, the "only true oracles" (1.53.2). Yet this change in Kroisos's alleged motives for his dedication to Amphiaraos makes sense when situated within the larger contestatory relationship between Apollo oracles, including Delphi, and the Amphiareion. Both 1.52 and the epigram feature a two-pronged assault on Amphiaraos's credibility: Kroisos's gifts to Amphiaraos are physically co-opted from his own sanctuary and transferred to the Theban Ismenion. Further, Kroisos's admiration of Amphiaraos is reassigned to the seer's non-oracular attributes, and this new rationale for the gifts also overlooks Amphiaraos's status as a legitimate oracle.

Finally, an anecdote from Herodotus's book 8 might be viewed as another attempt to disenfranchise Amphiaraos's oracle. In this anecdote, Amphiaraos issues the bizarre injunction that the Thebans must choose him as a military ally or an oracle. The Thebans chose the former (8.134):

---

43. Mackil 2013: 171.
44. See Pi. *O.* 6.17; Aesch. *Sept.* 568–69. Asclepiades of Mirlea says this line was taken from the *Thebaid* (PEG 1 F 10 = 7 EGF = 6 GEF). On converting this verse to its original hexameter line, see West 2011: 53.

ἐκέλευσε σφέας ὁ Ἀμφιάρεως διὰ χρηστηρίων ποιεύμενος ὁκότερα βούλονται ἑλέσθαι τούτων, ἑωυτῷ ἢ ἅτε μάντι χρᾶσθαι ἢ ἅτε συμμάχῳ, τοῦ ἑτέρου ἀπεχομένους· οἱ δὲ σύμμαχόν μιν εἵλοντο εἶναι. διὰ τοῦτο μὲν οὐκ ἔξεστι Θηβαίων οὐδενὶ αὐτόθι ἐγκατακοιμηθῆναι.

Amphiaraos, communicating through oracles, ordered them [the Thebans] to choose which of the following two options they wanted and to give up the other alternative—to have him as *mantis* or as a *summachos* [ally]. And they chose him as a *summachos*. And it is for this reason that no Theban is permitted to lie down and sleep in that spot [i.e., in his sanctuary].

Here Amphiaraos seems to participate actively in his own demise by devising a scenario whereby his oracle bans consultations from the local population, that is, from the clientele most likely to support it. The collocation of evidence from 1.52, 8.134, and the epigram, then, points to a concerted effort to effect the Amphiareion's diminution. Given the Ismenion's ties to Delphi, I would tentatively suggest that these attempts to bankrupt the Amphiareion stemmed not only from Apollo Ismenios's oracle but also, in some way, from Delphi, which viewed the seer's oracle as impinging on its own reputation.

Part 1 has traced a competitive dynamic between Delphi and the Amphiareion. Herodotus's Kroisos narrative repeatedly positions the Amphiareion as an oracle of comparable quality to Delphi. At the same time, both in the *Histories* and in the Boiotian inscription, we find evidence of attempts to discredit or disenfranchise the oracle of Amphiaraos, attempts in which Delphi itself may be implicated. In part 2, we will examine another individual over whom Delphi and Amphiaraos contest, namely, Amphiaraos's own son Alkmaion. Before turning to that contestation, I will close part 1 with a final image that again suggests a competitive and ongoing friction between the two oracles.

Pausanias's tour of Phleious, near Nemea, elicits the following digression (2.13.7):

ὄπισθεν δὲ τῆς ἀγορᾶς ἐστιν οἶκος ὀνομαζόμενος ὑπὸ Φλιασίων μαντικός. ἐς τοῦτον Ἀμφιάραος ἐλθὼν καὶ τὴν νύκτα ἐγκατακοιμηθεὶς μαντεύεσθαι τότε πρῶτον, ὡς οἱ Φλιάσιοί φασιν, ἤρξατο· τέως δὲ ἦν Ἀμφιάραος τῷ ἐκείνων λόγῳ ἰδιώτης τε καὶ οὐ μάντις. καὶ τὸ οἴκημα ἀπὸ τούτου συγκέκλεισται τὸν πάντα ἤδη χρόνον. οὐ πόρρω δέ ἐστιν ὁ καλούμενος Ὀμφαλός, Πελοποννήσου δὲ πάσης μέσον, εἰ δὴ τὰ ὄντα εἰρήκασιν.

Behind the marketplace is a house that the Phliasians call the House of Divination. Going into this house and spending the night there, Amphiaraos then began to prophesy for the first time, as the Phliasians say: for until then, according to their account, Amphiaraos was just an ordinary individual and not a *mantis*. And ever since this happened, the building has been permanently closed. Not far from there is a place called the Omphalos, the middle of the Peloponnese, if what they say is true.

The particular apposition that Pausanias formulates in this passage is curious. Near a house that transformed Amphiaraos into a seer is a place called the Omphalos, but, pointedly, not for the omphalos (naval stone) at Delphi. In other words, Pausanias constructs a juxtaposition between Amphiaraos and a term whose default association is with Delphi. Yet what initially seems to be a pairing between Amphiaraos and Delphi turns out to be misleading. Amphiaraos's House of Divination and the (Delphic) omphalos do not coexist in Phleious. Instead, Amphiaraos is paired with a strangely non-Delphic Omphalos, an omphalos now relocated to the center of the Peloponnese. This strange juxtaposition will be helpful to keep in mind in parts 2 and 3. For, as we will see there, Amphiaraos and Delphi almost never operate in tandem. When they are forced into close proximity, one is privileged over the other. What is more, the privileged entity, whether Amphiaraos or, more commonly, Delphi, effectively suppresses the other's salient attributes.

II. THE MYTH OF ALKMAION

It is hard to overestimate the popularity of the Alkmaion myth in antiquity. Alkmaion appears in the archaic Theban epics (the *Oidipodeia*, *Thebaid*, and *Epigonoi*, and as the eponymous hero of the epic sequel, the *Alkmeonis*.[45] Stesichoros wrote an *Eriphyle*. All three of the major tragedians produced plays that treated the Alkmaion myth in some way: Aeschylus wrote an *Epigonoi*, Sophocles an *Epigonoi*, an *Eriphyle*, and an *Alkmeon*, Euripides two Alkmeon plays, *Alkmeon in Psophis* and *Alkmeon in Corinth*. In addition, Achaeus wrote an *Alphesiboia*, Alphesiboia being the name of the first wife of Alkmaion, as well as an Alkmaion satyr play. The tragedian Agathon is also credited with an *Alkmeon*. In the fourth and third centuries, Alkmaion was the subject of tragedies by Timotheus (*Alkmeon* and *Alphesiboia*), Astydamas (*Alkmeon*), Evaretus (*Alkmeon*), Theodectes (*Alkmeon*), Chaeremon (*Alphesiboia*), and Nicomachus (*Alkmeon* and *Eriphyle*) and of comedies by Amphis and Mnesimachus.[46] The myth of Alkmaion endured into the Roman period. Ennius wrote an *Alcmeo*, and Accius wrote an *Alcmeo* and an *Alphesiboea*.[47] With the exception of a few fragments from the epic poems, Sophocles, and Euripides, all but the titles of most of these works is lost.

---

45. As West (2003: 5n3) notes, "Alcmaon is the epic form of the name, Alcmeon the Attic, Alcman the Doric; Alcmaeon is a false spelling." Since this "false spelling" has become the traditional spelling, I use it here, in its transliterated form, Alkmaion. I use the Attic spelling Alkmeon, however, when referring to titles from the Attic genre of tragedy. See Debiasi 2015: 261–63 for the *Alkmeonis*'s relation to the three main Theban epics. On the Theban epics and the *Alkmeonis*, see also Davies 2014.

46. For a comprehensive list of all known Alkmaion plays, see Jouan 1990: 157–58.

47. Propertius (1.15.5) and Ovid (*Met.* 9.407) also both refer to Alkmaion. Aristotle perhaps captures Alkmaion's perennial presence in tragedy best when he includes the hero in a list of other well-known subjects: "In the beginning poets recounted any sort of plot but now the best tragedies are composed about a few houses, like Alkmaion and Oidipous and Orestes and Meleager and Thyestes and Telephos and all the rest for whom it befell to suffer or to do terrible things" (*Poet.* 1453a18–22).

Apollodorus's *Bibliotheca* provides the most comprehensive extant account of the myth of Alkmaion (*Bibl.* 3.6.2; 3.7.2–6).[48] Because Apollodorus's purpose is to offer a complete survey of his material, he draws on a wide range of sources without privileging one variant over another.[49] In the case of the Alkmaion myth, his sources seem to depend on epic poetry, such as the *Epigonoi* and the *Alkmeonis*, but the genre of tragedy also clearly informs his account.[50] Given its exhaustive nature, the *Bibliotheca* preserves extended examples from what I will term the dominant or mainstream tradition of the myth of Alkmaion. Apollodorus's presentation intersects in significant ways with other instances of this mainstream tradition of the myth, such as those of Thucydides, Diodorus Siculus, and Pausanias.[51] Relying primarily on Apollodorus but enlisting these other authors as well, I will examine the two main episodes from the Alkmaion myth: first, Alkmaion's participation in the Epigonoi campaign and the matricide of Eriphyle, and second, his wandering, purification, and foundation following the matricide. Apollodorus's comprehensiveness will allow us to compare different takes on the same myth that are embedded in the *Bibliotheca* and also, importantly, to attend to certain patterns that emerge as a result of this inclusivity. As we will see, in both episodes, Alkmaion's connection with his father, Amphiaraos, is repeatedly undermined by Delphi. In the second episode, Delphi goes one step further by not only detaching Alkmaion from Amphiaraos but also transforming him into an oikist.

The Matricide of Eriphyle and the March on Thebes

The directive issued to Alkmaion to murder his mother, Eriphyle, appears t hree separate times in book 3 of the *Bibliotheca*. In the first two instances, it is also connected with an injunction for the Epigonoi to march on Thebes to avenge their fathers' own failed expedition. Comparing the three instantiations of this directive exposes a shift in the source of authority behind Alkmaion's acts of retribution.

In the *Bibliotheca*, Alkmaion makes his entrance on the mythic stage at the point of his father's departure as one of the Seven against Thebes (3.6.2). Foreseeing his

---

48. On the identity and floruit of Apollodorus (also known as Ps.-Apollodorus), see Higbie 2007: 243–45.

49. Higbie 2007: 243–45. See also Kenens 2011: 140: "Ps.-Apollodorus does not aspire to reconcile conflicting versions, nor does he show his preference for some variant."

50. Apollodorus mentions the "author of the *Alkmeonis*" at *Bibl.* 1.8.5 and also cites Euripides and summarizes the plot of his *Alkmeon in Corinth* at *Bibl.* 3.7.7. It is often assumed that the core of Apollodorus's account is based on the *Alkmeonis* (see, e.g., Debiasi 2015: 243), but this is not certain, given the fragmentary remains of the epic poem. Kenens (2011: 143–44) argues that Apollodorus read only prose summaries and did not have access to the original epic poems.

51. This overlap is not always the result of the authors drawing on the same sources (see Gantz 1993: 526). The mainstream tradition comprises epic, tragic, and prose variants from a wide range of ancient authors.

own death as well as the doomed outcome of the entire expedition, Amphiaraos had initially refused to take part in the campaign. But his wife, Eriphyle, bribed by Polyneikes with the necklace of Harmonia, betrayed her husband and compelled him to go.[52] Apollodorus succinctly captures the famous departure scene: Ἀμφιάραος δὲ ἀνάγκην ἔχων στρατεύεσθαι τοῖς παισὶν ἐντολὰς ἔδωκε τελειωθεῖσι τήν τε μητέρα κτείνειν καὶ ἐπὶ Θήβας στρατεύειν (And so, compelled to go to war, Amphiaraos issued commands to his sons, upon reaching adulthood, to kill their mother and march against Thebes, 3.6.2).[53] Proper retribution will come to Amphiaraos only if his sons avenge him in two separate ways: Alkmaion and Amphilochos must both kill their mother and attack Thebes.

We can compare this episode to the *Bibliotheca*'s two subsequent explanations for Alkmaion's course of action. After the departure of Amphiaraos, Apollodorus recounts the Seven's expedition up to Thebes and their fates there, including the seer's engulfment by the earth (3.6.8). When the mythographer next returns to the subject of Alkmaion, the hero appears together with the rest of the Epigonoi (3.7.2):

> μετὰ δὲ ἔτη δέκα οἱ τῶν ἀπολομένων παῖδες, κληθέντες ἐπίγονοι, στρατεύειν ἐπὶ Θήβας προῃροῦντο, τὸν τῶν πατέρων θάνατον τιμωρήσασθαι βουλόμενοι. καὶ μαντευομένοις αὐτοῖς ὁ θεὸς ἐθέσπισε νίκην Ἀλκμαίωνος ἡγουμένου. ὁ μὲν οὖν Ἀλκμαίων ἡγεῖσθαι τῆς στρατείας οὐ βουλόμενος πρὶν τίσασθαι τὴν μητέρα, ὅμως στρατεύεται· λαβοῦσα γὰρ Ἐριφύλη παρὰ Θερσάνδρου τοῦ Πολυνείκους τὸν πέπλον συνέπεισε καὶ τοὺς παῖδας στρατεύεσθαι. οἱ δὲ ἡγεμόνα Ἀλκμαίωνα ἑλόμενοι Θήβας ἐπολέμουν.

> And ten years later, the sons of the dead men, called the Epigonoi, chose to march against Thebes, desiring to avenge the death of their fathers. And when they consulted the oracle, the god prophesied victory to them with Alkmaion as their leader. Therefore Alkmaion, although not wanting to lead the campaign until he had punished his mother, nevertheless joined the expedition: for Eriphyle, having received the robe from Thersander, the son of Polyneikes, also persuaded her children to wage war. So, having chosen Alkmaion as their leader, they were making war on Thebes.

Delphi enters the picture with the arrival of the Epigonoi and immediately aligns itself with Alkmaion by selecting him as the leader who can bring victory to the Epigonoi.[54] The oracle's choice of Alkmaion is not necessarily expected: Adrastos's

---

52. Eriphyle is able to force Amphiaraos to join the campaign because of a former agreement worked out between Adrastos and Amphiaraos: if there should be a dispute between them, Eriphyle would arbitrate and make the final decision.

53. The departure of Amphiaraos was also a common subject in other media. See Davies 2014: 103–6 for a thorough survey of vase paintings featuring Amphiaraos and Alkmaion. Amphiaraos's departure scene is also included in Pausanias's ekphrasis of the chest of Kypselos (5.17.5–8).

54. The prophesying "god" here can only mean Delphi. See Apollod. *Bibl.* 3.7.5, where θεσπίζω is again used in the context of Delphi; see also *Bibl.* 1.9.16.

son Aigialeus would have been the more obvious candidate for the role and actually appears as the leader in at least one other version.⁵⁵ Perhaps by some kind of proleptic logic, the reasoning of this variant goes, Aigialeus cannot be leader of the successful expedition because he is doomed to die in Thebes. Yet Aigialeus's own fate alone does not fully account for Delphi's preference for Alkmaion here, as we will see below.

In Apollodorus's arrangement, Alkmaion's acceptance of his status as a Delphi-sanctioned leader is closely construed with his attitude toward Eriphyle ("Therefore Alkmaion, although not wanting to lead the campaign until he had punished his mother, nevertheless joined the expedition: for Eriphyle, having received the robe from Thersander, the son of Polyneikes, also persuaded her children to wage war," 3.7.2). In this scene, Eriphyle reprises her role as a woman who, seduced by bribes, betrays her family.⁵⁶ Taken at face value, however, the passage makes little sense. Alkmaion joins the expedition because of the oracle's pronouncement, but, in the same breath, Apollodorus also says that Alkmaion joins the expedition because Eriphyle persuaded him to do so. The correlation between and logical sequence of Delphi's and Eriphyle's constraints on Alkmaion are difficult to determine. Further, as Marie Delcourt once wondered concerning these lines, "What influence could she [Eriphyle] have on her son who is already designated to kill her?"⁵⁷ Indeed, the same question could be extended to Delphi's own role at this moment: What influence could Delphi have on Alkmaion when his father had already ordered him to march on Thebes? Delcourt's bewilderment over Eriphyle and the corollary question of Delphi's own presence in the episode reveal a curious aspect of the passage: in this chapter's rendering of Alkmaion's motivations, both parts of Amphiaraos's injunction have been reallocated to Delphi and Eriphyle, respectively. It is now Delphi who compels Alkmaion to march on Thebes by proclaiming that the Epigonoi can win only with him as leader. And, at the same time, Eriphyle, by betraying Alkmaion directly, generates a reason independent of her previous treachery for why her son should want to kill her.

Although Eriphyle's second betrayal may appear redundant, it allows this second scene to supersede the initial one centered on Amphiaraos's injunctions. The particular telling of the Epigonoi episode is thorough in its responsion and thus in its cancellation of the need for the earlier Amphiaraos episode. Yet, the results of the double erasure of Amphiaraos's demands are somewhat confused. The price

---

55. For Aigialeus as commander, see Eur. *Suppl.* 1213–26. Some scholars account for this discrepancy by assigning Alkmaion's role as leader to the version found in the *Alkmeonis* and Aigialeus's to the *Epigonoi* (see Debiasi 2015: 263).

56. For this second bribing as an epic motif, see Debiasi 2015: 265n28.

57. Delcourt 1959: 47 (my translation).

this passage pays for detaching these particular directives from the seer and reassigning them to Delphi and Eriphyle is a disjointed juxtaposition. Within the same statement, Delphi and Eriphyle seemingly act of their own accord and in parallel to one another as they each take on one half of Amphiaraos's former orders for vengeance. To be sure, Amphiaraos has not been completely expunged from the picture. His existence is implied by the καί ("Eriphyle had persuaded her sons also [*kai*] to go to war") that calls to mind Eriphyle's more notorious treachery against her husband. Nevertheless, in this second instantiation of accounting for Alkmaion's conduct, nowhere are Amphiaraos's original commands explicitly recalled. With the introduction of Delphi and Eriphyle into the story, the seer's own instructions are rendered gratuitous.

After the Epigonoi's successful campaign against Thebes, Alkmaion kills his mother, is pursued by her Erinys, and wanders the Peloponnese until he is purified. Apollodorus begins his final episode on Alkmaion with yet another version of how Alkmaion came to kill his mother (3.7.5):

> μετὰ δὲ τὴν Θηβῶν ἅλωσιν αἰσθόμενος Ἀλκμαίων καὶ ἐπ' αὐτῷ δῶρα εἰληφυῖαν Ἐριφύλην τὴν μητέρα μᾶλλον ἠγανάκτησε, καὶ χρήσαντος Ἀπόλλωνος αὐτῷ τὴν μητέρα ἀπέκτεινεν. ἔνιοι μὲν λέγουσι σὺν Ἀμφιλόχῳ τῷ ἀδελφῷ κτεῖναι τὴν Ἐριφύλην, ἔνιοι δὲ ὅτι μόνος.

> Following the capture of Thebes, having learned that Eriphyle had taken bribes also against him, Alkmaion was all the more angered and, with Apollo directing him through an oracle, killed his mother. Some say that he killed Eriphyle together with his brother Amphilochos, others that he did it alone.

In the *Bibliotheca*'s third reference to Eriphyle's matricide, Delphi itself claims responsibility for spurring Alkmaion to kill his mother. Alkmaion acts under the direction of an oracle from Apollo, with the result that Delphi alone now presides over Alkmaion's actions. As in the preceding example, the only remnant of Amphiaraos is as an adverbial hint (i.e., Alkmaion learns that Eriphyle has been bribed also [*kai*] with a view to his own demise).

It is surely not coincidental that, at the very moment in which Delphi blatantly solidifies its narrative hold on Alkmaion by taking over the injunction of matricide, Apollodorus acknowledges multiple versions of the myth of Eriphyle's murder ("Some say that he killed Eriphyle together with his brother Amphilochos, others that he did it alone"). Relying on the alternatives included in the *Bibliotheca* alone and without attempting to assign these discrepancies to their respective lost epic poems, we might even cautiously understand this editorial statement as signaling the acknowledgment of an "Amphiaraos version" and a "Delphi version" of events. In the Amphiaraos version (*Bibl.* 3.6.2), the seer enjoins both of his sons, Alkmaion and Amphilochos, to avenge him, while the Delphi version (*Bibl.* 3.7.5) is invested only in Alkmaion.⁵⁸ Such a division, in which Alkmaion appears with Amphilochos in connection with their father but acts alone in contexts that highlight Delphi, is in keeping with instantiations of the myth in other sources. Vase paintings, for example, frequently portray both Alkmaion and Amphilochos as present during the departure of Amphiaraos.⁵⁹ But, as we will see in the conclusion, Amphilochos, in stark contrast to his brother, has no traditional connection with Delphi. Generally speaking, Delphi appears to be interested only in Alkmaion.⁶⁰

Diodorus Siculus's rendition of both Amphiaraos's departure and the Epigonoi's campaign is more succinct than that of Apollodorus, but it is still possible to detect a comparable co-option of responsibility for Alkmaion's actions as we proceed from the departure scene of Amphiaraos to the Epigonoi's and Alkmaion's consultations at Delphi. Thus Diodorus also records that Amphiaraos ordered Alkmaion to kill Eriphyle and that Alkmaion eventually did so "in accordance with his father's commands" (4.65.6–7). But when the Epigonoi assemble to wage war on Thebes, they turn to Delphi for guidance (4.66.1). Delphi commands them to march against Thebes with Alkmaion as their leader, whereupon Alkmaion decides to consult Delphi himself (4.66.2–3):

ὁ δ' Ἀλκμαίων αἱρεθεὶς ὑπ' αὐτῶν στρατηγὸς ἐπηρώτησε τὸν θεὸν περὶ τῆς ἐπὶ τὰς Θήβας στρατείας καὶ περὶ τῆς Ἐριφύλης τῆς μητρὸς κολάσεως. τοῦ δ' Ἀπόλλωνος χρήσαντος ἀμφότερα τὰ προειρημένα πρᾶξαι διὰ τὸ μὴ μόνον τὸν χρυσοῦν ὅρμον δέξασθαι κατὰ τῆς ἀπωλείας τοῦ πατρός, ἀλλὰ καὶ πέπλον λαβεῖν αὐτὴν κατὰ τῆς τοῦ υἱοῦ τελευτῆς·

Alkmaion, having been chosen by them to be their leader, consulted the god concerning the expedition against Thebes and retribution against his mother, Eriphyle. And Apollo directed him through an oracle to accomplish both of these previous orders not only because she [Eriphyle] had received the golden necklace in exchange for the destruction of his father but also because she had taken the robe in exchange for the death of her son.

---

58. To be clear, I am not interested in matching up the contrasts acknowledged here between different versions of Alkmaion's matricide to different (lost) poems of the Theban epics, although others have attempted to do so (see Stoneman 1981: 47; and the following note).

59. Stoneman (1981: 47–49) notes how the earliest vase paintings depicting the departure of Amphiaraos include both sons. He connects this version with the *Thebaid*. Based on his survey of vase paintings of Amphiaraos's departure, Stoneman (48) argues that Alkmaion gradually became the more important son in the story "to the exclusion of Amphilochus." Pausanias also mentions both brothers in his description of the chest of Kypselos (5.17.5–8).

60. An exception to this discrepancy can be found in Euripides' *Alkmeon in Corinth* in which Apollo appears and commands Amphilochos to found Argos Amphilochion. Yet, in this version, Amphilochos is the son of Alkmaion, not his brother.

Diodorus's account features a double consultation at Delphi so that we hear of Delphi's endorsement of Alkmaion's leadership of the Epigonoi twice over. Delphi also sanctions the act of matricide by reminding Alkmaion of Eriphyle's second bribery and thus providing a reason separate from Amphiaraos's revenge for why she must be killed. In Diodorus's account, Delphi again has the last word on Alkmaion's conduct and fate.

Taken together, the three Alkmaion episodes in the *Bibliotheca*, and the corroborating sequence found in Diodorus Siculus, present a scenario in which Delphi repeats the earlier commands of Amphiaraos and, by repeating them, simultaneously replaces them. The result of this repetition is the conspicuous assertion of Delphi's connection with Alkmaion and the consequential suppression of Amphiaraos's own connection with and control of his son.

Wandering, Purification, and Foundation

The second episode of the Alkmaion myth relates the hero's wandering, purification, and eventual foundation of Akarnania following the death of Eriphyle. As we will see, the pattern of Delphic appropriation continues. What is more, the purpose of Delphi's claim to Alkmaion also finally makes itself known: in the productive and explicit connection that forms between Delphi and Alkmaion, Alkmaion is not merely purified of his matricide and successfully released from madness. He also transforms from the son of a seer to the Delphi-sanctioned oikist of Akarnania.

In the *Bibliotheca*, Alkmaion's ordeal unfolds in the following manner, beginning with Delphi's role in the matricide of Eriphyle discussed above (3.7.5):

μετὰ δὲ τὴν Θηβῶν ἅλωσιν αἰσθόμενος Ἀλκμαίων καὶ ἐπ' αὐτῷ δῶρα εἰληφυῖαν Ἐριφύλην τὴν μητέρα μᾶλλον ἠγανάκτησε, καὶ χρήσαντος Ἀπόλλωνος αὐτῷ τὴν μητέρα ἀπέκτεινεν. ἔνιοι μὲν λέγουσι σὺν Ἀμφιλόχῳ τῷ ἀδελφῷ κτεῖναι τὴν Ἐριφύλην, ἔνιοι δὲ ὅτι μόνος. Ἀλκμαίωνα δὲ μετῆλθεν ἐρινὺς τοῦ μητρῴου φόνου, καὶ μεμηνὼς πρῶτον μὲν εἰς Ἀρκαδίαν πρὸς Ὀικλέα παραγίνεται, ἐκεῖθεν δὲ εἰς Ψωφῖδα πρὸς Φηγέα. καθαρθεὶς δὲ ὑπ' αὐτοῦ Ἀρσινόην γαμεῖ τὴν τούτου θυγατέρα, καὶ τόν τε ὅρμον καὶ τὸν πέπλον ἔδωκε ταύτῃ. γενομένης δὲ ὕστερον τῆς γῆς δι' αὐτὸν ἀφόρου, χρήσαντος αὐτῷ τοῦ θεοῦ πρὸς Ἀχελῷον ἀπιέναι καὶ παρ' ἐκεῖνον παλινδικίαν λαμβάνειν, τὸ μὲν πρῶτον πρὸς Οἰνέα παραγίνεται εἰς Καλυδῶνα καὶ ξενίζεται παρ' αὐτῷ, ἔπειτα ἀφικόμενος εἰς Θεσπρωτοὺς τῆς χώρας ἀπελαύνεται. τελευταῖον δὲ ἐπὶ τὰς Ἀχελῴου πηγὰς παραγενόμενος καθαίρεταί τε ὑπ' αὐτοῦ καὶ τὴν ἐκείνου θυγατέρα Καλλιρρόην λαμβάνει, καὶ ὃν Ἀχελῷος προσέχωσε τόπον κτίσας κατῴκησε. Καλλιρρόης δὲ ὕστερον τόν τε ὅρμον καὶ τὸν πέπλον ἐπιθυμούσης λαβεῖν, καὶ λεγούσης οὐ συνοικήσειν αὐτῷ εἰ μὴ λάβοι ταῦτα, παραγενόμενος εἰς Ψωφῖδα Ἀλκμαίων Φηγεῖ λέγει τεθεσπίσθαι τῆς μανίας ἀπαλλαγὴν ἑαυτῷ, τὸν ὅρμον ὅταν εἰς Δελφοὺς κομίσας ἀναθῇ καὶ τὸν πέπλον. ὁ δὲ πιστεύσας δίδωσι μηνύσαντος δὲ θεράποντος ὅτι Καλλιρρόη ταῦτα λαβὼν ἐκόμιζεν, ἐνεδρευθεὶς ὑπὸ τῶν Φηγέως παίδων ἐπιτάξαντος τοῦ Φηγέως ἀναιρεῖται. Ἀρσινόην δὲ μεμφομένην

οἱ τοῦ Φηγέως παῖδες ἐμβιβάσαντες εἰς λάρνακα κομίζουσιν εἰς Τεγέαν καὶ διδόασι
δούλην Ἀγαπήνορι, καταψευσάμενοι αὐτῆς τὸν Ἀλκμαίωνος φόνον.

Following the capture of Thebes, having learned that Eriphyle had taken bribes also against him, Alkmaion was all the more angered and, with Apollo directing him through an oracle, killed his mother. Some say that he killed Eriphyle together with his brother Amphilochos, others that he did it alone. But the Erinys of his mother's murder pursued Alkamion and, going mad, he first went to Oikles in Arkadia and from there to Phegeus in Psophis. After being purified by him, Alkmaion married Phegeus's daughter Arsinoe, and he gave to her the necklace and the robe. But, later on, when the land became barren on account of him, the god prophesied to Alkmaion to go to Acheloös and to stand a second trial there. But first Alkmaion went to Oineus in Kalydon and was entertained by him, and then he came to the Thesprotians, but he was driven out of their land. Finally, having come to the springs of the Acheloös, he was purified by him and took his daughter Kallirhoe as a wife, and, having founded the land that the Acheloös had heaped up, he colonized it. But, later, when Kallirhoe desired to have the necklace and the robe and said that she would not live with him unless she received these things, Alkmaion went to Phegeus in Psophis and said that it had been prophesied that he would be released from madness whenever he took the necklace and the robe and dedicated them at Delphi. And Phegeus, believing him, gave them to him. But a servant revealed that Alkmaion was taking these things to give them to Kallirhoe, and Alkmaion was ambushed and killed by the sons of Phegeus at their father's command. And when Arsinoe chastised them, the sons of Phegeus carried her in a chest to Tegea and gave her to Agapenor as a slave, falsely accusing her of the murder of Alkmaion.

Upon killing his mother, Alkmaion first travels to Oikles in Arcadia and then on to Phegeus at Psophis. At Psophis, he is purified by Phegeus and marries Phegeus's daughter, Arsinoe. But the purification somehow fails, and the land of Psophis becomes barren as a result. Consequently, Delphi directs him to the Acheloös River, and, eventually arriving there, Alkmaion is purified a second time. The second purification proves effective, and Alkmaion proceeds to marry for a second time as well, this time Kallirhoe, the daughter of Acheloös. He also settles and colonizes (κτίσας κατῴκησε) the land, acts that, although not named explicitly in this version, refer to his foundation of Akarnania. Kallirhoe demands the necklace and robe of Harmonia, still in the possession of Arsinoe.[61] Alkmaion's attempt to retrieve the necklace and robe from his first wife and present it to his second precipitates his own death at the hands of Arsinoe's brothers.

---

61. Kallirhoe refuses to live with (συνοικήσειν) Alkmaion until she obtains the necklace. Συνοικήσειν, although here ostensibly meaning "to dwell with," may have a secondary, colonial resonance in this context, since the verb can also mean "to settle or found with."

In this way the myth of Alkmaion continually doubles back on itself, as if the particular form of madness thought up by Eriphyle's Erinys is for her son to endure everything twice over. But this web of redundancies organizes itself into a familiar pattern once we see that Alkmaion's movements are dictated by the same competing forces and resulting transference of authority discussed above. In need of purification, Alkmaion does not initially seek Apollo's aid, as we might expect, especially since the episode opens with Apollo himself giving the order of matricide. Instead Alkmaion heads for the house of Oikles, the father of Amphiaraos. From his grandfather, Alkmaion travels directly to Phegeus, and this progression strongly suggests that Alkmaion goes there to be purified at Oikles' instructions. Only after the land of Psophis suffers from his continuing pollution does Alkmaion turn to Delphi for help and is guided toward the location of a second and more efficacious purification. These two purifications of Alkmaion are clearly doublets of each other, and their equivalence is bolstered by the other recurring details associated with each act: a new home, a ruler with a daughter to marry, a wife in need of Harmonia's accoutrements. Just as Alkmaion receives the same injunctions from both Amphiaraos and Delphi to march on Thebes and kill Eriphyle, so he is assisted first by Oikles (who takes the place of his son Amphiaraos) and then by Delphi in his efforts to be released from madness.

Yet the doublets are more than a series of simple repetitions. They are also a powerful justification for the dominance of Delphi in the Alkmaion narrative. Delphi appears precisely because Oikles' own efforts prove to be ineffectual. Despite Oikles' implied directive to seek help from Phegeus, Alkmaion remains a polluted figure whose presence wreaks havoc in Psophis and who must turn to Delphi to receive any sort of lasting purification. Further, the implication of the earlier sequence of injunctions examined above concerning the march on Thebes and the murder of Eriphyle is now explicit. Delphi's role in Apollodorus's myth of Alkmaion is cast not as redundant or secondary but as crucial. As Apollodorus, and the sources on which he drew, present it, Alkmaion is better off with Delphi than with Oikles and Amphiaraos.

Delphi further solidifies its hold on Alkmaion through the final appearance of the necklace of Harmonia. Apollodorus tells us that Alkmaion attempted to reclaim the necklace and robe of Harmonia from his first wife because, Alkmaion alleged, it had been prophesied that he would be released from madness when he dedicated these objects to Delphi (*Bibl.* 3.7.5). A variation appears in Pausanias's account of the myth: the sons of Phegeus murder Alkmaion and, afterward, dedicate the necklace to "the god in Delphi" (8.24.10). In Ephorus's version, Delphi itself explicitly issues an oracle demanding the necklace (*FGrH* 70 F 96 = Athen. *Dein.* 6.22 p. 232 DF):

Ἔφορος δὲ ἢ Δημόφιλος ὁ υἱὸς αὐτοῦ ἐν τῇ τριακοστῇ τῶν ἱστοριῶν περὶ τοῦ ἐν Δελφοῖς ἱεροῦ λέγων φησίν· Ὀνόμαρχος δὲ καὶ Φάυλλος καὶ Φάλαικος οὐ μόνον ἅπαντα τὰ τοῦ θεοῦ ἐξεκόμισαν, ἀλλὰ τὸ τελευταῖον αἱ γυναῖκες αὐτῶν τόν τε τῆς Ἐριφύλης κόσμον ἔλαβον, ὃν Ἀλκμαίων εἰς Δελφοὺς ἀνέθηκε κελεύσαντος τοῦ θεοῦ.

And Ephorus or his son Demophilus, discussing the temple at Delphi, says: Onomarchos and Phaullos and Phalaikos not only seized all of the god's possessions but in the end their wives also took the ornament of Eriphyle, which Alkmaion had dedicated at Delphi at the god's command.

Whether through Alkmaion's excuse, the decision of the sons of Phegeus, or Delphi's own orders, the necklace (and robe) of Harmonia, having crisscrossed Greece, at last comes rest at Delphi. We might read this dedication as another moment in which Delphi attaches itself to an element more readily associated with Amphiaraos. Here Delphi physically secures possession of the token that above all symbolizes Eriphyle's betrayal of her husband. In this way, Oikles cedes authority to Delphi in the contest of Alkmaion's purification, and this transference of authority from Alkmaion's family to Delphi seems to be concretized in the closing image of the dedication of the necklace of Harmonia at Delphi. But the consequences of Delphi's successful advice for Alkmaion are more far reaching and penetrating than simply sending him to Acheloös to be purified properly. For, at the same time as the Oikles-Amphiaraos trajectory is cut short, the myth ramps up its colonial characteristics and becomes a full-fledged foundation tale.

Apollodorus's account is valuable because it exposes the myth's conversion to a foundation tale at the expense of Alkmaion's connection with his mantic family. Yet the colonial component of his presentation of the Alkmaion myth, while present, is relatively compressed in contrast to other accounts. When we collate the *Bibliotheca* with other representations of Alkmaion's wanderings, we are able to see more clearly the role Delphi plays in the foundation of Akarnania and the extent to which Alkmaion becomes an oikist under Delphi's direction. Pausanias and Thucydides are our best sources for fleshing out Apollodorus's episode of Alkmaion's foundation beside the Acheloös River. Here I will not present the two authors in chronological order but will rather begin with the later Pausanias, since the connections between Apollodorus's and Pausanias's versions are more predictable. I will then turn to Thucydides' own distinctive representation of Alkmaion as oikist of Akarnania.

Pausanias records the myth of Alkmaion after describing the cypress grove in Psophis that marks the hero's burial site (8.24.8–9):

ὁ δὲ Ἀλκμαίων ἡνίκα τὴν μητέρα ἀποκτείνας ἔφυγεν ἐξ Ἄργους, τότε ἐς τὴν Ψωφῖδα ἐλθών, Φηγίαν ἔτι ἀπὸ τοῦ Φηγέως ὀνομαζομένην, συνῴκησεν Ἀλφεσιβοίᾳ τῇ Φηγέως θυγατρὶ καὶ αὐτῇ δῶρα ὡς τὸ εἰκὸς καὶ ἄλλα καὶ τὸν ὅρμον δίδωσιν. ὡς δὲ οἰκοῦντι αὐτῷ παρὰ τοῖς Ἀρκάσιν οὐδὲν ἐγίνετο ἡ νόσος ῥᾴων, κατέφυγεν ἐπὶ τὸ μαντεῖον τὸ ἐν Δελφοῖς, καὶ αὐτὸν ἡ Πυθία διδάσκει τὸν Ἐριφύλης ἀλάστορα ἐς ταύτην οἱ μόνην χώραν οὐ συνακολουθήσειν, ἥτις ἐστὶ νεωτάτη καὶ ἡ θάλασσα τοῦ μητρῴου μιάσματος ἀνέφηνεν ὕστερον αὐτήν. καὶ ὁ μὲν ἐξευρὼν τοῦ Ἀχελῴου τὴν πρόσχωσιν ἐνταῦθα ᾤκησε, καὶ γυναῖκα ἔσχε Καλλιρόην τοῦ Ἀχελῴου θυγατέρα λόγῳ τῷ Ἀκαρνάνων, καί οἱ παῖδες Ἀκαρνάν τε καὶ Ἀμφότερος ἐγένοντο· ἀπὸ δὲ τοῦ Ἀκαρνᾶνος τοῖς ἐν τῇ ἠπείρῳ ταύτῃ τὸ ὄνομα τὸ νῦν γενέσθαι λέγουσι τὰ πρὸ τούτου Κούρησι καλουμένοις. ἐς ἐπιθυμίας δὲ ἀνοήτους πολλοὶ μὲν ἄνδρες, γυναῖκες δὲ ἔτι πλέον ἐξοκέλλουσιν.

When Alkmaion killed his mother, he fled from Argos and then, arriving in Psophis, which at that time was still called Phegia after Phegeus, settled there with Alphesiboia,[62] the daughter of Phegeus, and likely gave her, besides other things, the necklace. But since his sickness did not improve while he was living among the Arkadians, he fled to the oracle at Delphi, and the Pythia instructed him that the only land into which the avenging spirit of Eriphyle would not accompany him was a very new land and one that the sea had brought to light after the pollution of killing his mother. And Alkmaion, discovering the silting up of the Acheloös, settled there, and took as a wife Kallirhoe, the daughter of Acheloös, according to the Akarnanians. His children were Akarnan and Amphoteros: they say that those who live in this part of the mainland take their present name from this Akarnan, having been previously called Kouretes. Many men run aground on senseless passions, and even more women.

The trip to Oikles is absent from Pausanias's version, and we do not learn from him why Alkmaion initially travels to Psophis. At the same time, Pausanias provides a fuller account of Alkmaion's consultation of the Delphic oracle and includes the Pythia's riddling response that, in order to be released from madness, Alkmaion must discover a new land that has been brought to light since his mother's death.[63]

When taken together, Apollodorus's and Pausanias's accounts provide all the distinctive markers of an exemplary foundation tale: the composite story includes a murderer in exile (the polluted matricide Alkmaion), a crisis (the barren land of Psophis), a consultation at Delphi, the Pythia's geographical riddle of the sanctioned location, the resulting foundation (Akarnania), the marriage of the oikist to a local bride (Kallirhoe), and the oikist's naming of the land (after Alkmaion's son, Akarnan).

Thucydides' own rendering of the myth will serve as a final example of the mainstream tradition of the Alkmaion myth. Like Pausanias's account, Thucydides' version emphasizes the myth's riddling foundation oracle and thereby highlights the moment at which Delphi transforms Alkmaion into an oikist. What distinguishes Thucydides' account from those of Apollodorus and Pausanias,

---

62. Pausanias and the tragedians use the name Alphesiboia instead of Arsinoe for Alkmaion's first wife.

63. These details clarify certain aspects of the *Bibliotheca*'s comparable passage. Pausanias's inclusion of the oracular riddle explains Apollodorus's reference to the silting up of the Acheloös and why Apollodorus finds this detail worth mentioning (*Bibl.* 3.7.5).

however, is the way in which a conspicuous suppression of Amphiaraos shapes the configuration of Delphi's foundation oracle to Alkmaion.

Thucydides includes the story of Alkmaion as part of his discussion of Akarnania's unusual geography.[64] In presenting the myth, Thucydides departs from his normal narrative style and, drawing on oral tradition, appears to transform himself temporarily into another Herodotus.[65] The myth is a self-contained unit, marked off from the larger narrative with its own introduction and conclusion (2.102.5–6):

λέγεται δὲ καὶ Ἀλκμέωνι τῷ Ἀμφιάρεω, ὅτε δὴ ἀλᾶσθαι αὐτὸν μετὰ τὸν φόνον τῆς μητρός, τὸν Ἀπόλλω ταύτην τὴν γῆν χρῆσαι οἰκεῖν, ὑπειπόντα οὐκ εἶναι λύσιν τῶν δειμάτων πρὶν ἂν εὑρὼν ἐν ταύτῃ τῇ χώρᾳ κατοικίσηται ἥτις ὅτε ἔκτεινε τὴν μητέρα μήπω ὑπὸ ἡλίου ἑωρᾶτο μηδὲ γῆ ἦν, ὡς τῆς γε ἄλλης αὐτῷ μεμιασμένης. ὁ δ' ἀπορῶν, ὥς φασι, μόλις κατενόησε τὴν πρόσχωσιν ταύτην τοῦ Ἀχελῴου, καὶ ἐδόκει αὐτῷ ἱκανὴ ἂν κεχῶσθαι δίαιτα τῷ σώματι ἀφ' οὗπερ κτείνας τὴν μητέρα οὐκ ὀλίγον χρόνον ἐπλανᾶτο. καὶ κατοικισθεὶς ἐς τοὺς περὶ Οἰνιάδας τόπους ἐδυνάστευσέ τε καὶ ἀπὸ Ἀκαρνᾶνος παιδὸς ἑαυτοῦ τῆς χώρας τὴν ἐπωνυμίαν ἐγκατέλιπεν. τὰ μὲν περὶ Ἀλκμέωνα τοιαῦτα λεγόμενα παρελάβομεν.

And it is said also that by way of his oracle Apollo told Alkmaion, son of Amphiaraos, when he was wandering after the murder of his mother, to dwell in this place, adding that there would be no release from his terrors until he found and settled in that place which, when he killed his mother, had never been seen by the sun and was not land, on the grounds that the rest of the earth was polluted for him. And he being at a loss, as they tell it, at last noticed this deposit of the Acheloös, and it seemed to him that a place sufficiently able to provide for life would have been thrown up from the time he had killed his mother and engaged in his lengthy wanderings. And settling in the district around Oiniadai, he held power, and he named the country after his own son Akarnan. Such is the story we have received about Alkmaion.

Like Apollodorus and Pausanias, Thucydides deploys a number of prominent motifs associated with colonial discourse: the murderer in exile, the consultation

---

64. Thucydides' account of how Alkmaion came to settle Akarnania has garnered attention for just how un-Thucydidean it sounds. The passage is atypical not only for its mythological subject matter but also for the historian's use of poetic language, including the phrase λύσιν τῶν δειμάτων (release from terrors) and the culminating and "powerfully-positioned" μεμιασμένης, a word that Thucydides uses only here (Hornblower 2004: 106–7). According to Hornblower (106), both nouns in the phrase λύσιν τῶν δειμάτων are poetic. δεῖμα is only found one other time in Thucydides (7.80), and Hornblower compares the expression to Pindar's λύσις πενθέων (N. 10.76–77).

65. Conversely, Herodotus's own discussion of this region at 2.10.3 is more "scientific," i.e., more seemingly Thucydidean. Herodotus does not mention the myth of Alkmaion at all but focuses only on the geological phenomenon of the silting up of the Acheloös River. On the derivation of this mythological digression from oral tradition and popular legend, see Pothou 2009: 91. By Pothou's (88–89) count, there are only four mythological digressions of this sort in Thucydides in contrast to their frequent use in Herodotus.

with Delphi, and the oracular riddle whose correct interpretation divulges the authorized site for the oikist's foundation. Yet at the same time as we encounter a quintessential foundation tale, we also find Alkmaion's potential mantic ability evoked and, just as quickly, rejected. The particular form that the riddling oracle takes allows for the two options of seer and oikist to be in play simultaneously for Alkmaion. It is possible to discern Thucydides' evocation of Alkmaion's mantic abilities by comparing his formulation of the Pythia's riddle to the version presented by Pausanias. Again, Pausanias describes the oracle as follows (8.24.8):

ὡς δὲ οἰκοῦντι αὐτῷ παρὰ τοῖς Ἀρκάσιν οὐδὲν ἐγίνετο ἡ νόσος ῥᾴων, κατέφυγεν ἐπὶ τὸ μαντεῖον τὸ ἐν Δελφοῖς, καὶ αὐτὸν ἡ Πυθία διδάσκει τὸν Ἐριφύλης ἀλάστορα ἐς ταύτην οἱ μόνην χώραν οὐ συνακολουθήσειν, ἥτις ἐστὶ νεωτάτη καὶ ἡ θάλασσα τοῦ μητρῴου μιάσματος ἀνέφηνεν ὕστερον αὐτήν.

But since his sickness did not improve while he was living among the Arkadians, he fled to the oracle at Delphi, and the Pythia instructed him that the only land into which the avenging spirit of Eriphyle would not accompany him was a very new land and one that the sea had brought to light after the pollution of killing his mother.

Pausanias's Pythia emphasizes the newness of the land and the role played by the sea in creating it. What remains for Alkmaion to discover after this consultation is simply the precise location where the sea has created such a phenomenon. By contrast, for Thucydides, the Pythia's utterance is truly enigmatic; her vision is that of an "impossible landscape."[66] Delphi commands Alkmaion to settle in a place that the sun had never seen at the time of his mother's murder. To answer this riddle, to discover not only where such a place is but also what such a place could possibly be, entails a degree of interpretive talent that Pausanias's Alkmaion does not require.[67] Indeed, the difficulty of the riddle is registered by Alkmaion's reaction: *aporia* takes hold of him before "with difficulty" (*molis*) he grasps the answer.

As Alkmaion wavers, a solution to the riddle offers itself as an available, and perhaps even as the default, interpretation: the location to which Apollo directs Alkmaion is underground. Whereas Pausanias emphasizes the aftermath of the silting up of the Acheloös and the land's emergence into the light, Thucydides' riddle focuses on the region's initial state as a place shrouded in darkness and unseen by the sun. Yet the conjuration of a subterranean region is no arbitrary image when directed at the son of Amphiaraos, whose own defining moment was to be swallowed by the earth. Given the formulation of the riddle, I would suggest

---

66. "Impossible landscape" is Dougherty's characterization of the content of a number of foundation oracles: the oikist receives a description of a seemingly impossible landscape, and part of his task is to uncover how an actual geographical location fits the riddling terms of the Pythia's oracle. See Dougherty 1993: 45–60 for other examples.

67. See Dougherty 1993: 50–51 for the way in which foundation tales place a high level of importance on the interpretive abilities of the oikist.

that Delphi's injunction initially appears to encourage Alkmaion to become another Amphiaraos, to descend under the earth, and so to become a chthonic oracle like his father. That this option is a real prospect for Alkmaion is bolstered by the fate of Amphiaraos's other son, Amphilochos, whose purported tomb at the site of Mallos in Cilicia did become a chthonic oracle.[68]

We are perhaps meant to see the possibility of an Amphiaraos-like descent occurring to Alkmaion himself as he strains to decode the riddle. In this context, I revisit a suggestion by G. L. Huxley concerning a tantalizing fragment from the Theban epic *Alkmeonis*. The single line forms an address to Zagreus and Gaia (*PEG* F 3 = *Etym. Gud.* s.v. Ζαγρεύς):

> Ζαγρεὺς ὁ μεγάλως ἀγρεύων, ὡς·
> "πότνια Γῆ, Ζαγρεῦ τε θεῶν πανυπέρτατε πάντων,"
> ὁ τὴν Ἀλκμαιωνίδα γράψας ἔφη.

> Zagreus: the one who hunts greatly, as the writer of the *Alkmeonis* said: "Mistress Earth, and Zagreus, highest of all the gods."

Zagreus remains a shadowy figure. Aeschylus places him in the underworld, where he is possibly the son of Hades (frr. 5, 228). Callimachus says that the Titans tore him to pieces and that he was subsequently buried beside the oracular tripod at Delphi (*Aitia* frr. 43.117 and 643 Pfeiffer; Euphor. fr 13 Powell).[69] Plutarch lists Zagreus in a series of names associated with Dionysos at Delphi (*De E* 9.389a).[70] The evidence allows us at least to establish that Zagreus has chthonic associations and is linked to Delphi. Given Gaia's own connection with the sanctuary, Huxley reasonably conjectures that the epic fragment is part of an invocation made at Delphi. Further, the speaker is likely to be Alkmaion himself, who appeals to the two chthonic gods after receiving the Pythia's oracle. As Huxley observes, "In the circumstances the tainted hero's prayer to Earth and the buried Zagreus for help in his seemingly impossible search for land hidden from the Sun was intelligently apt."[71] That is, the *Alkmeonis* fragment best fits a setting in which Alkmaion appeals to these chthonic, Delphic gods to aid him in discovering a place beneath the earth.[72]

---

68. On the chthonic nature of Amphilochos's oracle at Mallos, see Bonnechere 2003: 170 and n. 7; and the conclusion.

69. See Arrigoni 2003.

70. The Orphics connect Zagreus with Dionysus as the son of Persephone (vs. Semele) and Zeus. But Zagreus seems to have been a god in his own right before becoming linked to Dionysus (Gantz 1993: 118).

71. Huxley 1969: 52.

72. Despite the associations that Zagreus and Gaia both have with Delphi, Debiasi (2015: 270–71) proposes that Alkmaion utters these lines in the *Alkmeonis* to the oracle of Amphiaraos. Although I find more convincing Huxley's reading, namely, that these lines are spoken at Delphi after Alkmaion receives the oracle, I think Debiasi's argument exposes our inclination to see Amphiaraos

The fragment also encourages us to decode Thucydides' oracular riddle, with it emphasis on a place unseen by the sun, as a directive for Alkmaion to head underground.[73]

Precisely because of its chthonic resonance, Thucydides' formulation of the Pythia's instructions seems to be constructed with a view toward eliciting an image of Amphiaraos's own oracle. This particular inflection is especially evident when compared to Pausanias's version with its lack of subterranean, and so oracular, implications. And yet, in Thucydides' account, this readily available solution to the riddle, namely, for Alkmaion to follow in his father's chthonic and mantic footsteps, is, of course, the wrong solution. That is to say, Thucydides' riddle cleverly constructs allegiance to Amphiaraos's oracular powers as a failure in oracular interpretation. After wavering in a state of *aporia*, Alkmaion instead eventually arrives at the correct, and, it should be noted, much less obvious answer: the Delphic oracle refers to the strange topographic phenomenon of the silting up of the Acheloös.

As traced above, Apollodorus also plays out both the mantic-paternal and Delphic options that are available to Alkmaion, but he does so in a paratactic succession of injunctions and then purifications. First Amphiaraos enjoins Alkmaion to kill Eriphyle, then Delphi issues the same statement. Likewise, Alkmaion first turns to his grandfather Oikles and only afterward seeks Delphi's assistance. In contrast, Thucydides contrives the Pythia's riddle as a synchronic synthesis of both options. Through the manner in which he constructs the oracle's "impossible landscape," Thucydides boldly plays with the possibility that Alkmaion could choose to follow his father below ground. In this way, Amphiaraos lurks beneath the surface of Thucydides' narrative. And yet, ultimately, the seer exists only as the false solution to a Delphic foundation oracle that, when correctly interpreted, transforms Alkmaion into the oikist of Akarnania.[74]

In part 2 we have seen that, as in the Kroisos narrative discussed in part 1, Delphi and Amphiaraos are engaged in a contest for authority. Taken together, the Kroisos narrative and the myth of Alkmaion point to a long-standing and ongoing tension between the Panhellenic oracle and the individual seer-turned-oracle that manifests itself in a variety of ways and in a range of ancient sources.

---

implicated in the chthonic resonance of Alkmaion's reaction. Similiarly, as I argue above, the specter of Amphiaraos is also evoked in Thucydides' construction of the Pythia's oracular riddle.

73. Huxley (1969: 51) conjectures that Thucydides actually took his version of the myth from the *Alkmeonis*. Cf. Debiasi 2015: 266.

74. Hornblower (1997 *ad* 2.102.5) notes that, unusually for Thucydides, Apollo is named in this passage: λέγεται δὲ καὶ Ἀλκμέωνι τῷ Ἀμφιάρεω, ὅτε δὴ ἀλᾶσθαι αὐτὸν μετὰ τὸν φόνον τῆς μητρός, τὸν Ἀπόλλω ταύτην τὴν γῆν χρῆσαι οἰκεῖν (And it is said also that by way of his oracle Apollo told Alkmaion, son of Amphiaraos, when he was wandering after the murder of his mother, to dwell in this place, 2.102.5). The appearance of Apollo's own name thus forms a stark contrast with that of Amphiaraos, who appears in this passage in the form of Alkmaion's patronymic.

In the Alkmaion myth, Delphi expunges Amphiaraos from the story by offering the only effective solution for Alkmaion's purification. But Delphi does not merely purify the matricide. The purification's requirement is that Alkmaion must also become an oikist. Reading these two features together, that is, the rejection of Amphiaraos and the simultaneous conversion of the story into a foundation tale, exposes how Delphi leverages a motif of colonial discourse, that of the fugitive homicide, to assert its oracular monopoly over Amphiaraos. Further, the roles of the Delphi-sanctioned oikist and seer are again positioned as mutually exclusive, as if locked in a zero-sum game. We encountered a similar phenomenon in chapter 4 in which we saw that Bacchylides excises the seer Melampous from the myth of the Proitids in *Ode* 11 at the same time as he transforms the myth into a foundation tale featuring Proitos as oikist. In the Alkmaion myth, the contest of who will win out, the seer or the oikist, is waged over a single individual, and we now also perceive the part that Delphi can play in determining the outcome.

The mainstream tradition of the myth with its insistent focus on the close connection between Delphi and Alkmaion, from Delphi's initial selection of Alkmaion as leader of the Epigonoi to the final dedication of Harmonia's necklace at Delphi, proves to be remarkably successful at detaching Alkmaion from his mantic family. With the exception of his appearance in Pindar's *Pythian* 8, which we will examine below, our sources make almost no connection between Alkmaion and seercraft. Thus Thomas Hubbard can note:

> There is no evidence that Alcmeon ever had an oracle anywhere in Greece or even that he had oracular powers. Greek tradition is univocal in representing Alcmeon's brother Amphilochus as the one who inherits Amphiaraus' prophetic powers. Indeed, the many myths surrounding Alcmeon all make it quite clear that he did not possess the ability to foresee the future. The entire story of the matricide and endless wandering in search of purification is incompatible with prophetic ability. Rather, we are told that Alcmeon throughout his career sought advice from the oracle at Delphi concerning his next step.[75]

As Hubbard's remarks reveal, Alkmaion is almost never represented as possessing *mantikē*. And yet, Akarnania, the region Alkmaion founds, did enjoy this association. It is as if the tradition, although successful at detaching Alkmaion himself from seercraft, could not curtail a more general connection between Akarnania and *mantikē*. Thus, according to Pausanias, the Boiotians assert that Hesiod was taught seercraft by the Akarnanians (9.31.5). Herodotus identifies two seers as Akarnanian, Amphilytos (1.62) and Megistias. Megistias, like Alkmaion, also claimed descent from Melampous (7.221). Megistias's identification as both an

---

75. Hubbard 1993: 195.

Akarnanian and one of the Melampodidai connects him with Alkmaion twice over and strongly suggests that it was as Alkmaion's descendant that he was able to become a seer. Further, Pausanias records a tradition that links Klytios, the progenitor of the Klytiadai clan of seers stationed at Olympia, to Alkmaion, saying that Klytios was the son of Alkmaion by the daughter of Phegeus. Klytios fled to Elis after his mother's brothers murdered Alkmaion (6.17.6). Finally, the very late source Clement of Alexandria reveals an explicit mantic link between Akarnania and Alkmaion when he reports that there was an oracle of Alkmaion in Akarnania, the land colonized by his son Arknan (*Strom.* 1.134).[76] Yet these are only fleeting intimations of Alkmaion's connection with *mantikē*, and to a certain extent, they only serve to reaffirm the thorough detachment of Alkmaion from Amphiaraos that the dominant tradition carries out. To encounter an explicit demonstration of Alkmaion's mantic potential, it is necessary to turn to Pindar.

III. THE *MANTIKĒ* OF ALKMAION

Pindar's *Pythian* 8 offers one final instantiation of the Alkmaion myth. The ode is considered Pindar's last epinikion and is dated, with the help of a scholiast's headnote, to 446 B.C.E.[77] The ode celebrates the Aeginetan youth Aristomenes for his victory in the wrestling contest at the Pythian games.

The ode is famously inscrutable and confounding in the way it defies expectations of genre and context. One striking and oft-noted feature is that the ode does not include an Aiakid myth in its main mythic portion, an unprecedented move that stands in contrast to the mythic portions of Pindar's other ten Aeginetan odes.[78] Another major concern is the identity of the ode's speaking subject, or *ego*, especially during the epiphany scene at lines 56–60. Scholars have variously argued that the *ego* represents the poet, the chorus, or the victor himself. I will address these issues at the end of the chapter when we are in a better position to attend to them. But, to begin, I turn to two other interrelated features of the ode that the rest of the chapter has prepared us to see as extraordinary, although traditionally they have not been viewed as such: first, the presence of Amphiaraos in a Pythian ode and, second, Alkmaion's characterization as another Amphiaraos, that is, as both a warrior-*mantis* and an epiphanic oracle.

---

76. A second late source, Christodorus (*AP* 393), seems to misidentify a statue of the poet Alkman by referring to it as a statue of the "*mantis* named Alkmaion."

77. On the date in light of schol. *ad P.* 8. inscr., see Hubbard 1993: 194n6 with bibliography.

78. The Aiakidai are mentioned at *P.* 8.22–23, but, as Hubbard (1993: 200n28) notes, they are "pointedly dropped as a theme here by the elaborate break-off formula of vv. 28–34." The Aiakidai are briefly mentioned again at *P.* 8.99–100 in the poem's closing prayer for Aegina.

As discussed above, the mainstream tradition of the Alkmaion myth works hard to discredit Amphiaraos and detach Alkmaion from his father. Alkmaion's allegiance to Delphi comes with a visible concommitant suppression of Amphiaraos. To encounter Amphiaraos in an epinikian celebration of Delphic Apollo, then, is to witness the seer's incursion into enemy territory. In fact, of the four references to Amphiaraos in the Pindaric corpus, his presence in *Pythian* 8's mythic portion marks his sole appearance in a Pythian ode. More striking still, however, is that Alkmaion himself not only appears conspicuously linked to Amphiaraos instead of Delphi, in the context of a Delphic ode, but is also characterized, uniquely among our archaic and classical sources, as a *mantis*. In light of the dominant tradition, then, we might think of *Pythian* 8's mythic portion and accompanying coda as "Amphiaraos's revenge," that is, an incomparable moment in which Amphiaraos is able to reclaim his son from Delphi and bestow on him the capacity for *mantikē*. Further, in a reversal of the pattern we encountered in Thucydides' passage, in *Pythian* 8 Alkmaion conspicuously inherits the gift of *mantikē* from Amphiaraos while his connection with Delphi and his potential as an oikist are suppressed. Indeed I would suggest that *Pythian* 8 positions itself in relation to the mainstream tradition of the Alkmaion myth in the same way that, as Nigel Nicholson has convincingly shown, Pindar's epinikia for Deinomenid athletes stand in ideological opposition to hero-athlete narratives.[79] The oppositions I trace here between the mainstream tradition's and *Pythian* 8's versions of Alkmaion, then, are not coincidental but rather part of a larger epinikian strategy to claim its superiority over other genres.

Before turning to the mythic portion of the ode, it is important to establish as best we can a terminus post quem for the tension between Delphi and Amphiaraos over Alkmaion. Strabo (10.2.9) mentions Akarnania in relation to the "author of the *Alkmeonis*," which suggests that Alkmaion's role as an oikist in the poem and, by implication, his attachment to Delphi go back to the epic tradition. Andrea Debiasi, among others, understands the core of Apollodorus's account of Alkmaion's matricide, wandering, and foundation to derive from the *Alkmeonis* (i.e., *Bibl.* 3.7.2–6), even with the assumption that the genre of tragedy also informs the events of the Alkmaion story in the *Bibliotheca*.[80] It is not certain whether the *Alkmeonis* itself belonged to the Theban epics proper, whose other poems were the *Oidipodeia*, *Thebaid*, and *Epigonoi*, or was a later sequel that continued its themes.[81] Given the poem's interest in both Delphi and the region of Akarnania, Debiasi posits that the *Alkmeonis* was the product of Kypselid Corinth. His argument connects these interests in the epic with the Kypselids' own close ties to Delphi and

---

79. See Nicholson 2016: 1–49, esp. 41–42.
80. See also Sakellariou 1958: 156–57n3, 159; Jouan 1989: 15.
81. See Debiasi 2015: 261–63.

their colonial interests in northwest Greece.[82] Drawing on the possible Kypselid connection as well as on other thematic factors, Debiasi dates the creation of the poem to between the second half of the seventh century and the beginning of the sixth century.[83] To be sure, the evidence for the *Alkmeonis* is extremely fragmentary, and it is difficult to determine the degree of tension that would have existed between Amphiaraos and Delphi in the epic.[84] If Debiasi is correct in seeing Delphi's prominence in the epic poem as the origin of its prominence in the *Bibliotheca*, we can reasonably suspect an antagonistic pairing of the oracle and Amphiaraos in the *Alkmeonis* as well. Malcolm Davies, who displays more caution in assessing how much the later mythographers can tell us about the Theban epics, nevertheless views Thucydides' source of the Alkmaion myth as the epic tradition.[85] The influence of epic thus likely lies behind what we have traced above, namely, that Thucydides constructs his account around the fraught interplay between Delphi and Amphiaraos. Finally, a sixth-century rivalry between Delphi and Amphiaraos is further supported by the contestatory dynamic traced in part 1 of this chapter between Delphi and the Amphiareion in Herodotus's Kroisos narrative and the sixth-century epigram from the Theban Ismenion. We can be fairly confident, then, that Pindar was aware of the mantic-oracular rivalry between Amphiaraos and Delphi when he composed *Pythian* 8 in the mid-fifth century.

Amphiaraos's Revenge

In the mythic portion of *Pythian* 8, Amphiaraos and Alkmaion appear in lieu of the expected Aeginetan heroes. The scene envisions Alkmaion fighting before the walls of Thebes and establishes for him two interdependent attributes: first, Alkmaion is connected with seercraft, and, second, he inherits this mantic ability from his father, Amphiaraos. In a coda to the mythic portion, Pindar returns the ode to the present day through the remarkable revelation that he himself encountered Alkmaion on the road from Thebes to Delphi. In this climactic scene, Pindar receives from Alkmaion a prophecy, suggesting that Alkmaion could also func-

---

82. Debiasi's argument depends particularly on seeing Apollod. *Bibl.* 3.7.3–4 (in which Delphi features prominently) as taken from the *Alkmeonis* (see Debiasi 2015: 262, esp. n. 12). Debiasi (277–78) makes a further association between the *Alkmeonis* and the Kypselids: "The dialectic insularity/mainland implied by the tale of the land formed by silting at the mouth of the Achelous (and possibly by the tale of the artificial mole made by Telamon on Aegina) can reflect the interests of the Cypselids in digging canals through isthmi, as it was planned in Corinth and accomplished in Leucas. Acarnania, with the relevant eponyms, plays a too significant role in the poem to be unrelated to the colonization conducted, with Delphic approval, by the Corinthian tyrants in Acarnania, Epirus, and Illyria."

83. See Debiasi 2015: 277 and n. 87.

84. We also know that Alkmaion played a part in the epic *Epigonoi*, but our problems of restoring the relationship between Amphiaraos and Delphi are the same there. On the *Epigonoi*, see Cingano 2015; Davies 2014: 107–14.

85. Davies 2014: 130.

tion, like his father, as an epiphanic oracle.[86] The central triad of the ode thus begins with the myth and concludes with the coda in the epode (38–60):

αὔξων δὲ πάτραν Μειδυλιδᾶν λόγον φέρεις,
τὸν ὅνπερ ποτ' Ὀϊκλέος παῖς ἐν ἑπταπύλοις ἰδών
υἱοὺς Θήβαις αἰνίξατο παρμένοντας αἰχμᾷ,

ὁπότ' ἀπ' Ἄργεος ἤλυθον
δευτέραν ὁδὸν Ἐπίγονοι.
ὧδ' εἶπε μαρναμένων·
'φυᾷ τὸ γενναῖον ἐπιπρέπει
ἐκ πατέρων παισὶ λῆμα. θαέομαι σαφὲς
δράκοντα ποικίλον αἰθᾶς Ἀλκμᾶν' ἐπ' ἀσπίδος
νωμῶντα πρῶτον ἐν Κάδμου πύλαις.
ὁ δὲ καμὼν προτέρᾳ πάθᾳ
νῦν ἀρείονος ἐνέχεται
ὄρνιχος ἀγγελίᾳ
Ἄδραστος ἥρως· τὸ δὲ οἴκοθεν
ἀντία πράξει. μοῦνος γὰρ ἐκ Δαναῶν στρατοῦ
θανόντος ὀστέα λέξαις υἱοῦ, τύχᾳ θεῶν
ἀφίξεται λαῷ σὺν ἀβλαβεῖ
Ἄβαντος εὐρυχόρους ἀγυιάς.' τοιαῦτα μὲν
ἐφθέγξατ' Ἀμφιάρηος. χαίρων δὲ καὶ αὐτὸς
Ἀλκμᾶνα στεφάνοισι βάλλω, ῥαίνω δὲ καὶ ὕμνῳ,
γείτων ὅτι μοι καὶ κτεάνων φύλαξ ἐμῶν
ὑπάντασεν ἰόντι γᾶς ὀμφαλὸν παρ' ἀοίδιμον,
μαντευμάτων τ' ἐφάψατο συγγόνοισι τέχναις.

But exalting the clan of the Meidylidai, you bear the word, the very one which once the son of Oikles prophetically riddled when he saw at seven-gated Thebes the sons standing fast in battle, when they came from Argos on a second road, the Epigonoi. Thus he spoke as they were fighting: "By nature noble determination from fathers is conspicuous in sons. I behold him clearly, Alkmaion, wielding the dappled snake on his fiery shield, first at the gates of Thebes. But the other, who suffered in a previous misfortune, now is possessed of a message of a better omen, Adrastos the hero. But at home he will fare the opposite. For he alone from the army of Danaans, having collected the bones of his dead son, will arrive through the fortune of the gods with his army unharmed at the wide streets of Abas." Such things Amphiaraos uttered. And I myself also rejoicing pelt Alkmaion with crowns, and I also sprinkle him with a hymn, because as my neighbor and the guardian of my possessions he met me going to the renowned-in-song navel of the earth, and he grasped hold of prophecies with his inborn skills.

86. In structural terms, this epode marks the center of the epinikion. As Mullen shows, the central epode of a Pindaric epinikion often signals the climax of the ode's myth (Mullen 1982: 100–11, with 105 for P. 8).

In the mythic portion of *Pythian* 8, we witness the collapse of distinctions between fathers and sons. To be sure, in all instantiations of the myth of the Epigonoi, the correlation between the campaigns of the Seven against Thebes and the Epigonoi is defined as one of generational repetition. Yet, Pindar does not leave the resumptive nature of the Epigonoi implicit in *Pythian* 8 but rather exploits this defining quality through the way in which he introduces the second expedition against Thebes.

The mythic portion's intense focus on the steadfast relationship between fathers and sons is already under way as soon as the relative pronoun leaves off praising Aristomenes' present victory and sends us back to Amphiaraos (38–41):

αὔξων δὲ πάτραν Μειδυλιδᾶν λόγον φέρεις,
τὸν ὅνπερ ποτ᾽ Ὀϊκλέος παῖς ἐν ἑπταπύλοις ἰδὼν
υἱοὺς Θήβαις αἰνίξατο παρμένοντας αἰχμᾷ,

ὁπότ᾽ ἀπ᾽ Ἄργεος ἤλυθον
δευτέραν ὁδὸν Ἐπίγονοι.

But exalting the clan of the Meidylidai, you bear the word, the very one which once the son of Oikles prophetically riddled when he saw at seven-gated Thebes the sons standing fast in battle when they came from Argos on a second road, the Epigonoi.

These opening moments of the myth initially seem to recount the Seven's original march against Thebes. Indeed, there is nothing in the myth's first three lines that signals that we are not in the time of the Seven. Amphiaraos's prophesying before the walls of seven-gated Thebes belongs far more readily to the first campaign.[87] Even the reference to sons (υἱοὺς, 40) does not necessarily put us in mind of the Epigonoi: the Seven themselves could easily be characterized in this way, given Pindar's frequent, periphrastic tendency to identify victors and mythical heroes as the sons of their fathers.[88] The preceding description of Amphiaraos as the child of Oikles perhaps encourages this initial understanding of υἱοὺς here as referring to the Seven. The third line of the myth, ὁπότ᾽ ἀπ᾽ Ἄργεος ἤλυθον (when they came from Argos), easily continues the impression that Pindar is recounting the Seven's own expedition. Thus it is only when Pindar reveals that the men arriving from Argos came δευτέραν ὁδὸν Ἐπίγονοι (on a second road, the Epigonoi) that we ourselves must double back and reenvision the scene a second time, as one belonging to the Epigonoi and not the Seven. The postponed position of Ἐπίγονοι as the final word captures perfectly the delayed or secondary nature of the Epigonoi

---

87. To my knowledge, there are no other extant versions of the myth of the Epigonoi in which Amphiaraos-as-oracle delivers a prophecy. In the Pindaric corpus, three of Amphiaraos' appearances are clearly placed during the time of the Seven (*O.* 6.13; *N.* 9.13, *N.* 9.24). *I.* 7.33 mentions Amphiaraos in a list of warrior-heroes who lost their lives.

88. See Slater 1969, s.v. υἱός for numerous examples.

themselves. I would argue that one effect of this surprise ending is to experience both campaigns synchronically and, in so doing, to acknowledge the seamless transfiguration of fathers into sons that is itself the central theme of the ode's mythic portion.

In this way, the mythic portion's opening endows us with a kind of double vision of fathers imperceptibly merging into sons even before we receive its confirmation in the gnomic pronouncement of Amphiaraos immediately following: ὧδ' εἶπε μαρναμένων: /φυᾷ τὸ γενναῖον ἐπιπρέπει / ἐκ πατέρων παισὶ λῆμα (Thus he spoke as they were fighting: "By nature noble determination from fathers is conspicuous in sons," 43–45). Fittingly, as he makes this claim, Amphiaraos himself is identified, uniquely within the Pindaric corpus, not by name but only as the child of his father (Ὀϊκλέος παῖς, 39).[89] The sentiment expressed in the seer's gnomic statement is no novel idea; it is a cornerstone of epinikian ideology. What makes the utterance so striking and, I would contend, even radical is not its ideological stance but rather that Amphiaraos will go on to envision his relationship with Alkmaion as the paradigmatic example of it. Further, in his pronouncement, Amphiaraos asserts that one's paternal inheritance is not only innate but also conspicuous (ἐπιπρέπει, 44).[90] That is to say, this inheritance is not capable of being suppressed. And yet, Alkmaion's detachment from his father is precisely what the mainstream tradition seeks to carry out.

The remainder of the mythic portion and its coda make specific the seer's theoretical claim, as Alkmaion is shown to embody the roles for which Amphiaraos himself is renowned, namely, as a warrior-*mantis* and, finally, as an epiphanic oracle. Following his gnomic statement, Amphiaraos's description of his son brings with it another startling realization: Amphiaraos must be speaking from beyond the grave, since the scene he beholds takes place after he has been swallowed by the earth and transformed into an oracle. His vision is that of Alkmaion as the leader of the Epigonoi, standing before the gates of Thebes and wielding a shield on which is emblazoned a dappled snake. The shield with its snake blazon once again collapses distinctions between father and son. For, as discussed above, Amphiaraos himself is known as a warrior-*mantis* whose own double nature is captured in Adrastos's estimation of him in *Olympian* 6: ἀμφότερον μάντιν τ' ἀγαθὸν καὶ /

---

89. Pindar mentions Amphiaraos five other times in his extant corpus of epinikia, and Amphiaraos's own name appears in all of them, including at the end of the mythic portion of *Pythian* 8, discussed below: μάντιν Οἰκλείδαν ποτ' ἐς Ἀμφιάρηον (*O.* 6.13); τοιαῦτα μὲν ἐφθέγξατ' Ἀμφιάρηος (*P.* 8.56); φεῦγε γὰρ Ἀμφιαρῆ ποτε θρασυμήδεα (*N.* 9.13); ὁ δ' Ἀμφιαρεῖ σχίσσεν κεραυνῷ παμβίᾳ Ζεὺς τὰν βαθύστερνον χθόνα (*N.* 9.24); μαχατὰν αἰνέων Μελέαγρον, αἰνέων δὲ καὶ Ἕκτορα Ἀμφιάρηόν τε (*I.* 7.33). We might note in particular his identification at *O.* 6.13, where his patronymic is paired with his own name. Identifying him only as the "child of Oikles" here at *P.* 8.39 thus seems exceptional.

90. The word occurs only here in Pindar (see Pfeijffer 1999: 532).

δουρὶ μάρνασθαι (both a good *mantis* and good at fighting with the spear, 16–17).[91] The shield itself concretizes Alkmaion's assumption of his father's military prowess, while the image of the snake upon it underscores his inherited mantic abilities.[92] Other scholars also understand the snake blazon to signal seercraft. The Greeks connected snakes with divination in general and, more particularly, with the Melampodidai, the mantic clan to which Amphiaraos and Alkamion belong.[93] At the same time, the image of the snake elicits a chthonic resonance.[94] The convergence of mantic-chthonic associations embodied in the snake thus fittingly evokes Amphiaraos's chthonic oracle.[95] As we will see, this combination also anticipates Pindar's presentation of the epiphany of Alkmaion in the coda.

Before turning to the coda, however, it is worth briefly noting the second father-son pairing in the mythic portion. Amphiaraos concludes his speech by foreseeing Adrastos's fate: although the Epigonoi will prove to be victorious in contrast to the Seven, Adrastos himself will experience a personal misfortune, since he alone will suffer the loss of his son (*P.* 8.48–55). The juxtaposition between the pairings of Amphiaraos-Alkmaion and Adrastos-Aigialeus is in keeping with a more pervasive tendency in *Pythian* 8 to follow a positive exemplum with its negative counterpart.[96] Yet, in the image of Adrastos's loss of Aigialeus, I wonder if we also receive an evocation of Amphiaraos's own experience in the mainstream tradition as a father regularly severed from his own son Alkmaion. Such an evocation of Alkmaion's detachment from Amphiaraos would simultaneously highlight its radical reversal in *Pythian* 8 and, in this way, would correspond to other allusions to the mainstream tradition that are similarly upended in this ode, as we will discuss below.

The Epiphany of Alkmaion

Pythian 8 leaves the mythic past of the Epigonoi and returns to the epinikian present through its coda (56–60):

χαίρων δὲ καὶ αὐτός
Ἀλκμᾶνα στεφάνοισι βάλλω, ῥαίνω δὲ καὶ ὕμνῳ,
γείτων ὅτι μοι καὶ κτεάνων φύλαξ ἐμῶν

---

91. See part 1 above for this passage and its epic pedigree.

92. Pfeijffer (1999: 533) makes this connection as well.

93. Melampous, Teiresias, and Trophonios are also connected with snakes. On snakes and divination, see, e.g., Ogden 2001: 84. If the Melampodid association with snakes is active in this description of Alkmaion's snake blazon, then it ties the hero to his whole mantic clan and not just to Amphiaraos.

94. See Ogden 2001: 84.

95. Ogden (2001: 85) notes that the place-name Knopia, one of the possible locations for Amphiaraos's Theban oracle, may mean "place of snakes." In this context, we might also note a later fourth-century relief of Amphiaraos from Oropos that depicts a sleeping patient whose arm is licked by a snake and to whom Amphiaraos himself appears (see Ustinova 2002: 269 with *LIMC* 1 no. 63.)

96. See *P.* 8.81–92 with Pfeijffer 1999: 439.

ὑπάντασεν ἰόντι γᾶς ὀμφαλὸν παρ' ἀοίδιμον,
μαντευμάτων τ' ἐφάψατο συγγόνοισι τέχναις.

And I myself also rejoicing pelt Alkmaion with crowns, and I also sprinkle him with a hymn, because as my neighbor and the guardian of my possessions he met me going to the renowned-in-song navel of the earth, and he grasped hold of prophecies with his inborn skills.

These lines have produced vigorous and ongoing scholarly disagreement over who prophesies to whom in the scene, and, moreover, what form the appearance of the prophesying figure takes. I would contend that part of the passage's underappreciated purpose is to be enigmatic, a quality that allows for the amalgamation of Amphiaraos and Alkmaion to continue, as we will see. Before examining this phenomenon, however, I will summarize briefly the most compelling solutions to the identities of the participants in this striking exchange en route to Delphi.

First, as many scholars recognize, the identity of the speaking subject, or *ego*, is most likely the poet himself and not, as others have suggested, the chorus or even the victor.[97] Second, the poet experiences an epiphany of the dead hero Alkmaion, who delivers a prophecy to him and to whom Pindar gives cult.[98] One of the most frequently cited dissenters to this scenario is Hubbard, who argues that Pindar witnesses the epiphany of Amphiaraos, not Alkmaion.[99] Ilja Pfeijffer convincingly refutes this possibility based on the internal logic of the scene as well as on syntactical grounds.[100] Hubbard's argument may be untenable, but it is valuable insofar as it exposes just how extraordinary and confounding Alkmaion's epiphany is. Pindar, apparently without precedent, inserts Alkmaion into the expected place of Amphiaraos. The moment thus forces a recalibration of our traditional assumptions about Alkmaion and leverages its polyvalence in order to drive home the passage's

---

97. For the poet as *ego*, see esp. D'Alessio 1994: 135–36; Robbins 1997: 270; Pfeijffer 1999: 540–45; Nagy 2000: 103; Martin 2004: 353–54. For the victor as speaking subject, see, e.g., Currie 2005: 59. For the chorus, see, e.g., Burnett 2005: 231; see 231n22 for a thorough bibliographical breakdown of these three different perspectives on the identity of the coda's *ego*.

98. As D'Alessio (1994: 136n61) observes, "The wording suggests that the episode was not simply an answer from an oracular shrine but rather a real epiphany." See Hubbard 1993: 194 for bibliography on a range of other possibilities (dream vision, shrine, statue at Delphi); Hubbard himself (1993: 201n33) sees the encounter as an epiphany, but an epiphany of Amphiaraos. Pfeijffer (1999: 544–45), who views it as an epiphany of Alkmaion, notes how this epiphany forms a parallel with the epiphany of Amphiaraos in the mythic portion. The double epiphanies thus mark another convergence between fathers and sons in the ode.

99. Hubbard 1993.

100. Pfeijffer 1999: 542–45. Pfeijffer (544) concludes, "Pindar's syntax leaves us no choice but to take Alcmaeon as the subject of the ὅτι clause; because the first person must refer to the poet, the traditional interpretation of the passage must be correct: it describes an encounter between the poet and the dead hero Alcmaeon on the road to Delphi."

central theme. That is to say, in keeping with the mythic portion of *Pythian* 8, the coda envisions an unbroken but simultaneously radical transfer of mantic power from Amphiaraos to Alkmaion. Its final phrase, in which Alkmaion prophesies because of his συγγόνοισι τέχναις (inborn skills, 60), delivers the theme's resounding conclusion.

At this climactic moment, Pindar also characterizes Alkmaion as his γείτων... μοι καὶ κτεάνων φύλαξ ἐμῶν (my neighbor and the guardian of my possessions, 58). This phrase has also produced much scholarly consternation.[101] The term *geitōn* (neighbor) suggests a local hero, an image supported both by the accompanying attribution of Alkmaion as the guardian of Pindar's possessions and by the poet's own actions in this scene, since crowning and sprinkling draw from the language of hero cult.[102] These attributes and actions ("neighbor," "guardian of my possessions," and Pindar's cultic gestures), all of which suggest a degree of personal contact and materiality, conjure a vision of a physical sanctuary.[103] Although Alkmaion's appearance itself may be an epiphany, I would argue that, given the absence of an actual sanctuary of Alkmaion and the inextricable correspondence that the scene establishes between Amphiaraos and his son, the coda simultaneously seems to evoke the physical space of the Amphiareion.

In this context, it is worth recalling Herodotus's report at 8.134 that Thebans were banned from consulting Amphiaraos's oracle. As I suggested in part 1, we should treat the Herodotean anecdote as a narrative that hints at efforts by other competing oracles, such as the Theban Ismenion and its ally Delphi, to disenfranchise the Amphiareion. By contrast, in *Pythian* 8, the native Theban Pindar closely aligns himself with both Alkmaion and, through the evocation of a sanctuary, the Amphiareion. It is possible, then, to view the coda as another opportunity for "Amphiaraos's revenge," an opportunity wherein a Theban at least notionally patronizes a local oracle from which, according to certain authorities, he is banned. In fact, Pindar's assertion of a Theban's right to approach the Amphiareion may have been especially charged during the period of *Pythian* 8's composition, since it was during this time that the Theban Amphiareion seems to have become defunct.[104] Hubbard postulates a compelling connection between Pindar's phrase "guardian of my possessions" and Herodotus's reference to Amphiaraos's own possessions being stored in his day in the Ismenion (1.52): "If indeed the Amphiareion did cease to be attended full-time and some valuables had to be transferred to Thebes, there may be a particular point to Pindar's phrasing his defense of the

---

101. As Pfeijffer (1999: 544) laments, "That there is no evidence of a cult of Alcmaeon near Thebes is annoying."

102. On *geitōn* as signifying a local hero, see Rusten 1983; Burnett 2005: 232.

103. See Martin (2004) for *Pythian* 8's distinctive interest in physical contact.

104. The Amphiareion was still functioning during the Persian Wars when it was consulted by Mys (Hdt. 8.134), but, by Herodotus's time, its diminution already seems to have occurred.

oracle's vitality by declaring it to be the 'guardian of my possessions.'"[105] This possibility as well as the more general contrast between the coda and Herodotus's anecdote at 8.134 supports the position that the coda's *ego* must represent the poet himself. The Theban Pindar's personal interaction with Alkmaion in Theban territory holds more contextual weight than an epiphany of Alkmaion to the Aeginetan victor or chorus.[106]

Even with the coda's evocation of the Amphiareion, the exact location of the meeting between Pindar and Alkmaion is ultimately left vague. We learn only that it happens as he travels to Delphi. Pfeijffer considers the possibility that Alkmaion's epiphany actually occurs at the sanctuary of Amphiaraos.[107] I find this suggestion attractive, since it both continues the collapse between Amphiaraos/the Amphiareion and Alkmaion and because a Theban location in the direction of Delphi is in keeping with where other sources place the site of the sanctuary.[108] At the same time, I would contend that the spatial indeterminacy of Alkmaion's appearance captures a fundamental component of his traditional character and that we should not dismiss its ambiguity. Alkmaion is a figure forever caught between the irreconcilable divinatory powers of Amphiaraos and Delphi. Hovering in the space between them, somewhere on the road from Thebes to Delphi, is, in a sense, precisely the place in which we should expect to find him.

Thus in the coda, Pindar further asserts Alkmaion's mantic inheritance, established in the mythic portion, through the claim that he himself experienced Alkmaion's epiphany and received a prophecy from him. Moreover, just as Pindar restores the relationship between Amphiaraos and Alkmaion, so too he rehabilitates a local Theban connection with this mantic family. Both assertions position *Pythian* 8 in opposition to attempts to marginalize Amphiaraos's authority and his connection with his son. More particularly, these assertions seem directed at Delphi, a point to which I will now turn.

Pindar's Alkmaion and Delphi

I will close the discussion of *Pythian* 8 by considering how Delphi and Delphic Apollo fit into the picture of Amphiaraos and Alkmaion developed above and how

---

105. Hubbard 1993: 201n32.

106. Burnett (2005: 232n24), for example, suggests that a cult of Alkmaion on Aegina (where she envisions the epiphany of Alkmaion appearing to the chorus) is possible based on a general Doric connection between the hero and the island. But, as far as we can tell, there is nothing at stake in a cult of Alkmaion on Aegina in the same way as there is in an epiphany of Alkmaion near or at the Amphiareion in Thebes.

107. Pfeijffer 1999: 544.

108. Pausanias (9.8.3) places the Amphiareion on the road between Thebes and Potniai, a possible route for traveling to Delphi (see Hubbard 1993: 196). See Foster (2017: 165) for how the crossroads of Oidipous are evoked and simultaneously countermanded by Pindar's own road to Delphi.

these observations refine our understanding of the marked divergence between the mainstream tradition of Alkmaion and Pindar's ode. The end of the coda coincides with the end of the third epode. Its closing image of traveling to Delphi sends us straight to the sanctuary itself at the opening of the fourth triad (61–63):

τὺ δ', Ἑκαταβόλε, πάνδοκον
ναὸν εὐκλέα διανέμων
Πυθῶνος ἐν γυάλοις...

And you, Far-Shooter, who govern the glorious all-receiving temple in the hollows of Pytho...

In direct opposition to the locative vagueness of the preceding coda, the strophe firmly attaches Apollo to the specific site of his temple at Delphi. The strophe celebrates Apollo's capacity to bestow on Aristomenes a victory, a role anticipated in the first epode's image of the god welcoming Aristomenes' *kōmos* (victory revel) to Delphi (20). The first triad also reveals a different side of Apollo, his capacity for violence, when it recounts how the god's arrows helped to subdue Typhos and the king of the Giants, Porphyrion.[109] Despite Apollo's multiple guises in the ode, however, Pindar never connects the god with prophecy, nor, despite repeated references to Delphi itself, does he include any mention of the Delphic oracle.[110] The absence of an oracular Apollo in *Pythian* 8 forms an obvious contrast to the highly visible and interconnected mantic performances of Amphiaraos and Alkmaion in the ode.

We can develop this contrast further by returning to one final peculiarity of the coda: the content of Alkmaion's prophecy to Pindar is never revealed. What exactly does Alkmaion foretell to Pindar? One convincing solution is to understand Alkmaion as transmitting to Pindar the contents of Amphiaraos's own prophecy, reported in the preceding mythic portion. This answer accounts for why Pindar himself would happen to know Amphiaraos's prophecy, and, more importantly, represents a further collapse between mantic father and son whereby Alkmaion relays his father's prophecy through one of his own.[111]

---

109. On Apollo's assistance in overthrowing Typhos and Porphyrion as a possible Pindaric invention, see Pfeijffer 1999: 497. The poem foregrounds in a variety of ways connections between fathers and sons.

110. In contrast, Apollo's oracular epithet, Loxias, appears in *P.* 3.28, *P.* 11.5, *I.* 7.49, and *Pa.* 6.60. Martin (2004) argues that Apollo also performs the role of a *koruphaios* (chorus leader) in *Pythian* 8.

111. I owe this point to Leslie Kurke. Yet Pindar's lack of specificity leaves open the possibility of other, simultaneous interpretations. A number of scholars view Pindar's ambiguity as a sign that Alkmaion addressed Aegina's current situation in 446 B.C.E.: perhaps the prophecy divined Aegina's eventual liberation from Athenian control and the defeat of pro-Athenian factions on the island, a message that Pindar did not wish to convey openly. For this theory, see Krischer 1985: 123; Hubbard 1993: 198 with n. 21, 203; Robbins 1997: 271.

The privileging of Alkmaion's prophetic powers over those of Delphic Apollo crystallizes the distinctions between *Pythian* 8's and the dominant tradition's treatment of Alkmaion. In the dominant tradition, Alkmaion repeatedly consults the Delphic oracle. Moreover, in this tradition, Delphi itself remains the one locative constant as the hero traverses Greece, first as one of the Epigonoi and then in his wandering after the matricide of Eriphyle. In *Pythian* 8, Alkmaion prophesies and, though appearing on Pindar's way to Delphi, is never himself placed there within the ode. These discrepancies produce a crucial implication, for their combination, namely, the absence of a prophetic Apollo, the presence of a prophetic Alkmaion who can rely on his own mantic abilities, and Alkmaion's absence from Delphi, means that there is no opportunity or need for Alkmaion to become a Delphi-appointed oikist.[112] *Pythian* 8 is pointedly not *ktisis* poetry. The lack of Alkmaion's status as an oikist is made all the more conspicuous because Alkmaion and Delphic Apollo share the space of *Pythian* 8 and yet as characters within the ode never actually coincide.

It is curious, then, that *Pythian* 8 exhibits a number of shared images and verbal parallels with *Pythian* 1, the earlier epinikion of 470 B.C.E. that celebrates Hieron as oikist of Aitna. So many similarities exist, in fact, that Tilman Krischer sees in *Pythian* 8 a deliberate evocation of *Pythian* 1.[113] It is difficult to understand why Pindar deploys the vocabulary and images of one of his greatest colonial odes unless it is to heighten a contrast and to draw attention to the degree to which *Pythian* 8 ignores these colonial themes and, more specifically, rejects Alkmaion's role as the founder of Akarnania. In this light, we might think of *Pythian* 8's strategy as the reverse of Thucydides' version of the myth of Alkmaion. In *Pythian* 8, Alkmaion as Delphi-sponsored oikist lurks beneath the surface, aurally present through the ode's elicitation of *Pythian* 1's colonial diction, but never realized.[114]

---

112. We might also note that *Pythian* 8 never alludes to the matricide of Eriphyle, so the opportunity for Alkmaion to be purified by becoming an oikist is never presented. On matricide as a topic avoided by epinikion, see Kurke 2013 on Pi. *P.* 11.

113. For example, in both odes, the enemy of the gods is Typhos, who is described in the same way (compare *P.* 1.16–17 to *P.* 8.16). As Krischer (1985: 115–16) contends, the shared description of Typhos is not formulaic, but rather *Pythian* 8 seems to be directly quoting *Pythian* 1. The conquest of the enemy is also represented by the same verb (compare *P.* 1.73 to *P.* 8.17). Finally, Hesychia (civic tranquility) also performs an important role in both odes. Burnett (2005: 227) compares the characterization of Hesychia in *Pythian* 8 to that of the golden lyre in *Pythian* 1. See also Martin 2004: 357n40 and 360.

114. *Pythian* 8 may also rework aspects of the *Alkmeonis*. A scholion to Euripides reports that the *Alkmeonis* contained the myth of the Aiakidai Telemon and Peleus's fratricide of their half brother Phokos (*PEG* F1 from schol. *ad* Eur. *Andr.* 687). The fragment suggests that the epic saw an analogy between these two acts of kin-killing, the matricide of Eriphyle and the Aiakidai's murder of their brother. As Debiasi (2015: 273–74) proposes, the *Alkmeonis* analogy between Alkmaion and the Aiakidai may even be closer if the aftermath of the murder of Phokos was also included in the epic. According to Pausanias (2.29.10), Telemon and Peleus were exiled from Aegina by Aiakos after the murder. Aiakos

I will end by returning to an issue raised at the beginning of this part of the chapter, namely, why Pindar devotes the mythic portion of *Pythian* 8 to an Argive/Theban myth in place of an expected Aeginetan one. To do so, I would like to connect a historical reading of the ode with a more general argument concerning the nature of Attic tragedy. First, *Pythian* 8 is frequently interpreted with a view toward understanding Aegina's current political environment in 446 B.C.E.[115] In particular, many have understood the ode's imagery, most notably Zeus and Apollo's battles against the hubristic Typhos and Porphyrion (12–18) and the closing prayer for Aegina's "voyage of freedom" (98), to signal metaphorically the island's struggle under Athenian control and its hope for liberation. Simon Hornblower, who advocates for a cautious assessment of how much we can know for certain about the Aeginetan situation following Aristomenes' victory in the wake of the Thirty Years' Peace, still concludes that *Pythian* 8 is one of the Pindaric odes that allows us to see "a subject or allied viewpoint on the Athenian empire."[116]

Second, as noted above, Amphiaraos and especially Alkmaion became incredibly popular subjects for Athenian tragic and comic playwrights in the fifth century. To recall the works of the three major tragedians alone, Aeschylus produced an *Epigonoi* (in addition to the *Seven against Thebes*), Sophocles both an *Epigonoi* and an *Alkmeon*, and Euripides two Alkmaion plays. The popularity of the Alkmaion myth in Athens may be due to the prominence of the Alkmeonidai family. No mythic genealogical ties existed between Alkmaion and the Alkmeonidai, who claimed descent from a grandson of Nestor, but one can see how a kind of folk etymology could have developed between them based on the shared name. Indeed, Huxley suggests that of the attested forms of the hero Alkmaion's name, Ἀλκμάων, Ἀλκμαίων, Ἀλκμαν, and Ἀλκμέων, "the last was preferred in Athens, perhaps

---

allowed Telemon, who asserted his innocence, to make his defense but only if he did not return to Aegina: he had to make his defense either from his ship or on a mole raised by the sea. Telemon sailed to the Aeginetan harbor known as "Hidden" and made a mole in the harbor. Debiasi suggests that the story of the mole, if included in the *Alkmeonis*, would form a parallel with the silting up of the Acheloös River that leads to Alkmaion's foundation of Akarnania. He also notes that there may have been one further analogy with Peleus, since, after his exile from Aegina, he too underwent a double purification like Alkmaion. If these later developments of the myth of Telemon and Peleus were included in the epic poem, then *Pythian* 8 may be responding to the analogies made there between Alkmaion and the Aiakidai and, from an epinikian perspective, rehabilitating them. That is, *Pythian* 8 avoids the nonepinikian topics of kin-killing, familial strife, and exile and recasts the analogy between Alkmaion and the Aiakidai as members of heroic families who all serve as models of inherited excellence. In this context we might note that the closing lines of *Pythian* 8 list the genealogy of the Aiakidai, including Telemon and Peleus, and envision Aegina receiving their blessings (99–100).

115. See, e.g., Wilamowitz-Moellendorff 1922: 443–44; Farnell 1932: 192; Figueira 1991: 89–91; Cole 1992: 101–11; Pfeijffer 1995; 1999: 426–56.

116. See Hornblower 2004: 231–35, at 234.

because of the Alkmeonid family name there."¹¹⁷ That is, the spelling favored in Athens more closely aligned the mythic Alkmaion with the Athenian aristocratic family. Another point of contact may have encouraged this association: the Alkmeonidai, like Alkmaion himself, famously enjoyed close ties to Delphi, even bankrolling the rebuilding of Apollo's temple there, as Pindar himself celebrates in *Pythian* 7.¹¹⁸ Our knowledge of the plots of these plays is extremely fragmentary. We do know that Sophocles' *Epigonoi* included the matricide of Eriphyle, and an unassigned fragment (fr. 880 R) mentions Alphesiboia, an alternate name for Alkmaion's first wife in Psophis.¹¹⁹ Euripides' *Alkmeon in Psophis,* performed in 438 B.C.E., recounts the rivalry between Alkmaion's two wives for the necklace of Harmonia.¹²⁰ From these two examples alone, we can see that at least some of the tragedies treated the subjects of Alkmaion's matricide, purification, and foundation.¹²¹

Attic tragedy's interest in Alkmaion, a non-Athenian hero, can be tied to the genre's propensity for appropriation. Barbara Kowalzig and Leslie Kurke show that Attic tragedy strikingly reworks the epichoric myths and cults of gods and heroes who are more readily found in other Greek poleis.¹²² Both also convincingly demonstrate that tragedy's propensity to do so functions as a form of Athenian imperialism taking place on the level of genre. Furthermore, Kurke examines not only tragedy's proclivity for the co-option of non-Athenian myths and cults but also how Pindar's own poetics react to this form of appropriation. Reading *Pythian* 11 as a targeted response to Aeschylus's *Oresteia* and, by implication, to tragedy in general, Kurke argues that, in *Pythian* 11, Pindar "emphasizes the locality and specificity of different communities' relations to the heroes of myth and cult as an important part of traditional choral and civic *harmonia*."¹²³ A similar phenomenon seems to be at work in *Pythian* 8, where it is possible to detect a reaction to

---

117. Huxley 1969: 54n1.

118. See also Hdt. 6.121–31, esp. 6.125, in which Alkmeon, the son of Megakles, is characterized as an assistant (συμπρήκτωρ) to Kroisos's ambassadors at Delphi. There may have also been a further perceived connection between the matricide Alkmaion, who flees to Delphi to be released from his mother's Erinys, and the Athenian family who, because of the so-called curse of the Alkmeonidai, were exiled from Athens and took up residence at Delphi.

119. Soph. *Epig.* = fr. 187 R (see Gantz 1993: 523). Sophocles may have also written an *Eriphyle* (mentioned by Jouan 1990: 158n16).

120. Jouan (1990: 158) also believes that Alkmaion's episode in Psophis also appeared in Sophocles' *Alkmeon*. For Euripides' *Alkmeon in Corinth,* performed posthumously, see Jouan (1990), who argues that Euripides' innovations in the myth promoted an anti-Corinthian and pro-Athenian perspective.

121. The two wives in *Alkmeon in Corinth* imply that Alkmaion had married the daughter of Acheloös as part of his foundation of Akarnania. In Euripides' *Alkmeon in Corinth,* Apollo appears at the end of the play and orders Amphilochos, here the son of Alkmaion, to found Argos Amphilochion in Akarnania.

122. See Kowalzig 2004, 2006; Kurke 2013.

123. Kurke 2013: 101.

Athenian imperialism operating on at least two levels. In the metaphors that speak to overcoming hubristic forces and in its explicitly stated desire for freedom, *Pythian* 8 seems to express Aeginetan resistance in the face of Athenian domination. At another level, the mythic portion reclaims the myth of Alkmaion not just from what I have referred to throughout this chapter as the myth's dominant tradition but more specifically from Attic tragedy as an instantiation of that tradition by reattaching Alkmaion to Amphiaraos and by locating mantic father and son in Thebes.[124]

. . .

In a Greek world full of oracles, Delphi enjoyed preeminence, not least of all in colonial discourse. But its status was not uncontested. This chapter enlisted Amphiaraos and Alkmaion as a case study for exploring evidence of resistance to Delphi's oracular monopoly and for demystifying Delphi's relationship with the figure of the oikist. Part 1 examined how Herodotus emphasizes Delphi's oracular monopoly in the Kroisos *logos* but simultaneously includes moments within the narrative that serve to undercut that monopoly. Amphiaraos and his oracle seem to pose a particular threat to Delphi by consistently matching Delphi's own correct oracular responses and by being acknowledged by Kroisos, together with Delphi, as the "only true oracles." At the same time, we also detected efforts both in Herodotus's account and in an inscription from the Theban Ismenion to disenfranchise the Amphiareion, efforts that suggest attempts by Delphi and its allies to curb competition. Part 2 explored another, more extensive manifestation of the contestatory dynamics between Delphi and Amphiaraos. In the dominant tradition of the Alkmaion myth, preserved in the works of Apollodorus, Diodorus Siculus, Pausanias, and Thucydides, among other ancient authors, Delphi repeatedly takes the place of Amphiaraos in directing the course of Alkmaion's actions. Yet Delphi's success does not only concern authorizing Alkmaion's leadership of the Epigonoi or successfully purifying him for matricide. Alkmaion's adherence to the oracle entails that the hero must also be transformed into an oikist and his connection with Amphiaraos and the rest of the mantic Melampodidai suppressed. Finally, part 3 demonstrated that Pindar, too, leverages a cultural segregation between the seer and the oikist but does so in order to produce a diametrically opposed vision to that of the mainstream tradition of the Alkmaion myth. In *Pythian* 8, Pindar attaches Alkmaion to his father by emphasizing Alkmaion's inherited *mantikē*. As a result, Alkmaion's own ability to prophesy obviates his reliance on Delphi and, by extension, Delphi's recruitment of him as an oikist.

This analysis suggests that when Delphi competes with a seer for authority, it can deploy the salient motifs of colonial discourse to its advantage. In contrast to

---

124. In Foster 2017, I examine in detail how *Pythian* 8 responds to Aeschylus's *Seven against Thebes*.

the seer, Delphi enjoys a productive relationship with the oikist and a prominent role in foundation tales. By converting the myth of Alkmaion into a foundation tale, Delphi not only becomes the dominant source of oracular power within the narrative but also effectively alienates Amphiaraos by operating within a discourse from which seers, given their incompatibility with oikists, are generally excluded. The broad range of authors explored in this chapter demonstrates how entrenched Delphi's position in colonial discourse was. In this way, chapter 6 builds on the work of chapters 2–5, which explored other ways in which the oikist and the seer are positioned as mutually exclusive. The cultural segregation of the roles of seer and oikist observed especially in chapter 4 and this chapter also allows us to appreciate further chapter 5's study of the extraordinary consolidation of these two positions in Pindar's *Olympian* 6.

Finally, I will close by briefly noting the following contrast. Alkmaion is frequently compared to Orestes: both avenge their fathers' deaths by killing their mothers, both are pursued by their mothers' Erinyes, and both seek refuge at Delphi.[125] Yet, at least as Aeschylus's *Oresteia* presents it, Orestes can remain loyal to Agamemnon even as he supplicates Delphic Apollo. He benefits from his allegiance to both the oracle and his father, and Delphic Apollo himself aids Orestes out of his own close personal ties to Agamemnon. Strabo tells us that Orestes too became an oikist and founded a city called Argos Oresticum (7.7.8). I would argue that although the myths of Orestes and Alkaion do display a number of parallels, the respective roles of their fathers, one a king, the other a seer, also reveal a profound discrepancy. Whereas Delphi's oracular and Agamemnon's political authority are viewed as compatible, this chapter has traced Delphi's and Amphiaraos's unbridgeable divide and the ways in which Alkmaion is forced to choose between them.

125. The definitive study of this pair remains Delcourt (1959).

Conclusion

"Any discourse is constituted as an attempt to dominate the field of discursivity, to arrest the flow of difference, to construct a centre."[1] This book has argued that the constructed center of late archaic and early classical colonial discourse is the Delphi-sanctioned oikist. It has also contended that the creation of this ideological edifice requires the necessary exclusion of the Greek seer. A discourse's strategies intensify the more forcefully it must overcome difference in order to establish and maintain its own angle of vision. A crowded oracular landscape, a widespread cultural fascination with the concept of talismanic power, the analogous authority of discrete figures who could claim it, the contestatory dynamic between seers and political leaders—all contributed to the ideological intensity of colonial discourse that we encounter in the late archaic and early classical periods.

By way of a conclusion, then, I would like to extend our gaze temporally beyond the parameters of the late archaic and early classical periods and spatially beyond Delphi's geographical area of influence in order to observe whether colonial discourse and the relationships between Delphi, the oikist, and the seer change significantly once we move past this temporal and spatial zone of discursive intensity. In fact, we began this exercise in chapter 2 when we considered how Theoklymenos aids Odysseus-as-oikist in effecting the metaphorical foundation of Ithaka. As I suggested there, the absence of Delphi facilitates Theoklymenos's and Odysseus's ability to operate as a collaborative, if still potentially competitive, pair.[2] In like

---

1. Laclau and Mouffe 1985: 112.

2. I also note in this context the discrepancy between different versions of the oikist Tlepolemos's foundation of Rhodes. In the *Iliad* version, Tlepolemos, a murderer in exile, leads a group of his people

manner, once we move past this discursive center in the opposite direction, that is, into the Hellenistic period, the model of suppressing the seer in colonial contexts also breaks down. Again, we anticipated this later collapse in our consideration of the seer Lampon and his involvement in the foundation of Thurii in the mid- to late 440s B.C.E. As discussed in chapter 6, while Lampon is initially recognized as one of the leaders of the colonial expedition, Delphic Apollo eventually decides to claim the title of oikist himself (Diod. Sic. 12.10.3, 12.35.3).

To this picture, I now add three Hellenistic examples in which the involvement of seers in a foundation is both conspicuous and presented as standard procedure. In the *Anabasis*, Xenophon describes how, arriving at the shores of the Black Sea, he was seized with a desire to found a city and settle his army there. To ensure that such a foundation would be propitious, he immediately sends for a seer: καὶ ἐπὶ τούτοις ἐθύετο πρίν τινι εἰπεῖν τῶν στρατιωτῶν Σιλανὸν παρακαλέσας τὸν Κύρου μάντιν γενόμενον τὸν Ἀμπρακιώτην (And with a view to these things, [Xenophon] was sacrificing before telling any of the soldiers, having sent for Silanos the Ambraciot who had been the *mantis* of Kyros, *An.* 5.6.16–17). The seer Silanos turns out to be hostile to the idea of Xenophon's Ten Thousand settling a new city, since he personally wants to head for home. For our purposes, however, it is simply worth noting that Xenophon calls attention to the need for a seer in order to begin the normal foundation process.

Delphi is markedly absent from Epaminondas's refoundation of Messene in 369 B.C.E.[3] In Pausanias's detailed account (4.26–27), the Messenian leader receives a foundation riddle for the precise location of the new site not from the Pythia but from a man resembling a priest of Demeter who appeared in a dream (4.26.7).[4] Once the sanctioned site had been found, Epaminondas in his role as oikist directs seers to confirm that the site was favored by the gods (4.27.5):

Ἐπαμινώνδας δέ, ὥς οἱ τὸ χωρίον, ἔνθα νῦν ἔχουσιν οἱ Μεσσήνιοι τὴν πόλιν, μάλιστα ἐς οἰκισμὸν ἐφαίνετο ἐπιτήδειον, ἐκέλευεν ἀνασκοπεῖσθαι τοῖς μάντεσιν, <εἴ> οἱ βουλήσεται ταύτῃ καὶ τὰ τῶν θεῶν ἐπιχωρῆσαι. φαμένων δὲ καὶ τούτων εἶναι τὰ ἱερὰ αἴσια, οὕτω παρεσκευάζετο ἐς τὸν οἰκισμόν.

And since Epaminondas considered the place where the Messenians now have their city especially suitable for a foundation, he ordered an examination to be made by

---

to the island seemingly of his own accord (*Il.* 2.661–69). In Pindar's *Olympian* 7, the poet inserts Delphi into the picture, and it is Delphic Apollo who orders Tlepolemos to sail to Rhodes and settle it (*O.* 7.27–33). On this discrepancy between the two versions, see Dougherty 1993: 120–29; Kowalzig 2007: 239–41.

3. See also Paus. 4.23.1–9 for an episode involving a seer and a foundation relating to the Messenian hero Aristomenes during the Second Messenian War. Aristomenes' floruit is dated to some time in the seventh century, but stories of this legendary figure are closely tied to Epaminondas and Messene in the fourth century, and it is perhaps better to understand Aristomenes in this context.

4. The man appears to the Argive Epiletes who accompanies Epaminondas. Earlier the same priest had appeared in a dream to Epaminondas himself (4.26.6).

the seers to see if it would be pleasing to the gods to follow him there. And when they said that the offerings were auspicious, he began to prepare for the foundation.

Finally, both Plutarch and Arrian mention the involvement of seers in Alexander the Great's foundation of Alexandria. In Arrian's account, the seers assure Alexander that the new city will prosper as they perform a series of foundation rituals (*An.* 3.2.2):[5]

τοῦτο δὲ ἐπιλεξαμένους τοὺς μάντεις καὶ μάλιστα δὴ Ἀρίστανδρον τὸν Τελμισσέα, ὃς δὴ πολλὰ μὲν καὶ ἄλλα ἀληθεῦσαι ἐλέγετο Ἀλεξάνδρῳ, φάναι εὐδαίμονα ἔσεσθαι τὴν πόλιν τά τε ἄλλα καὶ τῶν ἐκ γῆς καρπῶν εἵνεκα.

Thinking this over, the seers, and especially Aristander the Telmissian, who was said to have foretold correctly many other things to Alexander, said that the city would be blessed in other respects and also on account of the fruits of the earth.

In these Hellenistic accounts, seers assist oikists in the foundation rituals of a new city. Their presence in these contexts seems unremarkable and ordinary. In these instances as well, Delphi is nowhere to be found. Indeed, according to Plutarch, it is Homer who appears in a dream to Alexander and delivers instructions for the foundation site of Alexandria (*Alex.* 26). H. W. Parke and D. E. W. Wormell as well as Robert Parker have noted that the stature of the Delphic oracle seems to have diminished in the fourth century as Delphi itself became embroiled in the power struggles and shifting alliances that defined Hellenistic Greece.[6] As Parker observes, Delphic foundation oracles disappear in the early fourth century, followed by the disappearance of oracles concerning war and arbitration.[7] It would appear that as Delphi ceased to be used as a colonial oracle in the fourth century, colonial discourse's ideological assertion of the Delphi-oikist bond also dissipated. It was then that the seer could rise to the surface of the narrative.

The book's spatial focus comprises the Greek mainland and Magna Graecia, that is, all those places that fall within the orbit of Delphi. If we look to the East, however, we find a mythical seer who, at least for a time, seems to escape Delphi's notice and can perform the role of an oikist. Amphiaraos's younger son, Amphilochos, endures as a more shadowy figure who does not enjoy the robust mythographic

---

5. See also Plut. *Alex.* 26.5 for a different part of this foundation ritual in which seers are also mentioned.

6. Parke and Wormell 1956, 1: 244; Parker 1985: 307, 320. See also Miller 1997: 88. On Delphi in the Hellenistic period, see Arnush 2002; Scholten 2003. On divination in general in the Hellenistic period, see Trampedach 2015: 347–90.

7. See Parker 1985: 307: "With one doubtful exception, there is no evidence that the hellenistic kings ever consulted oracles before dispatching their military colonies." According to Parker (321), the Delphic oracle enjoyed a brief revival during the period of 230–180 B.C.E. This revival included a foundation oracle for the Parians' colony of Pharos in the first half of the second century.

tradition of his brother Alkmaion, the subject of chapter 6. Yet our sources characterize him as the counterpart to Alkmaion in a number of ways that further illuminate some of the arguments developed throughout the book. I begin with a passage of Pausanias in which he describes the altar of Amphiaraos at the seer's sanctuary at Oropos (1.34.3):[8]

> παρέχεται δὲ ὁ βωμὸς μέρη· τὸ μὲν Ἡρακλέους καὶ Διὸς καὶ Ἀπόλλωνός ἐστι Παιῶνος, τὸ δὲ ἥρωσι καὶ ἡρώων ἀνεῖται γυναιξί, τρίτον δὲ Ἑστίας καὶ Ἑρμοῦ καὶ Ἀμφιαράου καὶ τῶν παίδων Ἀμφιλόχου· Ἀλκμαίων δὲ διὰ τὸ ἐς Ἐριφύλην ἔργον οὔτε ἐν Ἀμφιαράου τινά, οὐ μὴν οὐδὲ παρὰ τῷ Ἀμφιλόχῳ τιμὴν ἔχει. τετάρτη δέ ἐστι τοῦ βωμοῦ μοῖρα Ἀφροδίτης καὶ Πανακείας, ἔτι δὲ Ἰασοῦς καὶ Ὑγείας καὶ Ἀθηνᾶς Παιωνίας· πέμπτη δὲ πεποίηται νύμφαις καὶ Πανὶ καὶ ποταμοῖς Ἀχελῴῳ καὶ Κηφισῷ. τῷ δὲ Ἀμφιλόχῳ καὶ παρ' Ἀθηναίοις ἐστὶν ἐν τῇ πόλει βωμὸς καὶ Κιλικίας ἐν Μαλλῷ μαντεῖον ἀψευδέστατον τῶν ἐπ' ἐμοῦ.

> The altar has different parts. One part is for Herakles and Zeus and Apollo the Healer, another is dedicated to heroes and the wives of heroes, and a third is for Hestia and Hermes and Amphiaraos and the children of Amphilochos: but Alkmaion, on account of his deed against Eriphyle, is neither honored in any part of the sanctuary of Amphiaraos nor yet with Amphilochos. A fourth portion of the altar is for Aphrodite and Panacea, and also for Iaso, Health, and Athena the Healer. The fifth part has been made for the nymphs and Pan and the rivers Acheloös and Kephisos. The Athenians also have an altar for Amphilochos in the city, and Amphilochos also has at Mallos in Cilicia an oracle, the most trustworthy of those in my day.

Keeping the conclusions of chapter 6 in mind, the passage offers a number of striking details. First, as elsewhere, a connection between Amphiaraos and Alkmaion is rejected. As Pausanias records, Alkmaion is not only shunned from the altar because of his status as a matricide but also from the entire sanctuary of Amphiaraos. At the same time, Alkmaion's exclusion is pointedly contrasted to Amphilochos's presence at the sanctuary. Even Amphilochos's children receive a part on Amphiaraos's altar. More noteworthy still, however, are Pausanias's concluding remarks concerning Amphilochos: he also receives cult in Athens and, further, enjoys the most trustworthy oracle of Pausanias's day at Mallos in Cilicia.

Amphilochos's connection with Mallos is part of a larger mythic narrative. Amphilochos is linked to the seers Kalchas and Mopsos in the *Nostoi* traditions, traveling throughout Asia Minor with them after the fall of Troy. Herodotus (7.91), for instance, describes the Pamphylians as the descendants of those of the Trojan diaspora who accompanied Amphilochos and Kalchas after the war.[9]

---

8. See also *IG* VII.421.
9. See also Theopompus *FGrH* 115 F 351; Lycoph. 439–46; Strabo 14.1.27, 14.5.16.

Quintus of Smyrna tells a similar story, making clear that Amphilochos himself was considered a seer (14.365–68):

μοῦνος δὲ θεοπροπίας εὖ εἰδὼς
Ἀμφίλοχος, θοὸς υἱὸς ἀμύμονος Ἀμφιαράου,
μίμνεν ὁμῶς Κάλχαντι περίφρονι· τοῖσι γὰρ ἦεν
αἴσιμον ἀμφοτέροισιν ἑῆς ἀπὸ τηλόθι γαίης
Παμφύλων Κιλίκων τε ποτὶ πτολίεθρα νέεσθαι.

Only Amphilochos, skilled in prophecy, the nimble son of blameless Amphiaraos, remained with wise Kalchas. For it was fated for them both to travel far from their homeland to the cities of the Pamphylians and Cilicians.

Amphilochos, in contrast to Alkmaion, readily inherits seercraft from Amphiaraos. Like his father, Amphilochos is a seer and also establishes an oracle. What is more, the oracle at Mallos may have been a chthonic dream oracle, a characteristic that further attaches Amphilochos to Amphiaraos and the Amphiareion.[10]

More than simply founding an oracle, however, Amphilochos founds the city of Mallos itself, together with Mopsos. That is to say, Amphilochos, in addition to his status as a seer, becomes an oikist, or, more specifically, a co-oikist with another seer. Strabo provides the fullest account of this joint foundation and its repercussions (14.5.16):

πλησίον δὲ καὶ Μαλλός, ἐφ᾽ ὕψους κειμένη, κτίσμα Ἀμφιλόχου καὶ Μόψου, τοῦ Ἀπόλλωνος καὶ Μαντοῦς, περὶ ὧν πολλὰ μυθολογεῖται· καὶ δὴ καὶ ἡμεῖς ἐμνήσθημεν αὐτῶν ἐν τοῖς περὶ Κάλχαντος λόγοις καὶ τῆς ἔριδος, ἣν ἤρισαν περὶ τῆς μαντικῆς ὅ τε Κάλχας καὶ ὁ Μόψος· ... οὐ μόνον δὲ τὴν περὶ τῆς μαντικῆς ἔριν μεμυθεύκασιν, ἀλλὰ καὶ τῆς ἀρχῆς. τὸν γὰρ Μόψον φασὶ καὶ τὸν Ἀμφίλοχον ἐκ Τροίας ἐλθόντας κτίσαι Μαλλόν· εἶτ᾽ Ἀμφίλοχον εἰς Ἄργος ἀπελθεῖν, δυσαρεστήσαντα δὲ τοῖς ἐκεῖ πολιν ἀναστρέψαι δεῦρο, ἀποκλειόμενον δὲ τῆς κοινωνίας συμβαλεῖν εἰς μονομαχίαν πρὸς τὸν Μόψον, πεσόντας δ᾽ ἀμφοτέρους ταφῆναι μὴ ἐν ἐπόψει ἀλλήλοις· καὶ νῦν οἱ τάφοι δείκνυνται περὶ Μάγαρσα τοῦ Πυράμου πλησίον.

Nearby is also Mallos, situated on a height, the foundation of Amphilochos and Mopsos, the latter the son of Apollo and Manto. Many myths are related about both of them. And in particular I myself have mentioned them in my account on Kalchas and the contest over seercraft (*mantikē*) in which Kalchas and Mopsos competed.... But it has been related in myth that the contest was not only about seercraft but also about sovereignty. For they say that Mopsos and Amphilochos, after leaving Troy, founded Mallos. Afterward Amphilochos went off to Argos but, frustrated by things there, came back to Mallos. Barred at Mallos from a share of the monarchy, he

---

10. On chthonic associations of Amphilochos, see Bonnechere 2003: 170 and n. 7. On the oracle of Mallos as a dream oracle, see Plut. *Mor.* 434d with Parke 1967: 106–7 and Eidinow 2007: 36. See also Lucian *Alexandr.* 29 and *Deorum concil.* 12; Cassius Dio 72.7.

clashed with Mopsos, and both men fell in the fight and were buried out of sight of each other. And now their tombs are visible in the area of Magarsa near the Pyramos River.

Amphilochos thus presents an exception to the model of colonial discourse explored throughout the book: he marks the convergence rather than the mutual exclusivity of the roles of seer and oikist. In this way, he represents the antithesis of his brother Alkmaion, who must choose between these competing claims. Drawing on the details of Strabo's account, then, I would like to consider a number of implications of this convergence.

In one further contrast to Alkmaion, Amphilochos has almost no connection with Delphi. Moreover, while his brother crisscrosses mainland Greece, Amphilochos travels at the fringes of the Greek world, and his foundation at Mallos is located in far off Cilicia.[11] Taking these two features together, I would contend that there may be spatial reasons for why Amphilochos can operate as both a seer and an oikist. He does so beyond Delphi's sphere of influence.[12]

Yet, at the same time, although he inhabits the role of both seer and oikist, Amphilochos does not, in the end, profit from possessing these two positions. As the Strabo passage quoted above relates, Amphilochos and Mopsos quarrel and kill each other, and this contestation explicitly concerns not only divination but also political power (οὐ μόνον δὲ τὴν περὶ τῆς μαντικῆς ἔριν μεμυθεύκασιν, ἀλλὰ καὶ τῆς ἀρχῆς, But it has been related in myth that the contest was not only about seercraft but also about sovereignty, 14.5.16). The end result of the seers Amphilochos and Mospos's cofoundation of Mallos thus ultimately underscores the cultural tension between religious and political authority that I have traced throughout the book, a tension distilled in the juxtaposition of the seer and oikist within colonial discourse. Finally, Amphilochos can only escape the notice of Apollo for so long. For, in another version of death of Amphilochos, the seer is killed not by a competing seer, but by Apollo himself at Soli near Mallos.[13]

I have suggested that the ideological intensity of colonial discourse explored in this book breaks down once we move temporally beyond Delphi of the late archaic and early classical periods and spatially beyond mainland Greece and Magna Graecia. Nevertheless, Delphi's centripetal pull on the oikist's allegiance was powerful and one that did not simply disappear. An inscription, a great temporal and

---

11. Malkin (1987: 252) notes the remoteness of Mallos. On the importance of Amphilochos and Mallos to Alexander the Great, see Scheer 2003.

12. One exception to Delphi's lack of interest in Amphilochos occurs in Euripides' *Alkmeon at Corinth*, but, in this version, Amphilochos is made the son of, not the brother of, Alkmaion. That is, as the son of Alkmaion, he inherits his father's personal connection with Delphi. On Amphilochos's connections to Akarnania and Amphilochion Argos, see Baron 2014.

13. Hes. fr. 279 M-W=Strabo 14.5.16–17.

spatial distance from the Delphi explored here, will serve as a final image of this enduring dynamic. The inscription was found in the city of Ai Khanoum in eastern Bactria (present-day Afghanistan) in the sanctuary of one Kineas, presumably the city's founder.[14] Ai Khanoum does not purport to have been sanctioned by a Delphic foundation oracle. The founder himself presumably never traveled to Delphi. And yet a certain Klearchos did go there and, copying down famous sayings of wise men, had them inscribed and set up in the oikist's shrine, as if to signal that an oikist even of this distant city could still enjoy Delphic Apollo's divine endorsement:

[…]
ε[ὐλόγει πάντας]
φιλόσοφ[ος γίνου]
[…]
Ἀνδρῶν τοι σοφὰ ταῦτα παλιοτέρων ἀνάκει[τα]ι
ῥήματα ἀριγνώτων Πυθοῖ ἐν ἠγαθέια·
ἔνθεν ταῦτ[α] Κλέαρχος ἐπιφραδέως ἀναγράψας
εἵσατο τηλαυγῆ Κινέου ἐν τεμένει.

Παῖς ὢν κόσμιος γίνου,
ἡβῶν ἐγκρατής,
μέσος δίκαιος,
πρεσβύτης εὔβουλος,
τελευτῶν ἄλυπος.[15]

[…] speak well of everyone; be a lover of wisdom […] These wise sayings of men of old, the maxims of renowned men, are enshrined at holy Pytho. There, Klearchos copied them carefully, and set them up here in the sanctuary of Kineas, to glitter from afar: as a child, be well behaved; as a young man, self-controlled; in middle age, be just; as an elder, be of good counsel; and when you come to the end, be without grief.

14. For this inscription and its connection with the sanctuary of Kineas, see Mairs 2015. Mairs convincingly argues that Kineas was most likely seen as the city's founder.
15. The text is from Robert 1968. The translation is from Mairs 2015, adapted.

BIBLIOGRAPHY

Adorjáni, Z. 2014. *Pindars sechste olympische Siegesode*. Leiden.
Althusser, L., and E. Balibar. 1979. *Reading Capital*. Trans. B. Brewster. London.
Amandry, P. 1975. *La mantique apollinienne à Delphes: Essai sur le fonctionnement de l'oracle*. Paris.
Amory, A. 1963. "The Reunion of Odysseus and Penelope." In C. Taylor, ed., *Essays on the Odyssey*, 100–121. Bloomington, Ind.
Antonaccio, C. M. 1999. "Colonization and the Origins of Greek Hero Cult." In R. Hägg, ed., *Ancient Greek Hero Cult*, 109–21. Stockholm.
———. 2001. "Colonization and Acculturation." In I. Malkin, ed., *Ancient Perceptions of Greek Ethnicity*, 113–57. Cambridge, Mass.
———. 2007. "Elite Mobility in the West." In S. Hornblower and C. Morgan, eds., *Pindar's Poetry, Patrons, and Festivals: From Archaic Greece to the Roman Empire*, 265–85. Oxford.
Argyle, A. W. 1970. "Χρησμολόγοι and Μάντεις." *Classical Review* 20: 139.
Arnush, M. 2002. "Argead and Aetolian Relations with the Delphic Polis in the Late Fourth Century BC." In R. Brock and S. Hodkinson, eds., *Alternatives to Athens: Varieties of Political Organization and Community in Ancient Greece*, 293–307. Oxford.
Arrigoni, G. 2003. "La maschera e lo specchio: Il caso di Perseo e Dioniso a Delfi e l'enigma dei Satiri." *Quaderni Urbinati di Cultura Classica* 73: 9–53.
Asheri, D. 1992. "Sicily, 478–431 B.C." In J. Boardman, J. K. Davies, D. M. Lewis, and M. Ostwald, eds., *Cambridge Ancient History*, vol. 5, *The Fifth Century BC*, 147–70. Cambridge.
———, ed. 2006. *Erodoto: Le storie*. Libro IX, *La battaglia di Platea*. Rome.
Asheri, D., A. Lloyd, and A. Corcella. 2011. *A Commentary on Herodotus, Books I–IV*. Ed. O. Murray and A. Moreno. Oxford.

Athanassaki, L. 2003. "Transformations of Colonial Disruption into Narrative Continuity in Pindar's Epinician Odes." *Harvard Studies in Classical Philology* 101: 93–128.

Athanassaki, L., and E. Bowie. 2011. *Archaic and Classical Choral Song: Performance, Politics, and Dissemination*. Berlin.

Aurigny, H. 2011. "Le sanctuaire de Delphes et ses relations extérieures au VII siècle av. J.C.: Le témoinage des offrandes." *Pallas* 87: 151–68.

Austin, J. N. H. 1972. "Name Magic in the *Odyssey*." *Classical Antiquity* 2: 45–63.

———. 1975. *Archery at the Dark of the Moon: Poetic Problems in Homer's "Odyssey."* Berkeley.

Bakker, E. 1997. *Poetry in Speech: Orality and Homeric Discourse*. Ithaca, N.Y.

Baron, C. 2014. "Adopting an Ancestor: Addressing Some Problems Raised by Thucydides' History of Amphilochian Argos (2.68)." *Ancient World* 45, no. 1: 3–17.

Beck, D. 2016. "The Voice of the Seer in the *Iliad* and *Odyssey*." In N. Slater, ed., *Voice and Voices in Antiquity*, 54–73. Orality and Literacy in the Ancient World 9. Leiden.

Beerden, K. 2013. *Worlds Full of Signs: Ancient Greek Divination in Context*. Leiden.

Bell, C. 2009. *Ritual Theory, Ritual Practice*. Oxford.

Bell, M. 1995. "The Motya Charioteer and Pindar's *Isthmian 2*." *Memoirs of the American Academy in Rome* 40: 1–42.

Belsey, C. 1980. *Critical Practice*. London.

Benardete, S. 1997. *The Bow and the Lyre: A Platonic Reading of the "Odyssey."* Lanham, Md.

Benveniste, É. 1973. *Indo-European Language and Society*. Trans. E. Palmer. London.

Bérard, J. 1957. *La colonisation grecque de l'Italie méridionale et de la Sicile dans l'antiquité: L'histoire et la légende*. Paris.

Bethe, E. 1922. *Homer*. Vol. 2. Leipzig.

Beye, C. 1966. *The "Iliad," the "Odyssey," and the Epic Tradition*. New York.

Boardman, J. 1999. *The Greeks Overseas: Their Early Colonies and Trade*. New York.

Boedeker, D. 1993. "Hero Cult and Politics in Herodotus: The Bones of Orestes." In Dougherty and Kurke 1993: 164–77.

Bohringer, F. 1979. "Cultes d'athlètes en Grèce classique: Propos politiques, discours mythique." *Revue des Études Anciennes* 81: 5–18.

Bolling, G. M. 1925. *The External Evidence for Interpolation in Homer*. Oxford.

Bonanno, D. 2010. *Ierone il Dinomenide: Storia e rappresentazione*. Pisa.

Bonifazi, A. 2001. *Mescolare un cratere di canti: Pragmatica della poesia epinicia in Pindaro*. Alexandria.

Bonnechere, P. 2003. "Trophonius of Lebadea: Mystery Aspects of an Oracular Cult in Boeotia." In M. B. Cosmopoulos, ed., *Greek Mysteries: The Archaeology and Ritual of Ancient Greek Secret Cults*, 169–92. London.

Bonnell, V. E., and L. Hunt, eds. 1999. *Beyond the Cultural Turn: New Directions in the Study of Society and Culture*. Berkeley.

Bouché-Leclercq, A. 1879–82. *Histoire de la divination dans l'antiquité*. 4 vols. Paris.

Bowden, H. 2003. "Oracles for Sale." In P. Derow and R. Parker, eds., *Herodotus and His World: Essays from a Conference in Memory of George Forrest*, 256–74. Oxford.

———. 2005. *Classical Athens and the Delphic Oracle*. Cambridge.

Bowra, C. M. 1964. *Pindar*. Oxford.

Braswell, B. K. 1992. *A Commentary on Nemean One*. Freiburg.

———. 1998. *A Commentary on Nemean Nine.* Berlin.
Bremmer, J. N. 1996. "The Status and Symbolic Capital of the Seer." In R. Hägg, ed., *The Role of Religion in the Early Greek Polis,* 97–109. Stockholm.
Broggiato, M. 2003. "Interpretazioni antiche e moderne della visione di Teoclimeno nell'*Odissea* (*Od.* 20. 351–357)." In R. Nicolai, ed., *Rhusmos: Studi di poesia, metrica e musica greca offerti dagli allievi a Luigi Enrico Rossi per i suoi settant' anni,* 63–72. Seminari romani di cultura classica, Quaderni 6. Rome.
Burkert, W. 1983. *Homo Necans: The Anthropology of Ancient Greek Sacrificial Ritual and Myth.* Trans. P. Bing. Berkeley.
———. 1992. *The Orientalizing Revolution: Near Eastern Influence on Greek Culture in the Early Archaic Age.* Trans. M. E. Pinder and W. Burkert. Cambridge, Mass.
Burnett, A. P. 1985. *The Art of Bacchylides.* Cambridge, Mass.
———. 2005. *Pindar's Songs for Young Athletes of Aigina.* Oxford.
Burton, R. W. B. 1962. *Pindar's Pythian Odes: Essays in Interpretation.* Oxford.
Cairns, D. 2005. "Myth and Polis in Bacchylides' Eleventh Ode." *Journal of Hellenic Studies* 125: 35–48.
Calame, C. 1977. *Les choeurs de jeune filles en Grèce archaïque.* 2 vols. Filologia e critica 20 and 21. Rome.
———. 2003. *Myth and History in Ancient Greece: The Symbolic Creation of a Colony.* Trans. D. W. Berman. Princeton, N.J.
Carey, C. 1980. "Bacchylides' Experiments: Ode XI." *Mnemosyne* 33, nos. 3-4: 225–43.
———. 1981. *A Commentary on Five Odes of Pindar.* New York.
———. 1993. "Pindar's Ninth Nemean Ode." In H. D. Jocelyn (with the assistance of H. Hurt), ed., *Tria Lustra: Essays and Notes Presented to John Pinsent, Founder and Editor of Liverpool Classical Monthly by Some of Its Contributors on the Occasion of the 150th Issue,* 97–107. Liverpool.
Carey, E. 1937. *Dionysius of Halicarnassus, Roman Antiquities, Volume 1, Books 1–2.* Cambridge, Mass.
Carlier, P. 1984. *La royauté en Grèce avant Alexandre.* Strasbourg.
Carson, A. 1984. "The Burners: A Reading of Bacchylides' Third Epinician Ode." *Phoenix* 38: 111–19.
Cartledge, P. 1987. *Agesilaos and the Crisis of Sparta.* Baltimore.
Casevitz, M. 1985. *Le vocabulaire de la colonisation en Grec ancien: Étude lexicologique; Les familles de κτίζω et de οἰκέω—οἰκίζω.* Paris.
———. 1992. "Mantis: Le vrai sens." *Revue des Études Grecques* 105: 1–18.
Chantraine, P. 1968–80. *Dictionnaire étymologique de la langue grecque.* 4 vols. Paris.
Christesen, P. 2010. "Kings Playing Politics: The Heroization of Chionis of Sparta." *Historia* 59: 26–73.
Ciaceri, E. 1911. *Culti e miti nella storia dell'antica Sicilia.* Catania.
Cingano, E. 2015. "Epigonoi." In Fantuzzi and Tsagalis 2015: 244–60.
Clay, J. S. 1980. "Goat Island: *Od.* 9.116–141." *Classical Philology* 74: 262–64.
———. 1983. *The Wrath of Athena: Gods and Men in the "Odyssey."* Princeton, N.J.
Clinton, K. 1974. *The Sacred Officials of the Eleusinian Mysteries.* Philadelphia.
Cole, T. 1992. *Pindar's Feasts or the Music of Power.* Rome.
Crahay, R. 1956. *La littérature oraculaire chez Hérodote.* Paris.

Crielaard, J.-P. 1995. "Homer, History, and Archaeology." In J.-P. Crielaard, ed., *Homeric Questions*, 201–88. Amsterdam.

Currie, B. 2005. *Pindar and the Cult of Heroes*. Oxford.

———. 2010. "L'*Ode* 11 di Bacchilide: Il mito delle Pretidi nella lirica corale, nella poesia epica e nella mitografia." In E. Cingano, ed., *Tra panellenismo e tradizioni locali: Generi poetici e storiografica*, 211–53. Alexandria.

D'Agostino, B. 2000. "Delfi e l'Italia tirrenica: Dalla protostoria alla fine del periodo arcaico." In A. Jacquemin, ed., *Delphes: Cent ans après la grande fouille; Essai de bilan*, 79–86. Athens.

D'Agostino, B., and D. Ridgway, eds. 1994. *Apoikia: I più antichi insediamenti greci in Occidente; Funzioni e modi dell' organizzazione politica e sociale: Scritti in onore di G. Buchner*. AION archaeol. 1. Naples.

D'Alessio, G. B. 1994. "First-Person Problems in Pindar." *Bulletin of the Institute of Classical Studies* 39: 117–39.

Daux, G. 1958. "Notes de lecture: Le devin Cléoboulos." *Bulletin de Correspondance Hellénique* 82: 364–66.

Davies, J. K. 1981. *Wealth and the Power of Wealth in Classical Athens*. Salem, N.H.

Davies, M. 2014. *The Theban Epics*. Washington, D.C.

Dawson, G. 1994. *Soldier Heroes: British Adventure, Empire, and the Imagining of Masculinities*. London.

De Angelis, F. 2016. *Archaic and Classical Greek Sicily: A Social and Economic History*. Oxford.

Debiasi, A. 2015. "Alcmeonis." In Fantuzzi and Tsagalis 2015: 261–80.

Defradas, J. 1954. *Les thèmes de la propagande delphique*. Paris.

De Jong, I. J. F. 2001. *A Narratological Commentary on the "Odyssey."* Cambridge.

Delcourt, M. 1959. *Oreste et Alcméon: Étude sur la projection légendaire du matricide en Grèce*. Paris.

Dench, E. 1995. *From Barbarians to New Men: Greek, Roman, and Modern Perceptions of Peoples of the Central Apennines*. Oxford.

Descoeudres, J.-P., ed. 1990. *Greek Colonists and Native Populations*. Canberra.

De Siena, A. 1998. "Metaponto: Problemi urbanistici e scoperte recenti." In *Siritide e Metapontino: Storie di due territori coloniali; Atti dell' incontro di studio, Policoro, 31 ottobre–2 novembre 1991*, 141–70. Naples.

Detienne, M., and J.-P. Vernant. 1978. *Cunning Intelligence in Greek Culture and Society*. Trans. J. Lloyd. Englewood Cliffs, N.J.

Dignas, B., and K. Trampedach, eds. 2008. *Practitioners of the Divine: Greek Priests and Religious Officials from Homer to Heliodorus*. Cambridge, Mass.

Dillery, J. 2005. "Chresmologues and Manteis: Independent Diviners and the Problem of Authority." In Johnston and Struck 2005: 167–231.

Dillon, M. 1996. "*Oionomanteia* in Greek Divination." In M. Dillon, ed., *Religion in the Ancient World: New Themes and Approaches*, 99–121. Leiden.

Donnellan, L. 2015. "*Oikist* and Archegetas." In Mac Sweeney 2015: 41–70.

Donnellan, L., and V. Nizzo. 2016. "Conceptualising Early Greek Colonisation: Introduction to the Volume." In Donnellan, Nizzo, and Burgers 2016: 9–20.

Donnellan, L., V. Nizzo, and G.-J. Burgers, eds. 2016. *Conceptualising Early Colonisation*. Brussels.

Dougherty, C. 1993. *The Poetics of Colonization: From City to Text in Archaic Greece.* Oxford.
———. 1994. "Archaic Greek Foundation Poetry: Questions of Genre and Occasion." *Journal of Hellenic Studies* 114: 35–46.
———. 2001. *The Raft of Odysseus: The Ethnographic Imagination of Homer's* Odyssey. Oxford.
Dougherty, C., and L. Kurke, eds. 1993. *Cultural Poetics in Archaic Greece: Cult, Performance, Politics.* Cambridge.
———, eds. 2003. *The Cultures within Ancient Greek Culture: Contact, Conflict, Collaboration.* Cambridge.
Dowden, K. 1989. *Death and the Maiden.* London.
Drachmann, A. B., ed. 1903. *Scholia vetera in Pindari carmina.* Vol. 1, *Scholia in Olympionicas.* Leipzig.
———. 1910. *Scholia vetera in Pindari carmina.* Vol. 2, *Scholia in Pythionicas.* Leipzig.
———. 1926. *Scholia vetera in Pindari carmina.* Vol. 3, *Scholia in Nemeonicas et Isthmionicas-Epimetrum-Indices.* Leipzig.
Dunbabin, T. J. 1948. *The Western Greeks: The History of Sicily and South Italy from the Foundation of the Greek Colonies to 480 B.C.* Oxford.
Eagleton, T. 2007. *Ideology: An Introduction.* London and New York.
Eidinow, E. 2007. *Oracles, Curses, and Risk among the Ancient Greeks.* Oxford.
Erbse, H. 1972. *Beiträge zum Verständnis der "Odysee."* Berlin.
Fantuzzi, M., and C. Tsagalis, eds. 2015. *The Greek Epic Cycle and Its Ancient Reception: A Companion.* Cambridge.
Farnell, L. 1932. *The Works of Pindar.* Vol. 2, *Critical Commentary.* London.
Fenik, B. 1974. *Studies in the "Odyssey."* Wiesbaden.
Figueira, T. J. 1991. *Athens and Aigina in the Age of Imperial Colonization.* Baltimore.
Finley, J. 1978. *Homer's Odyssey.* Cambridge, Mass.
Flower, H. 2013. "Herodotus and Delphic Traditions about Croesus." In *Oxford Readings in Classical Studies: Herodotus,* 1: 124–53. Oxford.
Flower, M. A. 2008a. "The Iamidae: A Mantic Family and Its Public Image." In Dignas and Trampedach 2008: 187–206.
———. 2008b. *The Seer in Ancient Greece.* Berkeley.
Flower, M. A., and J. Marincola, eds. 2002. *Herodotus, Histories, Book IX.* Cambridge.
Fontenrose, J. 1978. *The Delphic Oracle.* Berkeley.
Forrest, W. G. 1957. "Colonization and the Rise of Delphi." *Historia* 6: 160–75.
Foster, M. 2013. "Hagesias as *Sunoikistêr*: Seercraft and Colonial Ideology in Pindar's Sixth Olympian Ode." *Classical Antiquity* 32, no. 2: 283–321.
———. 2017. "Fathers and Sons in War: *Seven against Thebes,* Pythian 8, and the Polemics of Genre." In I. Torrance, ed., *Aeschylus and War: Comparative Perspectives on Seven against Thebes,* 150–72. London.
Foucault, M. 1972. *The Archaeology of Knowledge.* Trans. S. Smith. London.
Fränkel, H. 1973. *Early Greek Poetry and Philosophy.* Trans. M. Hadas and J. Willis. New York.
Friis Johansen, H. 1973. "Agesias, Hieron, and Pindar's Sixth Olympian Ode." In O. S. Due, A. Friis Johansen, and B. Dalsgaard Larsen, eds., *Classica et Mediaevalia: Francisco Blatt septuagenario dedicata,* 1–9. Copenhagen.
Gallagher, C., and S. Greenblatt. 2000. *Practicing New Historicism.* Chicago.

Gantz, T. 1993. *Early Greek Myth: A Guide to Literary and Artistic Sources.* Vol. 1. Baltimore.
Garland, R. 2014. *Wandering Greeks: The Ancient Greek Diaspora from the Age of Homer to the Death of Alexander the Great.* Princeton, N. J.
Garner, R. 1992a. "Countless Deeds of Valour: Bacchylides 11." *Classical Quarterly* 42: 523–25.
———. 1992b. "Mules, Mysteries, and Song in Pindar's *Olympia* 6." *Classical Antiquity* 11: 45–67.
Geertz, C. 1993. *Local Knowledge: Further Essays in Interpretive Anthropology.* London.
Gentili, B. 1988. *Poetry and Its Public in Ancient Greece.* Trans. A. T. Cole. Baltimore.
Giangiulio, M. 1989. *Ricerche su Crotone arcaica.* Pisa.
———. 2001. "Constructing the Past: Colonial Traditions and the Writing of History; The Case of Cyrene." In N. Luraghi, ed., *The Historian's Craft in the Age of Herodotus,* 116–37. Oxford.
———. 2010. "Collective Identities, Imagined Past, and Delphi." In L. Foxhall, H.-J. Gehrke, and N. Luraghi, eds., *Intentional History: Spinning Time in Ancient Greece,* 121–36. Stuttgart.
Gildersleeve, B. L. 1890. *Pindar: The Olympian and Pythian Odes.* New York.
Goldhill, S. 1991. *The Poet's Voice: Essays on Poetics and Greek Literature.* Cambridge.
Graham, A. J. 1983. *Colony and Mother City in Ancient Greece.* 2nd ed. Chicago.
———. 2001. *Collected Papers on Greek Colonization.* Leiden.
Gray, V. 2011. "Thucydides' Source Citations: 'It is Said.'" *Classical Quarterly* 61: 75–90.
Greengard, C. 1980. *The Structure of Pindar's Epinician Odes.* Amsterdam.
Griffith, M. 2006. "Horsepower and Donkeywork: Equids and the Ancient Greek Imagination." *Classical Philology* 101: 185–246, 307–58.
———. 2009. "Apollo, Teiresias, and the Politics of Tragic Prophecy." In L. Athanassaki, R. P. Martin, J. F. Miller, eds., *Apolline Politics and Poetics,* 473–500. Athens.
Hall, J. 2000. *Ethnic Identity in Greek Antiquity.* Cambridge.
———. 2002. *Hellenicity: Between Ethnicity and Culture.* Chicago.
———. 2008. "Foundation Stories." In G. R. Tsetskhladze, ed., *Greek Colonisation: An Account of Greek Colonies and Other Settlements Overseas,* 2: 383–426. Leiden.
Halliday, W. R. 1975. *The Greek Questions of Plutarch.* New York.
Hansen, W. 1972. *The Conference Sequence: Patterned Narration and Narrative Inconsistency in the "Odyssey."* Berkeley.
Harris, E. M. 1995. *Aeschines and Athenian Politics.* Oxford.
Harrison, T. 2000. *Divinity and History: The Religion of Herodotus.* Oxford.
Helms, M. 1988. *Ulysses' Sail: An Ethnographic Odyssey of Power, Knowledge, and Geographical Distance.* Princeton, N.J.
———. 1993. *Craft and the Kingly Ideal: Art, Trade, and Power.* Austin.
Henderson, J. 2000. *Aristophanes.* Vol. 3. Cambridge, Mass.
Henriques, J., W. Hollway, C. Urwin, C. Venn, and V. Walkerdine. 1998. *Changing the Subject: Psychology, Social Regulation, and Subjectivity.* London.
Heubeck, A., and A. Hoekstra. 1989. *A Commentary on Homer's "Odyssey."* Vol. 2. Oxford.
Heubeck, A., S. West, and J. B. Hainsworth. 1988. *A Commentary on Homer's "Odyssey."* Vol. 1. Oxford.
Higbie, C. 1995. *Heroic Names, Homeric Identities.* New York.
———. 2007. "Hellenistic Mythographers." In R. Woodard, ed., *The Cambridge Companion to Greek Mythology,* 237–54. Cambridge.

Hodkinson, S. 1999. "An Agonistic Culture? Athletic Competition in Archaic and Classical Spartan Society." In S. Hodkinson and A. Powell, eds., *Sparta: New Perspectives*, 147–87. London.
Horden, P., and N. Purcell. 2000. *The Corrupting Sea: A Study of Mediterranean History*. Oxford.
Hornblower, S. 1997. *Commentary on Thucydides*. Vol. 1, Books 1–3. Oxford.
———. 2001. "Epic and Epiphanies: Herodotus and the 'New' Simonides." In D. Boedeker and D. Sider, eds., *The New Simonides: Context of Praise and Desire*, 135–47. Oxford.
———. 2004. *Thucydides and Pindar: Historical Narrative and the World of Epinikian Poetry*. Oxford.
———. 2007. "The Dorieus Episode and the Ionian Revolt (5.42–8)." In E. Greenwood and E. Irwin, eds., *Reading Herodotus: A Study of the* Logoi *in Book 5 of Herodotus' Histories*, 168–78. Cambridge.
How, W. W., and J. Wells. 2002. *A Commentary on Herodotus*. 2 vols. Oxford.
Hubbard, T. K. 1992. "Remaking Myth and Rewriting History: Cult Tradition in Pindar's Ninth Nemean." *Harvard Studies in Classical Philology* 94: 77–111.
———. 1993. "The Theban Amphiaraion and Pindar's Vision on the Road to Delphi." *Museum Helveticum* 50: 193–203.
———. 2001. "Pindar and Athens after the Persian Wars." In D. Papenfuss and V. M. Strocka, eds., *Gab es das Griechische Wunder? Griechenland zwischen dem Ende des 6. und der Mitte des 5. Jahrhunderts v. Chr.*, 387–400. Mainz.
Hunter, R., and I. Rutherford, eds. 2009. *Wandering Poets in Ancient Greek Culture: Travel, Locality and Pan-Hellenism*. Cambridge.
Hutchinson, G. O. 2001. *Greek Lyric Poetry: A Commentary on Selected Larger Pieces*. Oxford.
Huxley, G. L. 1969. *Greek Epic Poetry from Eumelos to Panyassis*. Cambridge, Mass.
Immerwahr, H. R. 1986. *Form and Thought in Herodotus*. Cleveland.
Jameson, F. 1981. *The Political Unconscious: Narrative as a Socially Symbolic Act*. Ithaca, N.Y.
Jameson, M. H. 1991. "Sacrifice before Battle." In V. D. Hanson, ed., *Hoplites: The Classical Greek Battle Experience*, 197–228. London.
Johnston, S. I. 2005. "Introduction: Divining Divination." In Johnston and Struck 2005: 1–28.
———. 2008. *Ancient Greek Divination*. Malden, Mass., and Oxford.
Johnston, S. I., and P. T. Struck, eds. 2005. *Mantikē: Studies in Ancient Divination*. Leiden.
Jones, H. L. 1927. *Strabo: Geography*. Vol. 4, Books 8–9. Cambridge, Mass.
Jost, M. 1985. *Sanctuaires et cultes d'Arcadie*. Paris.
———. 1992. "La légende de Mélampus en Argolide et dans le Péloponnèse." In M. Piérart, ed., *Polydipsion Argos*, 173–84. Paris.
Jouan, F. 1990. "Les Corinthiens en Acarnanie et leurs prédécesseurs mythiques." In F. Jouan and A. Motte, eds., *Mythe et politique: Actes du colloque de Liège, 14–16 septembre 1989*, 155–66. Paris.
Katz, M. A. 1991. *Penelope's Renown: Meaning and Indeterminacy in the "Odyssey."* Princeton, N.J.
Kearns, E. 1982. "The Return of Odysseus: A Homeric Theoxeny." *Classical Quarterly* 32: 2–8.

———. 1991. "Review of Malkin, I., *Religion and Colonization in Ancient Greece* (Brill 1987)." *Journal of Hellenic Studies* 111: 236–37.
Kenens, U. 2011. "The Sources of Ps.-Apollodorus' *Library*: A Case-Study." *Quaderni Urbinati di Cultura Classica* 97: 129–46.
Kett, P. 1966. "Prosopographie der historischen griechischen Manteis bis auf die Zeit Alexanders des Großen." PhD diss., Universität Erlangen-Nürnberg.
Kindt, J. 2016. *Revisiting Delphi: Religion and Storytelling in Ancient Greece.* Cambridge.
Kirk, G. 1962. *The Songs of Homer.* Cambridge.
Kirkwood, G. 1982. *Selections from Pindar.* Chico, Calif.
Köhnken, A. 1974. "Pindar as Innovator: Poseidon Hippios and the Relevance of the Pelops Story in *Olympian* 1." *Classical Quarterly* 24: 199–206.
Konstan, D. 1995. *Greek Comedy and Ideology.* Oxford.
Kossatz-Deissmann, A. 1978. *Dramen des Aischylos auf westgriechischen Vasen.* Mainz.
Kowalzig, B. 2004. "Changing Choral Worlds: Song-Dance and Society in Athens and Beyond." In P. Murray and P. Wilson, eds., *Music and the Muses: The Culture of "Mousikē" in the Classical Athenian City,* 39–65. Oxford.
———. 2006. "The Aetiology of Empire? Hero-Cult and Athenian Tragedy." In J. Davidson, F. Muecke, and P. Wilson, eds., *Greek Drama III: Essays in Honour of Kevin Lee,* Bulletin of the Institute of Classical Studies of the University of London Supplement 87, 79–98. London.
———. 2007. *Singing for the Gods: Performances of Myth and Ritual in Archaic and Classical Greece.* Oxford.
Kraay, C. M. 1976. *Archaic and Classical Greek Coins.* Berkeley.
Krischer, T. 1985. "Pindars achte pythische Ode in ihrem Verhältnis zur ersten." *Wiener Studien* 19: 115–24.
Krummen, E. 1990. *Pyrsos Hymnon.* Berlin and New York.
Kurke, L. 1991. *The Traffic in Praise: Pindar and the Poetics of Social Economy.* Ithaca, N.Y.
———. 1993. "The Economy of *Kudos.*" In Dougherty and Kurke 1993: 131–63.
———. 1999. *Coins, Bodies, Games, and Gold: The Politics of Meaning in Archaic Greece.* Princeton, N.J.
———. 2009. "'Counterfeit Oracles' and 'Legal Tender': The Politics of Oracular Consultation in Herodotus." *Classical World* 102: 417–38.
———. 2011. *Aesopic Conversations: Popular Tradition, Cultural Dialogue, and the Invention of Greek Prose.* Princeton, N.J.
———. 2013. "Pindar's *Pythian* 11 and the *Oresteia*: Contestatory Ritual Poetics in the 5th c. B.C.E." *Classical Antiquity* 32: 101–75.
Kyriakou, P. 2007. "*Epidoxon Kydos*: Crown Victory and Its Rewards." *Classica et Mediaevalia* 58: 119–58.
Laclau, E., and C. Mouffe. 1985. *Hegemony and Socialist Strategy: Towards a Radical Democratic Politics.* London.
Lattimore, R. 2007. *The Odyssey of Homer.* New York.
Leschhorn, W. 1984. *"Gründer der Stadt": Studien zu einem politisch-religiösen Phänomen der griechischen Geschichte.* Palingenesia 20. Stuttgart.
Levine, D. B. 1983. "Theoclymenus and the Apocalypse." *Classical Journal* 70: 1–7.
Lloyd-Jones, H. 1976. "The Delphic Oracle." *Greece and Rome* 23: 60–73.

Löffler, I. 1963. *Die Melampodie*. Meisenheim am Glan.
Lomas, K., ed. 2003. *Greek Identity in the Western Mediterranean*. Leiden.
Lombardo, M. 1972. "Le concezioni degli antichi sul ruolo degli oracoli nella colonizzazione greca." *Annali della Scuola Normale Superiore di Pisa* 2: 63–89.
Londey, P. 1990. "Greek Colonists and Delphi." In Descoeudres 1990: 117–27.
Lonis, R. 1979. *Guerre et religion en Grèce à l'époque classique*. Paris.
Loraux, N. 1986. *The Invention of Athens: The Funeral Oration in the Classical City*. Trans. A. Sheridan. Cambridge, Mass.
Lord, A. B. 2000. *The Singer of Tales*. Cambridge, Mass.
Luraghi, N. 1994. *Tirannidi arcaiche in Sicilia e Magna Grecia*. Florence.
———. 1997. "Un *mantis* eleo nella Siracusa di Ierone: Agesia di Siracusa, Iamide di Stinfalo." *Klio* 79: 69–86.
———. 2011. "Hieron Agonistes or the Masks of the Tyrant." In G. Urso, ed., *Dicere laudes: Elogio, comunicazione, creazione del consenso; Atti del convegno internazionale, Cividale del Friuli, 23–25 settembre 2010: I convegni della Fondazione Niccolò Canussio*, 10, 27–47. Pisa.
Macan, R. W. 1908. *Herodotus: The Seventh, Eighth, and Ninth Books*. 2 vols. London.
———. 1973. *Herodotus: The Fourth, Fifth, and Sixth Books*. New York.
MacFarlane, K. 1998. "Bacchylides absolvens: The defeat of Alexidamus in Bacchylides 11." In J. P. Bews, I. C. Storey, and M. R. Boyne, eds., *Celebratio: Thirtieth Anniversary Essays at Trent University*, 42–49. Peterborough.
Macherey, P. 2006. *A Theory of Literary Production*. London.
Mackil, E. 2013. *Creating a Common Polity: Religion, Economy, and Politics in the Making of the Greek Koinon*. Berkeley.
Mac Sweeney, N. 2015. *Foundation Myths in Ancient Societies: Dialogues and Discourses*. Philadelphia.
Maehler, H. 2004. *Bacchylides: A Selection*. Cambridge.
Mairs, R. 2015. "The Founder's Shrine and the Foundation of Ai Khanoum." In Mac Sweeney 2015: 103–28.
Malkin, I. 1986. "Apollo Archegetes and Sicily." *Annali della Scuola Normale Superiore di Pisa* 17: 959–72.
———. 1987. *Religion and Colonization in Ancient Greece*. Leiden.
———. 1989. "Delphoi and the Founding of Social Order in Archaic Greece." *Mètis* 4: 129–53.
———. 1994. *Myth and Territory in the Spartan Mediterranean*. Cambridge.
———. 1998. *The Returns of Odysseus: Colonization and Ethnicity*. Berkeley.
———. 2003. "'Tradition' in Herodotus: The Foundation of Cyrene." In P. Derow and R. Parker, eds., *Herodotus and His World: Essays from a Conference in Memory of George Forrest*, 153–70. Oxford.
———. 2009. "Foundations." In N. Fisher and H. van Wees, eds., *Archaic Greece: New Approaches and New Evidence*, 373–94. London and Swansea.
———. 2011. *A Small Greek World*. Oxford.
———. 2016. "Greek Colonisation: The Right to Return." In Donnellan, Nizzo, and Burgers 2016: 27–50.
Marinatos, N. 1981. "Thucydides and Oracles." *Journal of Hellenic Studies* 101: 138–40.

Martin, R. 1989. *The Language of Heroes: Speech and Performance in the "Iliad."* Ithaca, N.Y.
———. 1992. "Hesiod's Metanastic Poetics." *Ramus* 21: 11–33.
———. 1997. "Similes and Performance." In E. Bakker and A. Kahane, eds., *Written Voices, Spoken Signs*, 138–66. Cambridge, Mass.
———. 2004. "Home Is the Hero: Deixis and Semantics in Pindar *Pythian* 8." *Arethusa* 37: 343–63.
Maurizio, L. 1995. "Anthropology and Spirit Possession: A Reconsideration of the Pythia's Role at Delphi." *Journal of Hellenic Studies* 115: 69–86.
———. 1997. "Delphic Oracles as Oral Performances: Authenticity and Historical Evidence." *Classical Antiquity* 16: 308–34.
McGlew, J. F. 1993. *Tyranny and Political Culture in Ancient Greece*. Ithaca, N.Y.
McInerney, J. 1999. *The Folds of Parnassos: Land and Ethnicity in Ancient Phokis*. Austin.
Meiggs, R., and D. Lewis. 1988. *A Selection of Greek Historical Inscriptions to the End of the Fifth Century B.C*. Oxford.
Merkelbach, R. 1951. *Untersuchungen zur "Odyssee."* Munich.
Merkelbach, R., and M. L. West. 1967. *Fragmenta Hesiodea*. Oxford.
Miller, T. 1997. *Die griechische Kolonization im Spiegel literarischer Zeugnisse*. Tübingen.
Mills, S. 2004. *Discourse*. London.
Montepaone, C. 1986. "L'apologia di Alexidamos: 'L'avventura del cavaliere.'" *Mètis* 1: 219–35.
Montiglio, S. 2005. *Wandering in Ancient Greek Culture*. Chicago.
Montrose, L. A. 1989. "Professing the Renaissance: The Poetics and Politics of Culture." In H. A. Veeser, ed., *The New Historicism*, 15–36. London.
Moretti, L. 1953. *Iscrizioni agonistiche greche*. Rome.
Morgan, C. 1990. *Athletes and Oracles*. Cambridge.
———. 1993. "The Origins of Pan-Hellenism." In N. Marinatos and R. Hägg, eds., *Greek Sanctuaries: New Approaches*, 18–44. London.
Morgan, K. 2015. *Pindar and the Construction of Syracusan Monarchy in the Fifth Century B.C.* Oxford.
Morrison, A. D. 2007. *Performances and Audiences in Pindar's Sicilian Victory Odes*. London.
Most, G. 2007. *Hesiod: The Shield, Catalogue of Women, Other Fragments*. Cambridge, Mass.
Muellner, L. 1976. *The Meaning of Homeric EYXOMAI through Its Formulas*. Innsbruck.
Mullen, W. 1982. *Choreia: Pindar and Dance*. Princeton, N.J.
Munson, R. V. 2001. *Telling Wonders: Ethnographic and Political Discourse in the Work of Herodotus*. Ann Arbor.
———. 2006. "An Alternate World: Herodotus and Italy." In C. Dewald and J. Marincola, eds., *The Cambridge Companion to Herodotus*, 257–73. Cambridge.
Murnaghan, S. 1987. *Disguise and Recognition in the "Odyssey."* Princeton, N.J.
Nafissi, M. 1999. "From Sparta to Taras: *Nomima, Ktiseis*, and Relationships between Colony and Mother City." In S. Hodkinson and A. Powell, eds., *Sparta: New Perspectives*, 245–72. London.
Nagy, G. 1986. "Pindar's *Olympian* 1 and the Aetiology of the Olympic Games." *Transactions of the American Philological Association* 116: 71–88.
———. 1990. *Pindar's Homer: The Lyric Possession of an Epic Past*. Baltimore.
———. 2000. "The Dream of a Shade." *Harvard Studies in Classical Philology* 100: 97–118.

Neer, R. 2001. "Framing the Gift: The Politics of the Siphnian Treasury at Delphi." *Classical Antiquity* 20: 273–344.

———. 2002. "How Geloan Is (or Was) the Geloan Treasury?" In *Archaeological Institute of America, 104th Annual Meeting, Abstracts,* 26: 64–65. Boston: Archaeological Institute of America.

———. 2003. "Framing the Gift: The Siphnian Treasury at Delphi and the Politics of Architectural Sculpture." In Dougherty and Kurke 2003: 129–49.

———. 2007. "Delphi, Olympia, and the Art of Politics." In H. A. Shapiro, ed., *The Cambridge Companion to Archaic Greece,* 225–65. Cambridge.

———. 2010. "Pindar and the Monuments." Lecture delivered at the Classical Arts Society, Chicago, March 2010.

Neer, R., and L. Kurke. Forthcoming. *Pindar's Sites: An Archaeology of Song.* Baltimore.

Nicholson, N. 2005. *Aristocracy and Athletics in Archaic and Classical Greece.* Cambridge.

———. 2007. "Pindar, History, and Historicism." *Classical Philology* 102: 208–27.

———. 2016. *The Poetics of Victory in the Greek West: Epinician, Oral Tradition, and the Deinomenid Empire.* Oxford.

Norwood, G. 1945. *Pindar.* Berkeley.

Ober, J. 1989. *Mass and Elite in Democratic Athens: Rhetoric, Ideology, and the Power of the People.* Princeton, N.J.

Ogden, D. 2001. *Greek and Roman Necromancy.* Princeton, N.J.

Oldfather, C. H. 1946. *Diodorus Siculus, Library of History.* Vol. 4, Books 9–12.40. Cambridge, Mass.

Oliver, J. H. 1950. *The Athenian Expounders of the Sacred and Ancestral Laws.* Baltimore.

Osborne, M. J. 1981, 1982. *Naturalization in Athens.* 2 vols. Brussels.

Osborne, R. 1996. *Greece in the Making, 1200–479 BC.* London. 2nd ed., 2009.

———. 1998. "Early Greek Colonization? The Nature of Greek Settlement in the West." In N. Fisher and H. van Wees, eds., *Archaic Greece: New Approaches and New Evidence,* 251–69. London and Swansea.

———. 2016. "Greek 'Colonisation': What Was, and What Is, at Stake?" In Donnellan, Nizzo, and Burgers 2016, 21–26.

Ostwald, M. 1986. *From Popular Sovereignty to the Sovereignty of Law: Law, Society, and Politics in Fifth-Century Athens.* Berkeley.

Page, D. 1955. *The Homeric Odyssey.* Oxford.

Papademetriou, J. 1957. "Αττικα III: ὁ θειος του Αισχινου Κλεοβουλος ὁ Μαντις." *Platon* 9: 154–62.

Papazarkadas, N. 2014. "Two New Epigrams from Thebes." In N. Papazarkadas, ed., *The Epigraphy and History of Boeotia: New Finds, New Prospects,* 223–51. Leiden.

Parke, H. W. 1967. *The Oracles of Zeus.* Oxford.

———. 1984. "Croesus and Delphi." *Greek, Roman and Byzantine Studies* 25: 209–32.

Parke, H. W., and D. E. W. Wormell. 1956. *The Delphic Oracle.* 2 vols. Oxford.

Parker, R. 1985. "Greek States and Greek Oracles." In P. A. Cartledge and F. D. Harvey, eds., *Crux: Essays Presented to G. E. M. de Ste Croix on His 75th Birthday,* 298–326. London.

———. 1996. *Athenian Religion: A History.* Oxford.

———. 2000. "Sacrifice and Battle." In H. van Wees, ed., *War and Violence in Ancient Greece,* 299–314. London.

———. 2004. "One Man's Piety: The Religious Dimension of the *Anabasis*." In R. L. Fox, ed., *The Long March: Xenophon and the Ten Thousand*, 131–53. New Haven, Conn.

———. 2005. *Polytheism and Society at Athens*. Oxford.

Partida, E. 2000. *The Treasuries at Delphi: An Architectural Study*. Philadelphia.

Pease, A. S. 1917. "Notes on the Delphic Oracle and Greek Colonization." *Classical Philology* 12: 1–20.

Peek, W. 1937. "Verbesserungen zu Boiotischen Epigrammen." *Hermes* 72: 232–39.

Petridou, G. 2016. *Divine Epiphany in Greek Literature and Culture*. Oxford.

Pfeijffer, I. L. 1995. "Pindar's Eighth Pythian: The Relevance of the Historical Setting." *Hermes* 123: 156–65.

———. 1999. *The Aeginetan Odes of Pindar: A Commentary on Nemean V, Nemean III, and Pythian VIII*. Leiden.

Philipp, H. K. 1994. "Olympia, die Peloponnes und die Westgriechen." *Jahrbuch des Deutschen Archäologischen Instituts* 109: 77–92.

Pleket, H. W. 1975. "Games, Prizes, Athletes, and Ideology: Some Aspects of the History of Sport in th Greco-Roman World." *Stadion* 1: 49–89.

Polanyi, K. 1968. *Primitive, Archaic, and Modern Economies: Essays of Karl Polanyi*. Ed. G. Dalton. Garden City, N.Y.

Pothou, V. 2009. *La place et le rôle de la digression dans l'œuvre de Thucydide*. Stuttgart.

Pritchard, D. 2012. "Public Honours for Panhellenic Sporting Victors in Democratic Athens." *Nikephoros* 25: 209–20.

Pritchett, W. K. 1971. *The Greek State at War*. Vol. 1. Berkeley.

———. 1979a. *The Greek State at War*. Vol. 3. Berkeley.

———. 1979b. "Plataiai." *American Journal of Philology* 100: 145–52.

Race, W. H. 1993. "First Appearances in the *Odyssey*." *Transactions of the American Philological Association* 123: 79–107.

———. 1997a. *Pindar: Nemean Odes, Isthmian Odes, Fragments*. Vol. 2. Cambridge, Mass.

———. 1997b. *Pindar: Olympian Odes, Pythian Odes*. Vol. 1. Cambridge, Mass.

———. 2014. "Achilles' κῦδος in *Iliad* 24." *Mnemosyne* 67: 707–24.

Raphals, L. 2013. *Divination and Prediction in Early China and Ancient Greece*. Cambridge.

Redfield, J. 1983. "The Economic Man." In C. A. Rubino and C. Shelmerdine, eds., *Approaches to Homer*, 218–47. Austin.

Reece, S. 1994. "The Cretan Odyssey: A Lie Truer Than Truth." *American Journal of Philology* 115: 157–73.

Richer, N. 1999. "Le recherche des appuis surnaturels topiques par les Spartiates en guerre." In J. Renard, ed., *Le Péloponnèse: Archéologie et histoire: Actes de la Rencontre international de l'Orient, 12–15 mai 1998*, 135–48. Rennes.

Robbins, E. 1997. "Public Poetry." In D. E. Gerber, ed., *A Companion to the Greek Lyric Poets*, 221–87. Leiden.

Robert, C. 1917. "ἡ ἱστορία παρὰ Φερκύδηι." *Hermes* 52: 308–13.

Robert, L. 1967. "Sur des inscriptions d'Ephèse." *Revue de Philologie* 41: 7–84.

———. 1968. "De Delphes à l'Oxus: Inscriptions grecques nouvelles de la Bactriane." *Comptes-Rendus de l'Académie des Inscriptions et Belles-Lettres*, 416–57.

Rose, P. 1992. *Sons of the Gods, Children of Earth*. Ithaca, N.Y.

Rosenberger, V. 2001. *Griechische Orakel: Eine Kulturgeschichte*. Darmstadt.

Roth, P. 1982. "Mantis: The Nature, Function, and Status of a Greek Prophetic Type." PhD diss., Bryn Mawr College.
Roux, G. 1976. *Delphes, son oracle et ses dieux*. Paris.
Russo, J., M. Fernández-Galiano, and A. Heubeck. 1992. *A Commentary on Homer's "Odyssey."* Vol. 3. Oxford.
Rusten, J. S. 1983. "ΓΕΙΤΩΝ ΗΡΩΣ: Pindar's Prayer to Heracles (*N.* 7.86–101) and Greek Popular Religion." *Harvard Studies in Classical Philology* 87: 289–97.
Rutherford, I. 2001. *Pindar's Paeans: A Reading of the Fragments with a Survey of the Genre*. Oxford.
Rutter, N. K. 1973. "Diodorus and the Foundation of Thurii." *Historia* 22: 155–76.
———. 1998. "The Coinage of Sicily in the Early Fifth Century BC." In R. Ashton and S. Hurter, eds., *Studies in Greek Numismatics in Memory of Martin Jessop Price*, 307–15. London.
———. 2000. "Coin Types and Identity: Greek Cities in Sicily." In C. Smith and J. Serrati, *Sicily from Aeneas to Augustus: New Approaches in Archaeology and History*, 73–83. Edinburgh.
Said, E. W. 1983. *The World, the Text, and the Critic*. Cambridge.
Sakellariou, M. B. 1958. *La migration grecque en Ionie*. Athens.
Santangelo, F. 2013. *Divination, Prediction, and the End of the Roman Republic*. Cambridge.
Schachter, A. 1967. "A Boeotian Cult-Type." *Bulletin of the Institute of Classical Studies* 14: 1–16.
———. 1981. *Cults of Boiotia*. 4 vols. London.
———. 1994. "The Politics of Dedication." In R. Osborne and S. Hornblower, eds., *Ritual, Finance, Politics: Athenian Democratic Accounts Presented to David Lewis*, 291–306. Oxford.
———. 2000. "The Seer Tisamenos and the Klytiadai." *Classical Quarterly* 50: 292–95.
Scheer, T. S. 1993. *Mythische Vorväter: Zur Bedeutung griechischer Heroenmythen im Selbstverständnis kleinasiatischer Städte*. Munich.
———. 2003. "The Past in a Hellenistic Present: Myth and Local Tradition." In A. Erskine, ed., *A Companion to the Hellenistic World*, 216–31. Malden, Mass., and Oxford.
Scholten, J. B. 2003. "Macedon and the Mainland, 280–221." In A. Erskine, ed., *A Companion to the Hellenistic World*, 134–58. Malden, Mass., and Oxford.
Scott, M. 2010. *Delphi and Olympia: The Spatial Politics of Panhellenism in the Archaic and Classical Periods*. Cambridge.
———. 2014. *Delphi: A History of the Center of the Ancient World*. Princeton, N.J.
Seaford, R. 1988. "The Eleventh Ode of Bacchylides: Hera, Artemis, and the Absence of Dionysus." *Journal of Hellenic Studies* 108: 118–36.
Segal, C. P. 1998. *Aglaia: The Poetry of Alcman, Sappho, Pindar, Bacchylides, and Corinna*. Lanham, Md.
Sewell, W. H., Jr. 1999. "The Concept(s) of Culture." In V. E. Bonnell and L. Hunt, eds., *Beyond the Cultural Turn: New Directions in the Study of Society and Culture*, 35–61. Berkeley.
Shapiro, H. A. 1990. "Oracle-Mongers in Peisistratid Athens." *Kernos* 3: 335–45.
Sineux, P. 2007. *Amphiaraos: Guerrier, devin et guérisseur*. Paris.
Slater, W. J. 1969. *Lexicon to Pindar*. Berlin.

———. 1984. "*Nemean* One: The Victor's Return in Poetry and Politics." In D. E. Gerber, ed., *Greek Poetry and Philosophy: Studies in Honour of Leonard Woodbury*, 241–64. Chico, Calif.
Smith, N. D. 1989. "Diviners and Divination in Aristophanic Comedy." *Classical Antiquity* 8: 140–58.
Smith, P. 1988. *Discerning the Subject*. Minneapolis.
Snodgrass, A. 1980. *Archaic Greece: The Age of Experiment*. London.
Sommerstein, A. 2009. *Aeschylus: Persians, Seven against Thebes, Suppliants, Prometheus Bound*. Cambridge, Mass.
Stallybrass, P., and A. White. 1986. *The Politics and Poetics of Transgression*. Ithaca, N.Y.
Stamatopoulou, Z. 2014. "Inscribing Performances in Pindar's *Olympian* 6." *Transactions of the American Philological Association* 144: 1–17.
Stanford, W. B. 2000. *Homer, Odyssey XIII–XXIV*. London.
Stehle, E. 1997. *Performance and Gender in Ancient Greece: Nondramatic Poetry in Its Setting*. Princeton, N.J.
Stein, H. 1908. *Herodotus, Historiae*. Berlin.
Steiner, D. 1993. "Pindar's 'Oggetti Parlanti.'" *Harvard Studies in Classical Philology* 95: 159–80.
Stern, J. 1970. "The Myth of Pindar's *Olympian* 6." *American Journal of Philology* 91: 332–40.
Stoevestandt, M. 2004. *Feinde—Gegner—Opfer: Zur Darstellung der Troianer in den Kampfszenen der Ilias*. Basel.
Stoneman, R. 1981. "Pindar and the Mythological Tradition." *Philologus* 125: 44–63.
Struck, P. T. 2016. *Divination and Human Nature: A Cognitive History of Intuition in Classical Antiquity*. Princeton, N.J.
Suarez de la Torre, E. 1992. "Les pouvoirs des devins et les récits mythiques: L'exemple de Mélampous." *Les Études Classiques* 60: 3–21.
Taita, J. 2001. "Indovini stranieri al servizio dello stato spartano: Un' 'epoikia' elea a Sparta in una nuova iscrizione da Olimpia." *Dike* 4: 39–85.
Tandy, D. W. 1997. *Warriors into Traders: The Power of the Market in Early Greece*. Berkeley.
Terranova, C. 2013. *Tra cielo e terra: Amphiaraos nel Mediterraneo antico*. Rome.
Thonemann, P. 2016. "Croesus and the Oracles." *Journal of Hellenic Studies* 136: 152–67.
Thornton, A. 1970. *People and Themes in Homer's "Odyssey."* London.
Trampedach, K. 2008. "Authority Disputed: The Seer in Homeric Epic." In Dignas and Trampedach 2008: 207–30.
———. 2015. *Politische Mantik: Die Kommunikation über Götterzeichen und Orakel im klassischen Griechenland*. Freiburg.
Travlos, J. 1988. *Bildlexicon zur Topographie des antiken Attika*. Tübingen.
Tsetskhladze, G., ed. 1999. *Ancient Greeks West and East*. Leiden.
———, ed. 2006a. *Greek Colonisation: An Account of the Greeks Overseas*. Vol. 1. Leiden.
———. 2006b. "Revisiting Ancient Greek Colonization." In Tsetskhladze 2006a: xxiii–lxxxiii.
———, ed. 2008. *Greek Colonisation: An Account of the Greeks Overseas*. Vol. 2. Leiden.
Turyn, A. 1924. "Lyrica greca." *Eos* 27: 110–12.
Ugolini, G. 1995. *Untersuchungen zur Figur des Sehers Teiresias*. Tübingen.
Ustinova, Y. 2002. "'Either a Daimon, or a Hero, or Perhaps a God': Mythical Residents of Subterranean Chambers." *Kernos* 15: 267–88.

Vannicelli, P. 2005. "Da Platea a Tanagra: Tisameno, Sparta e il Peloponneso durante la Pentecontaetia." In M. Giangiulio, ed., *Erodoto e il 'modello erodoteo': Formazione e trasmissione delle tradizioni storiche in Grecia*, 257–76. Trento.

Van Straten, F. T., ed. 1995. *Hiera kala: Images of Animal Sacrifice in Archaic and Classcial Greece*. Leiden.

Veeser, H. A. 1989. *The New Historicism*. London.

Vernant, J.-P. 1991. "Speech and Mute Signs." In F. Zeitlin, ed., *Mortals and Immortals: Collected Essays*, 303–17. Princeton, N.J.

Versnel, H. S. 1970. *Triumphus: An Inquiry into the Origin, Development, and Meaning of the Roman Triumph*. Leiden.

———. 1987. "What Did Ancient Man See When He Saw a God? Some Reflections on Greco-Roman Epiphany." In D. van der Plas, ed., *Effigies Dei: Essays on the History of Religion*, 42–55. Leiden.

Vian, F. 1965. "Mélampous et les Proitides." *Revue des Études Anciennes* 67: 25–30.

Vidal-Naquet, P. 1986. "Land and Sacrifice in the Odyssey." In P. Vidal-Naquet, ed., *The Black Hunter: Forms of Thought and Forms of Society in the Greek World*, trans. A. Szegedy-Maszak, 15–38. Baltimore.

Wallace, R. 2009. "Charismatic Leaders." In N. Fisher and H. van Wees, eds., *Archaic Greece: New Approaches and New Evidence*, 411–26. London.

Weber, M. 1978. *Economy and Society: An Outline of Interpretive Sociology*. Ed. G. Roth and C. Wittich. Berkeley.

Weniger, L. 1915. "Die Seher von Olympia." *Archiv für Religionswissenschaft* 18: 53–115.

West, M. L. 1978. *Hesiod, Works and Days*. Oxford.

———. 1997. *The East Face of Helicon: West Asiatic Elements in Greek Poetry and Myth*. Oxford.

———. 2003. *Greek Epic Fragments from the Seventh to the Fifth Centuries BC*. Cambridge, Mass.

———. 2011. "Pindar as a Man of Letters." In D. Obbink and R. Rutherford, eds., *Culture in Pieces: Essays on Ancient Texts in Honor of Peter Parsons*, 50–68. Oxford.

———. 2014. *The Making of the "Odyssey."* Oxford.

White, H. 1978. *Topics of Discourse: Essays in Cultural Criticism*. Baltimore.

Wilamowitz-Moellendorff, U. von. 1922. *Pindaros*. Berlin.

———. 1927. *Die Heimkehr des Odysseus*. Berlin.

Wilson, P. J. 2000. *The Athenian Institution of Khoregia: The Chorus, the City, and the Stage*. Cambridge.

INDEX

Acheloös, 159, 161–64, 166
Adrastos: Aigialeus and, 174; Amphiaraos and, 86, 116–18
Aigialeus, 154–55, 174
Aipytos, 119–21
Aitna: Chromios and, 131–32; foundation of, 124–25, 134; Hagesias and, 122, 125–35; Hieron as oikist of, 116; Hieron's plans for, 127, 134; *kōmos* to, 131, 135; mainland ties to, 134; Olympia as a paradigm for, 124–25; synoikism of, 128, 131, 134; Syracuse and, 113–15, 129, 134, 135; Zeus Aitnaios and, 134
Akarnania: Alkmaion as oikist of, 158–59, 161, 166, 179; *Alkmeonis* and, 169; Delphi and, 161, 162, 166; foundation of, 161–63, 179; as origin of seers, 167–68
Alexidamos, 90–92, 97, 103–7
Alkmaion: altar of Amphiaraos at Oropos and, 188; Amphiaraos and, 153–58, 160–61, 164–66, 168, 169, 170–77, 178, 182–83; Amphilochos and, 154, 156–57, 165, 188–90; Delphi and, 154–68, 177–82; epiphany of, 174–77; Klytios and, 168; as leader of Epigonoi, 154–55, 173; mainstream/dominant mythic tradition of, 138, 153, 162, 167, 182; matricide of Eriphyle and, 153–56, 158, 167; Oikles and, 159–61, 166; as oikist of Akarnania, 158–59, 161, 166, 179; Orestes and, 183; popularity of myth of, 152, 180–81; prophecy of, 175–76, 178; purification of, 158–61, 166, 167; seercraft and, 167–68, 169, 170–77

Alkmeonidai, 180–81
Alpheios: Hagesias's *kōmos* and, 134; Iamos and, 121, 124; as link between Peloponnese and Sicily, 132–34
altar(s): of Amphiaraos at Oropos, 188; Aristeas's altar of Apollo, 104; of Artemis at Lousoi, 91, 99–100; of Zeus at Olympia, 18n67, 112, 125–26
Amphiaraos: Adrastos and, 86, 116–18; Alkmaion and, 153–58, 160–61, 164–66, 168, 169, 170–77, 178, 182–83; altar at Oropos of, 188; Delphi, rivalry with in Kroisos *logos*, 141–47; Delphi, rivalry with over Alkmaion, 151–52, 157–58, 169, 170; Kroisos and, 141–47; matricide of Eriphyle and, 153–54, 153–58; as military seer, 117, 173–74; myth of Alkmaion's rejection of, 138, 152–70; shield and spear of, 142, 147–50; as *summachos* to Thebans, 150–51; Theban Ismenion and, 147–51. *See also* Amphiareion
Amphiareion: Alkmaion and, 176–77; Amphilochos and, 189; Delphi, rivalry with, 141–44, 147, 150, 170, 182; dimunition of, 151, 176; location of, 147–48, 149, 177. *See also* Amphiaraos
Amphilochos: Alkmaion and, 154, 156–57, 165, 188–90; Amphiaraos and, 156–57; Amphiareion and, 189; Apollo and, 157n60, 190; as co-founder of Mallos, 188–90; Delphi, lack of connection with, 190; as founder of

209

Amphilochos *(continued)*
  Argos Amphilochikon, 75; matricide of Eriphyle, 154, 156–57; as oikist-seer, 189–90; oracle at Mallos of, 188–89
Amphilytos, 145, 167
Antinoös, 69, 71–72
apoikia, Peloponnese as, 124–25
Apollo. *See also* Delphi; Delphic Apollo
  Amphilochos and, 190; Apollo Archegetas, 77n4, 137n3; Apollo Ismenios, 149, 151; Apollo Ptoieus, 138; Iamos and, 119–21, 125; seercraft as gift from, 17, 18, 121
Archias, 109, 115, 133
Arethousa, 132–34
Aristander, 187
Aristeas of Prokonnesos, 104–7
Aristomenes of Aegina, 168, 178, 180
Arsinoe, 159, 162
Artemis, altar of at Lousoi, 91, 99–100; Artemis Hemera/Hemerasia, 90, 96; Metapontine cult of, 90, 105; Proitids and, 90–92, 95–96; Proitos and, 102
Athena: Athena Pronaia and Apollo, 149–50; as bestower of *kudos*, 28; colonial narrative and, 62–64
Athens: foundation of Thurii and, 136–37; imperialism of, 180–82; Oropos and, 149
athletic victors, 8, 27–35, 48, 50
Attic tragedy, and myth of Alkmaion, 152, 180–82
augury, 16, 18, 19, 83

Bakis, 1, 139

charis, 140, 147
charisma and charismatic authority, 8, 12–13, 15, 18, 25, 39
chrēsmologos: Amphilytos as, 145; functions of, 19; Onomakritos, 84; seer and, 1–2, 1n1, 19, 84, 139
Chromios, 131–32
chthonic oracles, 165–66, 174, 189
colonial discourse: absence of seers from, 21, 76–82, 86, 116, 167; in archaic and classical periods, 6–8, 185; centrality of Delphi-oikist relationship in, 77, 79–82, 86–88; definition of, 6–7; Delphi's oracular monopoly and, 138–39, 167, 182–83; epinikion and, 8, 89; in Hellenistic period, 185–87, 190; motifs of, 11, 63–64, 66, 80, 81, 98–99, 100, 163–64, 167. *See also* colonial narrative
colonial ideology, 3, 11, 76–77, 79, 88, 107. *See also* ideology

colonial narrative: absence of Delphi in, 74, 185–87; characterization of oikist in, 9, 80–81; components of, 11, 78, 100, 162; definition of, 7; myth of Alkmaion as, 158–68; *Odyssey* as, 59–66; Proitid myth as, 98–101; role of Delphi in, 9, 116, 183; role of seers in, 10, 185–90. *See also* colonial discourse
colonial movement, Greek, 7–9, 60–61
crowns, *kudos*/talismanic power and, 27, 29, 30–31, 46, 81, 107

Deinomenidai, 108–10, 113, 115. *See also* Gelon; Hieron of Syracuse
Delphi: absence in colonial narratives, 74, 185–87; Alexidamos and, 107; Amphiareion, rivalry with in Kroisos *logos*, 141–47; Amphilochos and, 190; Aristeas and, 104–7; Kroisos and, 139–44, 182–83; Theban Ismenion and, 149–51. *See also* Apollo; Delphic Apollo/Delphic oracle
Delphic Apollo/Delphic oracle: Alkmaion and, 154–68, 177–82; Amphiaraos, rivalry with over Alkmaion, 151–52, 157–58, 169, 170; Battos and, 80; characterization of in *Pythian* 8, 178–79; in competition with other oracles, 138–39, 150–51; decline of, 187; Lampon and, 136–37; monopoly in colonial discourse of, 138–39, 167, 182–83; oikist and, 11, 22, 77, 79–82, 86–88. *See also* Apollo; Delphi
dēmioergoi and seers, 14–15
divination: forms of, 15–17; inherited divinatory ability, 18, 170–77; by military *manteis*, 17; role in Greek foundations, 10, 186–87; scholarship on, 8–9. *See also* intuitive divination; seercraft; technical divination
Dodona, 138
Dorieus, 48–50, 77n4

Elis, as origin of seers, 18, 36, 48, 123, 168
empyromancy, 16
entrails, 16
Epaminondas, 186–87
Epigonoi, 153–58, 172–73, 174
Epimenides, 19, 106n63
epinikion: in contrast to hero(-athlete) narratives, 105, 169; Deinomenidai and, 108; generic conventions of, 106n62, 110–12; historical framework of, 8; ideology of, 173; *laudandus* in, 110, 111, 115; relationship to colonial ideology, 88–89; suppression of seer in, 90–98, 101–3

epiphany: of Alkmaion, 174–77; of Apollo, 140; in battle, 25, 36; of Solon, 140
Eriphyle, 153–60
exēgētēs, 9, 19
extispicy, 16–17, 19

fathers and sons, 170–77
foundation myth and foundation tale. *See* colonial narrative

Gaia, 165
Gelon of Syracuse, 108, 113, 113n18, 115
genealogy, use of, 55–59
generational repetition, and epinikian ideology, 110–12, 172–73
gift-exchange model of reciprocity, 139–40, 144, 147

Hagesias: Aitna and, 112–15, 125; Amphiaraos as a model for, 116–17, 118n26; anchor metaphor and, 131; as *despotas*, 118n25, 134; as embodiment of Hieron's synoikism, 122, 127–28, 131; Hieron and, 114–18, 123–28, 135; hybridity of, 127–28, 130–31, 131, 135; Iamos as model for, 119, 121–22, 125–26; *kōmos* of, 134–35; as *mantis*, 116–22; Peloponnesian origins of, 122, 126–28; as *sunoikistēr*, 109, 112–15, 122–35; talismanic power of, 110–16, 130, 135; as *tamias* of mantic altar at Olympia, 109, 112, 126; treasury metaphor and, 130–31
Harmonia, necklace and robe of, 154, 159, 160–61, 167, 181
Hegesistratos: Mardonios and, 44; motivation of, 43; relationship with Sparta and, 42; "speaking name" of, 42; talismanic power of, 41, 44–45; Teisamenos and, 35, 41–45
Hellenistic period, 7, 14, 22, 78, 186–87
Hera, 91, 92, 94, 96, 102–3
Herakles, 27, 30, 125, 132n67
hiera, 17
Hieron of Syracuse: colonial agenda of, 113, 127, 135; Hagesias and, 108, 110, 116–18, 122, 124, 126n48, 135; as link between Syracuse and Aitna, 113–15; mainland ties and, 108, 132, 134; Pelops and, 123–25; synoikism of Aitna and, 122, 127, 128, 131, 134

Iamidai: as apolitical, 121–22, 135; as cofounders of Syracuse, 112; Kallias, 48–50; as mantic clan, 18; Melampodidai and, 118, 121–22; at Olympia, 18n67, 112; origins of, 126. *See also* Hagesias; Iamos; Teisamenos

Iamos: Apollo and, 119–21, 125; birth of, 119–20; foundation of Olympia and, 125–26; genealogy of, 118, 119, 120; Melampous and, 118; as model for Hagesias, 122, 124, 125, 126; Poseidon and, 119, 120–21, 124, 125, 135; seer-as-*sunoikistēr* construct and, 126. *See also* Iamidai
iatromantis, 19
ideology: definition of, 4–5. *See also* colonial ideology
intuitive divination, 15, 17–18
Ithaka: colonial narrative and, 62–64; Odysseus as oikist of, 62–66; refoundation of, 60–61, 73

Kalchas: Amphilochos and, 188–89; characteristics of, 17–18
Kallias, 48–50
Kineas, sanctuary of, 191
kleos, 59, 111, 115
Klytiadai, 18, 47, 168
Klytios, 168
kōmos: of Aristomenes, 178; Chromios and, 131–32; as colonial expedition, 131; Hagesias and, 126, 131–32, 134–5
Kroisos: Amphiaraos and, 142–44, 147–50; Apollo and, 139–40, 145–47; Delphi and, 139–44, 182–83; Herodotean *logos* of, 138–47, 182; Nicolaus of Damascus' pyre scene and, 145–47; Solon and, 140–41
Kroton, talismanic figures and, 48–50
ktisis poetry, 7, 179
kudos. *See* talismanic power
Kypselids, 169–70

Lampon: Delphic Apollo and, 137, 186; as oikist of Thurii, 136–37

madness: of Alkmaion, 158, 160; *mantis* and, 13; of Proitids, 90–91, 95–96, 100, 102
Mallos, 188–90
mantis, military. *See* military seer
mantic altar of Zeus at Olympia: empyromancy and, 16; stewardship of, 18n67, 112, 125–26
mantic authority: colonial ideology and, 108–35; of Hagesias, 116–22; Iamidai and, 122; oracular authority and, 8, 136–52, 166, 177; political authority and, 3, 77–82, 185; talismanic power and, 110, 115, 126, 130
mantic inheritance, 18, 164–65, 167, 168–77
mantic-oracular rivalry, 136–52, 157–58, 169, 170, 182–83
mantikē. *See* seercraft

mantis: definition of, 13; etymology of, 13. See also seer
mantosunē. See seercraft
matricide, 153–58, 183
Megistias, 85, 167–68
Melampodidai, 18, 74, 118, 121–22, 168, 174, 182. See also Alkmaion; Amphiaraos; Theoklymenos
Melampous: Aristeas and, 103–7; Artemis and, 95–96; as healer, 95; Iamos and, 118; mythographic tradition of, 92–98; Proitos and, 101–3; suppression of, 92, 102–3; talismanic power of, 106; Teisamenos compared to, 43
metaphor: anchor metaphor, 131; marriage metaphor in colonial discourse, 11; murderer metaphor in colonial discourse, 11; treasury metaphor, 128–30
Metapontion, 103–7
military seer(s): Amphiaraos as, 86, 117, 149–50, 174; as analogous to colonial seer, 78; divinatory sacrifice by, 17; Hagesias and, 117–18; paired with military commanders, 24, 84–86; talismanic power of, 20, 24, 35–48, 48–50. See also Teisamenos
Milo, 27, 30–31, 48–50
Mopsos, 118, 188–90
Mys, 147–48
Myskellos, 79

Nikias, 23, 24n4

Odysseus: as fugitive homicide, 63–64, 66; hidden identity of, 57–59; as oikist, 62–66; pairing of Theoklymenos and, 51–53, 66–69; parallels between Theoklymenos and, 53–59; post-Ithaka travels of, 65–66, 69–70
oikist(s): Alkmaion as, 158–67; Amphilochos as, 189–90; athletic victors and, 33–34, 80; bond between Delphi and, 9, 11, 77–82, 158–67, 190–91; charismatic authority and, 8; epinikion and, 88–89; interpretive skill of, 80–81; Lampon as, 136–37; Proitos as, 101–3; religious authority of, 9, 11, 77–82, 101–3, 116; religious status of, 9; seers and, 3–4, 10, 109, 186–90; selection of, 80; talismanic power of, 20, 33–34, 79–80
Oikles: Alkmaion and, 159–61, 166; Amphiaraos and, 172; Delphi and, 161
Olympia: empyromancy and, 16; foundation of, 124–25; Geloan treasury at, 129; mantic altar of Zeus at, 112
omens, 16, 17

oracles: Amphilochos's establishment of, 189; Kroisos's testing of, 141–42 ; rivalry between, 138–39; of Zeus Ammon, 138, 141. See also Amphiareion; Bakis; Delphic oracle; Dodona; Mallos
oracle monger. See *chrēsmologos*
Orestes, 64, 183
ornithomancy. See augury
Oropos, Amphiareion at, 147–48, 149, 188
Ortygia, 132–34

Peisetairos, 1–2
Pelops, 123–25
Phalanthos, 81
Phegeus, 159–60
political authority: of athletic victors, 30; Iamidai and, 121–22; mantic authority and, 122, 190; of oikist, 3, 87, 101–3; religious authority and, 10, 77–82, 101–3, 107, 190; seer as threat to, 82–87, 101; talismanic power and, 30, 34
Poseidon, 120–21, 124
Proitids (daughters of Proitos), 92–98
Proitos, 91, 92, 97, 98–103, 106–7
prophētēs, 19n73
Ptoion, sanctuary of Apollo, 138
purification: Alkmaion and, 158–61, 167, 181; Artemis's purification of Proitids, 95, 102; Melampous's purification of Proitids, 93, 95, 96; as motif of colonial discourse, 100; Proitos and, 103; seers and, 19, 83
Pythian games, 107, 168

refoundation: of Ithaka, 60–61, 66, 73; of Metapontion, 104–7; of Syracuse, 115
religious authority: contestation over, 2–3; of oikist, 9, 77–82, 101–3, 116; political authority and, 10, 77–82, 101–3, 107, 190; talismanic power and, 81, 82, 88

second sight, 17
seercraft (*mantikē, mantosunē*): of Alkmaion, 167, 168–77, 182; of Amphilochos, 189–90; as gift from Apollo, 17, 18, 121; Iamos and, 121–22; inheritance of, 17, 173–74, 177, 182, 189; techniques of, 15–18
seer(s): absence from colonial discourse of, 21, 76–82, 86, 116, 167; Aristander, 187; connected to foundation, 109, 136–37, 186–90; *chrēsmologos* and, 1–2, 1n1, 19, 84, 139; Hegesistratos, 41–45; itinerancy of, 14; Kalchas, 17–18; Klytios, 18, 168; Lampon, 136–37; oikists and, 3–4, 10, 109, 186–90; outsider

status of, 14; overview of, 13–20; redundancy with oikist, 74, 77, 87; shamans and, 106; as *sunoikistēr*, 109–10, 112–16, 122; talismanic power of, 35–50, 110–11; as threat to political authority, 82–87, 101. *See also* Alkmaion; Amphiaraos; Amphilochos; Hagesias; Iamos; *mantis;* Melampous; Teisamenos; Theoklymenos

Sibyl, 145–47

Silanos, 186

snake imagery, 174

Solon, 140–41, 144, 147

sphagia, 17

stasis: explusion of Adrastos due to, 86, 117; Iamidai and, 121; Melampodidai and, 74, 121; as motif of colonial discourse, 100; seer as instigator of, 77, 83–84, 86; in Thurii, 137

Stymphalos, 126–27, 128, 131, 135

sunoikistēr, Hagesias as, 109, 112–16, 122–35

Syracuse: Aitna and, 113–15, 129, 134, 135; Hagesias as *sunoikistēr* of, 109, 112–16; refoundation/synoikism of, 113

talismanic power: analogous figures of, 48–50; of Aristeas, 106; charisma and, 25; crowns and, 27, 29, 30–31, 46, 81, 107; crown victors and, 27–35; cultural and historical context of, 38–39, 185; Hagesias and, 110–16, 135; Kroton's victory and, 48–50; *kudos* as, 28–31; mantic inscriptions and, 45–48; of Melampous, 106; Milo and, 27, 30–31, 48–50; of oikists, 20, 33–34, 79–80; overview of, 24–26; recruitment of military seers and, 20, 35, 37, 44; related numinous phenomena and, 25, 30, 38; of seers, 35–50, 110–11; of Spartan kings, 38–39; Teisamenos, 35–45

technical divination, 15, 16–17

Teiresias, 18

Teisamenos: as athlete, 35–41; citizenship and, 36, 42–43, 80, 84; compared to Melampous, 43; Hegesistratos and, 41–45; inscription of, 47–48; "speaking name" of, 42; talismanic power of, 35–45

Telliadai, 18

Theban Ismenion, 147–51

Theban epics, and myth of Alkmaion, 152, 165, 169–70

Theoklymenos: genealogy of, 55–58; hidden identity of, 55–59; as navigator, 71–72; pairing of Odysseus and, 51–53, 66–69; parallels between Odysseus and, 53–59; refoundation of Ithaka and, 73; suitor's insult and, 67–73. *See also* Melampodidai

Thurii, foundation of, 136–37

Zeus: Zeus Aglaos, 90, 105; Zeus Aitnaios, 134; Kroisos and, 146–47; mantic altar at Olympia of, 112; oracle of Zeus Ammon, 138, 141

INDEX LOCORUM

Aeschines
De falsa legatione
78   45–47

Aeschylus
Prometheus Vinctus
484–99   15–16

Apollodorus
Bibliotheca
2.2.1–2   93, 95
3.6.2   153–54, 156–57
3.7.2   154–56
3.7.5   156–57, 158–60

Aristophanes
Birds
981–91   1–2, 138–39

Aristotle
Constitution of the Ithakans
fr. 507 Rose   65, 69
fr. 508 Rose   75

Arrian
Anabasis
3.2.2   187

Bacchylides
Ode 10
15–18   27–28

Ode 11
15–21   107
40–123   90–92, 97, 98–101
95–109   101–3

Carmina Epigraphica Graeca
328   47–48

Diodorus Siculus
4.66.2–3   157–58
8.17.1   79–80
8.21.3   81
11.49.1   127–28
12.9   27, 30–31, 48–50
12.35.2–3   136–37

Ephorus
Fragmente der griechischen Historiker
70 F 96   160–61

Euripides
Alkmeon in Psophis   181

Herodotus
Histories
1.46–92   139–47
1.46   141
1.48.1   141
1.49   142
1.52   142, 147, 150
1.53.2–3   143

216 INDEX LOCORUM

Herodotus *(contniued)*
1.53–55	143–44
1.62.4–63.1	145
1.66–68	25
1.92.2	142
4.15.2–4	104–7
4.88.2	28
4.155.3	80
5.44–45	48–50
5.46–47	32
5.102	32
6.92.2–3	31–32
7.228.3	85
8.134	150–51, 176
9.33	35–40, 43, 80, 84
9.35.1	40–41
9.37–38	41–44

Hesiod
frr. 132–33 M-W	93

Homer
Iliad
1.68–72	17–18
23.399–406	28

Odyssey
1.68–73	57
7.53–59	56–57
9.19–20	59
13.236–86	62–64
15.223–57	55–59, 74–75
15.271–78	64, 71
16.364–70	71–72
17.382–85	14
18.84–87	69
20.376–83	67–69, 73
23.118–22	65

Inscriptiones Graecae
VII.1670	47–48

Moretti 1953 no. 11	32–33

Nicolaus of Damascus
Universal History
Fragmente der griechischen Historiker 90 F68.11–15	145–47

Papazarkadas 2014	148–51

Pausanias
Description of Greece
1.34.3	188
2.13.7	151–52
3.11.5	37–38
3.14.3	33
4.26–27	186–87
5.7.3	133
6.3.8	34
7.17.13	34–35
8.18.8	95–96
8.24.8–9	161–62, 164
10.9.7	38

Pherekydes
Fragmente der griechischen Historiker
3 F114	94–95

Pindar
Isthmian Odes
1.10–12	29

Nemean Odes
1.1–6	114
1.1–7	132–34
9.1–2	131–32
9.13–14	86, 117–18

Olympian Odes
1.24	124–25
1.40–45	124–25
1.67–87	123–25
6.1–7	128–30
6.4–7	109
6.12–18	116–18
6.16–17	86, 173–74
6.36–51	119–20
6.57–70	120–21
6.65–66	129–30
6.74–76	111–12
6.92–96	114–15
6.92–100	126–27, 134–35
6.101–105	131

Pythian Odes
1	179
1.31	33–34
3.68–70	113–14
8.38–41	172–73
8.38–60	171–77
8.56–60	174–77, 178
8.61–63	178
11	181

Plutarch
De Pythiae oraculis
   407f–408a   81
Lysander
   12.1   38
Praecepta gerendae reipublicae
   812d   136–37

Poetarum Epicorum Graecorum
   F 3   165–66

Quintus of Smyrna
   14.365–68   189

Robert 1968   191

Scholia to:
   Aristophanes *Birds* 521   136–37
   Pindar *Olympian* 6.8   112

Supplementum epigraphicum Graecum
   15.195   95
   16.193   45–47
   16.304   47–48

Sophocles
Epigonoi
   fr. 880 R   181
Oidipous Tyrannos
   399–400   83

Strabo
Geography
   14.5.16   189–90

Theopompos
Fragmente der griechischen Historiker
   115 F 354   70

Thucydides
History of the Peloponnesian War
   2.102.5–6   163–66
   6.23.2–3   23–24

Xenophon
Anabasis
   5.6.16–17   186

www.ingramcontent.com/pod-product-compliance
Lightning Source LLC
Chambersburg PA
CBHW030650230426
43665CB00011B/1023